Greek Myth and the Bible

I0593019

This remarkable book undertakes to show that Greek myths were available to the writers of the Hebrew Bible and of the New Testament to serve both as models and as foils for their own religious purposes, just as John Milton adapted classical myths to make them fit Satan. Louden brings to light quite unexpected congruences from Homer to Euripides and shows repeatedly how old polytheistic stories could be reshaped as Biblical narratives about a single god, from Genesis to the Book of Revelation. Our picture of the complex dialog between Judaeo-Christian and pagan literature will never be quite the same.

Richard Janko, *University of Michigan, USA*

Since the nineteenth-century rediscovery of the Gilgamesh epic, we have known that the Bible imports narratives from outside of Israelite culture, refiguring them for its own audience. Only more recently, however, has come the realization that Greek culture is also a prominent source of biblical narratives.

Greek Myth and the Bible argues that classical mythological literature and the biblical texts were composed in a dialogic relationship. Louden examines a variety of Greek myths from a range of sources, analyzing parallels between biblical episodes and Hesiod, Euripides, Argonautic myth, selections from Ovid's *Metamorphoses*, and Homeric epic.

This fascinating volume offers a starting point for debate and discussion of these cultural and literary exchanges and adaptations in the wider Mediterranean world and will be an invaluable resource to students of the Hebrew Bible and the influence of Greek myth.

Bruce Louden is Professor in the Department of Language and Linguistics, the Humanities Program, and Philosophy, at the University of Texas at El Paso, USA.

Routledge Monographs in Classical Studies

For more information on this series, visit: www.routledge.com/classicalstudies/series/RMCS

Greek Myth and the Bible

Bruce Louden

 Routledge
Taylor & Francis Group

LONDON AND NEW YORK

First published 2019
by Routledge
2 Park Square, Milton Park, Abingdon, Oxon OX14 4RN

and by Routledge
52 Vanderbilt Avenue, New York, NY 10017

First issued in paperback 2020

Routledge is an imprint of the Taylor & Francis Group, an informa business

British Library Cataloguing-in-Publication Data
A catalogue record for this book is available from the British Library

Library of Congress Cataloging-in-Publication Data
Names: Louden, Bruce, 1954– author.
Title: Greek myth and the Bible / Bruce Louden.
Description: Abingdon, Oxon ; New York, NY : Routledge, 2018. |
Series: Routledge monographs in classical studies |
Includes bibliographical references and index.
Identifiers: LCCN 2018025600 (print) | LCCN 2018039344 (ebook) |
ISBN 9780429448553 (ebook) | ISBN 9780429828058 (web pdf) |
ISBN 9780429828041 (epub) | ISBN 9780429828034 (mobi/kindle) |
ISBN 9781138328587 (hardback : alk. paper)
Subjects: LCSH: Myth in the Bible. | Mythology, Greek. |
Greek literature–Relation to the New Testament. |
Greek literature–Relation to the Old Testament. |
Bible–Criticism, interpretation, etc. | Christianity and other religions–Greek.
Classification: LCC BS520.5 (ebook) |
LCC BS520.5 .L68 2018 (print) | DDC 220.6/8–dc23
LC record available at https://lccn.loc.gov/2018025600

ISBN 13: 978-0-367-66474-9 (pbk)
ISBN 13: 978-1-138-33486-1 (hbk)

Typeset in Times New Roman
by Out of House Publishing

Contents

Acknowledgments

Many chapters in this study began as conference papers, journal articles, or chapters in others' books. Much of the introduction began as a keynote address, "Agamemnon and the Hebrew Bible," for the annual conference, Swedish Exegetical Day, September 2015, in Lund. I am grateful to many in Lund for their invitation and hospitality: Tobias Hägerland, Göran Eidevall, Blazenka Scheuer, and Ola Wikander. The talk was subsequently printed under the same title in *Svensk exegetisk årsbok* 81: 1–24. Much of Chapter 1 was first presented as a paper at the Society for Classical Studies meeting, January 2012, in Philadelphia. An intermediate version was published in 2013 in *Illinois Classical Studies* (38): 1–22. An early version of Chapter 3 was given as a paper at the conference, Ancient Greece and Ancient Israel Interactions and Parallels (10th to 4th Centuries BCE), Tel Aviv. An earlier version of Chapter 4 was presented at the Melpomene Chair Greek Studies Conference, in honor of Dr. Donald Mastronarde's retirement, December 2015. An early version of Chapter 6 was presented at the Homer on the Range Conference, Austin, February 2012. An early version of Chapter 7 was presented at the annual meeting of the Classical Association of the Middle West and South in Grand Rapids, April 2011. An intermediate version was published in 2011 in *Interdisciplinary Humanities* (28.1: 21–31). An earlier version of Chapter 8 was published in 2014 as a chapter in *The Bible and Hellenism*, edited by Thomas L. Thompson and Philippe Wajdenbaum. An earlier version of parts of Chapter 10 was published in 2009 in *International Journal of the Classical Tradition* (16: 1–18). I am deeply grateful to these publishers and all those whose hard work and hospitality made my participation in these conferences possible.

Additionally, I want to thank several scholars for their time and patience as they commented on earlier drafts of several chapters. Clayton Bench patiently read an early version of "Agamemnon and the Hebrew Bible," which later became the introduction. Klaus Spronk offered suggestions on Chapter 4, "Euripides's *Hecuba* and Jael (Judges 4–5)." Carolina Lopez-Ruiz patiently read a draft of a chapter that I ended up removing from this book but will later pursue independently. Garth Tissol read and saved me from some glaring errors in drafts of Chapters 5 and 9. Lastly, Karl Olav Sandnes was extremely generous with his time and expertise, commenting on drafts of Chapters 6, 8, and 10. None of these scholars, however, should be held responsible for, or presumed to agree with, all the views expressed herein.

Introduction

In Genesis 28, Jacob pauses on his quest to the east, making a stop for the night at a place that initially does not receive any individuating details. Using one of the stones there for a pillow, he falls asleep and dreams his famous, fateful dream. Waking the next day, he dedicates the stone, on which he had laid his head, to his God. Commentators tell us that the stone Jacob dedicates to Yahweh is a component of a preexisting Canaanite sanctuary, originally used, therefore, in service of a previous god.

Fox (2008: 294–95), in his discussion of the "Corcyrian Cave," notes how, according to ancient tradition, this is where part of Zeus' battle with Typhoeus took place. Inscriptions unearthed at nearby Corcyros refer to "Zeus of Victory," referencing the outcome of the struggle. Near the mouth of the cave stood a temple to Zeus. As Fox notes, Christians later built a Christian church on the site of this earlier temple to Zeus (295), "the temple of the cave was laboriously replaced with a Christian church, *which reused its stones and pillars* c AD 500" (italics mine).

Christians have built on and appropriated elements from earlier polytheistic religion in other ways as well. In a rather well-known instance, Christmas, entirely postbiblical and extrabiblical as it is, appropriates a preexisting festival for the birth of the Sun god. As Fox notes, until well into the fourth century CE we lack records of Christians celebrating the holiday on December 25 (1992: 28), "Not until the mid-fourth century AD are Christians known to have been celebrating Christmas on 25 December." Fox continues (1992: 36),

> Previously the date had marked a pagan festival, the birth of the sun god at the winter solstice. It was a deliberate retort by Christians in the western parts of the Roman Empire to choose the date as a festival of the birth of their new god, Christ.

Many more instances could be added to these few examples: transformational activities of this sort were common practice among early Christians, and were arguably typical at some stage in the development of all three monotheistic religions.

This book is concerned with how both Jews and Christians did similar things in their sacred narratives. They often built them on or from preexisting sacred narratives, reusing the foundations, stones and pillars, appropriating elements, components, and even lengthy narrative sequences, from earlier myths. The building blocks are put to new use, but are the older stones and foundations completely obscured or still partly visible? As foundations, do they not still exert some overarching architectonic influence? Take away the foundation completely and a structure collapses. There is a key difference, however, between reusing stones to fashion a new temple and reworking parts of older sacred narratives to fashion new ones: we still have many of the earlier myths in their entirety, not just a few episodes or passages here and there. Thus, we have not merely glimpses but their earlier totality and their often originally different meanings remain.

We have known that this is the case since the rediscovery of the *Gilgamesh* epic in the nineteenth century (with its earlier version of the Flood myth): some narratives in the Hebrew Bible originated outside of Israelite culture. But the Flood myth, in its dependence on non-Israelite myth, is not an isolated instance, but rather is indicative of intercultural relationships evident in much of the Bible. As Mark Smith notes, "It is commonly accepted that parts of Gen 1–11 show literary dependence, either directly or indirectly, on Mesopotamian literary tradition."[1] A brief, only partial, list of examples in the Hebrew Bible, for which scholars have found antecedents outside of Israel, includes:

- Babylonian acrostics and some parts of Psalms 25 and 119;
- Mesopotamian oracle collections and the prophetic books;
- the Babylonian *Adapa* and some of the traditional features of revelations in the Hebrew Bible;
- Babylonian wisdom texts in general;
- the traditional god list and hymns of praise;
- an Aramaic blessing and Psalm 20;
- the Babylonian *Theodicy* and Job;
- Deuteronomy's central rubric of the covenant, and Hittite and Neo-Assyrian treaty documents;
- possible Persian impetus for formation of the Pentateuch.[2]

While some of these interconnections are now widely known, far less known are the Hebrew Bible's interconnections with Greek culture. It is not only the dominant cultures to the East of Israel that provided narrative models and sources for many of the various stories that would come together as the Hebrew Bible. This study will argue that Israel's oral traditions and scribal culture were not only acquainted with but were also influenced and shaped by ancient Greek culture. For those who think the similarities we will trace could have gone into either direction, I suggest that if one considers how widespread the respective languages were, Greek and Hebrew, which language has earlier documentation, which people enter the historical record first, which culture was a significant maritime power for over a millennium, and which established an empire including the other – if some form of diffusion, direct or indirect, accounts for correspondences between Greek and Hebrew narratives – the odds are far greater that the direction is from Greek to Israelite culture. I count myself, then, among those who regard the Bible as also responding to Greek culture, in addition to its engagement of Near Eastern cultural traditions.

I have argued elsewhere that the *Odyssey*, with its variety of settings and episodes, offered instances of several types of myth that proved germane to the interests of the scribal tradition behind the Hebrew bible. The recognition scenes in Joseph's myth (Gen 42–46), which are the same specific subtype of recognition found elsewhere only in the *Odyssey*, postponed recognition, are written in response to those in the *Odyssey*.[3] The Book of Jonah can be seen as a brief parodic version of key motifs from the *Odyssey*, those associated with "the fantastic voyage," and with the divine council between Zeus and Poseidon in Book 13.[4] The depictions of theoxeny in Genesis 18 and 19 have so many specific correspondences with those in the *Odyssey* that again it appears likely that they have been consulted as a rubric of sorts. Saul's consultation with the Witch of End-dor (1 Sam 28) has the same sequence of motifs as those the *Odyssey* present in Odysseus' encounter with Circe, and subsequent trip to the Underworld (Books 10–11). When Joshua sends two spies to consult Rahab in Jericho (Josh 2), the narrative follows the exact contours of Odysseus' disguised entrance into Troy and safe reception by Helen (4.242–58). When Jacob wrestles "the man" at the riverbank (Gen 32:22–32), the Hebrew Bible turns to a common genre of Greek myth, a hero wrestling a river god, but especially the subtype presented in *Odyssey* 4, when Menelaus wrestles the sea god Proteus and receives a blessing (4.351–586). Perhaps the most detailed correspondences of all are those between the crew's rebellion against Odysseus and desecration of Helios' cattle on Thrinakia in *Odyssey* 12 and Exodus 32.[5]

In this study, I pursue additional instances where episodes from the *Odyssey* prove apropos for the scribal tradition of the Hebrew Bible and for New Testament authors but include other Greek authors and texts as well. Hesiod's *Theogony*, I argue, is consulted by the Genesis scribes as they construct their primeval history, both immediately before and after their account of the Flood myth. Genesis' depiction of Noah's sons and grandsons adapts and refashions, in a classic instance of euhemerism, Hesiod's account of some of the Titans, Iapetos in particular. I will also demonstrate that episodes from the *Theogony* are consulted as a rubric for episodes in Revelation 4, 12, and 19–20.

I will argue that Argonautic myth is consulted as a rubric for many of the particulars of Genesis' account of Jacob. His heading east to win a wife, his labors to win her, which involve the use of magic, her own use of magic to conceive, and their flight from Laban during the night after she has stolen his household gods, all find close correspondences in Jason, Medea, Aietes, and the Golden Fleece. Closest of all are the correspondences between the devious fathers-in-law, Aietes and Laban. Even Jacob's friction with Esau appears to glance at Jason's difficulties with Heracles. Perhaps most unexpectedly, Rebecca's guiding role in his larger narrative, in a further instance of Euhemerism, adapts Hera's role as Jason's mentor deity.

For the relatively unique accounts of Jael in Judges 4–5, I will argue that both accounts draw on Euripides' *Hecuba* (somewhat as Römer has argued of Judges 11 and Euripides' Iphigenia plays), contrary to the view that these are some of the earliest passage in the Hebrew Bible. One of his most successful and well-known plays, the *Hecuba*, part of the larger Trojan War saga, offers corresponding equivalents for all the main characters and, unlike Judges 4–5, offers full motivations for why the characters acts as they do. Hecuba can be seen as a richly intertextual heroine, as Agoustakis notes (120).

In the *Ion*, Euripides presents all the expected motifs found in the Genesis patriarchs, particularly Abraham, as we explore in Chapter 2. As Athena prophesies at the end of the play, Ion will be a father of peoples. In his birth as a foundling, he also experiences many of the same motifs that the Israel scribal tradition employs for Moses. When the angel appears to Abraham and commands him not to sacrifice Isaac, the Genesis tradition draws not only on the basic rubric of the *deus ex machina* but also appears to be most influenced by Euripidean examples, particularly that which concludes the *Ion*.

For one of Christ's most well-known and climactic miracles, John's unique account of his raising of Lazarus from the dead, Euripides' *Alcestis* provides an antecedent for the entire sequence of motifs. Details of the larger myth of Heracles as the Son of God who cannot only triumph over death but bring others back as well, who, after dying an agonizing death will be translated to divine status and of Asclepius, son of Apollo, the principal Greek figure of the miraculous healer, who also figures in Euripides' play, appear to serve as a rubric for the account in John 11–12:8. In Chapter 8, we again consider Hesiod's *Theogony*. Here we will contemplate the possibility that Revelation authors intend that their audience perceive their reworking of Hesiod, seeing it as a *corrective* of his foundational narrative.

In Chapters 5 and 10, I argue that two episodes from Ovid's larger account of the myth of Phaethon in his *Metamorphoses*, Books 1–2, serve as rubrics for two well-known episodes in the New Testament. In the first, we consider that Ovid's account of the reckless offer the Sun makes to his child, Phaethon, on which, with further recklessness, he swears an oath, serves as a model for the Gospels' depiction of Herod and his daughter, when she asks for the head of John the Baptist on a plate. In the second, I demonstrate that Ovid's depiction of the Temple of the Sun serves as a rubric for some of the more elusive details and features in the divine-council structure in Revelation 4.

Finally, in Chapter 10 I show how traditional are two of the main structuring devices in Revelation, retrospective prophecy (also known as *vaticinatio ex eventu*) and "the vision," by comparing how Vergil uses the same two techniques in the *Aeneid*. We also consider the possibility that Revelations, in a few respects, is referencing Vergil's epic.[6]

This study has a deliberate focus on Genesis and Revelation, as the bookends of the Bible, with three chapters on each. I hope to demonstrate that much of the Bible has been written in a dialogue with Greek myth and culture.

The Hittites and the Ahhiyawa

Why would the Hebrew Bible have been impacted by Greek culture and Greek paradigms? Let us start with a brief overview of the earliest historical record of contacts between Greek culture and the Near East. Hittite treaties and royal letters record several place names and proper names associated with Greek culture of the Mycenaean period.[7] From the fourteenth century BCE are two references to Ahhiya, and from the thirteenth century are many mentions of the Ahhiyawa.[8] We now have a strong consensus that these are Hittite equivalents of terms common in Homeric epic, Achaia and Achaian, the latter being one of Homeric epic's collective terms for the Greeks.[9] Wilusa, a place name, is now understood as corresponding to Homeric Ilios/Ilium, and a phrase, "steep Wilusa," as Calvert Watkins argued,[10] is a seeming correspondent to "steep Ilios" (Ἴλιον αἰπεινήν), which occurs six times in the *Iliad*.

When we move to the names of individuals, Muwatalli II, a Hittite king, records in a treaty a god named Apaliunas, "Storm-god of the Army," which corresponds to Apeilon, an earlier spelling of *Apollo*. There is Tawagalawa, brother of a King of Ahhiyawa, whose name is an exact equation of *Eteocles*.[11] In Greek myth, a character by this name is prominent in the Theban cycle of myths, set in the generation before the Trojan War. Perhaps most intriguing of all, and taking us directly into the seminal myths of ancient Greece, is the name of a king of Wilusa (again, our *Ilium*) Alaksandu, clearly a Hittite rendering of the Greek name *Alexandros*, also known in the *Iliad* as Paris.[12] The "Indictment of Maduwatta,"[13] features a king of Ahhiya by the name of *Attarissiya*. More than a few scholars accept the equation of Attarissiya and *Atreus*.[14] In Homer, Atreus is the name of the father of Agamemnon and Menelaus. Elsewhere, a *Great King of Ahhiyawa* is mentioned but not named. Guterbock, considering the larger society that the Hittite references to Ahhiyawa suggest, notes (43), "I have argued that the Great King of Ahhiyawa, equal in rank to the king of Hatti and, by implication, to those of Egypt and Babylonia, can only be a ruler of the rank of an Agamemnon."[15]

While these attestations do not establish the *Iliad*'s historicity, nor is that my concern, they do demonstrate that the phase of Greek culture that we call Mycenaean was historically so prominent in the region in which the *Iliad* is set, that the Hittites, the other great power exercising control over the area, had extensive relations with them. Singer admirably sums up the situation (24),

The basic plot of the *Iliad* recounts the war between a Greek coalition headed by Mycenae and an Asiatic Trojan coalition including participants from Paphlagonia in the north to Lycia in the south. This geo-political map has hardly any relevance to Homer's days, but, on the other hand, it reflects quite accurately the division between the two major powers on either side of the Aegean in the thirteenth century B.C.E., Hatti and Ahhiyawa.

We call this phase of Greek culture Mycenaean because both the archaeological record and the *Iliad* agree that Mycenae was its most important and wealthiest city. In Greek myth, Agamemnon is king of Mycenae, wealthiest and most powerful of the many Mycenaean kings, an embodiment of its military might and widespread power. A few Ahhiyawa passages also record Greek doings at Cyprus and Miletus, considerably closer to the world of the Hebrew Bible.

The Philistines

Egyptian commemorative *stelae* from the reigns of Rameses II and III record unsuccessful invasions of Egypt by a coalition of "Sea Peoples," including the Philistines, and others, a few of which correspond to those featured in the *Iliad* as allies of the Greeks and Trojans.[16] As early as 1899, F. B. Welch suggested that fragments of Philistine pottery were linked in some way to those of the Mycenaean Greeks.[17] We now have a consensus that such is the case. Stager regards this and other correspondences as definitive (1991), "Throwing caution to the wind, I am willing to … state flatly that the Sea Peoples, including the Philistines, were Mycenaean *Greeks*."[18] Archaeologists have convincingly filled out other links between Philistine and Mycenaean Greek material culture.

At several major Philistine sites, deep changes are apparent that evidence Aegean migration in the twelfth century against the previous patterns of thirteenth-century Canaanite culture and reveal its interaction with the Aegean world.[19] For instance, the "Ashdoda" figurines are a local version of Mycenaean Mother Goddess figurines.[20] Sites in Philistia have Aegean-style hearths and Aegean wine-drinking sets and mixing bowls with spouted or strainer jugs and deep bowls not found in any significant use in Canaan prior to the Philistine migration. Aegean textile practices are in evidence, "Aegean-style imperforated loom weights show that domestic textile production was practiced according to an Aegean tradition."[21] Those taking part in the Aegean migration "kept their Aegean tradition of the domestic cult of an Aegean goddess, which seems to appear everywhere in Philistia."[22] At Miletus, where Hittite texts also document the presence of Ahhiyawa, we have "the remains of a Korridorhaus of the type common in the Aegean world": it imitates palatial architecture of mainland Greece.[23] Yasur-Landau further adds, "The rulers used Aegean symbols of rulership, mainly the central hearth, to consolidate their power by ritual feasting and drinking in the Aegean manner."[24]

As Yasur-Landau further notes, "The Cilician, Ugaritic, and Cypriot data show that in a relatively short time, within the first quarter of the twelfth century BCE, evidence for Aegean behavioral patterns appeared in vast areas of the eastern Mediterranean, sometimes but not in all cases following violent destructions."[25] He summarizes the new evolution in architecture,

> A deep change in the plan of a house and its interior arrangements reflects a conscious effort to replicate, in some cases, Aegean house forms and indicates a change in the cultural notion of what a house should look like … every aspect of everyday domestic life at the site mirrors behavioral patterns of Aegean origin previously unattested to in the Late Bronze Age Local, Canaanite tradition … the appearance of Aegean-style cooking and weaving, indicates that the most basic practices were carried out in a nonlocal manner … the deep change in the behavioral patterns in Philistia can be interpreted only by the arrival of people within the sphere of the expanding Aegean and Aegeanized world of the twelfth century.[26]

Furthermore, the introduction of Mycenaean culture starts to exert influence on the non-Aegean peoples, "Houses, whether built with or without Aegean-style installations, contain assemblages indicative of activities carried out in both the Canaanite and the Aegean manner, which hints at the birth of a multicultural society."[27]

There is continuity in Philistia over the next several centuries as well.[28] A seventh-century temple/palace complex at Tel Miqne/Ekron evidences worship of an Aegean earth goddess, in an inscription, in Phoenician,[29] detailing that an individual named Achish, with a lengthy list of his ancestors, built the temple for the goddess Ptgyh. The goddess' name is non-Semitic and is seen to correspond to the earth goddess at Ashdoda. Thus, the cult of the Aegean great mother-goddess Gaia seems to have been preserved in Philistia from the time of the Aegean migration in the twelfth century up to the seventh century. The name of the temple's builder, Achish, requires further comment. The ruler of Ekron, his name is also attested in an Assyrian inscription.[30] The Hebrew Bible has two Achishes. Twice (1 Sam 21:11–15, 27:1–6) David associates with a Philistine Achish, king of Gath. Later, 1 Kings 2:39–46 mentions another Achish during Solomon's reign, also king of Gath, perhaps grandson to the former. "The name is non-Semitic, and derives from … *ἈχαιϜός or *Ἀχαιός – meaning "the Achaean,"[31] and as Yasur-Landau notes, the name, "Achish … can be traced back to the fifteenth century BCE."[32]

This brings us full circle with the Hittite documents and Homeric epic, Ahhiyawa, Homeric Ἀχαιος, and biblical Achish. The one attested in the inscription at Ekron is perhaps a century later than Homer, still worshipping a goddess of Aegean descent. While he is with Achish, David performs acts that help the Philistines. He should perhaps be understood as acquiring aspects of Philistine culture during his lengthy sojourn among them. We return to him in the following text. Some archaeologists argue that proto-Israelite culture began to identify itself in opposition to Philistine culture.[33] Some of the most definitive markers of Israelite culture, including the taboo against eating pork, arose, they argue, so that the emerging Israelite sense of identity could better define itself against, in distinction to, the dynamic Philistine presence.

Javan

Let us now consider a few passages in the Hebrew Bible that openly reference Greek culture. Javan, a grandson of Noah in Genesis 10, is the same eponym as Greek *Ion* (from *Ἰαϝων). The name has widespread, international circulation from very early times. Chantrainne cites a Mycenaean form, "*iawone*."[34] It occurs in the *Iliad*, Ἰάονες 13.685, and was also current in ancient India, appearing some 50 times in the *Mahabhârata*, as Yavanas.

In Greek culture, Ion is patriarch and eponymous ancestor of the easternmost branch of the Greek people, the Ionians.[35] According to Euripides, and larger Greek traditions, Ion has four sons, as Athena explains at the end of Euripides' play (1575–78), "For, from him four sons, born from one root, will bequeath their names to the land, and the people by tribe."[36] Occurring first in the Bible in the Table of Nations (Gen 10:2, 4), Javan functions as Mr. Greece, if you will, progenitor of the people. As the Greek Ion, Javan also has four sons (Gen 10:4): Elishash, Tarshish, Kittim, and Rodanim. Genesis continues (10:5), "From these the peoples of the coasts and islands separated into their own countries."[37] Speiser explains that Elishash corresponds to Alashiya, a name for Cyprus; Kittim corresponds to Kition, a Greek city also on Cyprus, while Rodanim is clearly the inhabitants of Rhodes.[38] In additional passages in 1 Chronicles; Isaiah 66:19; Ezekiel 27:13; and Zechariah 9:13, "Javan" can be the entire country personified, but in Genesis and I Chronicles it signifies the Ionian Greeks of Asia minor, and, perhaps, of Cyprus in particular.[39]

Obscured by the proliferation of different ethnonyms for the people we call Greeks,[40] ancient Israelite culture, it is abundantly clear, had sustained contact with ancient Greek culture, through eras when we assume the Hebrew Bible was being composed and collected and earlier. In Homer, the Greeks, in something approaching our sense of the word, appear as Achaioi but also as Hellenes, Danaoi, and Argeioi.

Israelite scribal culture

The scribal culture that produced the Hebrew Bible may be seen, in some respects, as responding to larger paradigms in Greek culture. We should perhaps first keep in mind that the Hebrew Bible is not the product of authors, as we think of them, but *scribes*. Van der Toorn classifies into six categories the ways by which scribes produced written texts,[41]

1   Transcription of oral lore,
2   Invention of a new text,
3   Compilation of an existing text,
4   Expansion of an inherited text,
5   Adaptation of an existing text for a new audience, and
6   Integration of individual documents into a more comprehensive composition.

In five of these six, a scribe "does not invent his text but merely arranges it; the contents of a text exist first, before being laid down in writing."[42] Because, in five of the six methods, the scribe deals with a preexisting narrative, the possibility that some narratives are imported from outside of Israelite culture significantly increases.

Van der Toorn further notes, as abundant evidence demonstrates, that the Hebrew Bible exhibits "successive layers of scribal interventions. The final compositions reflect the involvement of generations of scribes. To the text as they had received it, they added their interpretations, framework, and other textual expansions."[43] This continues well after the Septuagint, in which the book of Jeremiah, for instance, is 15 percent shorter than in the eventual Hebrew text. Thus "Scholars have concluded that the Greek Jeremiah translates a Hebrew text earlier than that in the Hebrew Bible."[44]

As Van der Toorn and others have argued, the Hebrew Bible's most celebrated example of authorship, Moses as the reputed author of the Pentateuch, is attributed, or fictitious, designed "to legitimize a cultic reform that was carried out in 622 by King Josiah."[45] The Pentateuch should likely be seen as the result of the labors of Ezra, under the impetus of the Persian Empire. As Van der Toorn notes, "Ezra was a scholar who received his scribal training in Babylonia. His work on the Pentateuch compares to the editing of the *Gilgamesh Epic* by Sin-leqe-unninni and the editing of the prognostic compendium *Sakikku* by Esagil-kin-apli. The latter used disparate sources ('twisted threads') … to produce a 'new text' … Ezra did the same for the Law of Moses."[46] Positing 450 BCE as a reasonable date, he argues that, "Without the Persians, there would not have been a Pentateuch."[47]

Van der Toorn notes that books are a Hellenistic invention.[48] The Hellenistic period caused, he explains, "increasing demand for a national literature by an educated public."[49] In a further reaction, "The Hellenization of the Near East led to an increased production of national – and often nationalistic – historiography."[50] Thus, he argues that the publication of the Prophets, Psalms, and the Proverbs "can be viewed as a Jewish response to the cultural impact of Hellenism."[51]

Carr observes how, in the Hellenistic period in particular, Israelite culture is impacted by larger movements in Greek culture. He notes that only fifth-century and possibly sixth-century Greece provides "depictions of people reading texts."[52] References to buying texts become common in Greece in the fifth century. The first known instances of authors, in something like the sense that we understand the term, are Greek, seventh-, sixth-, and fifth-century lyric and dramatic poets. Carr also notes that a new form of cultural identity arises in Hellenistic Greek culture, "Hellenism introduced the idea of a transethnic 'Greek' identity defined by whether or not an individual had taken on Greek culture."[53] Sandnes (48) notes an even earlier record of this new sense of Greek identity. In Isocrates' assertion, 380 BCE (*Paneg* 50), "the title 'Hellenes' is applied rather to those who share our culture than to those who share a common blood" (τῆς παιδεύσεως τῆς ἡμετέρας ἤ τοὺς τῆς κοινῆς φύσεως μετέχοντας).

For Jews thus surrounded by Greek models of education, texts, and even the concept of authorship, Carr argues that the Hebrew Bible "is a counter-curriculum to that of Hellenistic education,"[54] a hybrid expression of cultural resistance. Evident in broader ways, the renewed focus on learning "Hebrew in the Hellenistic period would represent a form of hybrid cultural resistance to a textual educational system focused on gaining competence in Greek."[55] He notes as another hybrid form of cultural resistance,

> [T]he emergence for the first time of a Jewish identity not exclusively based in ethnic affiliation. It is around the early second century that we first see stories of "conversion" to Judaism and other indicators that Jewish identity, like Hellenistic "Greek" identity, is becoming a way of life, a *politeia*, rather than national identity.[56]

Perhaps most relevant for this study is Carr's summary of the hybrid conventions that evolved to make production of the Hebrew Bible possible,

> It borrowed Greek techniques for textual standardization to protect the emergent standardization of the Hebrew text. It used Greek-like paragraph markers to mark pericopes in the Hebrew corpus. It drew boundaries around the text that were modeled on yet surpassed the relatively sharp contours of the Hellenistic curriculum. It often was designated in Hellenistic categories like "ancestral laws," even as those categories were modified in often radical ways to fit the emergent Judean way of life ... provid[ing] the basis for a broadly aimed educational process that corresponded to the broader, non-temple focused aims of Hellenistic education ... [T]his body of indigenous Hebrew texts appears to have represented a hyperversion of the Greek forms of textuality it opposed.[57]

Carr finds the best examples of this hybridity in the Hasmonean dynasty, which he sees as embodying "an emerging form of Hellenized, and 'Hellenistic,' Torah-observing Judaism."[58] He uncovers a unique hybrid of "anti-Greek propaganda along with promotion and extension of a stylized non-Greek indigenous culture," but with "the use of Greek forms to advance such propaganda and culture within a monarchy adopting significant elements of Hellenistic culture ... this hybrid Hellenistic/anti-Hellenism mix shaped emergent Jewish education and textuality."[59] It is in 2 Maccabees, in particular, that "contradictions between Hellenistic and anti-Hellenistic elements emerge with particular clarity."[60] Though "saturated with Greek literary genres and ... written in Greek and reflect[ing] the author's thorough education in the Greek literary tradition ... and [promoting] Greek educational and character values like nobility, reason, beauty, self-control, and the ability to sacrifice familial relationships," to do so it employs "Hebrew examples and constant echoes of Jewish Scriptures like the *Aqedah*."[61] The text 2 Maccabees thus "is a Jewish example ... of Greek-language oral-written textuality."[62]

Van der Toorn argues that instruction in foreign languages would have been a standard element in Israelite scribal culture, "the knowledge of foreign languages was part of their profession ... The linguistic skills of the scribes would normally have included the mastery of one or more foreign languages ... In addition to Aramaic, the scribal program may have taught other languages as well, such as Egyptian and, later, Greek."[63] I suggest, however, there is no need to assume a particularly late date for knowledge of Greek by Israel's scribal culture. Smith, for instance, observes, of the postexilic period (2008: 234),

> Despite the stereotype that Greek was relatively minor in Jewish life in Judea at this time, it is clear that it was a considerable force in Judean culture. Even Qumran preserves Greek texts, and even Greek translations of sacred writings.

I will extend Carr's arguments to explore the motives behind the importation of myths from another culture. For instance, we can understand the examples here pursued in Chapters 1 through 4 as instances of a similar hybridity. When the scribal tradition uses Greek characters and forms to express traditional Israelite culture, the new Israelite version of a myth can also serve as a polemic against Greek culture. I thus argue that Israelite oral traditions and scribal culture were not only acquainted with, influenced, and shaped by ancient Greek culture and narratives but also were to such an extent that they formed their own variations on it to express their own, very different agenda.

Owing to diachronic interaction and acquaintance with Greek culture, Israel had more than a little knowledge of what we now call Greek myth. As to how they would have gained such acquaintance, we need to remain open to multiple possible scenarios, from different forms of oral performance – some of which should be assumed to go back to the period of Philistine incursion – to interactions between textual traditions. Recent discoveries have pushed back the date of the Greek alphabet, as Woodard notes, in conjunction with his study of the Fayum Tablets (3),

> [T]here is a network of affiliations that appear to draw the plaques into the world of the eastern Mediterranean, especially East Ionic Greeks ...

> Recent finds require an earlier date for the origin of the Greek alphabet than that advocated by many classicists throughout the twentieth century … late ninth century BC is reasonable.

This might allow for earlier circulation of Greek texts than is typically thought. But how does a myth pass from one culture to another?

Divine translatability

Mark Smith has written extensively on issues relevant to myths moving from one people to another in his work on "divine translatability." How did ancient peoples across the ancient Near East and their scribes, including those of ancient Israel, regard the gods of other peoples? Building on and responding to earlier work by Assmann, Smith offers a basic statement of the phenomenon (2008: 6), "[P]eople in one culture, most commonly at a highly elite level, explicitly recognize that the deities of other cultures are as real as its own." Those different peoples who participate would, from our perspective, understand their deities in cross-cultural discourse with each other (2008: 6): "translatability involves specific equation or identifications of deities across cultures and the larger recognition of deities of other cultures in connection to one's own deities." Smith notes the well-known example of Herodotus who, in his travels in foreign lands, understood an Assyrian, Arabian, and Persian goddess as versions of Aphrodite, Horus as Apollo, and Osiris as Dionysus (251–52).[64]

As Smith demonstrates, Israel during the monarchic period accepted other peoples' gods as real (2008: 10): "this translatability took the form, of a worldview that could recognize other national gods as valid for Israel's neighbors just as Yahweh was for Israel." Abundant in numerous Bronze Age sources, including Hittite treaties with Ramesses II, Ugaritic god lists, and the Amarna letters, evidence for divine translatability is widespread in earlier periods.[65] Passages he considers in the Hebrew Bible that demonstrate this understanding include Judges 11 (Smith 2008: 110–12); 2 Kings 1 (op. cit., 114–16); and 2 Kings 3 (op. cit., 116–18). Divine translatability extended far beyond written documents. On Cyprus, Greeks and Phoenicians shared a temple, in which the Greeks worshipped Athena and the Phoenicians worshipped the goddess Anat.[66] Apuleius offers an extensive list of goddesses in the *Golden Ass* 11.5. When the robed goddess appears to Lucius, in answer to his prayer to the Queen of Heaven, she asserts that she is known by many names, among them Minerva, Venus, Diana, Proserpina, Ceres, Juno, Bellona, and Hecate, but that her true name is Isis.

But such an understanding was not to last as Israel completed its transition away from its own earlier polytheism[67] to the resultant monotheism. Over time, owing to various pressures and changing conceptions of its god, Israel loses divine translatability. Smith partly ascribes this to fuller exposure to the more international empires emerging in Mesopotamia (2008: 10),

Israel's loss of translatability represented an internal development that corresponds with its experiences of the initial stage of the international age emerging under the Assyrians and the Babylonians ... the conceptual shift in this period involved a sophisticated hermeneutic that retained older formulations of translatability within expressions of non-translatability and monotheism.

In the Greco-Roman period, not only did Israel lose divine translatability but also scribes occasionally altered the passed-down biblical texts, censoring them to prevent audiences from perceiving too much common ground with polytheistic cultures (2008: 20),

> This situation changes dramatically during the Greco-Roman period. Within this time frame, biblical censorship serves to "protect" the biblical God from the appearance of horizontal translatability ... two cases of censorship against horizontal translatability, Deuteronomy 32:8–9 and Genesis 14:22 ... These show deliberate choices or alterations designed to protect against the appearance of polytheism.

The rejection of translatability also serves to advance other agendas, some of which we will consider repeatedly throughout this study. It becomes a means whereby *Israel can assert its control over some of the myths that it adopts and adapts for its own fairly different purposes* (183, italics mine),

> The eventual Israelite rejection of translatability in this context [Gen 1– 11] is arguably a form of reverse hegemony, whereby the dominant culture of Mesopotamia, its literary contribution and its understandings of divinity, are reduced and subordinated to Israelite visions of reality.

One new, *radical*, way of denying divine translatability that comes into play is euhemerism. Smith discusses euhemerism in connection with Philo of Byblos. Philo's *Phoenician History*, our sole surviving account of Phoenician mythology, engages in many of the usual practices of divine translatability. Thus, he refers to each of the Phoenician gods by the corresponding Greek figure. Astarte, for instance, is Aphrodite.[68] Some of the correspondences or translations of deities Philo argues for appear in earlier authors and were already traditional by his time. But, he applies the rationalizing element of euhemerism: he views the ancient gods as having originally been mortals, who, glorified through subsequent tradition, became understood as gods. Smith notes his approach at length (2008: 256),

> While Philo's treatment shows typologies of deities ... his presentation manifests methods of rationalist interpretation ... the theory of euhemerism ... which viewed deities of traditional mythology as human beings accorded divine honor after their deaths because of their

achievements or benefactions to humanity ... Philo indulges in classic euhemeristic interpretation of the gods as deified humans ... he makes them into Phoenicians.[69]

Euhemerism appears to be a well-known, widely circulating stance and methodology in the Hellenistic era, Euhemerus being fourth century BCE.[70] I will argue that forms of Euhemerism are broadly used in the Bible in both Hebrew Bible and New Testament narratives. In particular, in Chapters 1 (in the account in Gen 9–10 of the sons of Noah), 3 (the role of Rachel in Gen 27–33), 5 (the role of Herod), and 9 (various aspects of Revelation), I will argue that biblical scribes and authors present as mortals characters who are Greek gods in the Greek myths that these narratives, I suggest, are refashioning.

Smith also considers some of the broader implications that euhemerism has for the Hebrew Bible (2008: 270, italics mine),

> Even as Philo resists the intellectual project's purpose, he employs its intellectual methods and horizons, for example, Hellenistic euhemerism ... A similar effort may be at work in Judea in the production of scriptural works (contained in what later emerges as the Hebrew Bible). This may represent a local project to generate "a national literature," as a counterpoint to Hellenistic philosophy and literature. Perhaps ironically, *this project did so by drawing from Greco-Roman forms.*

Divine translatability gives one reason for understanding how and why ancient peoples would import other peoples' myths into their own repertoire. It demonstrates one reason for ancient peoples to regard another people's myths as significant because those narratives, after all, depict a god or gods who corresponds to their own.

Epic poetry and the Hebrew Bible

Of the many types of Greek myth that Israelite scribes found useful for their own agendas,[71] the larger cycle of Trojan War myth proved most relevant and most attractive for Joshua through 2 Kings. The crown jewel of Trojan War myth and the most prestigious narrative in ancient Greece, the *Iliad*, offered proud heroes and highly ambivalent depictions of warrior kings involved in national causes, kings who often quarrel with their prophets and lose the favor of their chief god. The *Iliad* not only became an epic paradigm within Greek culture but, I argue, also for Israelite scribes, much as *Gilgamesh* seems to have been. If we accept Janko's dating of the *Iliad*'s text to the last quarter of the eighth century,[72] but keep in mind the likelihood of earlier circulation of oral versions, it is easily early enough to impact a Hebrew Bible undergoing rewriting, revision, and editing, for centuries after that.

Epics build on, and can evolve out of, earlier epics. Both the *Iliad* and *Odyssey*, for instance, allude to an earlier epic about Jason and the Argonauts.[73]

We are still tracing the echoes of *Gilgamesh* in Homeric epic, though we will probably never know the nature of the contact. Did a bilingual Greek bard hear a live performance of a Babylonian version? Does the Homeric tradition reflect influence from a textual tradition of *Gilgamesh*?

Why does the Hebrew Bible lack epic?[74] Epic is inherently polytheistic. Typically, the epic hero has personal interactions with multiple gods.[75] The Hebrew Bible is largely a prose work, which suggests a closer affinity with archives, as Van der Toorn notes.[76] Moreover, the Hebrew Bible is not as fond of the figure of the hero, the default protagonist of an epic, as are other ancient myth traditions, particularly Greek myth. Almost entirely absent from the Pentateuch, which prefers patriarchs and prophets as protagonists, heroic protagonists feature in a few miniatures in Judges but are otherwise largely confined to Joshua and David.

Though lacking epic, nonetheless, the Hebrew Bible alludes to it and reworks it. We may have references to lost epics in the mentions of Shamgar (Judges) and Nimrod (Genesis), as well as the references to the Book of Yashar.[77] Furthermore, commentators have argued that the Hebrew Bible consciously applies epic models of organization and characterization. Smith, in his study of correspondences between David and Jonathan, Gilgamesh and Enkidu, and Achilles and Patroclus, suggests so: "I would sympathize with Cross's conviction that biblical books such as Samuel were 'interpreting the later history of Israel in Epic patterns.'"[78] But which "epic patterns"? Cross no doubt has in mind Ugaritic or Canaanite epic and, we can assume, additional Babylonian or Assyrian narratives. A case for *Gilgamesh* no longer needs to be made. However, I am making the case for including Greek epic as well.

In Trojan War myth, Israelite scribal tradition had, ready to hand, characters with developed dynamics between them, more than a little relevant for depicting Israelite saga, some of which, in the Philistines, reflected their own historical interactions with the Mycenaean phase of Greek culture. In particular the figures of Agamemnon, the prophet Calchas, and priest Chryseis, Achilles, Clytemnestra, Iphigenia, and the interrelations of these characters, were received as types, seen as appropriate vehicles to help depict several kinds of conflict. Of the six ways Van der Toorn posits by which scribes produced written texts, two are most relevant for my argument: "(5) adaptation of an existing text for a new audience; and (6) integration of individual documents into a more comprehensive composition."[79]

The larger David narrative suggests a prose epic in several respects, particularly if we apply Carr's model of hybrid cultural resistance. David's saga adopts many of Homeric epic's stylistic traits but employs them contrary to the norms and expectations of Greek culture. All is now subsumed under a Yahwist agenda, the expected type scenes of Trojan War myth, in which Greeks defeat Trojans, now articulate Israel's conflict with Philistines for a *reverse* outcome, in which Israel will prove victorious,[80] much as Vergil will later shift audience loyalty in his Roman refashioning of the Trojan War.

David moves freely back and forth in the zones between Philistine and Israelite culture. He should be understood as personifying the transmission of some aspects of Mycenaean Greek culture onto Israel. Whatever historical realities David's larger narrative may depict, it has been shaped by awareness of Trojan War saga: larger aspects of David's character correspond to key traits of the Homeric Achilles.[81] An even stronger case can be made for how Saul's character conforms to Agamemnon.

Agamemnon in the Hebrew Bible

As an example of some of the techniques I will use in this study, let us briefly consider how the traditional figure of Agamemnon has been adapted in the Hebrew Bible. What of his role in the *Iliad*? Whitman sees him as "a foil to Achilles," whom Homer undercuts throughout the *Iliad* by having him fail to meet audience expectations of how a king should behave.[82] As Whitman puts it, Homer uses "all his traditional eminence as a means of diminishing" him.[83] For instance, the *Iliad* has four major *aristeiai*, an episode in which a major warrior, inspired and propelled by a god, becomes virtually unstoppable, capable of inflicting massive casualties on his opponents. Agamemnon's *aristeia* achieves, as Whitman notes, "scarcely even a degree of victory."[84] Whitman concludes that Homer's aim is to depict Agamemnon, "as the opposite of Achilles – the nadir, as Achilles is the zenith, of the heroic assumption."[85] Agamemnon is "a magnificently dressed incompetence, without spirit or spiritual concern; his dignity is marred by pretension ... his prowess by a savagery which is the product of a deep uncertainty and fear."[86]

Greenburg focuses on Agamemnon's outrageous treatment of Apollo's priest, Chryses, in the *Iliad*'s first episode. When the priest comes to him to ransom his daughter, Agamemnon's potential concubine, the Greek commander treats Chryses with contempt. As Greenburg notes, not only does Agamemnon dishonor the priest, he misjudges the priest's influence with Apollo. Chryses' reference to Apollo "embodies a threat of sorts ... Agamemnon ... understands it and rejects it ... He is obviously and erroneously guessing that divinity will not respond to the priest's prayer."[87] He concludes, "It would be a crowning touch if Agamemnon is portrayed as being egotistically unaware of just how offensive he is."[88]

Van Nortwick builds on Whitman's observations, arguing, "The contrast between the expectations raised by his special status and the frequent lapses in leadership and judgment he displays is the key to his characterization in the *Iliad*."[89] He sees Agamemnon as "insecure about his judgment, prone to rash and ill-advised decisions."[90] When he finally issues an apology to Achilles, who does not fight for the first 19 books of the *Iliad* because of their quarrel, he claims he "is not responsible for his mistakes because Zeus sent 'blind distraction' ... upon him."[91]

As a warrior king who leads a large, national coalition to war, Agamemnon personifies many of the problems associated with kingship. Though a capable warrior, he is often petty, selfish, paranoid, and vindictive. He thematically finds himself on the wrong side of prophets and priests. Out of excessive self-concern he loses sight of the big picture, losing Zeus' favor in the process, which moves instead to Achilles. Israel's scribal tradition draws on him as a type for its own depictions of Saul and Ahab.

If I am correct, however, why are the correspondences not widely known? A few factors have hindered their due recognition. When a story rooted in a polytheistic tradition is adapted for a monotheistic tradition and audience, significant alterations are required. For instance, when Agamemnon loses Zeus' favor and support, this is far less traumatic than in monotheism. Agamemnon still retains the full support of Hera, Poseidon, and Athena. In a monotheistic adaptation, however, when Saul loses Yahweh's favor, that's it, game over. There are differences in degree in some of the corresponding elements. Agamemnon's bitter and recurring quarrels with his prophet, Calchas, and with Chryses, priest of Apollo, are significant aspects of his character, but for Saul with Samuel, and Ahab with Elijah and Micaiah, the corresponding quarrels are more central elements in the respective narratives: the prophets, Samuel and Elijah, are the main characters, in fact. Lastly, we might note the perspective of the vast majority of the Bible's readers. Popular culture, especially in the United States, assumes that David is fully "historical" but Agamemnon entirely mythical. How could a "historical" figure be partly shaped by a fictional one?

The figure of Agamemnon proved irresistibly paradigmatic for Israelite scribes to articulate issues about kingship within their own culture.[92] In different contexts, the scribes select different aspects of his character and relations with others. Saul and Ahab both share Agamemnon's serial confrontations with prophets; both lose God's favor and support, and both can be understood as embodying projected anxieties and concerns about monarchy. But only Saul, in his interactions with David, plays out a version of Agamemnon's dynamic with Achilles[93]; only Saul does so within the larger context of *confrontation with the Philistines*. Ahab, however, offers the most exact correspondences in friction between king and prophet, and a wife unexpectedly correspondent to Agamemnon's Clytemnestra.

We turn, then, to Saul. Like Agamemnon in so many ways, Saul is also a *foil*. The most powerful man in Israel, he spends much of his time nervously observing David's increasing popularity and rise, as Agamemnon does Achilles. Samuel is not only his almost constant antagonist but also, behind the scenes, exercises greater influence and authority than he. We thus have a set of three analogous characters: Saul and Agamemnon, David and Achilles, and Samuel and Calchas. The entire saga plays out against confrontation with the Philistines (1 Sam 14:52), indirect affirmation of its links with Homeric epic, if we accept that the scribal tradition is aware of the larger identity of Philistine and Greek culture.

Both Saul and Agamemnon are qualified warriors, capable of epic achievements on the battlefield. Agamemnon has his *aristeia* in *Iliad* 11; 1

Samuel 11:6 presents us with an equivalent scenario for Saul, "the Spirit of God suddenly seized him." However, while the motif normally initiates epic acts, as for Jephthah and Samson, here Saul proceeds to cut two oxen in pieces, which recapitulates Agamemnon summoning the Greeks to reclaim Helen (recounted in Apollodorus, E.3.6). After defeating the Amalekites, Saul erects a memorial to himself (1 Sam 15:12) like an Iliadic hero, whose overriding concern is with *kleos*, fame.

In his interactions with Samuel, and subsequent loss of Yahweh's favor, Saul moves into even-closer correspondence with Agamemnon. After anointing Saul as king, Samuel places the destruction of the Amalekites under the ban. When Saul elects to spare the king, his relationship with Samuel immediately disintegrates. Saul not only spares King Agag but also keeps some of the Amalekites' choicest possessions for himself. In so doing, he instantiates one of the *Iliad*'s central concerns and the prompt for Agamemnon's quarrel with Achilles: he distributes war winnings in a selfish manner. When Saul proceeds to set up a monument to his victory, he furthers our impression of excessive self-involvement.

What, then, of David and Achilles?[94] When David defeats Goliath, the Philistine's preliminary arming scene has long been recognized as conforming in almost every respect to those in the *Iliad*[95] and can be understood as referencing all three of its heroic duels, two of which, like that between David and Goliath, are to determine the entire battle between the opposing armies. The *Iliad*'s first duel between Paris and Menelaus employs a parodic arming scene. In 1 Samuel 17, the about-to-be-defeated Goliath's arming scene is so ironic as to also be parodic: for all his armor and weaponry he is easily slain. Of the three duels, that between Hector and Aias in *Iliad* 7 is far the closest to the preliminaries in 1 Samuel 17. The climax of the poem, however, is Achilles' duel with Hector, which seals the Fall of Troy.

Additional tensions between Achilles and Agamemnon serve as a rubric for Saul and David's interactions. After Achilles' quarrel with Agamemnon erupts, Zeus supports him, not Agamemnon, for the remainder of the epic. In 1 Samuel, the audience knows David has already been anointed as king, and has Yahweh's favor, from the beginning of his saga. After the quarrel, for the next three-fourths of the epic, Achilles does not fight for the Greek army and, in so doing, indirectly renders significant aid to the *Trojan* cause. David, after Saul threatens him repeatedly, goes over to the Philistines, twice entering into relationships with King Achish, the *Achaian* (1 Sam 21:10–15). During the second occasion (1 Sam 27.1–6), having earned the Philistine king's trust, Achish orders David to take the field against the Israelites (1 Sam 28). The unusual circumstance, an Israelite king working with the enemy, can be understood as Israelite scribes fashioning David's character to conform to a motif prominent in Achilles' interactions with Agamemnon, the harm he causes his fellow Greeks.

Both Achilles and David are depicted in connection with performances of epic poetry, both shown playing the lyre, as part of their larger frictions with Agamemnon and Saul. Midway through Agamemnon's quarrel with Achilles, he sends an embassy, attempting reconciliation. Reaching Achilles' tent, the embassy finds him (*Iliad* 9.186–89) playing the lyre, singing epic songs, Homeric epic's well-known self-referentiality: the subject of his own epic is singing about other epic heroes. David is also referenced as the subject of something like epic in the recurring refrain, which continues to put him in conflict with Saul: "Saul struck down thousands, but David tens of thousands" (1 Sam 18:6–8; 29:5). As Achilles plays before Agamemnon's embassy, while the deluded leader attempts reconciliation with him, so David plays the lyre before a troubled Saul. This motif is much more at home in Homeric epic: both Homeric protagonists, Achilles and Odysseus, are depicted as performers of epic poetry. Both Achilles and David are further noteworthy for their close relationships with another heroic male, Patroklos and Jonathan.[96]

Agamemnon and Saul are both depicted as visited by an *Evil Spirit*. When Agamemnon makes his public apology to Achilles for having begun their quarrel, he says it happened because Zeus sent the goddess *Ate* to delude him, as earlier Zeus also sent a Dream to deceive him. When Saul loses his support, Yahweh repeatedly sends an *Evil Spirit* (16:23; 18:10). The text 1 Samuel combines this motif with the motif of David playing lyre (1 Sam 16:23): "And whenever an evil spirit from God came upon Saul, David would take his lyre and play it, so that relief would come to Saul."

Even closer are correspondences between Agamemnon and Ahab. The latter, his interactions with prophets, his deportment on the battlefield, and his highly aggressive wife, all find virtually exact parallels in Agamemnon. Ahab's interactions with the prophets Elijah and Micaiah are even closer to Agamemnon's than Saul's with Samuel, including verbal equivalents. In Agamemnon, the scribal tradition had an established character type they knew to be a vehicle suited to how they wished to depict Ahab.

Ahab's animosity toward Elijah is more pronounced, has undergone a longer period of gestation than Saul's for Samuel, and resembles Agamemnon's toward Calchas in *Iliad* 1. Ahab's first words to Elijah are contemptuous (18.17): "As soon as Ahab saw Elijah, he said to him, 'Is it you, you troubler of Israel?'" One can't imagine Saul addressing Samuel this way, but this is precisely Agamemnon's tone to his prophet Calchas and to Apollo's priest, Chryses.

The most exact, most sustained correspondences occur in 1 Kings 22, when Micaiah recounts his vision of the *Enticing Spirit* that will fool Ahab into thinking he can now capture Ramoth-gilead. Let us review Agamemnon's circumstances in Book 2 of the *Iliad*. The night after Agamemnon's quarrel with Achilles begins, after a divine council, Zeus, who now supports Achilles over Agamemnon, sends a *Deceptive Dream* (2.6: οὖλος ὄνειρος) to Agamemnon. Zeus' purpose in sending the Dream, is to fool Agamemnon into thinking he can sack Troy the next day. The Dream works, leaving Agamemnon "believing in his heart things that are not going to be accomplished" (2.36).

Deliberations and discussion follow regarding how to proceed based on the Dream. Agamemnon orders the Greeks into assembly, but first convenes his executive council. Nestor, asserting no one would believe the dream if dreamt by anyone else, says it must be true because Agamemnon dreamt it (2.79–83). In his heated exchange with his prophet Calchas on the previous day, when Calchas made known how Agamemnon's abusive treatment of Apollo's priest brought the god's wrath upon them, Agamemnon replied (1.106–7),

> Seer of evil: never yet have you told me a good thing.
> Always the evil things are dear to your heart to prophesy.
>
> (μάντι κακῶν ... αἰεί τοι τὰ κάκ' ἐστὶ φίλα φρεσὶ μαντεύεσθαι).

Agamemnon fails to take Troy on that day, and suffers a major embarrassment before his troops, most of whom now contemplate going home to Greece.

In his confrontation with Micaiah, Ahab and his forces, including King Jehoshaphat, contemplate attacking the city Ramoth-gilead. Jehoshaphat suggests Ahab first consult with Yahweh. When he does so, all Ahab's prophets prophesy that God will give him victory. When Jehoshaphat asks if there is another prophet to verify their prophecy, Ahab responds in words that closely agree with Agamemnon's rebuke of Calchas (22.8; emphasis mine), "'There is one more ... but I hate the man, because *he never prophesies good for me, never anything but evil.* His name is Micaiah son of Imlah." Later in the confrontation Ahab repeats (22.18; emphasis mine), "'Did I not tell you that he never prophesies good for me, *never anything but evil?*'" Micaiah then recounts a vision (22.19–22),

> I saw the Lord seated on his throne with all the host of heaven in attendance on his right and on his left. The Lord said, "Who will entice Ahab to go up and attack Ramoth-gilead?" One said one thing and one said another, until a spirit came forward and, standing before the Lord, said, "I shall entice him." "How?" said the Lord. "I shall go out", he answered, "and be a lying spirit[97] in the mouths of all his prophets." You see, then, how the Lord has put a lying spirit in the mouths of all these prophets of yours, because he has decreed disaster for you.

Let us review the correspondences with *Iliad* 1–2:

1 Each king contemplates trying to take a city.
  a Each king leads a coalition of forces against another coalition.
2 Detailed deliberations and discussion precede his going into battle.
  a Jehoshaphat serves a similar function as Agamemnon's Nestor.
3 Each king receives a report of divine will ensuring his victory in the battle.
4 Each main god converses with a lesser divine being.

Zeus instructs the Dream, but the Spirit volunteers for Yahweh in corresponding terms: to fool the respective kings into thinking they will sack their respective cities that day.

5   The audience, however, knows the reports to be spurious. In the *Iliad*, typical of epic conventions, the audience is present at Zeus' deliberations, observing without any doubt that Agamemnon is being deceived. The text 1 Kings 22 maintains the Hebrew Bible's usual conception of having the prophet as somehow present at the divine council (cf. Isaiah 6), a monotheistic variation on the more traditional polytheistic divine council. Micaiah relays the corresponding information that Homeric epic gives through the principal narrator.

6   Each king proceeds, and fails, based on the false report of divine support.

In a key difference, Ahab's *Enticing Spirit* account repeats the motif from Elijah's earlier confrontation of *the one true prophet defeating the many false ones*. Thus, as Cogan notes, "[T]he issues of conflicting prophetic viewpoints and the royal response to the word of YHWH dominate,"[98] whereas for Agamemnon conflicting prophetic viewpoints is a nonissue. That the 1 Kings account derives from another is suggested by its being a secondary narrative, told in a tongue-in-cheek manner, how it retains polytheistic touches – but only to lampoon them – and its focus on conflicting prophetic viewpoints. Several of the motifs are more at home in the *Iliad* than in 1 Kings. Zeus or Athena sending a Dream is common in Homeric epic, for instance, whereas Yahweh's use of the Deceiving Spirit is less so. So also, as Cogan points out, is, "The consultation with prophets rather than priests in preparation for the attack on Ramoth-gilead comes as a surprise."[99] The triumph of the one true prophet over the many false subsumes the narrative under a Yahwist agenda, not relevant to the *Iliad*. Cogan, based on similarities between Micaiah's fortunes and the later Jeremiah, argues the episode "was written toward the end of the period of classical prophecy."[100] That it is thus so much later than the *Iliad* easily allows for some form of diffusion or adaptation of it. Ahab's encounter with Micaiah suggests a careful synthesis of Agamemnon's missteps at the opening of the *Iliad*.

Greek myth and the New Testament

Why would New Testament authors draw on Greek myth? Though such intersections remain underexplored, the case is easier to make than for the Hebrew Bible. The first-century CE era of the New Testament remains largely Hellenized, Greek the international language of the educated. Greek literature, philosophy, and rhetoric remain central to the larger educational system.

The earliest New Testament writings, Paul's letters, as Marquis demonstrates, reveal him to be fully conversant in Greek rhetorical strategies, and drawing on the larger Greek mythical tradition. In 2 Corinthians 1–9, as he describes his recent trip from Asia, Paul employs all manner of Greco-Roman tropes for travel. Figuring himself as a variety of famous wanderers, he draws on the larger myths of both Dionysus and Odysseus. Marquis notes how Alexander the Great had appropriated aspects of Dionysus' spread of his worship, and other details of Dionysian cult, to depict his own victories (27),

> The rise of the Alexander the Great, moreover, would usher in a new era of Dionysian fervor at a political level, as Hellenistic propaganda portrayed the conqueror of the world from Greece to India as a new Dionysius, traveling the earth and taking captive each city he conquered.

Accordingly, Marquis demonstrates how Paul employs motifs associated with Dionysian processions (as at 2:14: θριαμβεύοντι ἡμᾶς ἐν τῷ Χριστῷ) to color his own role in the spread of Christianity.[101]

Repeatedly uttering the Roman name for the province, *Achaia* (1:1; 9:2) – for us keeping active the Hittite, Homeric, and Hebrew Bible references with which we began – Paul activates epic tropes for crossing the Mediterranean. Marquis considers his specific naming of Troas (2:12) (68),

> More significant may be the placement of Paul's travelogue from Asia through Troas (that is, Alexandria Troas, a city founded by Alexander the Great near the ancient site of Troy) to Macedonia and eventually Greece. The path from East to West, from Asia to Europe, embarking from Troy, evokes Odysseus, hero of Troy, the most famous traveling demagogue.

He continues, noting how Paul here departs from his usual practice in his use of the place name, Troas (69),

> [A]ncient writers deployed the strait between Asia and Europe as a cultural boundary, often building upon its epic role separating the two sides in the Trojan War. Paul's normal practice in referring to locations on his international routes is to refer to cities (Ephesus, for example) as opposed to regions (Asia). By mentioning Asia and Troas, Paul evokes a host of traveling leaders who crossed the boundary between continents in order to found new worldwide regimes, from the legendary Greeks fighting Troy, to Persian invaders, to Alexander the Great. Additionally, Paul breaks off his travelogue before narrating his arrival in Macedonia and reunion with Titus. Much like Odysseus, his return is deferred, resulting in wandering.

Not only is Paul conversant with the mythic traditions but also in his dexterous play with these tropes, he clearly assumes that some of his audience is as well. Sandnes comes to a similar conclusion (249),

> The simple fact that Paul engages in written communication with his converts, and expects them to read aloud from his letters when coming

together (1 Thess. 5.27, cf. Col. 4.16), assumes the presence of literate participants in the Church … The presence of literate members of the congregation further implies some basic familiarity with Homer and the Greek legacy.[102]

When we turn to the Gospels we find the same is largely true. Though the use of rhetoric is less pronounced than in Paul, many narrative components are clearly indebted to those common in Greco-Roman myth. Why would it be otherwise? White records some of the initial reactions to early Christians (66–68),

Pagans looking at early Christianity were often amused by the stories about the resurrection and ascension of Jesus. After all, pagans knew of many such stories in their own tradition … For pagans, however, it was neither the miraculousness nor the preposterousness of the Christians that bewildered them; it was when Christians tried to argue that they were somehow unique.

The assumption of difference remains to this day, for the most part. We need to shake off centuries of reading habits to approach the Gospels anew.

If, for instance, we consider, as White notes, how multicultural the first-century CE Roman Empire was, some of the reasons for larger similarities are clear enough (20),

[N]either the authors nor their audiences lived in a vacuum. Rather they lived in the rich and complex cultural mix of the Roman Empire, one of the most pluralistic environments in the ancient world … Greek had become the common medium of communication and would remain so throughout the Roman period at least in the East. The political stability of Roman rule … also meant that people from all over the empire could move about with relative ease.

Reflecting these realities, the Gospels are products of their time, shaped by their authors to conform to the cultural expectations of their audience, as White notes (21),

What this means for the Gospel authors is that they could-in fact, *had* to-address the cultural backgrounds of their respective audiences. A storyteller must speak in terms, symbols, and metaphors the audience can understand … If anything, the rhetoric of persuasion is even more dependent on knowing where your audience is coming from and using their own background to get your message across.

As we will observe in Chapters 6 and 7, this is particularly true of Luke and John, chronologically later than Mark and Matthew.

In terms of more specific narrative details, White notes that the Gospels' depiction of Jesu' miracles conform to the expectations of the larger non-Christian audience (165), "[T]he miracles of Jesus as presented in the Gospels are patterned after standard types of miracle stories in both Jewish and Greco-Roman tradition." As we will note in Chapter 7, Christ's most climactic instances of healing are right in line with those of the miraculous Greek healer, Asclepios, son of Apollo.

The author of Luke in particular has consciously shaped his narrative to reflect larger engagement of the contemporary Greco-Roman world.[103] Several different currents connected with Greek philosophy are visible. As White observes, the larger contours of Luke and Acts, both by the same author, follow a rubric that comes from Greek philosophy (336–37),

> Charles Talbert ... has noted ... that the two volumes correspond to a pattern in the "Lives" of Greek philosophers, where the life of the "founder" is followed by a description of his successors and their school.

If we ask to which school or schools of Greek philosophy does Luke's Christ exhibit the closest ties, White argues that it is to the figure of Socrates in general, but especially as he had developed within the Cynics (340),

> This likening of Jesus to Socrates may also account for the Lukan slant on socioeconomic criticism, for Socrates by the first cent had been co-opted by several schools of Greek philosophy other than Platonism ... a prevalent view of Socrates as a "cynic" philosopher ... Central to these broader "cynicizing" ideals was a criticism of wealth and luxury ... Only by divesting oneself of care for worldly goods is one able to focus properly on moral self-improvement.[104]

Familiarity with the education system during the relevant period offers a further window into the interplay between the authors of the Gospels, their audiences, and earlier texts of Greek mythology. Sandnes notes the stability and longevity of the Greco-Roman educational system (214), "Teresa Morgan's survey of Egyptian papyri has demonstrated that both content and teaching methods remained the same throughout the Roman Empire for almost a millennium."[105] We have lists of the authors that typically comprised the core readings (Sandnes 61),

> At the beginning of encyclical studies, the students worked primarily with Homer in order to acquire the necessary skills in reading and writing ... Sextus Empiricus, living towards the end of the second cent CE, mentions the poets Homer, Hesiod, Pindar, Euripides, Menander and some others as well.

Noting Teresa Morgan's earlier work, Sandnes reiterates the uncontested position Homer held in encyclical education (42),

Texts from Homer and Vergil made up this core ... Other writers studied were Euripides, Menander, Demosthenes, Terence, Cicero and Horace ... The uncontested position of Homer in encyclical education formed the basis for ancient pan-Hellenism, and Homer's unique position in Greek education contributed considerably to the Greek character of the Roman Empire.

Products of this system thus had significant exposure to Homer, and to the other seminal texts by Hesiod and Euripides that we consider in this study.

Sandnes considers the example of Philo of Alexandria. His writings clearly document Jewish exposure to encyclical education (248), "Philo of Alexandria's writings antedate New Testament literature by some decades, and they address Jewish participation in encyclical studies quite extensively." In several ways he can be seen as a bridge, an example of continuity, between Jewish responses to Greek literature and approaches that Christians would later apply (ibid.): "He provides solutions and supportive biblical interpretations that would later appear among many Christians." Sandnes thus determines that the usual stereotype of Christian authors as somehow existing and writing in a cultural vacuum is erroneous (ibid.): "It is hard to believe that first-century Christians formed an isolated island when it came to the question of the Greek educational heritage."

Sandnes also documents the wide range of responses to encyclical education by early Christians. The varied positions, what he calls "the Christian *agôn* over encyclical studies in the first four centuries" (83), range from extremists who wanted little or no contact with the traditional educational system, to those who saw great value in the traditional Greco-Roman system. On the former, Sandnes (153) notes Celsus, as reported by Origen,

> Celsus says that Christians are not even able to give a reason for their faith, but instead lay restrictions on human reason and intellect ... that they are afraid of teachers; because teachers represent a challenge with which they cannot cope.

Christians found support for this position in Paul's epistles, particularly 1 Corinthians 1–2, as Sandnes notes (237–38), " 'So that your faith might rest not on human wisdom but on the power of God' (1 Cor. 2:5)."[106]

Christians who recognized continued value in encyclical studies often justified their doing so because of readings they derived by appropriating methods used in Homeric studies. For example, allegorical readings had become common in Neoplatonic and other readings of the epics. Sandnes cites a typical example from Seneca (66),

> Seneca *Ep.* 88 interprets Homer depicting Odysseus as storm tossed in ways that show us how "by the example of Ulysses, how I am to love my country, my wife, my father, and how, even after suffering shipwreck, I am to sail toward these goals, honourable as they are."

In a somewhat similar is the anonymous Christian author[107] who argues that Homer contains intimations of Christianity, much as Christians argue of the Hebrew Bible, as Sandes notes (95),

> Thanks to sophisticated exegesis of some Homeric passages, the author reaches the conclusion that Homer was, in fact, propagating monotheism. This is proved by reference to two Homeric passages... *Il.* 9.445 where Homer says θεὸς αὐτός, which, according to the author, means God himself; it is a reference to the only God (περὶ ἑνὸς καὶ μόνου θεοῦ)... *Il.* 2.204 in which Odysseus speaks against the rule of many: "let there be one [εἷς] ruler."

The same author finds Homeric references to Genesis, as Sandnes observes (96),

> The garden of Alkinoos (*Od.* 7.112–32) brought to mind the garden of Eden, and the story about Otus and Ephialtes (*Od.* 11.305–20) imitated the tower of Babel (Gen. 11). These examples demonstrate detailed work on Homer's text by some anonymous Christian intellectual.

Clement of Alexandria advocates applying the principle of *distinctio* to Greek literature, which, as Sandnes notes, becomes a common way of framing the issues early Christians had with traditional education (143), "the principle of *distinctio*, distinguishing between the useful and the unprofitable." Sandnes establishes Clement's position thusly (124–25), "his *Paedogogus* ... is a paradigm that assigns value also to Greek education." In his *Stromateis*, as Sandnes observes (125), he mounts what is in some respects a defense of Greek philosophy and the encyclical studies tradition,

> [H]e will not shrink from making use of (συγχρᾶσθαι) what is best (τὰ κάλλιστα) in philosophy and other preparatory instruction (προπαδεία) ... He adduces biblical support ... 1 Cor. 9:20–21, on becoming a Greek for the sake of the Greeks, and 1 Col. 1:28, on becoming perfect in wisdom. The resources of learning resemble the nourishment of athletes; they do not indulge in luxury, but strive after the good ... Searching out the good in Greek literature is thus the ideal of this text.

He characterizes Christian opponents in ways similar to Celsus (126), "the adversaries ... are not themselves acquainted with Greek literature, but are only talking about what they have heard." Clement, however, embraces a very open position on sources of wisdom (Sandnes 126),

> Clement emphasizes that all wisdom, whether human or divine, originates with God. In *Strom.* 1.4, he cites Homer, Hesiod, the Old Testament prophets, biblical wisdom texts and Paul the apostle, as examples of wisdom.

The episode in the Exodus myth, where Israelites obtain valuables from the Egyptians before leaving, became a touchstone for Christian authors who advocated the continued value of the traditional education. The curious account depicts the Israelites, before departing, as asking well-intentioned Egyptians to freely give them valuables, but later refers to them as having plundered the Egyptians (Exod 11:2, 12:35–36). Later, however (Exod 35:30–35, 36:1), in Origen's reading, the Israelites can fashion appropriate materials for use in their own worship from these "plundered" goods (Sandnes: 145). Origen thus counsels Christians to approach the Greek education system in similar fashion, taking what they find useful, in accord with the principle of *distinctio*.

Sandnes notes his unique response to those opposed to reading Greek literature (151), "Origen urges his opponent to read the narratives about Jesus in the gospels using methods commonly applied to Homer and Greek classical myths in general."[108] Sandnes spells out his approach in greater detail (152),

> (1.42) He (Origen) wants the Gospels to be read analogously with Homer's readings ... an openness to the text and a willingness to acknowledge levels of meaning within it, and at the same time to withdraw belief from that which is entirely unacceptable without rejecting the rest. This generous approach which Origen here calls for corresponds with the principle of critical use ... developed in Homeric interpretation.

In my study, then, we will also follow Origen's advice.

Sandnes also notes the unique, though lost, example of Apollinaris. Framing it as an instance of the struggle by Christians to attain intellectual equality (167), Sandnes considers Sozomen's references in his *Historia Ecclesiastica* (5.18.1–4), "Apollinaris ... employed his great learning and ingenuity in the production of a heroic epic on the antiquities of Hebrews to the reign of Saul, as a substitute for the poem of Homer [ἀντὶ μὲν τῆς Ὁμήρου ποιήσεως]." Thus, not only does Homeric epic remain monumental in the early Christian era but also some Christian authors clearly proceed by intuiting significant common ground between it and Hebrew Bible narratives. Ironically, Apollinaris thus reworked into the form of Homeric epic some of the same narratives from the Hebrew Bible that I have argued in the preceding text are responses to Homeric epic!

Jerome offers an intriguing instance of, in Sandnes's view (201), "the ascetic who is addicted to the Greek legacy." Though ambivalent about some aspects of traditional Greek education, he encouraged Christians to obtain familiarity with it, for, as Sandnes notes (202), "At the centre of his thought here is ... the necessity to know it in order to fight it." Elsewhere, as in Origen's example of the Israelites "plundering the Egyptians," Jerome, as others, uses the account of the pagan woman in Deuteronomy 21 as a metaphor for how Christians should approach Greek education (202),

> Jerome again draws on Deut. 21, about pagan women taken captive, and whom the Israelites were allowed to marry – on certain conditions.

Marriage must be preceded by the shaving of her hair and eyebrows. The attractive pagan woman ... This figurative speech recognizes beauty and value in Greek learning, but also emphasizes the necessity of critique and selection.

For an example of how a specific New Testament author evidences that he is a product of the larger Greek education system, Conzelmann also considers the author of Luke/Acts. He argues that this author's Greek reflects the greatest overlap with Greek literature (xxxv–xxxvi),

Elements of literary Greek are more pronounced in his work than else-where in the New Testament (with the exception of Hebrews). The vocabulary is considerable and exhibits points of contact with Josephus, Plutarch, Lucian, and most of all with the LXX.

He notes a few specific points of contact the author of Luke/Acts exhibits with Homer. Thus Acts 27:42, for instance, has ἐπικέλλειν τὴν ναῦν, "to run the vessel aground," which Conzelmann notes (221) "is found in Homer *Od.* 9.148–49, 546." ἐρείδω, "stick," is also found in Homer. He further offers a list of the Lukan author's general characteristics that evidence his exposure to Greek literature.[109]

Taylor's study of hospitality and recognition in the Bible, in both Hebrew Bible and New Testament narratives, provides significant support for many of the arguments I make in this study. On the one hand, he notes general affin-ities between sequences in the Hebrew Bible and Homeric epic (24): "Many stretches of Old Testament narrative both in the Pentateuch and in the his-torical books from Joshua to Chronicles are broadly similar to Homeric epic in their story-telling conventions." On the other hand, he argues for specific connections between Euripides and the New Testament (63–65),

The text of *Christus Patiens* ... borrows extensively from *Bacchae*, to the extent that a gap in the transmitted text of the Euripides play can be partially filled by lines from it. *Bacchae* was a popular play in antiquity ... For several passages in Acts a convincing case can be made for direct influence. The escape of Dionysus from prison in a miraculous earth-quake (*Ba.* 580–603) is very similar to the experience of Paul and Silas at Philippi (Acts 16:25–30) ... When later Paul recounts that incident before Agrippa, he says of the divine voice, "it is hard to kick against the goads" (Acts 26:14): this expression, unique in the New Testament, echoes Dionysus urging Pentheus not to "kick against the goads" (*Ba.* 795).

Taylor additionally points out general affinities between classical literature and a range of New Testament narratives, as well as a key difference (113),

[I]t is illuminating to read the gospels, Acts, epistles, revelation, as if they were classical texts. The gospels more specifically resemble philosophical biography: the story of a teacher, with a collection of illustrative incidents and memorable examples for disciples to follow ... They represent a mixture of genres ... They innovate by their focus on people of humble background.

Though we should observe that the *Odyssey*, in the prominence given Eumaios, already casts "humble" characters in prominent roles.

He notes considerable common ground between the second half of Acts and the *Odyssey* (132),

Above all this Mediterranean *periêgêsis* resembles the *Odyssey* ... the 2nd half of the story focuses almost entirely on Paul, putting him in the role of an epic or tragic hero. His successive arrivals at different places, with account of the people he meets and the good or bad treatment he receives, are broadly equivalent to the adventures of Odysseus.

He therefore concludes, much as Conzelmann (though using other means) demonstrated (133), "A debt to Greek literature is entirely plausible to Luke." He also notes an additional correspondence with Homer, which I address in the following text in Chapter 6 (134), "Luke likewise has his speakers address the reader at the same time as they address the inscribed audience." He reiterates the unique stance of Origen, as Sandnes, that he (158) "alone among early Christian authors explicitly compares the experience of reading Homer and reading the gospels (*Contra Celsum* 1.42)."

For a brief example of the possible influence of Greek narratives on those of the New Testament, we might explore for a moment the possibilities that Acts 14:8–19 presents. Several commentators have argued that the tale of Paul and Barnabas in Lystra, in which the two are likened by their audience to Zeus and Hermes, refers to Ovid's *Metamorphoses*. While Taylor notes several of the considerable correspondences (108 ff.), he suggests that both accounts, Ovid's and Acts', may derive from an earlier local legend or tradition. Robbins, however, argues for a direct connection with Ovid's account (59): "Interpreters regularly raise the possibility that the verse in Acts alludes to the story of the visit of the gods Zeus and Hermes to the elderly couple Baucis and Philemon in Ovid Metamorphoses 8:611–724." Among others whom he cites for support is Conzelman, who again remarks on the classical training of the Acts author (110),

It need not be asked whether Paul and Barnabas were seen as Zeus and Hermes, the Greek gods, or whether we have here a Greek interpretation of the native gods in this place. For the author (from his "classical" perspective) they are recognized simply as Zeus and Hermes.

Robbins concludes his discussion by noting Wordelmann's argument that Acts 14 also alludes to another famous myth of Zeus coming down among mortals, the story of Zeus' visit to Lycaon, which Ovid also narrates (ibid.),

> Recently, Amy Wordelman[110] has presented evidence that a reader only understands the dynamics of the Lukan episode if they have knowledge of the tradition of Zeus's visit to King Lycaon (cf. Ovid, *Metamorphosis* 1.226–261 … If this is true, Acts 14:11–12 contains cultural allusion to a particular episode in addition to cultural reference to these two Greek gods.

Finally, let me make a few brief comments about the oral tradition the stories about Christ passed through for some decades before the Gospels were written.[111] As White shows in some detail, Paul's letters give us a window into the earliest surviving versions of the circulating oral tradition. Two passages in 1 Corinthians depict Paul as having received an oral tradition and actively passing it on (White: 108). Both evidence what has become known as a "tradition summary formula." Perhaps most straightforward is that at 1 Corinthians 15:3–7 (Παρέδωκα γὰρ ὑμῖν ἐν πρώτοις ὃ καὶ παρέλαβον): "I handed on to you the tradition I had received." This appears earlier at 1 Corinthians 11:23–26 (γὰρ παρέλαβον ἀπὸ τοῦ Κυρίου ὃ καὶ παρέδωκα ὑμῖν): "For the tradition I handed on to you came to me from the Lord himself."

What is the abbreviated oral tradition to which Paul here refers? As White notes (110), 1 Corinthians 15:3–7 "gives us the basic outline of the story with a relative sequence of events … 'He died, he was buried, he was raised, and he appeared.'" The passion narrative, therefore, seems to have comprised the earliest core of stories passed down about Jesus. Paul makes no mention of many types of stories prominent in the later Gospels, no mention of Jesu' miracles, for instance.[112] The text 1 Corinthians 11:23–26, however, has the earliest enunciation of the Last Supper tradition and passes on a specific saying (White: 112–13): "Here we have an important additional component, namely, words spoken by Jesus himself in instituting dining as a commemorative practice." It will later develop into the establishment of the Eucharist as a rite. However, as White underscores (ibid.), here "there is no mention of Passover at all." Nor does either early account make any mention of a betrayal episode.[113]

With no evidence of antecedents for many major components in the later Gospels, it is clear, then, in many respects, that the tradition remains quite fluid during the time between Paul and the Gospels. In some instances, as we note in Chapter 6, the divergences between Paul's accounts and what will later be written in the Gospels are extraordinary. The authors of Luke and John in particular shape their Jesus along lines that reflect significant interaction with larger Greco-Roman culture. But this process is already evident in some manner near the beginning. At 1 Thessalonians 1:9, in what is often thought to be the earliest of Paul's letters, he addresses an audience that seems to consist largely of former "pagans." At various stages, then, Paul and the Gospel authors articulate their message in increasing degrees of inclusivity, moving outside the confines of earlier Jewish tradition and expectation, fashioning their narratives in ways that their increasingly non-Jewish audience would have found familiar.

Notes

1 Smith 2008: 182.
2 Van der Toorn 2007: 116, 177, 210, 1654 & ff., 120, 134, 215, 153 & ff., 248 & ff., respectively.
3 See discussion in Louden 2011a: 72–96.
4 Ibid.: 164–79.
5 Ibid.: 222–43
6 See also White 2010: 256: "[T]he Lukan narrative may well be playing directly off Roman imperial propaganda associated with the divine-man portrayal of Augustus' own birth and epic traditions from Vergil's *Aeneid*."
7 My discussion of Hittite proper names is based on Beckman et al. 2011.
8 See also Bachvarova (2016: 333–42) for discussion of some of these texts.
9 E.g., Singer 2013: 24: "The latter [Ahhiyawa] is exactly the name used by Homer to designate the Greeks, Achaioi, which, after many years of vain controversy, has been definitely shown to reflect Ahhiyawa."
10 Watkins 1995: 148–49.
11 Beckman et al.: 119–20.
12 Ibid.: 2.
13 Ibid.: 71, 99.
14 M. L. West 2001: 262–66.
15 Hans G. Guterbock, "Troy in Hittite Texts? Wilusa, Ahhiyawa, and Hittite History," in *Troy and the Trojan War: A Symposium Held at Bryn Mawr College*, John Lawrence Angel and Machteld Johanna Mellink, eds. (Bryn Mawr Archaeological Monographs, 1986), pp. 33–44.
16 See Louden (2011a: 326–28) for discussion of correspondences between the Egyptian stelae and two episodes in the *Odyssey*.
17 Yasur-Landau 2010: 2.
18 Lawrence E. Stager 1991.
19 Yasur-Landau: 8.
20 Ibid.: 306.
21 Ibid.: 343.
22 Ibid.
23 Ibid.: 64.
24 Ibid.: 331.
25 Ibid.: 189.
26 Ibid.: 280.
27 Ibid.: 281.
28 Though there is considerable variation at different sites. See, for instance, Maeir (2013) on how Gath gradually loses its Philistine identity under greater influence from Phoenician culture.
29 Yasur-Landau: 306.
30 Ibid.

31 J. Naveh, "Achish-Ikausu in the Light of the Ekron Dedication," *BASOR* 310 (1998): 35–37.

32 Yasur-Landau: 332.

33 Schlomo Bunimovitz and Zvi Lederman, "Canaanite Resistance: The Philistines and Beth-Shemesh – A Case Study from Iron Age I," *BASOR* (2011) 37–51; "A Border Case: Beth-Shemesh and the Rise of Ancient Israel," in *Israel in Transition: From Late Bronze II to iron IIa (c. 1250–850 B.C.E.), Vol. 1. The Archaeology*, ed. Lester L. Grabbe (Bloomsbury: T&T Clark, 2008), pp. 21–31.

34 Pierre Chantrainne, *dictionnaire étymologique de la langue grecque: historie des mots, A-K* (Paris: Editions Klincksieck, 1990), 475.

35 We consider him at length in Chapter 2.

36 Translations of Euripides and Homer are my own.

37 Translations of the Hebrew Bible are from Suggs et al.

38 Speiser 1962: 66.

39 Greek culture is also clearly referenced in the allusion to Alexander at Daniel 2:40.

40 We might compare how Americans in the twenty-first century refer, for instance, to "Germans" and "Japanese" rather than the terms these peoples use of themselves.

41 Van der Toorn: 110.

42 Ibid.: 47.

43 Ibid.: 7.

44 Ibid.: 131.

45 Ibid.: 34.

46 Ibid.: 250.

47 Ibid.: 251.

48 Ibid.: 9.

49 Ibid.: 259.

50 Ibid.

51 Ibid.

52 Carr 2005: 92.

53 Ibid.: 260.

54 Ibid.: 10.

55 Ibid.: 259–60.

56 Ibid.: 260.

57 Ibid.: 270.

58 Ibid.: 258.

59 Ibid.

60 Ibid.

61 Ibid.

62 Ibid.

63 Ibid.: 53.

64 *Histories*, 1.131, 2.144.

65 See discussion in Smith 2008: 37–90.

66 See discussion at Louden 2006: 247.

67 As apparent in many passages in the Hebrew Bible, e.g., Genesis 6:2, 4; Psalms 29:1, 89:7; Job 1:6, 2:1, 38:7, among many others, and Smith's discussion at 12–13.

68 See discussion at Smith 2008: 253.

69 Cf. ibid.: 256, "Philo indulges in classic euhemeristic interpretation of the gods as deified humans in a number of stories."

70 See Whitmarsh 2015: 152–55 for a brief account of Euhemerus' place in Greek intellectual history.

71 Cf. Smith: 182: "[T]he Bible shows not only the development of an indigenous literary corpus in the local language of Hebrew, but also translatability of literary works or motifs into this vernacular."

72 Janko 1982.

73 See, most recently, Louden 2018; cf. Louden 2011a: 135–63, and earlier, Crane 1987 and 1988. For previous work linking Jacob with Argonautic myth, see Wadjenbaum.

74 I repeat my definition of epic from Louden 2006: 6: "a *framework* that can contain within it almost any other type of myth, but which emphasizes a heroic modality, a hero's close interactions with the gods, and explores mortality, what it means to have to die."

75 On which see Louden 2005.

76 Van der Toorn: 16.

77 2 Samuel 1:18; Joshua 10:13.

78 Smith 2014: 39.

79 Van der Toorn: 116.

80 As Taylor notes (87), "The idea of an earlier war replayed with the sides reversed had been used by Herodotus and Thucydides (the Imperialist Athenians as the new Persians)."

81 Louden 2006: 157, 161–66, 170–79.

82 Whitman: 156.

83 Ibid.

84 Ibid.: 159.

85 Ibid.: 162.

86 Ibid.

87 Greenburg 1993: 197.

88 Ibid.: 205.

89 Van Nortwick 2011: 15.

90 Ibid.

91 Ibid.

92 In addition to the two contexts I discuss here, I argue that the figure of Agamemnon looms behind six additional episodes (Judg 4–5, 11, 19; 2 Sam 11; Gen 27, 34), which I will discuss in a future publication.

93 For fuller discussion of this see Louden 2006: 161–66.

94 For a sketch, see ibid: 161–66, 170–79, and Smith 2014, *passim*.

95 See Yadin 2004, and Louden 2006: 172–79.

96 On this see Smith 2014, throughout.

97 Sasson 2014 has "deceiving spirit," 391.

98 Cogan 2001: 496.

99 Ibid.: 497.

100 Ibid.

101 See further Marquis 2013: 42, 46, 71–77, 84–86, 134.

102 Cf., more broadly, Smith 2008: 22: "It is also evident that Christian texts of the New Testament sometimes drew on non-Christian notions bearing on divinity in order to build their communication between the Christian gospel and its audiences."

103   Cf. White: 318: "[T]he Jesus of Luke-Acts offers a wider outlook, with a view toward the Greco-Roman world. Several features of its construction help to make this point."

104   Cf. Marquis how in 2 Corinthians 4:18, "for things seen are temporary, but things unseen are eternal" (his translation), Paul expresses himself with language (115) "almost certainly of Platonic origin."

105   Here he cites Morgan 2007: 3–7.

106   On which, see, for instance, Sandnes 2009: 156: "1 Cor. 1–2 was crucial for Christians who abandoned Greek education"; 200: "Paul's text in 1 Cor. 1–2 on God's wisdom as opposed to worldly wisdom."

107   Referred to as Psalm Justin.

108   Sandnes reports (151, n. 80) that Lamberton (1989: 81) notes Origen is the only early Christian writer who explicitly does this.

109   Conzelmann (xxxvi): The following elements characteristic of literary Greek may be observed. First there is the use of the optative, rare in the New Testament: (1) potential opt in an independent clause (26:29); (2) in a direct question (8:31; 17:18); (3) in an indirect question (5:24; 10:17); (4) after εἰ, "whether" (17:27); (5) in a hypothetical protasis (20:16); and (6) without ἄν for the subjunctive of the direct discourse with ἄν (25:16). Next is the use of the future infinitive with μέλλειν (11:28; 27:10), and the future participle to indicate purpose (8:27; 10:22). Rhetorical devices may be observed, especially in the speeches: litotes (12:18 and often), paronomasia (17:30; 21:28; 24:3), and parechesis (17:25; 18:18). Only Luke continues to use indirect discourse to any considerable degree.

110   Wordelman 1994: 226–31.

111   On which see especially Dunn 2013.

112   White: 107: "Paul never mentions any of Jesus' miracles."

113   Note also 1 Thessalonians 4:14, for another brief passage of the early oral tradition.

Part I
The Hebrew Bible

1 Iapetos and Japheth

Hesiod's *Theogony*, *Iliad* 15.187–93, and Genesis 9–10

Though Hesiod's *Theogony* and the book of Genesis occupy analogous positions and serve similar functions in their respective ancient cultures, the many ways in which they overlap, and offer alternative versions of some of the same genres of myth, remain curiously understudied. Finkelberg (2005: 162–63) has called attention to one of the most conspicuous examples, the mythic tradition preserved at Genesis 6:2, 4, in which "the sons of the <u>gods</u>" (plural in the original, though often edited out of translations) mate with mortal women and give birth to a race of heroes, which corresponds surprisingly well to Hesiod's account of the genesis of the Bronze Age (*Works* 155–69; cf. Pindar *Olympian* 9, 53–56). Both works display common ground with several ancient Near Eastern mythic traditions. In Hesiod's case, correspondences with Anatolian myth have long been recognized (see especially West 1966), while more recent analyses (e.g., López-Ruiz 2010; West 1997) suggest Northwest Semitic ties in particular (Ugaritic, Syrian/Phoenician). In the case of Genesis, correspondences with Mesopotamian cultures have long been observed, especially in the myth of the Deluge. But more recent work (e.g., Smith 1990, 2001) has also pursued common ground with the Northwest Semitic group, in Ugaritic myth in particular (= the biblical Canaanites = Phoenicians).

Given their overlapping backgrounds, and that both employ forms of creation myth, we should not be surprised to find areas where Hesiod and Genesis *intersect*. Genesis includes specific allusions to Greek culture in the prominence it gives the eponymous character Javan (Gen 10:2, 4),[1] the son of Japheth in the *Table of Nations* (Gen 10:1–32). The same eponym as the Greek "Ion" (from Ἰάων[2] and earlier Ἰάϝων), according to Roberts, elsewhere in the Old Testament "Javan" can be the country personified, but in Genesis and I Chronicles it signifies the Ionian Greeks of Asia Minor and perhaps of Cyprus in particular, one of the likeliest locations for cultural dialogue between the Greeks and Phoenicians.[3]

But Javan's father may offer even more intriguing possibilities. Japheth, Noah's son, in what seems a specific intersection between the *Theogony* and Genesis, appears to be the same name, and, the corresponding figure, as Hesiod's Titan, Iapetos. However, both characters retain only a shadowy presence in their respective cultures, and, while they may have once been more fully fleshed out, in the narratives as we have them they barely exist as individuated characters, confined to only a few mysterious episodes. To bring the correspondences between Iapetos' role in the *Theogony* and Japheth's in Genesis into clearer focus, we will adduce that most Hesiodic of Homeric episodes, the *Dios Apate*, the "Deception of Zeus," and its aftermath at *Iliad* 15.187–95, and other cosmogonic myths involving a partitioning of the cosmos, as well as divine succession myths involving castration. These passages provide suggestive contexts for investigating Japheth's role in Genesis. Taken as a whole, the parallels between the two figures (key differences not withstanding), and the emphasis that Genesis, and other Hebrew Bible narratives, place on Japheth's son Javan, not only support J. P. Brown's argument (1995) that they are the same figure (78–83) but also Wadjenbaum's recent argument (2011: 103–4) that the biblical tradition has adapted both the figure and name of Iapetos, for the Hebrew Bible's Japheth.

Why would this be? To construct its larger sequence of primordial myth, Genesis appropriated individual myths from various cultures, including the myth of the Deluge from a Mesopotamian tradition. Though modern audiences tend to assume Genesis is of great antiquity, it is rather late in the form in which we have it. I subscribe to Auld's theory (2004) about the dating of the Hebrew Bible (which we briefly revisit in Chapter 4).[4] He posits that the earliest composed section of the Bible is 1 Samuel through 2 Kings. Deuteronomy through Judges was then constructed partly to provide anticipations of the royal Davidic story. Last of all, Genesis–Numbers was composed as a carefully intentioned preface to the larger work. In any case, it is clear that Genesis in the form we have it significantly postdates our text of Hesiod.[5]

Two recent studies argue that parts of Genesis are composed in response to, or in dialogue with, the *Odyssey*.[6] For the sons of the survivor of the Flood, and one's rebellion against his father, I argue that the Genesis tradition appropriates a version of the Titans' rebellion against Ouranos, euhemerized and reshaped to fit an Israelite agenda and conception.[7] Iapetos' status as a god in Hesiod and Homer, but Japheth's mortal status in Genesis, should be understood as an instance of monotheistic myth's tendency to euhemerize divine characters from other traditions. Elsewhere the Bible several times transfers other cultures' divine names to human characters (Nimrod: Ninurta; Esther: Ishtar; Mordecai: Marduk). As Carr notes (1996: 162), there is no evidence outside the Bible for the names of Noah's sons, and recent scholarship has considerably moved the dates up for much of the book of Genesis (Carr 1996: *passim*).[8] Though several of the motifs we will analyze also occur in Hittite and West Semitic narratives, which may well be where Hesiod encountered them,[9] the larger concatenation, and a few specifics, reveal unique correspondences between Hesiod and Genesis. I will argue, therefore, that Genesis 9–10 evolved in a dialogue with some form of Hesiod's *Theogony*.[10]

The names Iapetos and Japheth, and the sequence of the Sons

Neither Iapetós nor Japeth has a speaking part in our surviving texts. Both characters serve primarily as genealogical agents, connectors, sons of parents, and fathers of sons who are themselves more significant agents in their respective mythologies. Both are set in the primeval period of their respective mythologies and take part in several of the same genres of myth (or are sons or fathers of those who do). The first two mentions of Japheth (Gen 5:32, 6:10), phrases listing the three sons of Noah (Shem, Ham, and Japheth), both frame Genesis' brief but very Hesiodic reference, noted previously, to the Sons of the Gods mating with women and giving birth to a race of heroes (Gen 6:2–4): "they were the heroes of old, men of renown." From the perspective of source criticism, Speiser (1962: 41, 51) regards both these first mentions of Japheth as from the priestly source, the most recent layer. Iapetos and Kronos are the only Titans that are also named in Homer (*Iliad*, 8.478–81), as West (1966: 157) observes. West further explains their prominence (158),

> Iapetos and Kronos are the only two of the Titans who stand out later in the *Theogony* as constituting a serious individual danger to Zeus: Kronos who nearly swallows him, and Iapetos who rears a brood of dangerous sons against whom measures have to be taken individually.

The two are well known, then, but in terms of their notoriety, both with respect to interfamilial relations and their relations with the chief god.

The *Theogony* and Genesis both confuse the sequence of the two characters among their fathers' several children. Genesis establishes a canonical order of the three sons of Noah as Shem, Ham, Japheth, occurring five times (5:32, 6:10, 7:13, 9:18, 10:1), implying an eldest-to-youngest sequence, as Speiser (62), and many others, note, "the explicit order of the sons of Noah, which indicates age, is invariably Shem-Ham-Japheth." But when Noah wakens from his drunken sleep (discussed in the following text), and realizes what his "youngest son" has done to him (9:24; the Septuagint has νεώτερος), the culprit, on this most important occasion, is Ham, not Japheth. We further consider this violation of the expected sequence in the following text.

When Hesiod enumerates the Titans' offspring (133–38), Iapetos is fifth and Kronos is last, clearly designated as the youngest. In a later section, however, Hesiod alters the sequence, detailing Kronos' offspring (453–506) before Iapetos' (507–616). Caldwell (1987) offers a possible motive for the change (53),

> We would expect the family of Kronos to come last, since Kronos is the youngest of the Titans, but Hesiod puts Kronos before Iapetos so that Zeus' victory can be mentioned before telling the story of Iapetos' son Prometheus (a story in which Zeus is already king of the gods).

The resulting order in this lengthy, well-known section of the *Theogony*, with Iapetos last, after Kronos, thus ends up corresponding to the usual sequence in Genesis of Ham, then Japheth. Is there a connection, then, in both myths having a prominent violation of their usual sequence for the sons? Genesis' Ham, as we will argue, corresponds in many ways to Hesiod's Kronos: each is the son who most directly challenges his primordial father. The correspondences will prove unexpectedly close.

In keeping with their primeval status, Iapetos and Japheth are both associated with, but not the central actors in, their respective versions of the Flood myth.[11] Iapetos is grandfather of Deukalion, the Greek character corresponding to Noah (and the earlier Utnapishtim). Pindar, at a fairly early date (roughly 470), knows a complete version of the myth (*Olympian* 9, 40–56), and makes prominent mention of Ἰαπετιονίδος φύτλας ("of Iapetos' race"). Japheth, as we have seen, is a son of Noah, and is on the Ark, a survivor of the Deluge.

Castration of the father

The only other event in which Japheth plays a role is the bizarre episode in Genesis 9:20–27 in which his brother Ham sees Noah's genitals, when their father is passed out, drunk, in his tent. The episode, in its present form, is enigmatic and resists attempts at convincing analysis and interpretation, other than the specific outcome: a curse placed on the Canaanites because Canaan is Ham's son. Here is Alter's translation (1996),

> [Noah] exposed himself within his tent. And Ham ... saw his father's nakedness and told his two brothers outside. And Shem and Japheth took a cloak and put it over both their shoulders and walked backward and covered their father's nakedness, their faces turned backward so they did not see their father's nakedness. And Noah woke from his wine and knew what his youngest son had done to him.

Noah then pronounces a curse, not on Ham but on Ham's son, Canaan, while bestowing blessings on Japheth and Shem.

Alter (40), noting some of the episode's notorious inconsistencies, connects the passage both with Hesiod and with the rather Hesiodic account of the race of heroes at Genesis 6:1–4,

> Like the story of the Nephilim, this episode alludes cryptically to narrative material that may have been familiar to the ancient audience but must have seemed to the monotheistic writer dangerous to spell out ... Ham, the perpetrator of the act of violation, is mysteriously displaced in the curse by his son Canaan, and the whole story is made to justify the ... subject status of the Canaanites in relation to the descendants of Shem ... (Ham also figures now as the *youngest* son, not

the middle one). No one has ever figured out what exactly it is that Ham does to Noah. Some commentators, as early as the classical Midrash, have glimpsed here a Zeus Chronos [*sic*] story in which the son castrates the father, or, alternately, penetrates him sexually … Lot's daughters, of course, take advantage of *his* drunkenness to have sex with him.

While Alter here confuses the generations involved in Hesiod's castration account, other scholars have nonetheless come to similar conclusions in their attempts to understand the episode and its aftermath.

From these and other inconsistencies, many commentators assume Genesis 9:20–27 is an abbreviated excerpt from a longer tale, which the authors of Genesis have altered and adapted to make the resultant version serve their own narrative purpose: providing an etiology for a curse on the Canaanites. Independent of any possible correspondence with the *Theogony*, the *Talmud* (b. Sanhedrin 70a) suggests that Ham originally committed a much greater offence, as Alter hints that he castrated Noah or sexually abused him (partly based on parallels between the phrase "and he saw," which at Gen 34:2 is used of Shechem violating Dinah). Shinan and Zakovitch (2012: 132) note that Noah's reaction, again in Alter's rendering, "knew what his youngest son had done to him" is "a bit strong for referring to the consequences of merely being 'seen.'"

In Hesiod, of course, Iapetos' youngest brother Kronos *does* castrate his father Ouranos (*Theogony* 159–210), while Iapetos has also committed unspecified offences for which he is punished in Tartaros (*Iliad* 8.478–81). Chantraine (453) derives the name from ἰάπτω, "lancer, atteindre, blesser, lacérer … Seul terme apparenté Ἰαπετός 'celui qui est projeté.'" If Chantraine is correct, Iapetos' very name alludes to his punishment (somewhat as does Pentheus), as in Hesiod's use of the verb ἰάπτω at *Catalogue of Women*, frag. 204.118: πολλὰς Ἄϊδηι κεφαλὰς ἀπὸ χαλκὸν <u>ἰάψειν</u>, and in the *Iliad*'s proem, πολλὰς δ' ἰφθίμους ψυχὰς Ἄϊδι προΐαψεν (1.3).

When Noah wakens, "And Noah woke from his wine and he knew what his youngest son had done to him," he places the curse not on Ham, now the youngest son, but on Ham's son Canaan. This leads Speiser to wonder (62), "Have two divergent traditions been fused?"[12] In the *Theogony*, Kronos, who castrates his father Ouranos, *is* the youngest of his brothers. But Iapetos, as we have seen, is also associated with some unstipulated kind of wrongdoing, and of the four sons he and his wife Klymene produce, three of them are also subject to severe punishment: Atlas, Menoitios (who seems most like Ham: *Theog.* 514–16: ὑβριστὴν … ἀτασθαλίης τε καὶ ἠνορέης ὑπερόπλου), and more famously, Prometheus, whom Hesiod refers to eight times as "Son of Iapetos."

Ion and Javan

Japheth's other main function, as is also true of Shem and Ham, is to be the father of several sons. It is at this point that Genesis most explicitly

demonstrates awareness of Greek myth. In the Table of Nations that immediately follows the incident in Noah's tent, Genesis list Japheth's four sons
as Gomer, Magog, Madai, and Javan (Gen 10:2, 4). As noted, Javan is the
same eponym as the Greek Ion (from *Ἰαϝων).[13] The name has widespread,
international circulation from very early times. Chantraine cites a Mycenaean
form: "*iawone.*" It is in the *Iliad*, Ἰάονες, 13.685, as Brown notes (82), and
was also current in ancient India, found frequently, as Yavanas, in the
Mahabhârata. Speiser, noting the larger parallels and overlap between the
names Japheth and Iapetos, concludes (65), "It is significant, therefore, that
the descendants of Japheth include the Ionians."

Javan, in turn, has four sons (Gen 10:4): Elishash, Tarshish, Kittim, and
Rodanim. Genesis continues, as explanation (10:5), "From these the peoples
of the coasts and islands separated into their own countries."[14] Speiser (66)
explains that Elishah corresponds to Alashiya, another name for Cyprus,
Kittim corresponds to Kition, a Greek city also on Cyprus, while Rodanim
clearly designates the inhabitants of Rhodes. According to Euripides, and
larger Greek traditions,[15] Ion also has four sons. Athena explains near the
end of Euripides' play (1575–78), "For, from him four sons, born from one
root, will bequeath their names to the land, and the people by tribe."[16] Ion is
a few generations from Iapetos (Prometheus: Deukalion: Hellen: Xouthos: I
on), according to Apollodorus.

Noah's divine attributes

Let us now consider these passages from some other perspectives, placing
them in revealing contexts. In several particulars, Noah, in the episodes
following the actual Flood narrative, acts, or is depicted, in ways more reminiscent of a divine character than a mortal. It is worth emphasizing that
these episodes do not express any particular continuity with the larger Flood
narrative, which supports the possibility of their having been originally independent narratives, now used as transitioning elements. In the episode that
serves as prelude to the mysterious events in the tent, Genesis credits Noah
with inventing viticulture (9:20, and perhaps suggested earlier at 5:29). On the
one hand, the focus on wine seems generally surprising, given its far less central place in Israelite culture than Greek.[17] On the other hand, this is the type
of accomplishment that in Greek myth would be credited to a god. Psalm
80:8–9, as J. P. Brown argues (135), depicts Yahweh as a vintner, "The God of
Israel brought Israel as a vine out of Egypt and planted it,"[18] showing that a
similar association could hold in Israelite culture. Genesis 9, in contrast, does
not say Yahweh showed or taught Noah but instead presents Noah as the
primary agent.

Genesis credits Noah with a supernatural life span. He is said to be
500 years old when he fathers Shem, Ham, and Japheth (5:32). His own father
Lamech lived to be 777 (5:31); Noah is 600, the three sons apparently 100,
when the Deluge comes (7:6).

Carr traces some intriguing correspondences between Genesis 9:20–24 and Genesis 2–3. In several respects, Noah suggests strong thematic parallels with Adam, as Carr demonstrates,

> Both stories portray the father of humanity as a primeval farmer (Genesis 2:7; 9:20) ... Adam is made from the "*'adâmâh*" ("ground") to work it (Genesis 2:7–8, 15), and Noah is a "Man of the *'adâmâh*" (Genesis 9:20) ... Both stories deal with the products of their gardens, whether fruit in the Garden of Eden (Genesis 2:17; 3:2–6), or wine, in the case of Noah (Genesis 9:20–21) ... in both cases consuming this product leads to trouble: eyes are opened (Genesis 3:7; 9:22), nakedness is seen (Genesis 3:7; 9:22), and a curse is soon given (Genesis 3:14–19; 9:25–27).

In other respects, however, Noah suggests parallels with Yahweh, as Carr notes (1996: 237),

> In Genesis 2–3 God planted the garden, cursed Cain, and expelled him from the ground. Now in Genesis 9:20–27, however, a human (Noah) plants the vineyard, curses his grandson, and metaphorically expels him from Shem's tent (cf. 9:27).

These particulars, and some others, suggest we here have characters (Noah, his father, and his sons) who, in an earlier version of the narrative, may have been immortals but now, according to the demands of monotheism, are here euhemerized.

Threefold division of the cosmos

If we accept that some elements of Genesis' postdiluvian portrayal of Noah and his sons draw upon narratives in which gods originally played the roles here played by a human father and his three sons (as we have argued all along in the case of Japheth < Iapetos), we can bring parts of Genesis 9–10 into clearer focus by placing them in context with two other genres of myth. On the one hand, we need to consider the type of myth that Burkert (2004: 35) characterizes as "threefold division of the cosmos and the respective gods." On the other hand, myths that depict the succession of the king of the gods also offer valuable contexts for interpreting the roles of Noah, Japheth, and Ham.

In the famous *Table of Nations* that follows Noah's curse (Gen 10:1–32), all the different peoples of earth are depicted as springing from his three sons. The *Iliad*'s *Dios Apate* and its resolution in Book 15, the most Hesiodic episode in Homer, provide valuable contexts for understanding Noah's blessings and curses on his three sons, and for contemplating Japheth's role in Genesis. While plotting to seduce Zeus, so that, while he sleeps, she can act contrary to his prohibition of divine intervention in the

Trojan War, Hera claims, first to Aphrodite, then to Zeus, that she is going to see Okeanos and Tethus to reconcile their marital strife (14.200–10, 301–11). As Janko notes (1992: 181), the episode derives "from a theogony, one, moreover, where Okeanos and Tethus are the primeval parents." While in Hesiod, both are Titans, the *Iliad* here alludes to an alternate cosmogony, known in the Near East.

The episode also offers multiple connections to the Book of Genesis. First, it is worth emphasizing that in all of Homer and Hesiod the word γένεσις occurs only in this episode (14.201 = 302, 14.126).[19] More fundamentally, as Janko explains (1992: 182), the primordial coupling of Okeanos and Tethus not only corresponds to that of Apsu and Tiamat in the *Enuma Elish* but also some version of the latter underlies Genesis 1:2, in its primordial emphasis on "the deep" (*tehom* = Tiamat).[20]

In the episode's conclusion (*Iliad* 15.187–93), Poseidon recounts how the three sons Rhea bore to Kronos (mention of the Titan couple further edges the narrative toward a Hesiodic modality) each once drew lots.

> Ζεὺς καί ἐγώ, τρίτατος δ' Ἀΐδης, ἐνέροισν ἀνάσσων.
> τριχθὰ δὲ πάντα δέδασται, ἕκαστος δ' ἔμμορε τιμῆς·
> ἤ τοι ἐγὼν ἔλαχον πολιὴν ἅλα ναιέμεν αἰεὶ
> παλλομένων, Ἀΐδης δ' ἔλαχε ζόφον ἠερόεντα,
> Ζεὺς δ' ἔλαχ' οὐρανὸν εὐρὺν ἐν αἰθέρι καὶ νεφέλῃσι·
> γαῖα δ' ἔτι ξυνὴ πάντων καὶ μακρὸς Ὄλυμπος.

> ... Zeus, and I, and Hades, who rules those below, as third.
> All was assigned in thirds, and each received his portion of honor:
> when the lots were shaken, I drew as mine, to always inhabit
> the hoary salt seas, and Hades drew the misty depths,
> and Zeus drew the wide heaven, clouds, and upper sky.
> But Earth is common to us all, and great Olympos.

Before considering some of the details more closely, and their possible relevance to Genesis 9–10, let us first note other instances of this same genre of myth.

As Burkert in particular has noted, the *Atra-Hasis*, perhaps the oldest of the several Mesopotamian myths of the Deluge, opens with a scene depicting very similar interactions among members of the pantheon of Babylonian gods. Dalley's (1991) rendering of Tablet I, 11–16 includes the relevant account,

> They took the box (of lots) ...,
> Cast the lots; the gods made the division.
> Anu went up to the sky,
> [And Enlil (?)] took the earth for his people (?).
> The bolt which bars the sea
> Was assigned to far-sighted Enki.

As Burkert explains (2004: 35), with the restoration of Enlil to the text, the division establishes "the usual trinity of Anu, Enlil, and Enki, sky god, weather god, water god." Burkert summarizes the key differences between this instance and that in *Iliad* 15 (36),

> In the oft-quoted verses of the *Iliad,* the world is divided among the appropriate Homeric gods ... This differs from the system of *Atra-Hasis* in that the earth together with the gods' mountain is declared to be a joint dominion ... in both instances the division is claimed to have been made by a mythical act, the gods drawing lots.

For our purposes, we note that in both *Iliad* 15 and the opening of the *Atra-Hasis* the division is tripartite, and in both a sky god appears to receive the most prestigious lot.

Hebrew Bible scribes are familiar with, and employ a variation of this same genre of myth, gods casting lots to determine their realms or responsibilities. Deuteronomy 32:8–9 briefly presents a very polytheistic account in which the supreme god, here named Elyon, apportions different peoples to different gods, with Yahweh, here in the role of a lesser god (!), receiving the Israelites as his share. Smith (2008: 140) offers a recent translation,

> When the Most High (Elyon) gave the nations their inheritance,
> and divided humanity (literally, "the sons of a human being"),
> He [Elyon] established the boundaries of peoples,
> [according] to the number of the sons of God/the children of Israel.
> For the portion of Yahweh is his people,
> Jacob his inherited measure.

Plainly descending from a fully polytheistic tradition, the surprising account differs from those at *Iliad* 15.187–93 and in the *Atra-Hasis* in that it does not depict drawing lots, nor does it specify a tripartite division. Here a Supreme god, called Elyon, dispenses the various peoples of the world to various gods, with only Yahweh specified as one of the latter.[21] In other respects, however, it suggests broad generic affiliations with the passages from *Iliad* 15 and the *Atra-Hasis. Iliad* 15, for instance depicts why it is that Zeus has dominion over the heavens. Deuteronomy 32 depicts why Yahweh has the people of Israel as his special responsibility.[22]

An intriguing textual variant exists, as Smith points out (2008: 139), "[T]here is an older reading of this verse that the divine allotment was made according to the number of the 'sons of God,' but in the Masoretic text, it is according to the number of the children of Israel." As Phillips notes (216–17), the variant, the more polytheistic reading of the Septuagint, which is very close to the feel of *Iliad* 15.187–93, is confirmed in the Dead Sea Scrolls,

[T]his Septuagint reading has been confirmed from the Dead Sea Scrolls over against the Hebrew "sons of Israel." The poet, drawing on Canaanite mythology, identifies Yahweh with the pre-Davidic Canaanite Elyon, who has not only laid out the boundaries of the nations, but allotted them to their gods, subordinate members of the pantheon, called sons of God (cp. Ps. 82:6). But Israel he reserved for himself, who should in consequence be supreme among nations.

An abbreviated Phoenician account also survives in Philo of Byblos, *The Phoenician History*, which might be seen to bridge the kind of account *Iliad* 15.187–93 and that in Deuteronomy 32:8–9. Smith offers a summary (2008: 142), "According to Philo, the god Kronos, who is identified explicitly with El, went about the world assigning different lands to various gods (*PE* 1.10. 32, 38)." He continues (2008: 142), "Thus Deuteronomy 32:8–9 reflects an old version of the divine founding of the world known in broader West Semitic tradition, one that is otherwise eclipsed in the biblical record by Israel's specific foundational traditions."[23]

The terms the Septuagint uses drive home the episode's underlying similarity to Poseidon's account in the *Iliad*, διεμέριζεν ὁ ὕψιστος ἔθνη ... καὶ ἐγενήθη μερὶς Κυρίου λαὸς αὐτοῦ ... κληρονομίας. However, contra Smith's assertion here ("otherwise eclipsed"), I will argue that Genesis 9–10 reflects largely the same mythical concept, although now transformed, euhemerized, if you will, shaped exclusively around *mortal* agents. If we consider all four passages together, Deuteronomy 32:8–9 might be understood as medial, and transitional, between the fully polytheistic versions of the mythic type evident in *Iliad* 15 and the *Atra-Hasis*, and the anthropomorphized version in Genesis 9–10.[24]

What is the meaning of Ham "seeing his father's nakedness" at Genesis 9:21–24? Many commentators agree that something far more serious may have originally transpired between Ham and Noah, than the son seeing his father's genitals. Alter (40) notes a suggestive parallel in Genesis 19:32–35, " 'to see the nakedness of' frequently means 'to copulate with' ... Lot's daughters, of course, take advantage of his drunkenness to have sex with him." If the parallel holds, this implies that Ham, in some sense, sexually violates his father, in his drunken sleep. Alter (40) and Wadjenbaum (103) note that the Midrashim interpret Ham's act as constituting an actual castration.

López-Ruiz (2011) has traced how the castration motif occurs not only in Hesiod's version of the succession myth (*Theogony* 159–200) but also in the Hittite *Song of Kumarbi*, Philo's *Phoenician History*, and in the Orphic theogony. It is thought that the succession myth involving Kumarbi, with its roots in Hurrian culture, could reflect traditions going back to the middle of the second millennium. Philo's account is also thought to retain and refract elements going back to the Ugaritic era. López-Ruiz summarizes the relevant details (92), "Anu ... confronted by Kumarbi ... flees up to the heavens, but Kumarbi chases him, bites off his genitals, and swallows them." Somewhat as Aphrodite's birth from Ouranos' severed members, as well as Athena being born from Zeus' head after he has swallowed Thetis, a new god is born, the storm god, Teshub, from Kumarbi's combination castration/swallowing of Anu's member. Lacunae in the text prevent our knowing the outcome of this ancient intrigue, though presumably Teshub will emerge victorious. In a key difference with Hesiod, as López-Ruiz notes (2011: 93), Kumarbi is not Anu's son, but the offspring of an earlier god, Alalu.

According to Philo, in the *Phoenician History*, Elos, whom he equates with Kronos, castrates Ouranos. In Philo's summary (López-Ruiz, 2011: 96–97),

> In the thirty-second year of his dominion and reign, Elos, that is Kronos, trapped his father Ouranos in an island location and, having him in his power, castrated him in the vicinity of some springs and rivers ... The blood of his genitals dripped into the springs and the waters of the rivers.

An Orphic theogony (according to the Derveni Papyrus, which contains a commentary on it) presents an unusual variation on the castration motif as it appears in Hesiod, combined with the version in the *Song of Kumarbi*. López-Ruiz summarizes (2011: 139–40),

> Zeus is said to swallow the phallus of Sky ... αἰδοῖον κατέπινεν ... The Derveni commentator ... seeks a physical explanation for the passage ... as an allegory for the sun's life-generating power, which Zeus needs in order to become absolute king ... The allegory is easy to grasp if we think of the Sun as part of the Sky ... and, simultaneously, as the life-giving element in the Sky ... the castration attested in the Derveni theogony is ... closer to the Hurro-Hittite myth than is Hesiod's ... in the Hurro-Hittite epic, Kumarbi castrates Anu (Sky God) with his own mouth.

The end result has Zeus "impregnated with the cosmos."

Harvest, wine, and castration

Of these four interrelated myths of a son castrating his father, set in primeval times, the *Theogony*'s account of Kronos' castration of Ouranos offers the greatest correspondence with the circumstances of Genesis 9–10. Perhaps most significant is the central function of harvest motifs in both myths. Noah is portrayed as a farmer, the first to plant grapes (9:20). Though a specific word for *harvest* does not occur, the narrative implicitly requires that he has produced a harvest of grapes to have created the wine that here intoxicates him.

Hesiod's Kronos uses a sickle, an iconic emblem of the harvest, to castrate Ouranos. West considers the evidence that Kronos, in fact, was originally a god of the harvest, concluding (1997: 291), "If Kronos was originally a harvest god, it [the sickle] was an appropriate implement for him." He further argues (1997: 282) that a central epithet of Kronos, ἀγκυλομήτης (conventionally rendered as "devious, having crooked counsel"), first meant "of the curved sickle." West (1966: 217–18) catalogues how the sickle, ἅρπη, figures in numerous Greek myths, concluding, "In short, it is the normal weapon in Greek mythology for the amputation of monsters." As Brown points out in his discussion of ἅρπη (78, on *Theog*. 179–81), "The verb ἤμησε ["reap"] shows awareness of the normal farm use of the implement." Hesiod thus depicts Kronos' castration of Ouranos employing terms typically figuring in a harvest.

Brown (78–80) presents an intriguing analysis of the parallels between Hesiod's word for sickle (ἅρπη: *Theogony* 175, 179; *harpê*), and a Hebrew form, *hereb*, the Hebrew Bible uses of Yahweh smiting the dragon. Though West appears to dismiss the idea that they are in any way cognate,[25] Brown views them as interrelated (80), "And then it is too much for coincidence that Zeus in Apollodorus strikes the monsters with his inherited *harpê* of adamant, while Yahweh in Isaiah strikes it with the *hereb*."

Wine and wine making in Genesis 9 can also have another thematic function. As Brown demonstrates (135), both Greek and Israelite cultures share the metaphor of wine as blood, as the following passage from Isaiah graphically reveals,

> "Why are your clothes all red,
> like the garments of one treading
> grapes in the winepress?"
> I have trodden the press alone ...
> I trod the nations in my anger,
> I trampled them in my fury,
> and their blood bespattered my garments ...
> I stomped on peoples in my anger,
> I shattered them in my fury
> and spilled their blood over the ground.
>   Isaiah 63:2–6[26]

Isaiah juxtaposes a description of Yahweh slaying the dragon Leviathan, wielding the *hereb*, with a description of Yahweh figured as a vintner,

> On that day the Lord with his cruel sword (*hereb*),
> his mighty and powerful sword, will punish
> Leviathan that twisting sea serpent,
> that writhing serpent Leviathan;
> he will slay the monster of the deep.
> On that day sing of the pleasant vineyard.
> I the Lord am its keeper.
>   Isaiah 27:1–3

Philo's summary of the castration of Ouranos concludes with his blood running into springs, a winey image, "The blood of his genitals dripped into the springs and the waters of the rivers."[27]

Noah's longevity, in several respects, suggests an overall thematic correspondence with Hesiod's account of Ouranos' stifling repression of his offspring, transformed to a human plane. His own father, Lamech, lives to be 777 (5:31). As earlier noted, Noah is said to be 500 years old when he fathers Shem, Ham, and Japheth (5:32). For another 100 years before the Flood, he serves as their father. Though Genesis gives no indication of motives on Ham's part, the extraordinary spans of time, Noah's age at the birth of his sons, and how long he serves as their father after they have been born but before the onset of the Flood could imply a lingering resentment that he is preventing his sons from obtaining their own positions in life. In a similar broad correspondence, Ham's/Canaan's subsequent sentence of enslavement (9:25–26) suggests a thematic equivalent for Kronos' imprisonment in the underworld[28] (although in the *Theogony*, imprisonment in the underworld is a consequence of his battles with Zeus).

One might also posit a thematic correspondence between castration and circumcision, given the partial parallels of the acts involved. Although Genesis postpones specific introduction of the rite until a little later, to the episode where Yahweh proclaims his covenant to Abraham (Gen 17), a passage often understood as late, and assigned to P,[29] several commentators have suggested a connection between episodes depicting castration, and the rite of circumcision in the broader culture. West, in a discussion of why Kronos would use the sickle (1997: 291, n. 38), observes, "One could well imagine a castration myth serving as the *aition* of circumcision ritual." Similarly, Brown, in a wide-ranging discussion of instances of castration, remarks (80), "Hesiod shows that the *harpê* is suitable for castration, of which circumcision seems like a mitigation." Brown continues, adducing consideration of the tale of Onan, concluding (81),

> But Onan in his act of *coitus interruptus* (Gen 38:9) spills his seed on the ground as if it were a sowing. Thus some connection could be seen between the harvesting of grain and castration or circumcision.

There remain tenuous possible connections between Ham and the myth of Kumarbi. On the one hand the Table of Nations emphatically associates Ham with Hittite culture. Heth, the eponymous ancestor of Hittites is the second of Canaan's sons (Gen 10:15), grandson, therefore, of Ham. Canaan is also father (10:16–17) of the Jebusites and Hivites, concerning which, as Speiser notes (69), both the MT and LXX[30] have a tendency "to confuse Hittites, Hurrians and Hivites." In the *Theogony*, Hesiod's adjective for the sickle, καρχαρόδοντα, "having jagged teeth" (175, 179), comes close to suggesting an element of personification in the instrument, aligning the episode with the specific form of castration Kumarbi employs. While there are several suggested etymologies for Ham, does the lack of consensus leave open any possible connection between the names Ham (Χάμ in the LXX) and *Kum*-arbi?

Noah and Zeus

The conclusion of the *Dios Apate* suggests a further correspondence both with Genesis 9–10, and with Hesiod's version of the succession myth, if considered from one further perspective. When Zeus wakes from his post-coital slumber (*Iliad* 15.4), he immediately takes in the damage his inopportune sleep has abetted: a wounded Hector vomits blood; confused battle on the plains of Troy. Angered at Hera for having seduced him, he reminds her of an earlier occasion when, after she had intervened to harm Heracles, he enchained her, and hurled down to earth any god who came to her aid (15.18–24).

The overtones of theomachy are again quite Hesiodic, as Janko, who points out several corresponding themes in the *Theogony*, notes (1992: 230–31), and in the earlier episode in the *Iliad* when Hephaistos describes how he was so hurled (1.580–94). Continuing the Hesiodic tone, Hera swears by Gaia, Ouranos, and Styx (15.36–38), that Poseidon, not she, has intervened (causing Hector to be wounded) entirely of his own accord. Zeus then bids her to summon Iris and Apollo to him, which she does after further brief mischief. When Iris, ordered by Zeus to go and tell Poseidon to cease his interventions, delivers the command, the sea god complains (15.184–217) that Zeus is unfairly treating him as a subordinate, when, really, in his view, they are equals. Poseidon goes on to relate the lot drawing among the three brothers that distributed the heavens to Zeus, the seas to Poseidon, and the underworld to Hades, as noted previously.

The larger arc of the *Dios Apate* presents a sequence of events very reminiscent of Genesis 9, especially Ham's interactions with Noah, their outcome, and their possible connections with the *Theogony*. If we can momentarily see Zeus as resembling Noah, deep asleep (his postcoital siesta resembling Noah's intoxicated slumber), Poseidon, who is plotting mischief while Zeus sleeps, resembles Ham. Zeus' inopportune sexual activity would partly parallel Noah's drinking as forms of behavior through which the chief players voluntarily incapacitate themselves, making possible mischief by the other male relatives, Ham and Poseidon.[31] In a far more specific parallel, when Zeus and Noah awaken, and perceive the mischief that has transpired while they slept at the wrong time, both narratives culminate in accounts of a cosmic threefold division, an etiology that explains present-time relations on earth, in which the Zeus/Noah figure remains as the adjudicator.

When Noah awakens, "and learnt what his youngest son had done to him" (9:24), concerning which, as we argued previously, the parallels with the *Theogony* point to a castration, he pronounces a curse upon him, "Cursed be

Canaan! / Most servile of slaves / shall he be to his brothers" (9:25). Noah continues, now assigning portions of mortal existence, as it were, to each of his three sons,

> Bless, O Lord,
> the tents of Shem;
> may Canaan be his slave.
> May God extend Japheth's boundaries,
> let him dwell in the tents of Shem,
> may Canaan be his slave.
>
> 9:26–27

A clear hierarchy is implied: Shem is assigned the most fortunate portion, a position endorsed by God, above and over both of the other brothers. Japheth receives a medial position, while Canaan (Ham's son), is clearly given the inferior, subordinate lot.

In *Iliad* 15, contrary to Poseidon's assertion of equivalence, the lot drawing (15.189–93) establishes and confirms a clear hierarchy, as does the division between Noah's sons. I suspect the *Iliad* intends us to see Poseidon's remarks as fully cognizant of this fact, but designed instead to serve a face-saving purpose, allowing him to retreat with dignity, so to speak. As part of this rhetorical face-saving strategy, Poseidon puts himself first in sequence, Hades second, and Zeus last, a clear inversion of the actual hierarchy. The vertical positions assigned the three brothers, among other factors such as visibility, frequency of their appearances in myth, designated objects of mortals' prayers, potency of their weapons, and so forth, clearly establish Zeus as holding sway over the other brothers, the traditional role of the sky father, Poseidon as medial, and Hades, though quite a potent figure, never to be taken lightly, nonetheless as subordinate.

Beyond the structural parallels, the three brothers receiving hierarchical portions of a share of humanity (rather than of the cosmos, as at *Iliad* 15 and in the *Atra-Hasis*), there remain some further interconnections between the two scenes. As many commentators have observed, Noah, in his blessing on Japheth (Gen 9:27), makes a wordplay on his name, "May God *extend* Japheth's boundaries," where "extend," is the Hebrew *yapt* (Speiser 60), echoing the name *Yepet* (the basis of the form "Japheth" in our time zone). Hesiod's account of the Titans features a very similar wordplay (*Theogony* 207–9), Τιτῆνας ἐπίκλησιν καλέεσκε ... φάσκε δὲ τιταίνοντας. While the wordplays are quite typical, even generic, and perhaps best understood as mnemonic devices, intended to facilitate a listening audience's (as well as an oral performer's) ease in remembering broader aspects of the respective episodes, the precise location and sequence of the two wordplays seem *far* from coincidental.

Unexpectedly, in a most specific parallel, both wordplays occur at the same precise point in their larger sequences. In the *Theogony*, the Τιτῆνας/

τιταίνοντας wordplay immediately follows the account of Kronos' castration of Ouranos (178–200); in Genesis the *yapt/Yepet* wordplay immediately follows the episode of Ham violating Noah's nakedness in the tent, additional indirect support for our reading that a castration is implied in Genesis 9:22–25. The *yapt/Yepet* wordplay may have additional relevance to Greek culture. Wadjenbaum (101–3) argues that it is a sign of the passage's lateness, regarding "extend Japheth's boundaries" as a Hellenistic era reference to Alexander's conquests, because Japheth, through his fathering Javan (10:2), is a clear acknowledgment of Greek culture.

Much of Hesiod's *Theogony* is best understood as a version of the succession myth. Kronos' castration of Ouranos, the war between the Titans and Olympians, and, in the *Iliad*, the extra-Hesiodic account of the three brothers drawing lots to determine the threefold division of the cosmos represent pivotal stages in the larger movement. Genesis, in its account of humanity springing from Noah's three sons, euhemerizes and refashions this mythic type, intending instead a version that provides an etiology for the succession of *mortals*. Not only are multiple points of contact suggested with Hesiod (and Homer), especially in having the first two mentions of Japheth frame the reference to the race of Heroes in Genesis 6, but also after the Flood, Japheth becomes the father of Javan (10:2), a clear borrowing of the same eponym Greek myth uses for the Ionian people, which the Hebrew Bible earlier uses as a reference to Greek culture outside of Genesis (1 Chro 1:5, 7, Isa 66, Ezek 27).

Genesis 9–10 bears extensive signs of modification, that it has been transformed to fit other purposes and agendas than those the stories originally served. Our analysis confirms Brown's assertion (82),

> Now behind Genesis there seems to lie a story in which Noah's sons did more than see him naked: Gen 9:24 "When Noah awoke from his wine and knew what his young son had done to him …" What can this have been but castrating him? The association of Iapetus with Kronos, and hence with the castration of Ouranos, suggests that he is the same figure as Japheth youngest son of Noah.[32]

Carr (1996: 162, 310–11) and others have concluded that there are clear indications of modification of Genesis 9, for instance, in how the curse has been reassigned to Canaan, though it must have originally applied to Ham.[33] Since the nineteenth century, we have known that the authors of Genesis took a preexisting Mesopotamian tale of the Deluge and its survivor, and adapted it to fit within an Israelite mythic conception. The Deluge in Genesis, as we have it, is framed, at both ends, by seeming references to Greek myth. Noah's interactions with his sons, and how their offspring are thought to become progenitors for all humankind, may be based upon myths in which the main characters were originally gods, an instance of Euhemerism. Like Euhemerus, Israelite authors could interpret the gods acting in the primeval myths of other cultures as really having been "illustrious humans, later idealized and worshiped as gods."[34]

In some earlier versions of the Flood myth, including the account of Utnapishtim in *Gilgamesh*, the survivor of the Flood, has no children. This vacancy leaves ample room for a developing Israelite tradition not only to append a variety of different types of myth as sequel to the survivor of the Flood also but a relatively free hand as to the names of his sons, and how they might connect with other cultures. I suggest, then, that to connect the Flood myth with stories set in subsequent eras, Israelite tradition utilized a combination of two common types of myth set in primeval times: one in which intergenerational conflict among gods resulted in a son taking power by castrating his father, the former king of the gods; and another in which three brother gods draw lots to determine their own portions of rule and to establish hierarchical relations between themselves. While these two mythic types are extant in several different traditions, the versions in Genesis 9, though highly truncated, not only seem closest to the forms the same two mythic types assume in Greek myth but also correspond in four particulars absent from the other known versions: the corresponding names, Iapetos/Japheth; the altered sequence given of the punished sons; the connection with the eponymic Ion/Javan; and the closely corresponding wordplays (*yapt/ Yepet*; Τιτῆνας/τιταίνοντας).

The Genesis tradition thus appears to have carefully interwoven the two types of myth, taking the myth of Kronos' castration of Ouranos, but combining it with some version of the myth of three fraternal gods, drawing lots to determine their subsequent portions. Ham's role, if we are persuaded that Genesis 9:20–27 glances at the Greek version of a divine succession myth, corresponds to Kronos', the youngest Titan.

In Genesis 9:20–26, when he commits his mysterious offence, Ham is clearly Noah's youngest son. As noted previously, a large section of the *Theogony* (the episode detailing Kronos' offspring: 453–506 precedes that detailing Iapetos' offspring: 507–616) has Kronos sequentially precede Iapetos, which could conceivably serve as a model for those instances where Genesis has Japheth as youngest (Gen 5:32, 6:10, 7:13, 9:18, 10:1). In the *Iliad*'s sole reference to Iapetos, 8.477–83, Zeus reminds Athena, as she considers crossing him, that he presently sits, with Kronos, a prisoner in Tartaros. The Titan serves as an implicit warning to her of the danger she risks should she rebel against her father.[35] In Greek myth there is a generational difference in the agents in the two respective myths: Zeus, Poseidon, and Hades, the three brothers who receive shares are themselves the sons of Kronos, the agent who castrated his father Ouranos. Whereas Genesis has collapsed the separate generations into one: Ham corresponds to Kronos, on the one hand, and to Hades, on the other, and even Zeus in *Orphic Fragment* 222, in which it is Zeus who castrates Kronos, intoxicated to incapacity from mead.[36]

The Genesis tradition could have combined and transformed the two myths either by using the versions that we have, or conceivably Genesis may have been aware of and influenced by earlier versions of these myths, possibly different than our Hesiodic *Theogony*, perhaps a slightly different lot drawing than that at *Iliad* 15. If, for instance, as Janko (247) suggests, the lot drawing in *Iliad* 15 took place shortly after a Titanomachy, the situation of a deposed, weakened (imprisoned) father brings the correspondences even closer to the situation in Genesis 9:20–27. If Genesis draws on earlier versions than those we have, we might best see this part of Genesis as having evolved in a dialogic relation with Hesiod's account.[37] However, some recent studies have been moving up the dates for the composition of Genesis to more recent times. Finkelstein and Silberman, for instance, place initial compilation of the Torah in the seventh century (23, 40, 46, etc.). If these dates are accepted,[38] reference to the myths as we have them in Hesiod and Homer becomes more likely.

Based on the congruence of these motifs, the characters' occurrence at similar stages of larger creation myths, and Japheth's explicit connection to Greek culture (as father of Javan), we can, I suggest, presume that Japheth bears some connection with Iapetos. As Brown notes (82), Milton already made the equation in *Paradise Lost*. Asserting Eve's beauty is "more Lovely than Pandora," the epic poet continues with a brief reference to her marriage to Epimetheus,

> ... when to the unwiser Son
> Of Japhet brought by Hermes, she ensnar'd
> Mankind with her fair look.
> Paradise Lost 4.716–18[39]

Where we expect the Greek name Iapetos, Milton instead weaves his Hebrew correspondent. Though the resultant versions lack an exact match between the two characters (e.g., they do not occupy the same sequential position in their Flood myths), Japheth, who is absent from all other Near Eastern accounts, may well derive from the Hesiodic Iapetos. If we accept that Noah's postdiluvian acts seem to be modeled on those a god might perform, should it surprise us, then, if the authors of the narrative followed the same process in the case of his sons?

Notes

1   With several other mentions in the Old Testament: 1 Chronicles 1:5, 7; Isaiah 66:19; Ezekiel 27:13; Zechariah 9:13.
2   See, e.g., Aeschylus, *Persians*, 178, 563: Ἰαόνων.
3   There is a vast bibliography on the subject. For a recent sample see Louden 2011a: 318–19, 324.
4   See Auld 2004: 63–70.
5   I follow Janko's dating for the *Theogony*, 700–665 BC (2011: 35).
6   Brodie 2001: 451–94, Louden 2011a.

7   Cf. Shinan and Zakovitch 2012: 135: "These traditions parallel the Greek myth about Kronos, who castrated his father, Uranus (the sky), and ruled in his stead. Each of these traditions speaks about a multi-generational conflict, but what was told in the polytheistic nations surrounding Israel about the battle of gods was transferred, in the monotheism of the bible, to the human realm."

8   See also Finkelstein and Silberman 2001: 23, 36–40, 46, 65, 67; cf. Brodie 2001: 450.

9   See López-Ruiz 2011.

10 See also Doak (2012), who argues that the Hebrew Bible's depiction of the destruction of giants draws on the heroic age of Greek myth (153), "the characteristics apparent in the Greek heroic age have been 'transferred to,' and negativized in, the figures of non-Israelite Giants." See Doak 119–52 for fuller discussion, and 153–99, on possible influence of Greek traditions of heroes in cult on the Biblical giants.

11 Also noted by J. P. Brown 1995: 83, and Wadjenbaum 2011: 73, 101, 105.

12 Though Shinan and Zakovitch (132) see in this "the 'measure for measure' principle: the son's violation of his father causes his own son to be harmed."

13 As J. P. Brown (1995: 82) records, Milton also notes the correspondence in *Paradise Lost* 1.508, "Th' Ionian Gods, of Javan's Issue."

14 Suggs et al. 1992, *Oxford Study Bible*.

15 See especially Rhodes 1981: 66–70.

16 Translations from Greek are my own, unless noted otherwise.

17 Though see J. P. Brown 1995: 134–48, on some underlying parallels in the status of wine in the two cultures, nonetheless.

18 Cf. Isaiah 27:1–3, discussed in the following text.

19 Janko 1992: 182.

20 Cf. Burkert (2004: 30–33), who argues that "Tethus" descends from Tiamat.

21 Compare Smith 2008: 141: "In this picture, El Elyon is the head god who oversees the division of the world into nations given to the various gods of the world, and in this scenario, Yahweh is one of the gods who receives his inheritance from El."

22 Cf. Smith 2008: 139; 135: "the traditional 'inheritance' of this deity, as we noted in 1 Sam 25:19, and as we will see shortly in Deut 32:9. Israel as the 'inheritance' of Yahweh is a widespread image in the Bible" (1 Sam 10:1, 1 Kings 8:53, 2 Kings 21:14, Isa 19:25, Mic 7:18, Ps 33:12, 68:10, 106:5, cf. 2 Sam 20:19, 21:3).

23 Cf. also brief discussion in López-Ruiz 2011: 105.

24 Other narratives relevant for understanding the dynamics of such myths include the contest between Athena and Poseidon to determine which god would have Athens as its people (Apollodorus, *The Library*, III.14.1; see especially: ἔχειν τιμὰς ἰδίας ἕκαστος, and how Zeus appoints the gods to arbitrate), and the "contest" or strife Prometheus instigates with Zeus concerning the division of sacrifice, *Theogony* 534–57.

25 West (1997: 291) in a discussion on the two cultures' words for *sickle*, "its fortuitous similarity."

26 Cf. Genesis 49:11, and Isaiah 5:1–10, especially 5:7.

27 López-Ruiz 2011: 97

28 On this as a general tendency in myth – slavery and excessive confinement corresponding to a state of death, see Frye 1976: 104, 129; cf. Louden 2011a: 69–72, on the same tendency in the story of Joseph.

29 Speiser 1962: 26; cf. Alter 1996: 72.

30   That is, the Masoretic Text, the canonical Hebrew and Aramaic text of the Tanakh, reaching the form in which we have it perhaps as late as the eighth century CE, and the Septuagint, the translation of earlier versions of the Hebrew Scriptures into Greek, perhaps in the third to second century BCE.

31   *Orphic Fragment* 222 preserves a tradition in which it is Zeus who castrates Kronos, after having incapacitated him with mead (López-Ruiz 2011: 99), the same motifs, but here affixed to different generations.

32   Cf. Wadjenbaum 2011: 103–4: "It seems likely that the biblical writer ... modified the detail of Cronos castrating his father into Ham seeing his father naked ... some Jewish midrashim interpret Ham's deed as an actual castration ... The biblical writer used a myth from Hesiod but transformed it ... this story is not about gods, but about humans."

33   Cf. Speiser 1962: 61–62.

34   López-Ruiz 2011: 97, in a discussion of Philo's version of Ouranos, Kronos and Zeus; cf. López-Ruiz 2011: 131, and West 1966: 13.

35   Finkelberg 2011a.

36   On which see López-Ruiz 2011.

37   Again, cf. Louden 2011a: 10–15, 320–24, and Brodie, on other episodes in Genesis as composed, or evolved, in a dialogic relation with *The Odyssey*.

38   And again, cf. Auld's larger argument.

39   Though Milton may well have assumed influence running in the opposite direction.

2 Euripides' *Ion* and the Genesis patriarchs

The paradigmatic figure for the book of Genesis is the patriarch. After the creation myth, the Flood myth, and the myth of Noah's sons serving as progenitors of the peoples of Earth, Genesis segues to a sustained focus (chs. 11–50) on the interlocking fortunes of three patriarchs (Abraham, Jacob, Joseph) with the less significant Isaac sandwiched between the first two. Though Greek myth prefers heroic protagonists,[1] in the character of Ion we can recognize a figure who not only combines the same traditional motifs found in the four patriarchs of Genesis, and, in several specific respects, in Moses, as well, but also is clearly known to the Genesis authors, as we observed in Chapter 1. A foundling, preserved in a basket, a special given name, the parents' painful childlessness, the covenant or special promise given by god, ultimately serving as the father of a nation or nations – so many motifs in Ion's story, unusual aspects of his character, and the defining qualities of other central characters in his myth, come into clearer focus when we read them across the Hebrew Bible patriarchs. Put another way, if we consider the Genesis patriarchs and Moses from the context of Greek myth, we can recognize many of their defining acts and gestures in the character of Ion. While in Chapter 3 we will explore numerous correspondences between Jacob and Jason,[2] we here concentrate most on Abraham, Isaac, and the birth of Moses.

However, there are a few profound differences, especially in terms of larger narrative agendas, between Euripides' *Ion* and Genesis' myths of the patriarchs, which have perhaps obscured the considerably greater number of close correspondences. Some are larger cultural differences; some result from Euripides' distinctive traits and techniques as an author. The *Ion*, in its mixture of tragic and comic, fantastic and realistic elements, questioning and accepting the gods, is virtually *sui generis* and has provoked some of the most divergent interpretations of any Greek tragedy. For the most part, Genesis lacks all these tendencies and characteristics. In one of the most traditional of all mythical motifs, Ion is the son of a god, a trait that monotheistic Hebrew Bible myth shies away from, though it may occasionally be hinted at, nonetheless (discussed in the following text under "The miraculous birth"). The *Ion* has a central thematic concern with autochthony: Creusa is a child of

Erechtheus, granddaughter, in Euripides' version, of Erichthonios. Genesis, while not employing the mythic type, hints at it in its repeated depictions of how Abraham acquires the land, first through divine promises (Gen 12:7; 13:15), later through less mythical means.

Euripides' distinct characteristics as an author are responsible for other stark distinctions between the *Ion* and the Genesis patriarchs. The *Ion*'s mortal characters, especially the Old Man (most extreme in his desire to burn Apollo's temple), the Chorus, and to a lesser extent Creusa and Ion, openly question Apollo, not only his motives but also his *morals*.[3] Such a stance is almost completely unimaginable in Genesis, other than in Genesis 18, where the briefest instance of this motif, gently treated in a comic modality, occurs with Sarah (discussed in the following text). The Genesis patriarchs have a greater acceptance of divine will than do Euripides' characters, and do not question God. The single character in the *Ion* most accepting of divine decrees and plans, Xuthus, emerges as a comic figure in part *because* of his blind acceptance. From the perspective of Genesis, the *Ion*'s characters have a more limited and faulty understanding of the gods' larger purposes than does Abraham, in particular. Creusa's repeated mentions of Apollo's act as a rape, are thus, on the one hand, quite accurate, but, on the other hand, do not comprehend any larger purpose in the god's agenda for Ion. Some of this is due to the different perspectives mortals and gods have on time in Greek myth.[4] At play's end Creusa, fully informed by Athena's *dea ex machina* appearance, becomes reconciled,[5] a movement that would not be necessary for characters in Genesis.[6]

In a fourth marked difference, gender, Euripides' Creusa has a far more central and aggressive role than do the women in Genesis 12–50, except, briefly, Rebecca. By play's end, as Saxonhouse notes (1986: 272), "Euripides ... exalts the role of both women and motherhood."[7] In these key differences with the Genesis patriarch myths, Euripides is simultaneously more traditional (god as parent, autochthony) and more "modern" (questioning gods, gender).

The miraculous birth

One of the most unusual features of Euripides' *Ion* is the treatment and coloring given to the protagonist's extraordinary, but at the same time, utterly traditional, conception and birth. Taking one of the most well-attested motifs from ancient mythologies, that an exceptional human is the offspring of a mixed marriage, an immortal of either gender coupling with a mortal,[8] Euripides subjects a patently unrealistic event to a form of realistic scrutiny. Rather than present some neutral omniscient narrator giving an account (other than Hermes' brief remarks 10–11), as would be likely in epic or the Hebrew Bible, Euripides largely limits his presentation to the mortal's perspective, a woman, for whom the experience is a brutal rape at the hands of a seemingly callous god (887–901, 912–13).[9] The Hebrew Bible explicitly employs the motif of mortal/immortal coupling producing special offspring in Genesis 6:2 and 4, and perhaps implicitly in other stories, Samson's miraculous birth (Judg 13:2–25),[10] and perhaps in vestigial form in the case of Isaac (discussed in the following text).

Creusa is able to conceal her pregnancy and her giving birth (14–15). Safely delivering Ion in her father's palace (16–17), afterward, she conveys him back to the cave where Apollo had raped her (17–18). Placing him in a wicker cradle (κοίλης ἐν ἀντίπηγος: 19; cf. 1380, 1391), she leaves various of her youthful possessions with him (discussed in the following text under recognition scenes) and two snakes as guardians (19–27). Hermes, at Apollo's request, retrieves the newborn infant, cradle, and swaddling clothes from the cave (32: σπαργάνοισί; cf. 1351), leaving him at the steps of the oracle at Delphi, opening the cradle, so someone will see the child (38–40). The priestess then discovers him, and, after a moment's hesitation, decides to raise him.

Abandoned by his mother, the foundling who, born in secret, having matured, becomes a pivotal, privileged figure in his culture[11] is known in the Hebrew Bible as Moses. Exodus relates how the pharaoh, fearing a possible revolt, orders midwives to slay newborn male Israelites (1:12–16). However, an unnamed Levi woman bears a son, does not slay him, and hides him for three months (2:3–5),

> But she could conceal him no longer, so she took for him a vessel of papyrus and tarred it with tar and with pitch, and put the boy in it and set in the rushes on the Nile's lip … Now Pharaoh's daughter went down to wash by the Nile … And she saw the vessel among the rushes, and sent her maidservant, and she took it.[12]

The unnamed pharaoh's unnamed daughter, through the machinations of the baby's sister, who had watched her sister set it on the bank of the Nile, ends up having the baby's anonymous mother serve as wet nurse, while she raises the child as her own (Exod 2:7–10).

We can, without difficulty, see not only the same basic underlying series of motifs as in the *Ion* but also observe that a few variants have unexpected correspondences. Like Creusa, Moses' unnamed mother conceals her giving birth, and then prepares to expose her baby, setting it in a special vessel. Both infant cradles are locomotive, perhaps predicting the protagonists' future movements. Ion's ἀντίπηξ is specifically a wheeled carriage (19); Moses' is distinctively intended to keep him afloat in the Nile. Pharaoh's daughter encounters the infant Moses in much the same way that the Pythia does in the *Ion*, each highly placed woman going on to serve as foster mother.

In each case a third party ensures the infant's transit to the foster mother. In the *Ion* this is Hermes' main role in the play's backstory (32–40, 1598–99); in Exodus 2 it is Moses' mysterious unnamed sister. Here, in Alter's translation, is everything we are told about her,

> And his sister stationed herself at a distance to see what would be done to him.
>
> Exodus 2:4

> And his sister said to Pharaoh's daughter, "Shall I go and summon a nursing woman from the Hebrews that she may suckle the child for you?" And Pharaoh's daughter said to her, "Go." And the girl went and summoned the child's mother.
>
> Exodus 2:7–8

Aside from the different treatment of time (these actions all occur during Moses' infancy), from the perspective of the *Ion*, the sister very closely corresponds to Hermes, watching until someone discovers the baby, arranging for it to reach first a foster mother, then, ironically, reuniting it with its birth mother. Propp, based on source analysis, argues that this sister is *not* Moses' sister Miriam (1998: 150),

> Who is she? Moses has a sibling Miriam in P and a kinswoman Miriam in E … But since the Yahwist never again refers to this sister, it is futile to inquire after her name in J or JE. In the redacted Torah, one naturally identifies her as Miriam.[13]

Does this allow for the possibility that the unnamed sister in Exodus 2 is modeled on a character adapted from another source? It is worth noting that, assuming Yahweh is orchestrating the events of Moses' life, he does so with a remoteness that rivals Apollo's in the *Ion*.

We thus have a fairly complete homology between the main characters in the two myths:

> The special son who will grow up to be a leader: Ion > Moses;
> His mortal mother, separated from him: Creusa > Moses' anonymous mother;
> A transporter who sees to it that he is cared for: Hermes > Moses' unnamed sister;
> An exceptionally placed, high-status, foster-mother: Pythia > Pharaoh's daughter;
> A remote god, guiding his destiny: Apollo > Yahweh.

The lack of names for Moses' parents is striking, given his central importance in his culture, when compared with other figures such as the Genesis patriarchs, Samson, David, Aeneas, or Christ.[14] The *Ion*'s version is the more traditional in having a known and divine father, and in the Pythia, a far more orthodox or traditional figure than pharaoh's daughter. Have the Exodus authors innovated, changing the more traditional character types, to accommodate an emerging monotheism, resulting in a partial instance of euhemerism?

Patriarch myths highlight the previous painful childlessness of the parents, making the subsequent miraculous birth of the future patriarch more dramatic. In the *Ion* this is almost obsessive. References both to Xuthos' and Creusa's previous lack of a child pop up at regular intervals (65–57, 303–6, 356, 469–91, 658, 680, 729, 748–49, 761–62, 817, 824, 840, 950, 1302, 1461).[15] Perhaps most intriguing of these is Creusa's ironic dialogue with Ion at 303–8.

Childlessness is not only thematic in Abraham's larger story, but Genesis' account is constructed to create considerable drama in his prolonged childlessness. Immediately after the first mention of his wife, Genesis emphasizes, "And Sarai was barren, she had no child" (11:30). At Genesis 15:2 Abraham complains to God of his childlessness, "O my Master, Lord, what can you give me when I am going to my end childless?" When Sarai continues to be barren, she persuades her slave-girl Hagar to have sex with Abraham (a pattern that will recur with Jacob), Hagar subsequently becoming pregnant with Ishmael (Gen 16:1–16). After childlessness within their marriage has been established as a recurring theme for over six chapters, Genesis 18 and 21 narrate the miraculous conception and birth of Isaac to his 90-something parents,[16] Abraham and Sarah. To do so Genesis 18 employs a genre of myth particularly well attested in Greek myth, theoxeny, in which mortal hosts, having unwittingly received divine guests in mortal guise, display their exemplary morality through correct observance of guest/host relations, and receive a boon. Here implicitly God causes the conception of a son for the too-old-to-bear-children parents. Alter notes (1996: 86) how Genesis emphasizes the extraordinary circumstances,

> [O]nly here is the barren woman actually post-menopausal; and only here is there a long postponement, filled in with seemingly unrelated episodes, until the fulfillment of the promise (chapter 21).

By depicting the conception as an act of God, a reward for exemplary hospitality, Isaac's birth shares some common ground with the *Ion* and its underlying motifs of divine paternity and autochthony. Genesis, in giving a divine *masculine* power the larger responsibility for the birth, significantly lessens the female agency and responsibility for this crucial procreative act. Furthermore, because Genesis 18 depicts the circumstances of Isaac's birth by employing a genre of myth well known in other cultures, one attested earlier in Greek myth,[17] we must consider the possibility that other aspects of Abraham's myth might also be adopted from other mythical traditions.

The patriarch's significant name

The special child, on learning his destiny, that he is to be a patriarch, receives a speaking name, reflecting the unique circumstances of his upbringing, or his relation to god. In the *Ion*, although it is Hermes who first performs this act of pronouncing Ion's name,[18] the play is so constructed to make Xuthus think that he serves this traditional paternal office. To conclude his introductory monologue, Hermes twice names Ion,

> Ἴωνα δ' αὐτόν, κτίστορ' Ἀσιάδος χθονός
> ὄνομα κεκλῆσθαι θήσεται καθ' Ἑλλάδα.
>   74–75

Throughout Greece he shall be called by the name
Ion, the founder of the Asian land.

> Ἴων' ἐγω <νιν> πρῶτος ὀνομάζω θεῶν
> I first of the gods will name him Ion.
>   81

Hermes thus foregrounds Ion's role as patriarch, progenitor of the Ionian people, that he is their eponymous ancestor, but gives no indication of what the play will argue is the name's literal meaning.[19] Before this, Ion is nameless, as he notes, τοῦ θεοῦ καλοῦμαι δοῦλος, "I am called the god's slave" (308).

A third of the way through the play, however, Xuthus receives an oracle that the first person he encounters as he exits (ἐξίοντα: 516, *exionta*) the shrine will be his son. The myth of Jephthah has a similar motif but in a tragic version (Judg 11:30–34): the hero vows to sacrifice the creature that first comes out of his door when he returns, which unexpectedly proves to be his unnamed daughter. Xuthus repeats the prophecy to the incredulous Ion, as he first encounters him, again uttering the same participle (ἐξίοντι: 535). When he is finally able to persuade Ion that, because of and according to Apollo's prophecy, he is his father, he repeats the verbal association, making it explicit (661–63),

> Ἴωνα δ' ὀνομάζω σε τῆι τύχηι πρέπον,
> ὁθούνεκ' ἀδύτων ἐξιόντι μοι θεοῦ
> ἴχνος συνῆψας πρῶτος.

I name you Ion, as fits your destiny,
because you first met me, as I came out
from the god's sanctuary.

The play repeats the association even twice more (800–2, 831: Ἴων, ἰόντι δῆθεν ὅτι συνήντετο).[20]

Exodus, in its depiction of Moses' naming, presents a surprisingly close correspondence, though the event is set earlier in his life. At some indeterminate time[21] ("and the boy grew"), the wet nurse (his actual birth mother) brings him to pharaoh's daughter, "And she called his name 'Moses' and said, 'For I drew him from the waters'" (Exodus 2:10). Alter explains (2004: 314),

"The folk etymology relates it to the Hebrew verb *mashah*, 'to draw out from the water.'" It is a folk etymology because, as many commentators point out, the name Moses is Egyptian, as Propp (152) notes, "*Môse(h)* derives from Egyptian *mose* '(is) born.'" However, it is intriguing, I suggest, that, as with Ion, Moses is named for the circumstances of his foster parent's first meeting him. For both Ion and Moses, it is a foster parent who names the child. Each names their respective child with respect to themselves in motion, going out of Apollo's shrine at Delphi, for Xuthus, drawing out of the Nile, for pharaoh's daughter, each patriarch receiving a folk etymology.

All four Genesis patriarchs receive speaking names, connected in some way with God, two, like Ion, after they have reached maturity. Abraham is originally Abram, until God, as part of his larger covenant (discussed in the following text), appears to him, at the advanced age of 99,[22] declaring, "And no longer shall your name be called Abram but your name shall be Abraham, for I have made you father to a multitude of nations" (Gen 17:5).[23] North (5) explains Abram as coming from *'ab-hâmôn*, "father of many." In both forms the meaning of the name Abram/Abraham thus instantiates the literal meaning/definition of "patriarch."

A middle-aged Jacob, having spent 14 years laboring to win his two sister wives, and apparently another seven to increase the flocks that will also be his wages from Laban, during an eerie nocturnal encounter, wrestles "a man" at the Jabbok ford. The most heroic of the Genesis patriarchs, Jacob holds his own, refusing to let go of his opponent all night.[24] As daybreak approaches, he declares that he will release his hold on his opponent only if he will pronounce a blessing on him. His opponent concedes, declaring, "Not Jacob shall your name hence be said, but Israel, for you have striven with God and men, and won out" (Gen 32:29). Again, Genesis bestows a folk etymology. A more accurate rendering of "Israel," according to Alter (2004: 181), would be "God will rule/prevail."

Unlike Abraham and Jacob, Isaac and Joseph are both given their "patriarchal names" at birth, the former in ways that seem connected with his thematic roles throughout his myth (discussed in the following text). When the guest declares that when he later will visit them again, Abraham's wife will have given birth to a son (Gen 18:10), Sarah laughs, incredulity getting the better of her. But the guest corrects her,

> Why is it that Sarah laughed, saying "Shall I really give birth, old as I am?" … And Sarah dissembled, saying, "I did not laugh," for she was afraid. And He said, "Yes, you did laugh."
>
> Genesis 18: 13–15

Shortly before, Abraham, expressing similar incredulity, also *laughed* at God's prophecy that he and Sarah would soon have a son (17:17). Alter (2004: 83) explains, "The verb *yitshaq* is identical with the Hebrew form of the name Isaac that will be introduced in verse 19."[25] Isaac thus bears a name that sounds like *He/She Laughed*, another folk etymology, or mnemonic device, but one that instantiates his largely ironic function in his myth (discussed in the following text).

In Rachel, Jacob's favorite wife, Genesis again emphasizes the thematic patriarchal motif of painful, long-term childlessness,

> And Rachel saw that she had borne no children to Jacob, and Rachel was jealous of her sister [Leah], and she said to Jacob, "Give me sons, for if you don't, I'm a dead woman!"
>
> Genesis 30:1[26]

After apparently employing a form of magic, use of the mandrake root (30:14–16),[27] Rachel successfully conceives,

> [A]nd she conceived and bore a son, and she said, "God has taken away my shame." And she called his name Joseph, which is to say, "May the Lord add me another son."
>
> Genesis 30:23–24

As Alter explains (2004: 162), Genesis here offers not one, but two folk etymologies for the name "Joseph,"

> *taken away my shame, ...'asaf*, is proposed as an etymology of *Yosef*, Joseph ... *May the Lord add me another son*. 'Add,' *yosef*, Rachel's second etymology, is a perfect homonym in Hebrew for Joseph.[28]

Euripides' depiction of Ion's naming thus finds correspondence in all four Genesis patriarchs. Exodus' depiction of Moses, however, offers the most specific parallel.

The patriarch's divine promise

In the introductory monologue, Hermes first hints at Ion's greater destiny (74–75), as noted previously. At play's end, Athena gives a more specific and detailed account (1572–93), stressing several elements or motifs that recur in Genesis in the corresponding divine proclamations to the four patriarchs. First, Athena stresses that because Ion is descended from Erechtheus (1572–74), he has the right to rule her (Athena's) land (τῆς γ' ἐμῆς ὅδε χθονός), and, consequently, he will become famous throughout Greece (1575). He will have four sons, who, in turn, will become the progenitors of four tribes, "For from this man, / four sons will be born" (1575–77). Their descendants will colonize the Cyclades, island cities, and the coasts (1582–84). The eponymic Ionians will become famous, spreading throughout Europe and Asia (1584–87). Creusa and Xuthus will also have children, progenitors of the Dorians and Achaeans (1587–94).[29]

On the one hand, this is a classic retrospective prophecy (or *vaticinatio ex eventu*),[30] meaning everything Athena here prophesies, casting as future events, has already taken place for the play's original external audience. The real function of retrospective prophecy in a myth, however, is to reveal that what may *appear* to mortals as haphazard history is the result of the gods' plans and steerage of human affairs, as Athena declares, "Apollo has brought everything about well" (1595: καλῶς δ᾽ Ἀπόλλων πάντ᾽ ἔπραξε).[31]

On the other hand, Athena's proclamation is also closer than often realized to Genesis' account of Javan, son of Japheth. Like Euripides' Ion, Genesis' Javan will also have four sons, "Elishah and Tarshish, Kittim, and Rodanim. From these the people of the coasts and islands separated into their own countries" (10:4–5).[32] Gibert, in his commentary [on 1581–88], notes that Athena "divides the future colonies into two groups, islands and coastal areas." Genesis 10:5 does very much the same, "From these the people of the coasts and islands." As we also noted in Chapter 1, Speiser (66) finds sound equivalents for all but the second,

> *Elishah* corresponds to cun[eiform] Alashiya "Cyprus." *Rodanim.* Inhabitants of the island of Rhodes … *Kittim* is the Kition of the Greeks, which is modern Larnaka in Cyprus.[33]

Though not precise equivalents, both accounts suggest a similar basic conception of Ion's/Javan's descendants as populating well-known Aegean islands, and nearby coastal areas.

Earlier Greek myth has some elements of what might be understood as a blessing or covenant, in the prophesy Menelaus receives from Proteus, and that Odysseus learns from Teiresias in the underworld. However, because the two men are less patriarchal than heroic figures, the corresponding motifs are a little different. Having already learned from the sea god how he can accomplish his voyage home, and the fates of Aias, Agamemnon, and Odysseus, Menelaus hears a startling prophecy of his own destiny,

> σοὶ δ᾽ οὐ θέσφατόν ἐστι … θανέειν καὶ πότμον ἐπισπεῖν,
> ἀλλά σ᾽ ἐς Ἠλύσιον πεδίον καὶ πείρατα γαίης
> ἀθάνατοι πέμψουσιν, ὅθι ξανθὸς Ῥαδάμανθυς
> … οὕνεκ᾽ ἔχεις Ἑλένην καί σφιν γαμβρὸς Διός ἐσσι.
> 4.561–69

> but it is not your fated destiny to die,
> rather, to the Elysion plain and the ends of earth
> the immortals will send you, where fair Rhadamanthys is
> … for you have Helen and are son-in-law to Zeus.

The notion of a privileged destiny, because of a privileged relation with God, is hinted at in Abraham, whose *descendants* are explicitly tied to the notion of a kind of eternal existence, "all the land you see I shall give to you and your descendants forever. I shall make your descendants countless as the dust of the earth" (Gen 13:14–17). The covenant is to be everlasting, "I shall maintain my covenant with you and your descendants after you, generation after generation, an everlasting covenant" (Gen 17:7); "As a possession for all time I shall give you and your descendants after you the land in which you now are aliens, the whole of Canaan." (Gen 17:8). A privileged afterlife for a special individual is explicit, if mysterious, in the case of Enoch, "And Enoch walked with God ... 300 years ... and then was no more, for God took him" (Gen 5:22–24).

Teiresias' prophesy of Odysseus' later pilgrimage inland corresponds with Genesis' accounts of Abraham and Jacob, on the one hand, and with Cadmos, on the other. Having journeyed so far from the sea that the people he encounters do not know what ships are (11.121–28) and mistake his oar for a winnowing fan, he is to sacrifice a ram, bull, and boar. Returning home, he is to perform hecatombs to all the Olympian gods. Then, declares Teiresias, his sacred task completed, his life will end, many years later,

> ... θάνατος δέ τοι ἐξ ἁλὸς αὐτῷ
> ἀβληχρὸς μάλα τοῖος ἐλεύσεται, ὅς κέ σε πέφνῃ
> γήρα' ὕπο λιπαρῷ ἀρημένον; ἀμφὶ δὲ λαοὶ
> ὄλβιοι ἔσσονται.
>
> 11. 134–37

> ... Death will come to you,
> worn down by pleasant old age, such a very gentle
> one - from the sea - will slay you; and your people will be
> prosperous around you.

Heubeck (86) sums up the prophecy's account of Odysseus' life, "to rule long and wisely over a happy country blessed with riches." Abraham meets his death in a broadly parallel manner, "And Abraham breathed his last and died at a ripe old age, old and sated with years, and he was gathered to his kinfolk" (Gen 25:8). Even closer to Teiresias' prophecy is the version in LXX: ἐν γήρᾳ καλῷ πρεσβύτης. According to Carr's analysis (94, 126–27), this passage is late, the Priestly source. The two Homeric passages we adduce as partly corresponding differ from those describing the Genesis patriarchs in that they apply more to the individual protagonist at a personal level, in keeping with overall epic tendencies. But both traditions would seem to agree on special dispensation for the patriarch/hero, his people prosperous around him, partly owing to his special relationship with god.

As tribes or peoples are to come from Ion (1575–87), so, explicitly are they to come from Abraham. In the first version of God's promise to him, it is a single nation, "I shall make you into a great nation" (Gen 12:1–3); in a later instance it is several, "You are to be the father of many nations" (Gen 17:4).[34]

Isaac receives one short prophecy in line with Ion's, but it is subservient to Abraham, "I shall bless you and give you many descendants for the sake of my servant Abraham" (Gen 26:24). Jacob receives one with a similar geographical focus as Ion's (1584–85), "They will be countless as the specks of dust on the ground, and you will spread far and wide, to west and east, to north and south" (Gen 28:14).[35] Near the end of Jacob's life, God specifically connects the move to Egypt with the promise of his patriarchy, "Do not be afraid to go down to Egypt, for there I shall make you a great nation" (Gen 46:3).

The culmination of the Genesis patriarch myths is the 12 sons of Jacob, each serving as eponymous ancestor of the 12 tribes of Israel. Jacob accomplishes this feat of paternity through multiple partners, Leah, Rebecca, and the slave girls Zilpah and Bilhah (Gen 29:31–30:24; 35:23–27; 49:1–27). In Ion's myth, Creusa corresponds to Jacob in having the multiple partners, Apollo and Xuthus, accomplishing a corresponding feat of *maternity* as parent for the several tribes. Our analysis of her thematic parallel with Jacob confirms Saxonhouse's observation, noted on the preceding text (272), "Euripides ... exalts the role of both women and motherhood."[36] In being female rather than male, Creusa's thematic parallel with Jacob as parent of several different tribes, by means of multiple partners, additionally confirms Saxonhouse's further observation (260) that Euripides, in his departure from a more autochthonous version of Athens' mythical origins that had deemphasized the maternal role, "has also asserted a new vision, one that introduces the female into the origins of the cities."[37]

Ion and Isaac: attempted murder/human sacrifice by the parent

In one of the most well-known stories in the Hebrew Bible, God commands Abraham to offer his son Isaac as a sacrifice. But an angel intervenes at the last minute, declaring he has already shown his dedication to God (Gen 22:1–19). In the *Ion* Creusa, aided and encouraged by the chorus and the old man, plots to kill her son Ion, though unaware he is her child. Considerable differences notwithstanding, each episode is set within a larger patriarch myth; each death is prevented by indirect divine intervention; and each depicts the gods guiding the larger destiny of the respective cultures, emphasizing divine motives as beyond mortals' understanding. Despite some diametrically opposed tendencies, all the separate motifs involved in the depiction of Abraham (Gen 22), about to sacrifice Isaac, occur in the *Ion*.

Both Ion and Isaac are depicted as innocent and sacred. Segal (69) describes Ion's opening song (82–183) as reflecting "the sheltered innocence of the adolescent boy."[38] Burnett offers a similar interpretation (104), "[H]is unworldly childlike purity is the subject of the song that marks his first entrance ... this temple play gives us instead the closing moments of his enchanted childhood."[39] Isaac is even younger, his innocence conveyed through the narrative's stark juxtapositions. The audience hears God's command to Abraham, but Isaac does not. We observe, therefore, as he unknowingly obeys his father's commands, with no comprehension of what their unique purpose is on this occasion. Isaac's role in Genesis 22 is entirely passive, as Ion has largely been in his preceding years, happily confined to his existence in the temple at Delphi.

Both episodes employ several different forms of irony concerning the son's identity. In their innocence, both sons address their parents, ironically, in complete ignorance of their actual intentions toward them. Isaac asks Abraham, "Here is the fire and the wood but where is the sheep for the offering? And Abraham said, 'God will see to the sheep for the offering, my son'" (Gen 22:7). In the brief exchange between mother and son mentioned previously, ironic in several ways, Ion is surprised at Creusa's declaration that she has no children (305). Earlier in the same dialogue, Ion *himself* raises the issue of parent/child sacrifice when he asks her if it's true that her father sacrificed her sisters (277).[40] Each myth employs the same additional irony connected with the patriarchal theme of prolonged childlessness. Despite the tremendous difficulty both parents have had in obtaining offspring, *each is now willing to slay their son*.[41] There are significant differences. In the *Ion* the idea originates from mortals, not as a command from god, with the chorus first suggesting and the old man vigorously seconding the idea that Creusa murder Ion (836–56).

Both sons unwittingly help further the attempt on their lives. Isaac helps obtain the implements to be used for his own sacrifice (Gen 22:6), "And Abraham took the wood for the offering and put it on Isaac his son." Ion's supervision of the erection of the tent and other elaborate rituals (1133–45, 1165–66) corresponds closely to Isaac's helping prepare the specifics of his sacrifice. In so doing, both sons again instantiate their status as sacred.[42] Creusa's plot to poison Ion *amid the sacrifices* corresponds to Isaac, bound by Abraham, and placed on top of the altar. A death does occur, but in each myth a substitute, an animal that wanders into range, ends up dying in place of both sons. For Isaac it is a ram,

> And Abraham raised his eyes and saw and, look, a ram was caught in the thicket by its horns, and Abraham went and took the ram and offered him up as a burnt offering instead of his son.
>
> Genesis 22:13

For Ion it is a dove that drinks the poisoned drink meant for him (1204–8).[43] In both myths the audience knows that the son will not be slain. Genesis 22 foregrounds this, explicitly declaring in the first verse that God is "testing" Abraham. In the *Ion* the audience deduces this, as Burnett (116) argues, "The spectator ... has known all along that this murder will not be done."

In response, Ion seeks Creusa's death, an episode that functions, structurally, like a parody of her attempt on him. Perhaps surprisingly, some of the motifs Genesis 22 uses of Abraham and Isaac find their closest correspondences to acts in this part of the *Ion*. Unlike the completely passive and too-young Isaac, Ion retaliates against his parent, though, like Creusa before, still unaware of his actual relation to her. His intent to slay her despite her position at the altar again associates the attempted violence with a sacrifice. Abraham specifically builds an altar (Gen 22:9) on which to sacrifice Isaac. Burnett notes how the episode, because Ion threatens to slay Creusa even as she seeks refuge at Apollo's altar, makes mother and son equivalents of each other (119), "Ion's interrupted gesture clearly makes him the equal of his mother ... both are now guilty of an unintended religious crime."

In each myth, the god most centrally involved in the plot remains offstage while the sacrifice is averted. Ion and Abraham are both in essentially the same threatening posture when the god-sent intervention stops them. As Speiser notes (165), "The blade is in mid-air when his hand is stayed by a voice from heaven." Burnett argues similarly of Ion (119), "[H]is arm is clearly raised against the suppliant when the Pythia bursts upon the scene crying 'Hold!'" At this point both Yahweh and Apollo accomplish divine interventions, not personally, but through other agents. In Genesis 22 an angel intervenes, "And the Lord's messenger called out to him from the heavens" (Gen 22:11). The angel's intervention, explicitly to prevent violence, is very like a *deus ex machina* from Greek myth. Whether Athena's paradigmatic appearance at *Odyssey* 24.528–44, to stop further violence between Odysseus' family and the suitors' relatives, or those that often conclude Euripidean dramas, not only as Athena in the *Ion* but also those at *Helen* 1642–79 and *Iphigenia at Tauris* 1435–89.

Euripides has a two-part divine intervention with Apollo's priestess first intervening to prevent Ion from taking Creusa's life, prompting instead, through the introduction of the cradle, the recognition scene between mother and son (1320–69).[44] Athena subsequently appears to deliver the retrospective prophecy noted previously and bring closure to the story, both characters thus together corresponding to Isaac's angel. In Genesis, the intervention successful, the angel now gives a speech that corresponds to Athena's at *Ion* 1553–605,

> By My own Self, declares the Lord, that because you have done this thing and have not held back your son, your only one, I will greatly bless you and will greatly multiply your seed, as the stars in the heavens and as the sand on the shore of the sea ... And all the nations of the earth will be blessed through your seed because you have listened to my voice.
>
> Genesis 22:16–17

Apollo's nonappearance at the end of the *Ion* is a supposed problem, a touchstone for vastly differing interpretations. Whitman's initial assessment is representative of many (100), "[M]ost critics have felt that his [Apollo's] failure to appear in person at the end and do his own explaining is less than morally responsible." Burnett and Saxonhouse offer what seem to me to be more balanced appraisals. But, before proceeding, we should reiterate that the same motif occurs at the end of Genesis 22, with Yahweh sending an angel, as Apollo does Athena. I am unaware of any similar criticism directed at Yahweh.

During the play both Creusa and Ion make accusatory speeches openly questioning Apollo (339–400, 859–922). According to Saxonhouse (264), "Apollo does not appear at the end of the play lest his presence call forth old recriminations."[45] However, we have to be aware of identifying too much with either Ion's or Creusa's perspective, I suggest.[46] Burnett, on the one hand, notes shortcomings in Ion's perspective (129), "Ion's speech, in which he chides the god, is proven mistaken in its assumptions." On the other hand, she also argues for applying a larger perspective that would be more indicative of the author, than of an individual character (127–28), "The poet seems ... to be describing the nature and the working of divinity in general, and his revelation is, at first sight, a difficult one to take in." Whitman, analyzing Apollo's nonappearance at play's end (101), also suggests a position that could, just as well, apply to Yahweh's way with Abraham in Genesis 22, "leaving the god instead in the familiar tragic perspective, mighty, mysterious, aloof."

The angel and Hagar

If we enlarge the context for our consideration of the angel's *deus ex machina* appearances to Abraham (Gen 22:11–12, 15–18) by including the angel's appearances to Hagar (16:7–13; 21:17–20), we find even closer correspondences with Athena's intervention and other actions in the *Ion*. Seen from the *Ion*'s perspective, Hagar and Sara both embody complementary aspects of Creusa's character, and experience complementary aspects of her circumstances. However, Abraham, from the perspective of the *Ion*, *combines* the functions of Apollo and Xuthus.

Unable to conceive, it is Sara who suggests that Abraham have sex with her slave girl, Hagar (16:1–3). Creusa's actual legal status, as line 298 makes clear,[47] is that of a slave. Throughout the play, she is troubled by her inability to conceive by her soon to be patriarch husband, Xuthus. When Hagar becomes pregnant, she acts haughty toward Sara, who, complaining to Abraham, arranges to have her cast out (16:4–6). Alter well captures the unexpected postures of wife and husband (2004: 77), "[H]er [Sara's] bitterness and resentment against the husband who, after all, has only complied with her request; his willingness to buy conjugal peace at almost any price." Creusa's corresponding bitterness or resignation appears especially at 790–91. Sara drives Hagar out of the house here (16:6), as Creusa and her servants fear they will be (808–10). When Hagar flees, taking refuge at a spring in the wilderness, an angel appears to her, commanding her to return,

> Return to your mistress and suffer abuse at her hand ... I will surely multiply your seed ... you have conceived and will bear a son / and you will call his name Ishmael.
>
> 16:9–11

Very like Athena to Creusa, perhaps remarkably so, the angel gives purpose to Hagar, and supplies the name for her son, decreeing he will be a patriarch – all this with God offstage, as Apollo throughout the *Ion*.

Having given birth, she remains in highly ambivalent status and circumstances. When Sara sees Ishmael laughing, on the day Isaac is weaned, she resumes her earlier posture (21:10), "Drive out this slavegirl and her son, for the slavegirl's son shall not inherit with my son, with Isaac." Again, Hagar is in the position Creusa *fears* she is in, but at the same time Sara's role is that which Creusa, at the suggestion of her servants, temporarily adopts: to get rid of her husband's, but not her own, son (836 ff.). In their presumed helplessness, both Hagar and Creusa weep (21:16; 242, 248). Giving her only some bread and a water skin, Abraham sends her out into the wilderness,

> And when the water in the skin was gone, she flung the child under one of the bushes, and went off and sat down at a distance, a bowshot away, for she thought, "Let me not see when the child dies." And she sat at a distance and raised her voice and wept.
>
> 21:15–16

Hagar here briefly abandons her child (21:15), as Creusa.

But also like Creusa, she has two divine encounters, at virtually the same times in her child's life: at or near conception, and when the boy is an adolescent or young man. Alter calculates, as to Ishmael's age (104), "the boy would be about sixteen," within reach of Ion's youthful, if undetermined, age. At God's direction, the angel now *speaks to Hagar from heaven*, very clearly corresponding to the *deus ex machina* apparatus. As with Athena in the *Ion*, the angel brings mother and the endangered child back together, saving both from danger, and prophesying a great future for her son (21:18), "Go, lift the child, and hold him in your arms, for a great nation will I make him." As Carr argues (1996: 194), "God interacts directly with her in a way similar to the way he interacts with Abraham and his heirs," again reminiscent of Creusa's initial relations with Apollo. Though cast out, Ishmael receives God's support, "God was with the lad, and he grew up" (21:20), suggesting rough correspondence with Apollo's divine steerage of the key events in Ion's life.

Abraham thus becomes, for Ishmael, the distant, high-status father that Apollo is to Ion. Much about Abraham, unique in the Bible in so many ways, suggests the status of a god. He several times performs acts and functions more typical of a god than a mortal. God personally appears to him more than to any other character in the Bible, except Moses. At the opening of Genesis 17, God tells him, "Walk in my presence." In the entire Bible, only Enoch, who is given a unique afterlife, is treated in a similar manner (Gen 5:22–24). Their curious dialogue at Genesis 18:16–33 is clearly an adapted divine council,[48] that is, it is modeled on typical exchanges between *two gods*. Even more curious, Abraham there fulfills the dynamic traditionally associated with the Sky Father, while Yahweh serves that of the traditional wrathful, and lesser, god. The only other corresponding scene in the Hebrew Bible is that between Moses and Yahweh (Exod 32:7–14).[49] But as for Ishmael, Abraham remains entirely distant from him, as Apollo to Ion, taking no part in the scene, having minimal contact with his son hereafter. At the same time, his sending Hagar and Ishmael into the wilderness with only a water skin and some food not only resembles the motif of exposing an infant (21:15–16) but also of his own coming sacrifice of Isaac, as subsequent details and correspondences between the two episodes make clear.[50] Yet in his dealings with Sara about Ishmael, Abraham is curiously reminiscent of Xuthus. Consider again Alter's characterization, "his willingness to buy conjugal peace at almost any price."

Ismael's future occupation, an archer, is a fairly rare one in the Bible. Again, however, this may come into clearer focus, coming from Euripides' play. Ion is not only a capable archer – evidence of his divine paternity – but his ability figures prominently in the play (107, 524).

Xuthus and Isaac in Genesis 27: the deceived father

Xuthus' peculiar role in the *Ion*, completely left in the dark as to his actual relationship with Ion, corresponds in several ways to Isaac's role in Genesis 27.

Isaac is here virtually in his dotage, easily deceived, duped by his wife, who, in league with the son he does not prefer, manipulates him to suit her own preferences. The dynamics between the three characters, Creusa, Ion, and Xuthus, correspond to those between Rebecca, Jacob, and Isaac.

Both Isaac and Xuthus, in these episodes at least, share several larger character traits and functions. Isaac is the least developed as a character of the four Genesis patriarchs, Barton (325) noting, "Isaac is a more shadowy figure than the other patriarchs." The same holds for Xuthus, who is scarcely mentioned in Apollodorus (passing mention in just three passages that only link him to other characters). Both are substitutes, thematically, through their myths. In the case of Isaac, a substitute, his father's servant, wins his wife (Rebecca) for him (Gen 24). Xuthus will now function as a substitute or surrogate father for Ion. Both function more as "genealogical place holders," links between their offspring and other more significant relatives, than biological fathers. Both men come across as comic or comedic characters, highly ironic figures (in a passive, not active sense). In Isaac's case, this seems to be a functional application of the folk etymology of his name. Again, consider Alter's explanation (83) of Genesis 17:17, "17. and *he laughed*. The verb *yitshaq* is identical with the Hebrew form of the name Isaac." The folk etymology instantiates Isaac's largely ironic function in Genesis 27, I suggest.[51]

Creusa and Rebecca both display greater mental agility than their husbands, and easily outmaneuver them.[52] When Rebecca learns that Isaac plans to give his blessing to Esau, she initiates her own plot to promote Jacob over Esau (Gen 25:28, 27:1–28:5). When she further learns that he has asked Esau, a hunter, to get him some game for a meal, prior to blessing him, Rebecca instead has Jacob retrieve two kids, which she cooks for the meal.

Knowing Isaac is almost dim, she has Jacob wear the skins of the slain kids to pass himself off as the hairy Esau. Completely fooled, Isaac, after eating the savory dish Rebecca prepared, mistakenly bestows his blessing on Jacob (Gen 27:18–19). Only after he has already finished blessing Jacob does Esau return.

Creusa offers parallels with Rebecca in advancing plans to promote certain offspring at the expense of others. Her use of a libation ceremony (1029 ff.) to cover the intended poisoning of Ion partly corresponds to Rebecca using the cooking of a meal to shortchange Esau. Her motive for murder resembles Rebecca's agenda: prevent/secure advancement of a specific son. Though Xuthus is not blind, as old, or infirm as Isaac, he has other weaknesses that similarly incapacitate him. Mueller (371) notes his "striking absence of memory ... of Ion's conception ... [he] can remember nothing, an amnesia." Creusa's and Ion's subsequent deception of him (corresponding to Rebecca's and Jacob's of Isaac) works because Xuthus cannot remember any particulars of his paternity of Ion. Creusa, on the contrary, has formidable powers of recollection (cf. Mueller 371), corresponding to Rebecca's mental acuity.

Both men are thus tricked, unknowingly, into serving the gods' larger designs. As Saxonhouse notes, on the one hand (269), Xuthus appears "very much the dunce throughout," and, on the other (271), he is ignorant "of the fact that he is the dupe of both Apollo and Creusa." Xuthus' ignorance will remain complete. Athena commands Creusa to tell no one that Ion is her son (1601), so Xuthus will remain happy in his false belief (1602). Both wives, however, Creusa and Rebecca, are in on the larger divine plan but not their husbands; this is quite explicit in the *Ion*, implicit in Genesis 27. It is according to Athena's specific instruction that Xuthus be kept in the dark as to Ion's actual paternity (1601–2: νῦν οὖν σιώπα, παῖς ὅδ' ὡς πέφυκε σός, / ἵν' ἡ δόκησις Ξοῦθον ἡδέως ἔχῃ). Rebecca is implicitly validated in engineering Isaac's deception about Jacob's blessing when the latter receives repeated assurances from God of his future as a patriarch (Gen 28:13–15, 32:28–29). As Mueller notes (366), "Creusa effectively displaces her husband, Xuthus, as 'father' of her son." Virtually the same could be said of Rebecca regarding Isaac and Jacob.

Aegeus, in Euripides' *Medea*, is a further instance of the same basic figure, his relations with Medea and Theseus offering another instance of the dynamic found in Xuthus, Creusa, and Ion. In Aegeus, as for Xuthus, and repeatedly for the Genesis patriarchs, childlessness is again a motivating issue (667–73, 717–18, 721–22), when he first meets Medea. We see again a father whose paternity is problematic (is he or Poseidon the father of Theseus), a husband easily deceived by a strong-willed woman (his future wife). Aegeus complements Medea as to her foresight (προμηθίαν: 741).

Medea has more than a few traits in common with both Creusa and Rebecca. She easily outwits her husband, Jason (and Aegeus),[53] as Creusa does Xuthus. Her ability to interpret the oracle for Aegeus (667–81) is evidence that Medea is connected with the gods' larger designs, as is Creusa.[54] Creusa and Medea both want revenge against their children (though Creusa is ignorant of her relation to Ion while she does, whereas Medea is "fully cogni-zant of the details of her attempted murder").[55] Creusa attempts to have Ion drink a poison; Medea will apparently attempt to have her stepson Theseus drink a poison.[56] Medea is a master of manipulating oaths,[57] a thematic cor-respondence to Rebecca's thorough manipulation of Isaac's blessing.

Ion and Joseph: the patriarch as romance protagonist

Of Genesis' four patriarchs, Ion offers the greatest number of correspondences with Joseph, because of the climactic recognition scenes near the conclusion of both characters' larger myths, and certain character traits. Elsewhere, in the *Helen* and in *Iphigenia in Tauris*, Euripides places his recognition scenes in the middle of his plots. The *Ion*, however, corresponds to Genesis' account of Joseph (37, 39–47), first in postponing the actual recognition (Ion and Creusa have a lengthy scene together, unaware of their relationship), and in having it serve as the climax of the myth.

Ion and Joseph both embody a prissy kind of youthful innocence. As Joseph's myth begins he is seventeen (Gen 37:2), a close correspondence to Ion's approximate (but unstated) age.[58] Both retain a childish simplicity in their relations with others. Ion's opening speech about his life at Delphi (82–183) corresponds thematically to Joseph's narration of his first two dreams to his brothers (37:5–9). Alter's (207) assessment is relevant, "a young Joseph who is self-absorbed, blithely assuming everyone will be fascinated by the details of his dreams."[59] Owen arrives at a closely corresponding view of Ion (xxvi), "[He] has a naïve curiosity, an occasional love of showing off." Both retain this boyish state, perhaps suggesting a partial failure to become mature males capable of fully engaging a female counterpart, in that they remain unmarried for the greater part of their myths, as they are depicted in the accounts we have.[60]

Both have a sense of privilege and entitlement that can offend others. This is especially prominent in Joseph. His brothers are already jealous of the favoritism Jacob shows him (Gen 37:4) when he recounts his first two dreams, prompting their outraged response, "Do you mean to reign over us, do you mean to rule us?" (Gen 37:8). Joseph does not even know where his brothers are pasturing their father's sheep (Gen 37:12–17), suggesting that he, for unstated reasons, is exempt from the chores they perform.[61]

Both, while in their youth, are abandoned by their closest family members. Ion is abandoned by Apollo at his conception and by his mother shortly after his birth, though Ion bears responsibility for neither act. Joseph, how-ever, is at least partly responsible for provoking his brothers' subsequent behavior: selling him into slavery. Though Joseph, for some time after this, is a prisoner with no resources, he soon rises to a position of considerable power. Kugel finds it noteworthy that during this time he makes no attempt to contact his father, though he now has considerable resources to do so.[62] Though the circumstances and chronology are quite different, nonetheless, it seems significant that both share the similar situation of having a literally distant father.

Partly because of the distancing from their fathers, both have family members, who, out of bitter resentment at the protagonists' good fortune, attempt to take their lives. Joseph's brothers are depicted as nursing considerable hatred of him over Jacob's earlier favoritism, and Joseph's own behavior toward them, his narration of his first two dreams serving as a catalyst, "And they hated him all the more, for his dreams and for his words" (Gen 37:8). This hatred soon prompts most of them to contemplate his murder, "and they plotted against him to put him to death" (Gen 37:18). Several factors conspire in Creusa (unaware that Ion is her son) to encourage her to agree to the old man's suggestion that she slay him (843–50).[63] The final straw is her resentment over Xuthus' good fortune, which makes her see him as a traitor (864: προδότης), added to her own frustrations over not knowing what became of her own child, her prolonged state of childlessness since then, and long-simmering anger at her seemingly shabby treatment by Apollo. Both sets of relatives will have a cover story to mask their attempted murder. Creusa will use a libation ceremony to cover the poisoning (1029 ff). Joseph's brothers will claim a wild animal slew him, "And so now let us kill him and fling him into one of the pits, and we can say a vicious beast has devoured him" (Gen 37:20).[64]

Despite their initial elite status, both Ion and Joseph occupy a largely servile status for much of their myths. In both instances, this partly results from their separation from family. Euripides' play thematically depicts Ion as the servant or slave of Apollo. Ion gives a lengthy description of his daily, menial tasks of sweeping the temple floors (102–24). He declares that he is a servant of the gods (131–33), a figure Genesis also uses of Abraham (Gen 26:24). He concludes his monody reiterating the same notion (181–83; cf. 794–95, 1343, 1372–73). When Creusa asks his name, he declares he is Apollo's slave (309: τοῦ θεοῦ καλοῦμαι δοῦλος).[65] When she compliments him on his robes, he says they belong to the god he serves (327). Joseph is not only sold into slavery (Gen 37:25–28) but thrown into prison shortly thereafter for two years (Gen 39:20–41:14). Nonetheless, both protagonists find comfort in their servitude. Ion is quite content performing his tasks. Joseph finds a similar fulfillment.[66]

Ion's ability to read oracular signs corresponds to Joseph's ability to interpret dreams. The play foregrounds Ion's sign-reading ability in the two-sided attentiveness he pays to the birds in his opening monody (179–80): aware that they convey divine signals. But more crucially, his understanding of *kledonism* (1187–91) helps him avoid the old man's poisoning attempt, his interpretation immediately confirmed by the doves.

Genesis first shows Joseph recounting his dreams to his brothers but not interpreting them (37:5–11). Nonetheless, his brothers call him "dream-master" (Gen 37:19), which will later prove an accurate designation during his stay in Egypt, when he is able to interpret the dreams of the cupbearer, the baker, and pharaoh (Gen 40:5–41:32). However, their corresponding ability to interpret signs from the gods also forms the complement of another close correspondence: The respective gods, Apollo and Yahweh, shape the entire arc of their lives; "as the Lord was with him, and whatever he did, the Lord made succeed" (Gen 39:23).

Both myths conclude in a climactic recognition scene, the traditional culmination of a romance myth, in which characters are reunited with their long-lost relatives in highly emotional circumstances.[67] The myth of Joseph employs the same subtype as that preferred by the *Odyssey*: *postponed recognition*, in which the protagonist is fully aware of his other family members' identities, but nonetheless, refrains from disclosing his own identity until a later time, after having first interrogated and tested his relatives in earlier scenes. In the *Ion* Euripides employs the type preferred by some later authors, including the *History of Apollonius King of Tyre* and Shakespeare,[68] in which neither family member (Ion, Creusa) is initially aware of the other's identity. However, Euripides creates a variant of the type, in many respects a tour de force exploration of the possibilities the type-scene affords, a virtuoso treatment by a scholar of myth.

When the famine drives Joseph's brothers to Egypt (Gen 41:53–42:4), they come face to face with the official in charge of distributing grain, their unrecognized brother, Joseph. They cannot recognize him because they "know" he is dead (42:32, 38; 44:20, 28), his greatly elevated status, position as royal insider, foreign dress, and his own deceit, "and he played the stranger to them and spoke harshly to them" (Gen 42:7). Eager to see if they have changed since they sold him into slavery, he has them falsely accused of theft by planting his own silver in their goods as they leave (42:28) to see if they will betray their brother Benjamin, as they earlier betrayed him. When they return with Benjamin, Joseph again has silver planted in their baggage (44:7–13). When they refuse to betray Benjamin, Joseph finally reveals himself to them (45:1–15). Overall, the evolution of Joseph's postponed recognition is very close to several episodes in the *Odyssey*, especially Odysseus' recognition scene with Laertes.[69]

Euripides features a substantial earlier encounter between Ion and Creusa (237–452), but unlike corresponding scenes in the *Odyssey* or Joseph's myth, neither character knows the other's actual identity, nor tests the other, as do Odysseus and Joseph. But the scene is full of ironic *near* recognitions. Remark after remark ricochets, in one way or another, off their true identities and actual familial bond with each other (especially at 303–6, 308, 313, 316, 318, 324–25, 328, 330–32, 338–40, 342–46, 354, 356, 359–60, 364–65, 433–34), in a virtuoso dialogue that stretches the traditional conventions of the recognition scene.

The *Odyssey* and Joseph's myth both thematically employ a specific form of irony in which the protagonist remains unrecognized in the presence of family members, but they, nonetheless, are prompted to think of their presumably absent relative. This applies to characters throughout the poem (e.g., as at 8.564–71, 9.506–17, 13.172–78), not just to the immediate family members.[70] Common ground between those episodes and the first dialogue between Creusa and Ion suggests Euripides has adapted the *Odyssey*'s series of postponed recognitions, especially that between Odysseus and Penelope in Book 19, but removed the element of one character testing the other. In a sense, his doing so makes Ion and Creusa more equal partners and participants in the scenes (both 237–452 and 1261–509), neither in full control of the events as they unfold, the opposite of Odysseus' and Joseph's encounters.

In what may be Euripides' biggest innovation, however, he includes a *false* or *seeming recognition scene* between Xuthus and Ion, placing it shortly after (515–675) the nonrecognition scene between Ion and Creusa.[71] The scene anticipates, and even parodies, the same dynamics and sequence of events and moods that occur in the true recognition at play's end between mother and son, as a number of parallel details reveal.[72] Both parents are immediately utterly convinced of Ion's identity as their son. Both parents at once call Ion their child: ὦ τέκνον: 516, ὦ τέκνον μοι: 1398. Ion in return thinks each parent is insane: σ' ἔμηνε θεοῦ τις: 520; θεομανής: 1402. Both parents insist on embracing him (519, implicit in 1404). When he demurs, both parents say Ion may now kill them (527, 1404). He incredulously repeats their claim to be his relative (πατρὸς ... πατὴρ: 527–28, φίλος ... φίλος: 1407–8). Xuthus then recounts the oracle he received, about which Ion closely interrogates him. With Creusa, the inspection of the cradle and Ion's interrogation of her knowledge about the tokens within serve the same corresponding function. Larger correspondences continue, and as with Xuthus, Ion briefly finds fault with his future life as Xuthus' son (585–647), whereas with Creusa he finds fault with Apollo (1512–52). Euripides' Xuthus again corresponds partly to Isaac in wanting to bless the wrong son but also to Abraham in being utterly convinced by God.

The Pythia, Apollo's priestess and Ion's surrogate mother (1324–25), triggers (1320–69) the climactic recognition between mother and son (1261–509).[73] The *Odyssey*'s recognition scene between Odysseus and Eurykleia, and its position (19.353–505), falling between Odysseus' testing of Penelope (19.53–251) and his actual recognition with her (23.1–232), may have served Euripides as precedent or inspiration. The supremely loyal old woman is no blood relation, but in serving as Odysseus' wet nurse (19.492–93) and having taken part in his naming ritual (19.399–412), she comes close to being a surrogate mother for him. As in the first dialogue between Creusa and Ion, additional ironic remarks touching on their relationship (563, 669–70, 787–95, 803, 837–38, 915–18, 1276–78, 1307) reverberate through the intervening portions of the play, prefiguring the recognition.

The Pythia's entrance was prompted by Ion's threat to slay Creusa at Apollo's altar. To prevent him from committing a religious crime she calls his attention to the basket she carries (1337–38), to which Ion refers with Hermes' same word from the opening monologue (ἀντίπηγ': 19). At Apollo's urging (1347) she has kept the basket and its contents safe. Ion's swaddling clothes (1351: σπάργαν') are within, also earlier mentioned by Hermes (32) and by Creusa (918). As Ion quickly realizes, the clothes are clues (known to no other person: 1361–62) that could lead to his mother, which the Pythia now commands him to investigate (1355). As Ion ponders the possibilities, as to who his mother may be, his reflections again abound in ironic remarks pertaining to Creusa (1376–77), who sits nearby, again instantiating Euripides' reworking of the *Odyssey's* relevant form of irony.

Intimate personal tokens (1386: τὰ μητρὸς σύμβολ'), as so often in a romance, will prompt the recognition. As she glimpses the basket, Creusa, first flooded with hope (1395: φάσμα τῶν ἀνελπίστων), now declares Ion is her son, exposed by her in the same basket (1398–400). The incredulous Ion, as in his scene with Xuthus, first accuses her of madness but agrees to a test of her claim. Under penalty of death, Creusa will name the tokens the basket contains (1412–16).[74] The first item is a weaving sampler, depicting the Gorgon, with serpents as a fringe, like the aegis (1417–25). The second again involves serpents, golden, comprising a child's necklace (1427–31). The final item is an olive wreath, still green, taken from Athena's tree on the Acropolis (1433–36).

The olive as the climactic token of recognition again points to the *Odyssey's* recognition scenes. When Penelope tricks Odysseus into proving his identity, she tests him about their unique marriage bed, carved into the trunk of a *living* olive tree. As he accurately divulges the information no one else knows (23.227–29), only now does Penelope accept that he is her long-lost husband. Similarly, no one else in the *Ion* knows of the basket and tokens (1341–42, 1361–62). The olive tree from which Penelope's marriage bed is carved has distinctive traits, θάμνος ἔφυ τανύφυλλος ἐλαίης ... ἀκμηνὸς θαλέθων (23.190–91), in particular, it is "fully grown, flourishing." Creusa's olive wreath, στέφανον ἐλαίας (1433), retains a similar quality, developing it to a higher degree, θάλλει δ' ἐλαίας ἐξ ἀκηράτου γεγώς (1436). In both myths the olive maintains its traditional association with Athena.

Though Euripides builds on some elements of the *Odyssey's* recognition scenes, in other respects the *Ion* departs from the most conventional expectations of a romance, as, in one respect, does Joseph's myth. Creusa and Joseph's brothers both come *to* the protagonist, opposite romance's more frequent pattern in which the protagonist returns home after a long absence. Both myths share the same apparent innovation, owing to a similar motivation: providing an etiology for a people's presence.

The *Ion* thus provides a valuable context for studying all four Genesis patriarchs, as well as for Moses' birth and name. Not only does Ion's myth contain all the principal motifs used for the Genesis patriarchs, in several instances it preserves them in a more traditional form than does Genesis. At the very least, then, comparison of the *Ion* and the patriarchs brings out in greater detail how traditional so many of the individual components are.

Weinfeld has well demonstrated Genesis' dependence on the Greek *ktisis*, or foundation, story type,[75] though his concern was more to demonstrate correspondences between Abraham and Aeneas. As I argue here, the *Ion* (which also incorporates aspects of a *ktisis* narrative) is perhaps even more relevant, and perhaps more broadly demonstrates the Pentateuch's larger dependence on different aspects of Greek culture.

While Ion's "speaking name" instantiates the same naming conventions as those given to Moses and the Genesis patriarchs,[76] it seems stronger than mere coincidence how the meanings of Ion's and Moses' share several specific correspondences. Both names embody mobility predictive for their peoples. Each foster parent articulates the corresponding circumstances: "as I came out," "I drew him from." Before the names are given the notion of mobility is already there in Ion's stroller and Moses' floating basket. The five main characters that play roles in their miraculous births offer a close homology:

> Ion > Moses,
> Creusa > Moses' unnamed mother,
> Hermes > Moses' unnamed sister,
> Pythia > Pharaoh's unnamed daughter,
> Apollo > Yahweh.

The striking *serial* anonymity of so many characters in Moses' early story strongly suggests the Exodus tradition is reshaping a narrative imported from elsewhere, in which the characters crucial to such a significant figure had more specific status.

Moreover, the slot for "father" is conspicuously absent in our homology. Shinana and Zakovitch, pursuing their argument that an earlier account of Moses with more prominent supernatural elements has been suppressed, argue that because Matthew presents Christ as a second Moses, we can reconstruct some elements now missing in Exodus (169), "he shaped his story about Jesus' birth by using motifs known to readers from the ancient Jewish traditions about the birth of Moses." If their argument is valid, however, logically the ultimate parallel suppressed in earlier accounts about Moses would be his original divine paternity, as for Christ, and as for Ion. Does the *Ion* thus help us make better sense of the seemingly deliberate anonymity so prevalent in Moses' origin myth?

But clearly the repeated correspondences between the *Ion* and the Abraham cycle are of particular note. The *Ion*'s divine economy, the interrelations between Apollo and Athena, provides a highly suggestive context for considering when and where the angel intervenes in the Abraham cycle, as opposed to when God does. While Greek tragedy's *deus ex machina* scenes in general provide a useful context for considering the angel's appearances in Abraham's myth, Athena's in the *Ion* (1553–605) should henceforth be considered particularly relevant. Her appearance, as both by the angel, is prompted by the events in the narrative.

Unable to fully accept what Apollo has done and intended for him, Ion questions the god and his oracle (*Ion* 1537–38, 1546–48). Immediately, Athena appears. The monotheistic Genesis tradition does not allow an Abraham that questions God, whereas in polytheism, this may seem a more reasonable, more realistic response. Athena's dramatic *deus ex machina* resolution addresses the questions and anxieties of each of the two central characters, Creusa and Ion, in much the same way that the angel does in its two separate interventions for Hagar and Abraham.

Unexpectedly, Athena's concluding prophecy is centered far more around (and largely addressed to)[77] Creusa than Ion. As Athena resolves Creusa's issues and anxieties, so at Genesis 16:9–11, the angel's first appearance to Hagar does the same. As Athena validates Creusa as Ion's mother, and declares a glorious future for him, so the angel to Hagar, "I will surely multiply your seed … you have conceived and will bear a son / and you will call his name Ishmael." After Sara does arrange to have Hagar and Ishmael cast out, the angel again appears to her (21:18), "Go, lift the child, and hold him in your arms, for a great nation will I make him." Ishmael will be a skilled bowman (21:20; cf. 21:16), as Euripides emphasizes of Creusa's Ion as we first meet him (106–8).

Though addressed largely to Ion, Athena's prophecy has the same elements found in God's repeated promises to Abraham (12:1–2, 7; 15:5–14; 17:1–14), Isaac (Gen 26:24), and Jacob (Gen 28:14; 46:3). We can adduce the somewhat analogous promise to Moses, depicted as a direct extension of the covenant (Exod 2:23–25), that he is to lead the Israelites out of Egypt (Exod 3:10, etc.).

Because we have a growing consensus that Abraham's narrative is among the more recent in Genesis,[78] we can consider the possibility that the many correspondences it exhibits with the *Ion* are not merely generic, but result from the authors reacting or responding to the myth of Ion. Of the Genesis patriarchs, Ion's foundational role is closest to that of Abraham as father of nations. Creusa's unusual prominence and centrality should be seen as more than merely relevant to the Abraham cycle's concerns with Hagar. Might we even reinterpret Genesis' anachronistic references to the Philistines (Gen 21:32, 34; Gen 26), as the redactors' way of signaling connections with larger Greek culture, as we argue in the Introduction of 1 Samuel–1 Kings?

As Weinfeld notes (23), the basic rubric or paradigm that the Pentateuch employs for colonization[79] is already present in Homer, "This basic pattern of settlement, which includes the erection of a temple and the division of the land by lot, can be found earlier, in Homeric literature." He refers to the account at *Odyssey* 6.9–10 of how Nausithoos is said to have founded the Phaiacians' city on Scheria,

> ἀμφὶ δὲ τεῖχος ἔλασσε πόλει, καὶ ἐδείματο οἴκους,
> καὶ νηοὺς ποίησε θεῶν, καὶ ἐδάσσατ' ἀρούρας.

> He drove a wall around the city, and built homes,
> and made temples of the gods, and apportioned the land.[80]

In the *Ion* these portions of the larger myth remain in the future, as Athena declares of the descendants of Ion's four sons (1582–84),

> At the appointed time the children born
> of them shall colonize (ἐποικήσουσι) the Cyclades,
> Possess the island cities and the coasts.

As with Abraham, it is Ion's descendants who shall spread and inhabit the lands, the very lands specified in Genesis 10:4–5 as inhabited by the sons of Javan.

Notes

1 Old Testament myth articulates its devaluing of heroic protagonists by elevating Jacob at the expense of the more stereotypically heroic Esau (Gen 27); cf. David's defeat of the Philistine Goliath (1 Sam 17), perhaps a direct allusion to and editorial comment by biblical redactors on Greek myth.

2 See Louden (2011a: 57–104) on correspondences between Joseph in Egypt (Gen 39–47) and the *Odyssey*.

3 Of course, this tendency is also seen elsewhere in Greek culture, appearing first in some of the pre-Socratics. But of the authors of mythic texts, it is most pronounced in Euripides.

4 On which see Segal (1999: 74), regarding "the transcendent time of the gods."

5 Segal (72): "In the recognition scene, however, Creusa looks back over the course of her life and sees the wounds as healed."

6 See especially Lape (2010: 120–21), on how extraordinarily different is Euripides' treatment of the traditional motif of a god parenting a special child with a mortal partner than other authors'.

7 On Euripides' treatment of gender, see Saxonhouse (1986) throughout, Lape, and Mueller (2010).

8 Cf. Whitman 1974: 73: "The whole myth is also of a common aetiological kind, in which a god engenders the founder of a nation or familial line ... Pindar ... in the sixth *Olympian Ode* relates how Apollo seized Evadne and begat Iamus, the father of a famous line of prophets."

9 On the jarring aspects of Euripides' presentation, see Whitman (74): "We are invited, or rather compelled, to see the whole action through the eyes of the violated girl, hapless victim of a god's lust."

10 Judges 13:2–35, in turn, seem so close to the circumstances of Christ's conception as depicted at Matthew 1:18–25, that they must have served as an ante-text. Boling (1975: 220) notes a parallel between them.

11 Cf. Propp's formulation (1998: 155): "the tale of an imperiled child of illustrious lineage, abandoned by its natural parents and raised in obscurity by foster parents, only at length to come into its own."

12 Propp's translation. Other Hebrew Bible translations, unless otherwise noted, are by Alter.

13 Further problematizing the relations between the siblings are Propp's additional observations (214): "E's language in 4:14 indicates, however, that Moses and

Aaron are nothing more than *fellow* Levirates … we note that 15:20 (E) calls Miriam 'Aaron's sister,' implying that she is more closely related to Aaron than to Moses."

14 Cf. Shinan and Zakovitch 2012: 165: "It is a remarkable fact that Moses – the first prophet, the one who delivers the Israelites from Egypt, gives them the Law, and leads them through forty years of wandering in the desert – did not warrant an elaborate birth story." They go on to offer what they consider to be the original version of his birth, based on apocryphal accounts that, they argue, preserve early elements (166) "that the Pentateuch had sought to blur and suppress, traditions that continued to be told orally."

15 Lape (106) "Creusa's childlessness is mentioned more than twenty times in the play." Cf. Whitman (89): "[T]he affront to her Athenian pride is nothing to her grief at being childless."

16 According to Genesis 17:17, Abraham is 100, Sarah 90.

17 See Louden (2011a: 30–56) for analysis of parallels between theoxeny in the *Odyssey* and in Genesis 18–19. We return to theoxeny again in Chapter 6.

18 See Mueller 2010: 370.

19 Segal (74): "Hermes … is the first to call Ion by the name that he will have as the founder of Ionian Greece … an act which in itself implies the divine view over the whole trajectory of Ion's life."

20 See Mueller (369–70), on Greek fathers' traditional role as name givers.

21 Alter 2004: 313: "The verb clearly indicates his reaching the age of weaning, which would have been around 3."

22 Shinan and Zakovitch (138) observe that the Bible says almost nothing about Abraham until he is 75.

23 Alter's translation.

24 For a discussion of thematic parallels with Menelaus' wrestling Proteus at the sea-shore, see Louden 2011a: 113–23.

25 Cf. Speiser 1962: 125: "Heb. *way-yishaq* anticipates, of course, the personal name Isaac (*Yishaq*). P does this here, J offers a variant explanation in xviii 12, and E still another in xxi 6."

26 Alter underscores how thematic childlessness is within her larger myth (158): "It is a general principle of biblical narrative that a character's first recorded speech has particular defining force as characterization."

27 We consider her use of the mandrake root in some detail in Chapter 3.

28 Cf. Speiser's perspective, utilizing source criticism (232): "[W]hereas J derives 'Joseph' from *ysp* 'to add' … E connects the name with '*sp* 'to gather, remove.'"

29 As Lape (98) notes, Euripides is offering a particularly Athens-centered account, "Athena closes the play with a genealogical tale that effectively remakes the Hellenic world as offshoots of the Athenian family tree."

30 In Chapter 10 we discuss how retrospective prophecy/*vaticinatio ex eventu* functions in *The Aeneid* and the Book of Revelation.

31 Though Euripides considerably problematizes Apollo's interventions in his play.

32 Translation here is from *The Oxford Study Bible*.

33 However, the *Midrash Rabbah* interprets the four as "i.e. Hellas and Taras [Tarantum], Italia, and Dardania … Especially the southern part of Italy, called Magna Graecia."

34 Cf. "I shall make your descendants countless as the dust of the earth; only if the specks of dust on the ground could be counted could your descendants be

counted" (Gen 13:16); "Look up at the sky, and count the stars, if you can. So many will your descendants be" (15:5)

35 Cf. "a nation, a host of nations will come from you" (Gen 35:11).
36 On Euripides' treatment of gender, see Saxonhouse throughout, Lape, and Mueller.
37 Cf. also Lape (136): "It seems no accident that Euripides has made Apollo, the spokesman of purely paternal heredity in the *Eumenides*, the guarantor of maternal inheritance."
38 Cf. Segal (75): "his recurrent concern with purity," and 76.
39 Cf. Burnett (105) on how Ion "will carry an immaculate Delphic purity of heart down to Athens." I also adduce Whitman (89–90).
40 The circumstances to which Ion refers, a king sacrificing his child for success in war (on which, see Owen 1939: 93) are the same for two other instances of human sacrifice in Hebrew Bible myth: Jephthah's sacrifice of his daughter (Judges 11:30–37) and King Mesha's sacrifice of his son in 2 Kings 3. See discussion in Louden 2006: 205–6.
41 Speiser (164): "To sacrifice Isaac, as God demanded, was to forego at the same time the long-range objective itself."
42 Cf. Speiser's comment, ibid., "the boy burdened with the wood for his own sacrificial pyre."
43 On the dove as a substitute for Ion, see Burnett (117): "[O]ne of them dies Ion's death."
44 Cf. Burnett (126): "He [Apollo] acts here by means of a dove and a priestess ... And finally he sends Athena."
45 Cf. Burnett (122): "The god makes a point of saving Creusa from an open blasphemy, just as he saved her from killing and being killed. He will not allow a confrontation, for fear she might with further blasphemy put herself beyond even his mercy."
46 Compare Mastronarde (2002: 16), though speaking of the *Medea*, "The divergent views are not to be judged as completely right or completely wrong or as mutually exclusive, but as elements to be weighed and evaluated by the audience, with due attention to speaker, context and rhetorical purpose."
47 Φερνάς γε πολέμου καὶ δορὸς λαβὼν γέρας.
48 See discussion in Louden 2011a: 26–27.
49 Ibid.: 25–26.
50 Alter, noting that the phrase used here of Abraham, "rose early in the morning," will recur at 22:3, in the binding of Isaac, remarks the connection (2004: 104) "as part of an intricate network of correspondences between the two stories."
51 Note the further plays on his name, 21:6, 9.
52 A marriage dynamic Greek myth also depicts in the marriage of Helen and Menelaus, both in *Odyssey* 4, and in Euripides' *Helen*; cf. the *Medea*, discussed in the following text.
53 See discussion at Mastronarde (18), as to whether she later marries him.
54 Cf. Burnett (115): "[T]hough she is a rebel against Apollo, Creusa yet has divine favor and protection."
55 Burnett (102). See Mastronarde (8–15), for discussion of the *Medea* as a revenge play.
56 Burnett (111): "Medea, we assume, poured her own poison into Theseus' cup." Cf. also *Ion* 1269–70: "I met with good fortune before going to the city of Athens

and perishing at my step-mother's hands," as Ion's circumstances evoke Theseus' encounter with Medea.

57 Mastronarde (283): "Medea ... is engaged in a deceptive manipulation of oaths and *philia*."

58 Owen (76): "What is Ion's age at the time of the play? On the one had he shows the naïve curiosity of a boy ... on the other hand, he is old enough ... to discharge various offices for visitors."

59 Alter (207): "his own wide-eyed amazement, and perhaps his naïveté."

60 Cf. Kugel 1990: 278: "[T]he text (Gen. 37:2) specifically states that Joseph was seventeen years old, yet goes on to describe him as a 'youth' ... Is this term, used even of the three-month-old Moses (Exod 2:6) appropriate for a young man of 17?"

61 Kugel's analysis of other facets of Joseph's behavior toward his brothers is also relevant (276), "the Genesis narrative notes that he used to bring back 'evil reports' about his brothers – he was a tattle-tale."

62 Kugel (276) "A still more problematical element in Joseph's picture was the fact he made no attempt to contact his beloved father, not when he was set in charge of Potiphar's household (and presumably could have done so without difficulty), and not even when he became a high official in Pharaoh's court. That he felt no attachment to his brothers is understandable, but his father?"

63 Cf. the chorus' earlier wish for Ion's death (720).

64 Creusa's brief reference to her slain sisters takes the *Ion* unexpectedly close to the imagery Genesis employs for the plot by Joseph's brothers: σκόπελον ἥμαξαν πέτρας (274).

65 Cf. Mueller (370): "Ion refers to himself as the property of Apollo."

66 Kugel (278): "as a result of his elevation to the top of Potiphar's staff that Joseph, slave that he is, has found a measure of comfort and well-being."

67 For a typology of recognition scenes, as well as analysis of parallels between those in the *Odyssey* and the myth of Joseph, see Louden 2011a: 72–96. For discussion of the *Ion*'s recognition scene, see Owen: xvii–xviii.

68 See especially the scene between father and daughter in *Pericles* 5.1.

69 Cf. Louden 2011a: 90: "The behavior most often criticized, Odysseus' decision to test his father with mocking words (24.240), is closely paralleled in Joseph's treatment of his brothers in their recognition scene." See further Louden 2011a: 92–93.

70 For discussion of the well-known technique see, most recently, Louden 2011a.

71 See Gibert 1995: 85.

72 Ibid.: 162, n. 4.

73 The *History of Apollonius King of Tyre* (48–49, Diana's priestess) and Shakespeare's *Comedy of Errors* (Emilia in 5.1) both feature a priestess/abbess figure who triggers a recognition scene, and seem descended, one way or the other, from Euripides' Pythia.

74 Plautus employs the same dynamic in the *Rudens*'s recognition scene, where a father tests a daughter's knowledge of the tokens (1045–190).

75 For a recent extension of Weinfeld's studies see Gmirkin 2017, particularly 221, 230–31.

76 We will further address the meaning Genesis finds in "Jacob" in Chapter 3.

77 See Gibert on 1571–75, "Athena now addresses Creusa alone and speaks of Ion in the third person until 1604."

78 E.g., Carr 1996: 268; Weinfeld 1993: 11; among many others.
79 See Gmirkin for a sustained argument that the Pentateuch responds to Plato's *Laws*, which concerns itself with matters largely implied by *Odyssey* 6.9–10.
80 See Weinfeld (24) for further discussion of the *Odyssey* passage. Also relevant as a Homeric antecedent is *Odyssey* 11.121–34, where Odysseus is depicted as introducing the worship of Poseidon to an inland region where he has not previously been worshipped.

3 Jason, Hera, Medea, and Aietes; Jacob, Rebecca, Rachel, and Laban

Argonautic myth and Genesis 27–33

Owing to a dispute over his inheritance, a young man undertakes a journey to the east. Receiving divine aid along the way, he reaches the foreign land where the devious father of his future bride imposes a series of labors upon him. When, using magic, the young hero accomplishes the daunting tasks, involving an unusual harvest, the cunning father-in-law reneges on the terms of their agreement. Consequently, the hero and his young bride flee in the middle of the night after she has stolen her father's prized possession. Her father angrily arranges their pursuit. This abstract could serve as an outline for the larger Argonautic myth, but also as a capsule of Jacob's journey to Haran to win Rachel from the devious Laban. Not only do the myths correspond in several specific motifs but also there are homologies for four principal characters (Jason: Jacob, Medea: Rachel, Aietes: Laban, and Hera: Rebecca), with Laban's household gods unexpectedly corresponding to the Golden Fleece. Because the parallels are too many and too close to ascribe to coincidence, I will argue that the authors/compilers of Genesis 27–33 are responding to a version of, perhaps a distillation of, Argonautic myth.

Differences in modality, as well as larger cultural issues, have hindered recognition of the parallels.[1] Argonautic myth is heroic, and epic, its central characters heroes, kings, princesses, and the occasional monster. Jacob's story, however, is a patriarchal myth, set more in desert tents than the exotic peoples and locales of Argonautic myth. Jacob's myth is foundational, his offspring central to Israelite culture: his 12 sons are progenitors of the 12 tribes. Jason's children are comparative nonentities, with few significant roles to play in other Greek myths.

Despite the different modality, and differences between polytheism and monotheism, there are significant correspondences in how both myths figure the gods and their interactions with mortals. Gods appear to both protagonists to give aid, and to test them, en route to their quests and on their return. These theophanies, and other forms of interaction, confirm the protagonists' special relations with the gods and validate their quests and other concerns. Both protagonists respond by constructing altars and establishing cultic observances. Though the divine aid is busier, more overt, in Argonautic myth, as is the way of polytheistic epic, with its larger cast of immortals, specific instances correspond well with episodes in Jacob's myth, particularly the encounter with Triton in Apollonius' *Argonautika* (4.1551–618, 1733–64) and Genesis 32:22–32.

Though study of the myths' correspondences is handicapped by the lateness of the only complete version of Argonautic myth, Apollonius' *Argonautika*, multiple references to an early oral epic of Argonautic myth make it clear that some complete version was in circulation, as several commentators have argued.[2] In fact, the numerous references in Homeric epic, in the *Iliad*, 7.468–69, 21.41, 23.747, and in the *Odyssey*, 10.137, perhaps most importantly 12.70, demonstrate that some oral epic version of Argonautic myth predates our *Iliad* and *Odyssey*. This last mention declares that the Argo is πασιμέλ ουσα, "a concern to all," underscoring the myth's broad circulation *before* the *Odyssey*. Jason, Aietes, the return voyage, and the Wandering Rocks are all specified, suggesting acquaintance with a fairly complete account of the myth. Additionally, the mentions of Hekamede (*Iliad* 11.624–40, 14.6) and Agamede (*Iliad* 11.740–41), "who knew as many drugs (φάρμακα) as the wide earth yields," both clearly shaped around the figure of Medea and, given corresponding names, demonstrate that Homeric epic is well aware of her character.[3] In the *Odyssey*, specific attributes of Circe and Nausikaa are also thought to be based on earlier depictions of Medea.[4] In a fragment from the *Nostoi* epic, Medea restores Aison's youth through her magic,[5] suggesting she is a key principal in the myth from early on.

Brief hints in Mimnermus, the scant remains of Eumelus'[6] *Korinthiaka* and the *Naupaktia*, Pindar's *Fourth Pythian*, multiple mentions in Herodotus, and Euripides' *Medea*, all demonstrate the earlier existence of a full, if fluid, version of the narrative, with individual authors treating the sequence and certain details with considerable flexibility. In several instances, these earlier texts reveal very different versions of some of the episodes than in Apollonius. Most intriguingly for our purposes, in several instances the correspondences between Genesis 27–33 and Argonautic myth are closer to these earlier versions, which strongly suggests that the Genesis authors/compilers are working from a version earlier than Apollonius'.

We can most easily trace the correspondences between the two myths by considering the following sequence of motifs. While some of these motifs are generic, their concatenation into a whole is unique:

- The Dispute over Inheritance
- The Young Male Protagonist Is Morally Ambiguous
- An Authoritative Female Directs His Journey to the East
  - Hera in Iliad 19.96–133 and Rebecca in Genesis 27
- God(s) Appear(s) in Theophany to the Hero
- The Heroes Establish Cultic Etiologies, Especially as to Why Something Is Not Eaten
- The Malevolent Father-in-Law Imposes a Series of Labors on the Hero
- The Bride Employs Magic and Uses the Mandrake Root

- The Hero Executes His Labors Aided by Magic
- The Father-in-Law Reneges on the Terms of the Labors
- The Bride Steals Her Father's Sacred Article (The Fleece, Household Gods)
- The Hero Sneaks off in the Night with His Wife, His Entourage, and the Sacred Article; the Father-in-Law Pursues with a Band
- The Fathers-in-Laws' Bands Overtake Them and Negotiate a Settlement

We will then conclude by considering how the two myths may be related with each other.

The dispute over inheritance

Earlier versions of Jason's myth (though Apollonius is less specific) begin with circumstances frequent in Greek heroic myth: a usurping king attempts to do away with the rightful heir to the throne, the protagonist, by sending him away to perform a presumably lethal task (Gantz 342; Green 430–31). The *Iliad*'s account of Bellerophon (6.155–202) resembles an *Argonautika* without a Medea.[7] The larger trajectory of Herakles' labors, with Eurystheus in the role of illegitimate king, offers the fullest development of this dynamic.

The *Theogony* (996) refers to Pelias as *hubristés* and *atásthalos*. In Mimnermus, Jason "accomplishes a difficult test for arrogant Aietes" (11.3: ὑβριστῇ Πελίη τελέων χαλεπῆρες ἄεθλον).[8] As Gantz notes (342), in some accounts Pelias has usurped the throne of his half-brother Aison, Jason's father. Gantz concludes (342) that in all versions "Pelias notes the missing sandal, remembers the prophecy, and plots [J]ason's destruction via the Fleece." Though lacking a specific depiction, "Apollonius stresses Pelias's brutality and lawlessness" (Green 202). His Pelias clearly assumes that his test is lethal, that Jason will not return.[9] His underlying motive is to remove a legitimate claimant to the throne.

In Jacob's myth the tension over inheritance is between him and his brother Esau, with Jacob, though at his mother's urging (Gen 27:6–41), the actual cause of the friction. Esau, enraged over Jacob's cheating him out of his father's blessing (Gen 27:1–40), and his having earlier induced him to sell his birthright (Gen 25:29–34), threatens to kill Jacob, prompting the latter's journey. Rebecca advises him to flee to her brother in Haran, until Esau's temper cools (Gen 27:42–45).

Both Jason and Jacob have prior family connections to the people to whom they now travel. In the complex backstory of the Fleece, Phrixos and Helle, Athamas' children by Nephele (Gantz 176–79), fled destruction at the hands of Ino (alluded to in *Argonautika* 2.1181–82), their stepmother, whereupon Nephele obtained the Golden Ram to save them. Athamas and Jason's grandfather, Salmoneus, are brothers, sons of Aeolus. Thus, when Phrixos' sons, sailing west to reclaim their inheritance in Orchmenos, shipwreck, and Jason encounters them, he declares that they are his kin (2.1160) and takes them on board (2.1093–167). In Haran, Rebecca sends Jacob to her brother, Laban.

The young male protagonist is morally ambiguous

Though our period may see epic heroes such as Odysseus and Akhilleus as morally ambiguous, Jason's behavior is far more slippery. The same holds for Jacob, who, though a future patriarch and father of the 12 tribes, lies to his father and cheats his brother to obtain the former's blessing (discussed in the following text). Alter comments on the tendency in general (2004: 180), "[O]f all the patriarchs Jacob is the one whose life is entangled in moral ambiguities," and when Jacob deceives his father (2004: 140), "It is surely noteworthy that Jacob expresses no compunction, only fear of getting caught."

Jacob's behavior corresponds with Jason's moral ambiguities, though Jason's troubling behavior comes at a later stage of his story, *after* he meets Medea, and on his return journey. Exploiting Medea's love for him, he uses her to win the Fleece. The *Odyssey* briefly suggests a similar scenario in Odysseus' interactions with Nausikaa. Odysseus plays on her implicit interest in marriage to win her favor, so he can obtain clothing and make his way to the Phaiakians' palace (*Odyssey* 6.149–85).[10]

Not only do both protagonists not hesitate to perform questionable acts but also both do so *against members of their own families*. Though Hera's manipulation of Medea (in Apollonius) to revenge herself on Pelias may let Jason off the hook to some extent, the same could be said of Jacob, that God uses him as part of his larger designs for the Israelites. Apollonius, focalizing Book 3 around Medea, offers detailed depictions of her motivations in the encounters but not of Jason's own inner workings (Vergil's model for his similar treatment of Dido and Aeneas in Book 4 of the *Aeneid*). Jason's subsequent career in Greece and inglorious end (reminiscent of Bellerophon's in *Iliad* 6.200–2) may imply divine retribution for his questionable deeds.

An authoritative female directs his journey to the east

Jacob and Jason both receive crucial direction from a dominant female who influences events on their behalf. Hera supervises Jason's enterprise, thematically lending help as a mentor god.[11] He earns her aid from the encounter at the river, helping her, disguised as an old woman, cross the river (right before Apollonius' *Argonautika* begins), to which event the goddess later refers (3.66–73). However, Hera also helps him to punish Pelias, who earlier neglected to sacrifice to her (1.10–12).[12] As Hera, Rebecca in Jacob's myth steers and directs his larger quest. She first prompts Jacob's deception of Isaac and Esau, the very circumstance that compels Jacob to leave his home, then, when Esau threatens to kill him, directs him on his journey east (Gen 27:42–44) to Haran. Her direction corresponds to Hera's repeated interventions on Jason's behalf. Though transforming an imported divine character into a mortal one is a classic instance of euhemerism, nonetheless, Genesis loosely associates Rebecca's actions with those of a god. When Isaac is startled by how quickly Jacob has brought the venison he desired, Jacob claims that Yahweh brought it to him (Gen 27:20), assigning divine agency to what Rebecca did. When Jacob hesitates to follow her advice, she insists, "Just listen to my voice" (Gen 27:13).

Hera in Iliad 19.96–133 and Rebecca in Genesis 27

Rebecca also corresponds to Hera in another myth outside of Jason's. When she deceitfully arranges for her husband to bless the son she favors, she follows Hera in the well-known account of Herakles' birth. When Zeus declares his plans for his special son Herakles (*Iliad* 19.96–133), Hera subverts his wish, manipulating him into swearing an oath that designates Hera's choice of Eurystheus, not Herakles. Again, there is a precise homology between all the main characters. Both fathers, Zeus and Isaac, carelessly misuse the status they intend to bestow upon their favored sons, Herakles and Esau. Deceived by their wives, Hera and Rebecca, they unknowingly bless *her* favorite (Gen 27:30, 33; *Iliad* 19.112–13), Eurystheus and Jacob, her reason for having intervened. While Rebecca is Jacob's mother, Hera approaches a maternal relationship to Eurystheus, acting almost as a midwife to encourage his birth and delay Herakles' (*Iliad* 19.118–19).[13]

The father's favorite son, Herakles and Esau, is the more heroic of the two, a hunter (Gen 25: 27–28; 27:5, 39–40) who uses the bow (Gen 27:3), who is so hairy that Jacob must wear animal skins to resemble him (Gen 25:25, 27:11–24; on Herakles as hirsute see Hard: 212), who is known for his appetite (Gen 25:29–34). Like Esau to Jacob, Herakles is the first born of twin brothers, born the night before Iphicles (Apollodorus II.4.8). These defining characteristics, all less common in the Hebrew Bible, establish Esau as a typological equivalent of Herakles. But despite his father's favor, and his own physical endowment, he is made subservient to the mother/stepmother's favorite (Gen 27:37; *Iliad* 19.122–33). So close are the two traditions that Alter's assessment (2004: 145) of how Esau is disadvantaged by Isaac's blessing applies just as well to Herakles' subsequent laborious life, "Deprived by paternal pronouncement of political mastery, he must make his way through violent struggle." The authors of the Jacob myth demonstrate their familiarity with Hera by having her euhemerized as Rebecca in not one but *two* separate myths. Apollonius depicts considerable tension between Jason and Herakles (1.863–76, 1290–95), which suggests that the Genesis compilers, as in the case of Hera, have also drawn on Herakles' roles in two separate Greek myths, his composite roles in *Iliad* 19 and in Argonautic myth, to inform Esau's functions in the larger Jacob saga.

Both protagonists now journey to the east. Aietes' kingdom Aia is firmly in the East: Mimnermus (11.5–7) describes how Helios' rays are stored there (cf. Gantz 340). Aietes is Helios' son. Jason's journey to the east is thus clearly connected with things solar. In archaic Greek myth the Sun is closely identified with life, as evident in the common formula: to be alive = to see the sun (*Iliad* 18.61, 442; 24.558; *Odyssey* 4.540, 10.498; 14.44; 20.207). Jacob's journey (Gen 29:1) opens as follows, "And Jacob lifted his feet and went on *to the land of the Easterners*," for which the Septuagint has γῆν ἀνατολῶν, reminiscent of the *Odyssey*'s ἀντολαί Ἡελίοιο (12.4) for Circe's isle, and its use of solar motifs. Owing to the landlocked nature of the Hebrew Bible (other than Jonah), Jacob's journey is only by land, covers less distance than Jason's, and takes up a much smaller portion of the myth.

Jacob and Jason both go abroad because of a crisis at home unconnected with winning a wife. When Rebecca learns that Esau plots to kill Jacob, she orders him to go stay with her brother, Laban (Gen 27:43–45). When she explains to Isaac, Rebecca adds, as a pretext for his going abroad, her insistence that Jacob not marry a local woman, but one of her own kin. But the root cause and original motivation for Jacob's leaving is first to avoid Esau's wrath (Gen 27:42–45). For Jason, Medea only becomes a factor after his arrival in the east. Both Jason and Jacob return from their journeys to the East with wives, and in possession of a sacred implement. Accomplishing the journey to the East thus suggests successful maturation, successful navigation of rites of passage,[14] an acquisition of knowledge that enables the protagonist to become king or patriarch.

God(s) appear(s) in theophany to the hero

In both myths the gods appear in theophany to the protagonists as they journey. On their outward voyage, Glaukos appears, rising out of the sea, declaring to the Argonauts that it is Zeus' will that Herakles not continue with them, but fulfill his own destiny (1.1311–25). For the Argonauts, who had been quarreling about what to do about Herakles' absence, Glaukos' appearance resolves their quarrel and validates their voyage. On the return voyage, Thetis appears, visible to Peleus alone (4.842–65). Apollonius uses the scene, and the immediately preceding section, to comment obliquely on the *Argonautika*'s backstory (that Hera had given Thetis in marriage to Peleus: 4.805–9) and on events that take place after the conclusion of Apollonius' poem. References to problems in the marriage of Thetis and Peleus (4.815–17) also offer implicit commentary on problems in the union of Jason and Medea.

Like Jason and his crew Jacob receives theophanies both on his outward and his return journeys. On the trip east to Haran, he stays the night at Bethel, and dreams of the ramp to heaven, angels going up and down it. Yahweh stands over him and declares he will give this ground to Jacob and his descendants, who will be as plentiful as the dust. He will protect and be with him until all this is accomplished (Gen 28:10–15). Source criticism reveals the dream belongs to the E strand, whereas mention of Yahweh speaking to him is the J strand, meaning actual theophany, not just dream, may have been the earlier version of the episode.[15]

On his return from Haran angels appear and encourage him (Gen 32:2–3). A short time later at the ford of Jabbok, Jacob wrestles all night with "a man," not loosening his grip until the man blesses him (Gen 32:24–32).[16] Neither dream nor vision, god appears to Jacob alone, as would be typical of epic. The startling physicality of the encounter finds a parallel in Menelaus wrestling with the god Proteus (*Odyssey* 4.351–586), after which he too receives a "blessing."[17]

Triton's theophany to the Argonauts on their return voyage (4.1551–618, 1732–64) corresponds in several particulars both to Jacob's vision in Genesis 28 and his encounter by the ford in Genesis 32. Amid their difficulties in Libya, having buried Mopsos by Lake Triton, the Argonauts set out a tripod to placate local deities. Triton then appears: a young man, claiming to be Eurypylos, son of Poseidon, who offers them a clod of earth as a guest gift. Euphemos receives the clod and asks for directions from the inland lake to the sea. After responding in detail, Triton and tripod disappear. But after a further sacrifice by the Argonauts, Triton reappears in his true form, thrusting the Argo forward to the sea. In the episode's conclusion (4.1732–64), Euphemos remembers a dream, courtesy of Hermes, in which the clod seemed to turn into a young woman, with whom he has sex, who then seems to be his daughter. She informs him that she is not his daughter but the offspring of Triton, bidding him to set her down in the ocean, for she will always be a source of help for him and his descendants. At Jason's urging, Euphemos now throws the clod in the sea, and it becomes the island Thera, Euphemos its founder and patriarch.

As with Jacob in Genesis 28, the theophany in the concluding section is confined to a dream, though, as is the way of myth, the dreams are nonetheless "real." What the gods say not only happens but also is foundational for the external audience. Both gods in the respective dreams proclaim very similar futures: both dreamers will be patriarchs,

> I, the Lord, am the God of Abraham your father and the God of Isaac. This land on which you lie, to you I shall give it and to your seed. And your seed shall be like the dust of the earth, and you shall burst forth to the west and the east and the north and the south, and all the clans of the earth shall be blessed through you, and through your seed. And, look, I am with you and I will guard you wherever you go, and I will bring you back to this land.
>
> Genesis 28:13–15

Apollonius imparts corresponding information, divulging some in the dream and some in Jason's subsequent interpretation of it,

> Triton's offspring I am, friend, nurse of your children,
> no daughter of yours, for Triton and Libya are my parents.
> Set me down in the keeping of Nereus' maiden daughters,
> to dwell in the sea off Anaphe. In time hereafter
> I'll return to the sun's rays, ready aid for your descendants.
>
> 4.1741–45

My good friend, fate has willed you a great and splendid honor!
When you throw this clod into the sea, the gods will make it
an island, and it shall be peopled by your children's
descendants, for Triton handed it to you as a guest-gift,
this piece of the Libyan mainland: it was he, and no other
immortal, who made you this present at your meeting.

4.1749–54

We can note the following common motifs:

Each god identifies himself (I am the Lord / Triton's offspring I am);

Each connects the dreamer with a specific land (This land on which you are lying / When you throw this clod in the sea);

Each declares he will be that land's patriarch, with innumerable descendants (They will be countless as the specks of dust / it shall be peopled by your children's descendants); and

Each promises future aid and protection (I shall be with you to protect you / I'll return to the sun's rays, ready aid for your descendants).

The clod of earth, central to the Argonautic episode, suggests a variation of a motif from creation myths. Euphemos hurling the clod into the sea to become a populous island seems a smaller degree, a more local instance of Deukalion and Pyrrha hurling rocks after the flood to repopulate the earth (Apollodorus 1.46–49). The sewn men in the *Argonautika* (3.1281–363: discussed in the following text) suggests a further variation on the same motif, as do the Spartoi (Apollodorus 3.21–27), Cadmus' sewn men, again in smaller degree, constitute a local instance. In each instance the protagonist displays, or is associated with, godlike procreative powers. But the clod also offers a general correspondence with Jacob's stone.[18]

Before Jacob has his dream, he uses a stone as a pillow (Gen 28:11). After the dream he takes the stone and sets it up as a pillar, pouring oil over it, dedicating it as the first stone for an eventual temple. Jacob's act resembles something out of epic, as Alter suggests (2004: 150), "Cultic pillars ... were generally several feet high ... it would have required ... Herculean strength to lift the stone." However, it also corresponds to Euphemos' dream, and the motif of the clod, Deukalion's stones, or the sewn men, though here the outcome is directed toward the establishment of a place of worship rather than a population. Jacob's stone and foundation pillar also seem a variant of the same motif, combined with another traditional motif of Israelite myth, discussed in the following text. If we are correct in seeing a parallel with Euphemos' clod, Cadmus' participation in this motif, as a Phoenician, is close to a specific intersection of Greek and Israelite culture.

Genesis affords a further correspondence with Euphemos' episode in the story of Lot. Surviving the destruction of Sodom and Gomorrah, but losing his wife in flight, as Aeneas Creusa, Lot makes it to safety accompanied by his daughters, settling in a cave (Gen 19:21–30). On two successive nights each daughter gets her father drunk and has sex with him, both becoming pregnant (Gen 19:31–36). Lot becomes progenitor or patriarch of two peoples, the Moabites and the Ammonites (Gen 19:37–38), thus enacting[19] what Euphemos dreams (4.1732–39). Lot earns this status by having given exemplary hospitality to the disguised angels (Gen 19:1–3), a negative theoxeny because of the mob's violations of hospitality, earning a boon from god as a result.[20] Euphemos takes part in something resembling a positive theoxeny. Because Triton first appears in the form of a young man they may not know that he is a god. But it is not quite a theoxeny because the Argonauts are the foreigners and strangers, and he is closer to a host, a reversal of theoxenic norm in which the god is guest and the mortal host. Apollonius refers to the clod as a guest gift (*xeinia*: 4.1553), clearly marking the encounter as an exchange of hospitality.[21]

The heroes establish cultic etiologies, especially as to why something is not eaten

En route to Aia, and returning from it, Jason and his crew, in their encounters with other peoples and places, perform acts that become foundational for the ancient audience. Their epic acts set precedents and establish rituals, explaining why a certain custom is practiced.[22] In the Doliones episode, after a hospitable reception, the Argonauts help King Kyzikos and his people defeat their monstrous opponents, a six-armed aboriginal race. But the next day, after a full day's sail, violent blasts of wind drive them right back to the Doliones, without their realizing. Mistaken for invaders, a disastrous battle erupts in which they slay many of the Doliones, Jason slaying Kyzikos. Afterward, in their grief the Doliones eat uncooked food, not even grinding their grain, which present-day Ionians commemorate in ritual (1.1070–77). Though regarded as the first cultic etiology in Apollonius' poem,[23] four immediately preceding passages offer brief etiologies of other phenomena, the stone to which they tied Argo (1.1019–20), slain heroes worshipped in cults (1.1048), a still-visible tumulus (1.1061–62), and the tears of Kyzikos' wife gathered by nymphs into a fountain (1.1066–69). The passage at 1.1070–77 might thus be regarded as forming a cap for these earlier, briefer, cultic etiologies.

Jacob's myth follows the same procedure: specific episodes account for religious practices current at the time(s) of its composition or compilation. Like Jason, Jacob has such encounters both on his way east and on his return. The episode discussed previously, his famous dream, concludes with a cultic etiology, an explanation for the existence of a cultic center, earlier known as Luz, now renamed by Jacob as Bethel, "Temple of El."[24]

The cultic etiology in Jacob's myth most relevant to this study is that which concludes his mysterious "wrestling with god" episode, which, as *Argonautika* 1.1070–77, provides several etiologies, including one for a specific dietary practice. Right before this Jacob is met by angels and renames that place

Mahanaim, "twin camps" (Gen 32:1–2), described by Westermann (86) as an "onomastic etiology." When he wrestles the mysterious "man," the most heroic act of his journey, Jacob dislocates his hip, a consequence of God touching him there (Gen 32:24–28). The encounter concludes with at least three more etiologies. Jacob is given the new name, Israel, making him the eponymous ancestor of his people (Alter 2004: 180–81). He renames the locale Peniel (ibid.: 181: "The name builds on 'face-to-face' [*panim 'el panim*]"). But the unique encounter concludes with an etiology of a dietary prohibition. The myth declares, "the children of Israel do not eat the sinew of the thigh which is by the hip-socket to this day, for he had touched Jacob's hip-socket at the sinew of the thigh." Both corresponding episodes commemorate a heroic act by the protagonist, which not only provides a cultic etiology about an eating practice but also explains why something is *not* eaten.

The malevolent father-in-law imposes a series of labors on the hero

On arrival in the eastern land, Jason, because of the Fleece, and Jacob, because of his quest for a bride, both meet up with a figure common in Greek myth, the malevolent father of the hero's future bride.[25] Jacob's Laban has more than a little in common with Jason's Aietes as devious fathers of the young women the protagonists will marry after accomplishing a series of difficult tests. The protagonists' interactions with the malevolent fathers-in-law play out under the very different time schemes that inform the two myths. Aietes' opposition and hostility are immediately apparent as soon as he learns Jason's reason for coming (3.367–68). Whereas, in keeping with the distended time scheme of Jacob's myth, Laban's antipathy emerges only gradually, the first hints coming after Jacob has been with him for a month (Gen 29:14–15). Rebecca originally intends that Jacob stay with Laban until Esau's anger cools, an indeterminate time (Gen 27:44–45). But when avoiding Esau combines with finding a wife for whom he must perform a series of labors, his stay grows to years, due to Laban's deviousness. Jason's interactions with Aietes are synchronic, taking up only a few days; Jacob's with Laban are diachronic, expanding to cover 20 years (Gen 31:38).

Apollonius characterizes Aietes as *huperphialos*, "arrogant" (3.17; cf. 4.1083, and βαρύφρονος: 4.731). In his first remarks to Aietes Jason characterizes Pelias as *atasthalos*, "reckless" (3.390).[26] Jason essentially trades one negative father figure for another, with Aietes imposing labors on top of those Pelias earlier imposed.[27] Jacob similarly leaves friction at home to find new familial conflict from the father of his prospective bride.

Aietes' immediate response, on learning of Jason's quest for the Fleece, is to accuse the sons of Phrixos of plotting for his throne and kingdom, not the Fleece (3.372–76). When Jason explains how Pelias imposed the quest for the Fleece upon him and offers to subdue a hostile people in exchange for it, Aietes considers having the Argonauts slain then and there (3.396–99), before deciding to impose a test upon him. The test is explicitly deadly (3.407–8: ἄεθλος ... ὀλοόν).[28] He is to yoke two brazen-footed, fire-breathing bulls, then use them to plough and sew dragon's teeth, from which will spring a race of armored men he must then slay. If he accomplishes these labors, Aietes says he will give him the Fleece.

Like Aietes, Laban imposes a series of labors on Jacob, but to win Rachel. While he initially greets Jacob with apparent warmth, "Indeed, you are my bone and my flesh" (Gen 29:14), after a month passes without elaboration, Laban asks, "[W]hy should you work for me for nothing simply because you are my kinsman?" (Gen 29:15). As Alter notes (2004: 154, n. 15), this means Laban has already put Jacob to work for a month without pay. Speiser (227) paints Laban's treatment of Jacob in starker terms,

> Laban's elaborate pretense of politeness and family solidarity is maintained for just one month. Immediately thereafter he puts into operation a scheme of singular cunning and duplicity.

In reply Jacob says he would work seven years for Laban's beautiful younger daughter, Rachel, to which Laban agrees (Gen 29:19).

In Jacob's myth the labors are explicitly to win his wife/wives, whereas Jason's labors for Aietes, originally to win the Fleece, quickly involve him with Medea. It is in the execution of the labors that the synchronic/diachronic dichotomy between the two myths is strongest. Laban ends up imposing *multiple* sets of labors on Jacob, requiring *decades* to accomplish. Jason executes Aietes' labors in a day. The stark difference instantiates the different sense of time at work in Greek epic and Israelite myth.

Both protagonists, before meeting their prospective fathers-in-law, earlier demonstrate the ability to accomplish related kinds of labors. En route to Aia, Jason and his Argonauts propitiate Rhea/Kybele, leaping and dancing wearing full armor (1.1134–49). The episode clearly anticipates aspects of Jason's labors for Aietes, as Hunter (83) notes, "[T]hey perform as a group what Jason will later enact by himself." Polydeuces' defeat of Amykos (2.1–97), the Bebrycian king who makes guests box with him, predicts Aietes' treatment of the Argonauts and his defeat at their hands. In the episode's conclusion (2.142–45) the Argonauts take his abundant flocks, corresponding to the outcome of Jacob's encounters with Laban (Gen 30:25–31:18).

When Jacob first arrives in Haran, shepherds are waiting to water their flocks at a well. Normally, they jointly roll away the stone that rests on top of the well. But as Jacob sees Rachel approach with her father's flocks, he rolls the stone away singlehandedly, a surprisingly heroic feat.[29] Implicitly, he defeats the other shepherds in so doing, and symbolically wins Rachel as his bride. In one of Jason's labors, he hurls a great stone among the sewn men (3.1365–67).[30] Jacob easily rolls away a large stone that normally requires a group of shepherds; Jason hurls a great stone that four men together could have only raised an inch. After rolling the great stone off, Jacob waters

Laban's flock for Rachel (Gen 29: 7–10). Kissing her, he tearfully tells her he is Rebecca's son, her father's kinsman, whereupon she runs home to tell Laban (Gen 29:11–12). This first meeting between Jacob and Rachel has some rough parallels with the first meeting between Jason and Medea in the *Argonautika* (3.956–1147).

The bride employs magic and uses the mandrake root

Medea's knowledge of drugs (φάρμακα) and use of magic are central to her character. The *Argonautika* and earlier accounts specify that Jason could not perform Aietes' tasks without her help (3.1247 ff; 4.143–61, 4.364–65; cf. Euripides, *Medea* 478–82). Her knowledge of drugs, not real interest on Jason's part, first involves her with him, when Hera suggests that if Aphrodite were to make Medea, πολυφάρμακον (*polypharmakon*), "of the many drugs/ roots," fall in love with him, she would be able to advise him how to obtain the Fleece (3.25–28).

Though a smaller component in her myth, and her character, Rachel is also associated with drugs and depicted using them. Unable to conceive after marrying Jacob, when she learns that Leah's first son, Reuben, has found some mandrakes (Gen 30:14, μῆλα μανδραγροῶν, in the Septuagint), Rachel asks if she may use them. Alter explains (2004: 160), "[T]hese plants ... were used for medicinal purposes and were thought to be aphrodisiac, and also to have the virtue of promoting fertility, which seems to be what Rachel has in mind."[31] Upset that she has borne no children and that her sister Leah has, Rachel uses the mandrakes to get pregnant.

Central to Medea's magic is *cutting roots*. Apollonius' fullest depiction of her performing magic (3.845–66) features her use of the "Prometheion" drug. Particular emphasis is placed on the plant's root, said to resemble "newly-cut flesh" (3.857). The plant's description juxtaposes the two terms *cutting* and *roots* (ῥίζης τεμνομένης: *Argonautika* 3.865).[32] R. L. Hunter argues for the *Prometheion* plant's identity with the mandrake (1989: 188),[33] "Scholars have sought a real plant lying behind Apollonius' description ... The most likely candidate is mandrake, around which there was extensive folklore." If we accept the identification, both young wives are thus depicted with the same plant, both aware of its magical properties, but putting it to different uses in their differing contexts. Euripides' Medea knows how to use drugs to produce children, as she so advises Aegeus (717–18: τοιάδ' οἶδα φάρμακα). Do her unspecified drugs here include the mandrake? Mandrake is otherwise mentioned in the Hebrew Bible only in the Song of Songs (7:13), where it is again associated with sex and fertility. Apollonius' description of Medea first seizing it as she goes to meet Jason strengthens the *Prometheion*'s likely identity as the mandrake, "having plucked it, she tucked it away within the fragrant breast-band, which was wound around her ambrosial breasts" (3.867–68; cf., 3.1013–14), instantiating the mandrake's erotic and sexual associations.[34]

The hero executes his labors aided by magic

As noted previously, Jason cannot perform Aietes' tasks without Medea's help, which is crucial to his success throughout the labors. She provides him with a drug (3.1013–14) that makes him virtually invulnerable for one day, strengthening his might and his weapons (3.1042–50). While Jason executes Aietes' labors, the drug protects him from the fire-breathing bulls' lethal exhalations (3.1305, 3.1313–15, 1326–27). Later Medea lulls the dragon to sleep with her spells, sprinkling juniper branches in his eyes (4.87–88, 149–51).

Jacob's use of magic to accomplish his labors is more pronounced than Rachel's. When she gives birth to Joseph (a consequence of the mandrake), Jacob wishes to leave, having now spent 14 years with Laban. He suggests that he keep, as his wages, "every spotted and speckled animal and every dark-colored sheep and the speckled and spotted among the goats" (Gen 30:32). Agreeing to these terms, Laban has his sons remove all livestock meeting the specifications. But Jacob then uses a form of magic[35] to produce abundant livestock of the types specified. Taking rods of poplar, almond, and plane trees, and strips of bark, he has animals mate before them (Gen 30:37–39), later giving birth to the desired offspring, "the flocks bore brindled, spotted, and speckled young" (Gen 30:39). Most newborn are the types Jacob is to keep, tremendously increasing his holdings, greatly lessening Laban's (Gen 30:25–43). He employs freshly cut plants, corresponding to Medea's "root cutting" and her lulling the dragon to sleep by sprinkling juniper branches in his eyes (4.87–88, 149–51.[36]

Aietes requires (3.413–16) Jason, in his first labor, to sow fields with the dragon's teeth to produce a race of warrior men. We earlier noted parallels between Jason sewing the crop of warrior men and Euphemos using the clod Triton gave him to form an island, soon fully populated (4.1551–618, 1732–64). As Jason plows the furrow in which he will sew the dragon teeth, he leaves groaning clods of earth behind. Apollonius uses the same term here for the fertile clod (3.1336: βῶλον) as for that Triton gives to Euphemos to generate the island Thera. Yoking the bulls, sewing the fields, and fighting the sewn men, all, as Gantz notes, suggest Jason may be seen as harvesting a crop (361), "rushing among them and mowing them down while they are still in the ground, as if he were a harvester." Aietes refers to the tests as "a dreadful harvesting" (οὐλομένου … ἀμήτοιο: 3.436). In Jason's myth this motif is present at least from Eumelus on.[37] When he slays the sewn men, Jason uses his sword like a sickle (3.1381–91).[38]

Jacob employs the tree shoots and bark strips to engender offspring from Laban's livestock. Rachel uses the mandrake to obtain offspring, children. Both activities depend upon the character's ability to exert control over a form of procreation, as Jason's labors for Aietes. When Jacob declares his wages, black lambs, brindled and spotted goats, he must already intend to use the magic breeding technique, as Jason knows Medea's magic will aid him in accomplishing Aietes' labors.

The father-in-law reneges on the terms of the labors

Medea characterizes Aietes as a man who does not hold to covenants (3.1105–6, already implicit in Hesiod and Mimnermus' characterizations of him as *hubristes*), much as Laomedon in early Greek myth.[39] Having assumed Jason could not perform his tasks, outraged that he has (3.1404–6; 4.6–11, 4.212–35), Aietes has no intention of handing over the Fleece and immediately plots his opposition (3.1406: ἀντιόωτο; cf. 4.6–9). He intuits Medea's necessary involvement (4.9–10) and calls the Colchians into assembly, demanding her return (4.230–35). In so doing, Aietes breaks the terms he proposed (*Argo* 3.400–21; 4.7–10, 228–35).

Instantiating the type, Laban reneges on terms in *multiple* sets of labors. When Jacob completes the seven years he agreed to work for Rachel, Laban breaks the bargain, giving him Rachel's older sister Leah (Gen 29:20–26). Having his sons remove all the agreed-upon types of livestock that should be Jacob's repeats his earlier behavior (Gen 30:35–36). As Jacob notes to Rachel (Gen 31:7), "But your father has tricked me and has switched my wages ten times over."[40]

The bride steals her father's sacred article (the Fleece, household gods)

When Aietes breaks the terms he proposed, Jason and Medea steal the Fleece. Rachel's stealing her father's household gods (Gen 31:19–35) is a close thematic parallel, though less central to her myth, and Jacob is not directly involved. Laban's household gods have not been previously mentioned (whereas the Fleece is the *telos* throughout the *Argonautika*). Her motivation[41] for doing so is how Laban has treated her (Gen 31:14–16). It is Rachel's idea to steal her father's household gods, Rachel who steals them.

As Argonautic myth never demonstrates the function or purpose of the Fleece, so Jacob's myth never does with the household gods.[42] Though Laban's household gods lack the Fleece's complex backstory, parallels in other myths are suggestive. Alter (2004: 169) elaborates on their functions and their association with polytheism,

> The household gods, or *teraphim* … are small figurines representing the deities responsible for the well-being and prosperity of the household … There is no reason to assume that Rachel would have become a monotheist through her marriage, and it is perfectly understandable that she would want to take with her in her emigration the icons of these tutelary spirits, or perhaps, symbols of possession.

Suggs further suggests (40), "Possession of the household gods insured safety and prosperity and possibly the right of inheritance."[43] As for the Fleece, Morris (430–31) finds parallels in the bulbs (not breasts) of the Ephesian

Artemis. In an oft-cited parallel (e.g., Alter 2004: 169) Aeneas, as commanded by Hector's ghost, takes the Trojan Penates as he flees Troy's destruction (*Aeneid* 2.289–95, 320–21), an early part of the myth because, as Weinfeld (12) notes, a *fifth*-century Etruscan amphora depicts his wife Creusa carrying them. Theano offers a relevant parallel when she hands over the Palladium, the sacred statue of Athena to Odysseus and Diomedes.[44] The Philistines' capture of the Ark (1 Sam 4–7) is a comic or parodic instance of a similar subgenre of myth (but lacking a cunning female figure who hands it over), in their inability to maintain possession of the sacred article.

Household gods function in a corresponding manner at 1 Sam 19:13–16. David, avoiding Saul's guards as they attempt to kill him, escapes when his wife Michal, Saul's daughter, stages a deception using their household gods. As David escapes through a window, Michal places the *teraphim* on the bed, setting some woven goat hair above its head, covering it with a cloak. Alter (1999: 120) argues 1 Sam 19:13–16 is in dialogue with Rachel's theft of Laban's household gods,

> She adopts the familiar trick … of concocting a dummy to mask an escape. But the means she chooses introduce another elaborate allusion to the Jacob story. The household gods (*teraphim*) are what Rachel stole and hid from her father when Jacob fled from him. Like Rachel, who pleads her period and does not get up from the cushions under which the *teraphim* are hidden, Michal also invokes "illness" to put off the searchers. Both stories feature a daughter loyal to her husband and rebelling against a hostile father. Michal puts goat's hair at the head of the bed because, being black or dark brown, it would look like a man's hair, but goats (and the color of their hair) are also prominent in the Jacob story.

This episode also corresponds closely to Medea's theft of the Fleece. The juxtaposition of David's household gods with a twist of goat's hair even creates a visual similarity to the Fleece. Like Medea, Michal deceives her father to enable her husband's escape.[45] Like Aietes, and Laban, Saul sends a band of men pursuing David.

In stealing (ἔκλεψε, in the Septuagint) her father's gods, Rachel replicates the central role Medea plays in Jason's obtaining the Golden Fleece from her father. Medea, priestess of Hecate, helping Jason take the sacred Golden Fleece also corresponds to Theano, priestess of Athena in Troy, and to Rachel, though not depicted as priestess. Material remains demonstrate that such acts occurred between different cultures. Yasur-Landau (336–37) notes an ancient gender requirement perhaps relevant to Medea, Rachel, and Theano's acts, "The foundation of cult is done by transfer of an *Aphidrum*; a statue or another sacred object … The participation of a priestess is in this, as perhaps in other cases of transfer of cult of female deities, an essential one: only women could wash and adorn a female cult image."[46] The notion of the transference of a cult from one people to another may underlie the mythic accounts of Theano, Rachel, and Medea. Rachel stealing Laban's household gods also pivots the remainder of the myth to a more heroic modality, looking ahead to Jacob wrestling with god (Gen 32:24–31) and his anxiety over meeting with Esau. While in Apollonius a dragon guards the fleece, in earlier accounts, including the *Naupaktia*, Aietes merely kept it in his palace.[47] As Huxley says (71), "[S]he simply brought the fleece with her to the Argos," a virtual equivalent of Rachel's acts in Genesis. Again, it is clear again that the Genesis compilers are often referencing an earlier version than Apollonius, whether the *Naupaktia* or some other.

In its only present-time function in the *Argonautika*, Jason and Medea make love on the Fleece – the hurried consummation of their wedding (4.1141–43) – "the bravest thing Jason ever does in this poem," as Green (40–41) wryly observes. Green adduces a parallel in the Hebrew Bible. Their physical contact with the Fleece, he suggests, is (41) "an act as potentially dangerous as laying impious hands on the Ark of the Covenant." Rachel offers a most unexpected correspondence when she sits on the household gods, stashed in her camel's saddle, as they flee. She evades Laban's search by claiming that she cannot get rise to be searched because she is having her period (Gen 31:35). In both myths, then, the respective daughters profane their fathers' stolen sacred implements, their only actual use in the myths, by associating them with a bodily function, while their fathers are engaged in their pursuit.

The hero sneaks off in the night with his wife, his entourage, and the sacred article; the father-in-law pursues with a band

Jacob and Jason both now sneak off with their wives, their entourages, and the sacred implements. In the face of such malicious fathers-in-law, they have little choice than to act as they do. The dynamics of their flights, the pursuit by the livid fathers and his sons, correspond closely. Aietes, enraged that Jason successfully accomplished the labors, correctly intuits that Medea helped him to do so (4.8–10). Each daughter now switches sides, so to speak. Hera prompts Medea to flee to the Argives from fear of her father (4.11–24). When Jacob tells Rachel that God appeared to him in a dream, telling him to leave (cf. Mercury to Aeneas), she complains of her father, "Why, we have been counted by him as strangers, for he has sold us, and he has wholly committed our money" (Gen 31:15). Both make this shift in their relations with their fathers before stealing their sacred implements. When Medea reaches the Argonauts, she asks them to save her from Aietes (4.83–84), corresponding to Rachel's declaration. Each bride only now steals her father's sacred implement, Rachel without Jacob's knowledge (Gen 31:19), Medea now directing Jason on how to do so (4.123–82).

Each father, enraged over the theft of the sacred article, and his daughter's role and flight, launches an extensive pursuit in which his son(s) also take part. In epic's more heroic style, Aietes formulates his response in an assembly (4.212–36), threatening the lives of those present if they fail to bring Medea back (4.230–35).[48] The pursuing Colchians split into two bands, one led by Aietes' son Apsyrtos.

Rachel's theft of the household gods is subordinated under Jacob's decision to leave. In both instances, flight by stealth is key, necessary due to the malevolence of the father-in-law.[49] Keeping his departure secret, Jacob flees with his wives, his flocks, and Rachel in possession of her father's household gods. Before Laban knows, they are three days' journey distant (symmetrical with Laban earlier removing the speckled goats the same distance: Gen 30:36).

The fathers-in-laws' bands overtake them and negotiate a settlement

Apsyrtos, Aietes' son, leading a contingent of Colchians, and Laban and his sons, both pursue and overtake the two protagonists in flight with their wives' entourages, the former's Fleece, and the latter's household gods. Though in Apollonius Aietes does not pursue Jason but requires his son and others to do so, in earlier versions Aietes pursues the Argonauts into Greece. Herodotus cites a version in which Aietes pursues Jason all the way back to Greece (1.2.2–3).[50] Again, the Genesis tradition references an earlier version. The band of Colchians led by Apsyrtos overtakes Jason at the mouth of the Ister (4.302–37). Outnumbered, the Argonauts are on the verge of battling the Colchians, when both sides agree to terms. The *Argonautika* presents two versions of this motif, *two* sets of negotiations by the multiple pursuing parties representing Aietes' interests. In the first instance, the Argonauts, and Apsyrtos' band of Colchians representing Aiestes' interests, all take oaths, making a covenant, that Jason is entitled to keep the Fleece, but that Medea is to be turned over to a priestess of Artemis, until her status is resolved (4.340–49). In a second scene (4.1170–222) at Drepane, Alkinoös, king of the Phaecians, adjudicates Medea's status before a contingent of Cochians. The negotiations Laban and Jacob undergo at Genesis 31:44–54 function like a composite of the *Argonautika*'s two episodes.

Though Jacob's flight is by land, Laban's seven-day pursuit (Gen 31:23) corresponds closely to Aietes' and Apsyrtos'. In both myths a god appears, warning the pursuing band not to press the chase too far. In the *Argonautika*, Hera sends lightning as a sign to the Colchians to cease their pursuit (4.507–10). God appears to Laban in a dream, limiting his conduct, "And God came to Laban the Aramaean in a night-dream and said to him, 'Watch yourself,' lest you speak to Jacob either good or evil" (Gen 31:24). Laban nonetheless overtakes Jacob, camping opposite him in the hill country in Gilead (Gen 31:25). Though Laban takes the lead in the pursuit, his sons, who earlier express an aggressive, threatening attitude toward Jacob (Gen 31:1), accompany him.[51] In a speech that could easily be delivered by Apsyrtos on Aietes' behalf, if Fleece is substituted for "household gods," Laban accuses Jacob of having deceived him, kidnapping his daughters, fleeing in secret, and stealing his household gods (Gen 31:26–30).

In both myths subsequent negotiations result in Jason and Jacob keeping the sacred article *and* the daughters of the malevolent fathers-in-law, though the nature of the negotiations differs considerably. Because Jason satisfied Aietes' own terms for obtaining the Fleece, Apsyrtos, negotiating on Aietes' behalf in the first negotiation scene, determines that he may keep it (4.338–49). More incensed by Medea's role (4.228–35), Aietes has Apsyrtos attempt to negotiate her return. Laban likewise criticizes Jacob at greater length for taking his daughters than for stealing his household gods, which Rachel does without his knowledge (Gen 31:19). At this juncture each myth compares the daughter to a woman captured as a slave in war (*Argonautika* 4.400; Gen 31:26, "driving my daughters like captives of the sword").

Why does the *Argonautika* have two separate arbitration scenes? In between the two scenes is the myth's most jarring act, Medea's and Jason's treacherous murder of her brother Apsyrtos (4.415–85). Although Jacob's myth has no close parallel, his earlier conduct toward his family members, cheating his brother and deceiving his father, and his anxiety over again meeting with Esau offers thematic correspondence to Jason proposing to trick Apsyrtos to slay him (4.404–5). Immediately before, when Medea fears Jason will have her taken back to Aietes, she accuses him of breaking his oaths to her (4.358–59, 388), suggesting Jacob's deceitful dealings with his family members. But it is Medea who converts Jason's broad suggestion into a plot to murder her brother at Artemis' temple (4.15–22, 468–81) and dispatch the pursuing Colchians in similar fashion (4.482–89). After the murder Jason performs a gruesome expiation ritual, cutting off Apsyrtos' limbs, licking the blood thrice, and thrice spitting it out (4.477–79). Medea holds high a torch, a signal for the Argonauts to treacherously slay the others. The surviving Colchians, learning of the slaughter, but warned by Hera not to pursue the Argonauts (discussed in the following text), decide to settle in the area, fearing Aietes' wrath if they return without Medea (4.511–21).

When Jason and Medea later reach the Phaiakians (4.993–99), a third band of Colchians comes, demanding Medea be handed over to them (4.1001–7). The atmosphere resembles the particulars of Laban's negotiations with Jacob, except Alkinoös' third-party mediation is decidedly more Greek than Israelite. The Colchians begin insisting Medea be released to them without discussion (4.1005), threatening battle otherwise, and hinting at Aietes' arrival. Laban's blustering, and refusal to concede any points to Jacob after the latter's lengthy complaint (Gen 31:36–42), corresponds well.[52]

Alkinoös is determined to bring the two opposed parties to a peaceful reconciliation (4.1008–10). Before he does so, however, Medea first pleads her case to his wife Arete (4.1013–29), then to the Argonauts (4.1030–54). While Alkinoös decides to wait a day before coming to a decision, he briefly considers raising an armed force to drive the threatening band of Colchians away (4.1098–99). However, he informs Arete that, if Medea and Jason have had sex, he will rule that they should stay together; if not, she is to return to her father. When Arete has a herald report this to Jason and Medea, they make love for the first time, on the Fleece (4.1141 & ff.). It is worth emphasizing that Medea and Jason using the Fleece as bedding occurs at precisely the same point in sequence as does Rachel's sitting on Laban's household gods claiming her period. The next morning, accompanied by rows of Phaiakian warriors, Alkinoös proclaims his judgment, holding the respective parties to his determination by making them swear oaths: the Colchians must honor the agreement or not set foot in Drepane (4.1170–210).

Though lacking a figure corresponding to Alkinoös, Jacob's and Laban's negotiations have more than a little in common with the scene at Drepane. While Jacob's myth is landlocked, on his way back from Laban "he crossed the Euphrates" (Gen 31:21), marking his escape from Laban's sphere of power. At Genesis 31:20, Laban is referred to as non-Israelite, "And Jacob deceived Laban the Aramaean," preparing the way, as Alter notes (2004: 169), "for the representation of the encounter between Jacob and Laban as a negotiation between national entities." When Laban proposes the terms by which he and Jacob will abide, they swear oaths, Laban swearing by "the god of Nahor" (Gen 31:53), emphasizing the cross-cultural nature of the pact.[53] Jacob sets up a stone pillar, and his kin gather stones for a mound, to serve as a witness (Gen 31:45–46), perhaps serving as ring composition with the episode at Genesis 28:10–22, and his use of the cultic stone.

Why would the Genesis authors appropriate and adapt Argonautic myth from the Greeks? On the one hand, in both Greek and Israelite cultures the myth serves the same basic function. It depicts the coming of age of a leader; his successful accomplishment of difficult labors; his winning a wife, daughter of a foreign man of substance; and his taking possession of a significant item that denotes the gods' favor and secures his own standing. By taking the distinctive article away from his father-in-law, he acquires, in some sense, the latter's former prestige or figurative position. All this confers a heroic dimension upon Jacob, by far the most heroic of the Genesis patriarchs. Thus, Argonautic myth supplies for the Genesis compilers a ready-to-hand heroic rubric to add more of an epic dimension to this particular pastoralist. The appropriation of Argonautic myth also suggests a direct engagement of, even confrontation with, larger Greek culture by the Israelite scribes, as we consider in the following text.

To strengthen the case as to the Greek provenience of the tale, we can demonstrate that the correspondences cannot be explained by arguing the story passes from Israelite culture to Greek. Quite the contrary, several definitive elements are far more at home in Greek myth than in the Hebrew Bible, strengthening the likelihood that some form of Argonautic myth is the earlier version of the two. For instance, wrestling is thematic in Jacob's myth, closely associated with him.[54] Emerging from Rebecca's womb, he grasps Esau's heel, a classic wrestling move, but also wordplay on his name (Gen 25:26), which could here be understood as "heel-grabber" or "leg puller."[55] When he, in his most heroic act, wrestles "the man" at the Jabbok ford, he acts far more like a Greek hero such as Herakles, who, among other nonhuman opponents,[56] wrestles the river Achelous. In an indication of how unusual the subject matter is for the Hebrew Bible, Jacob's exploit features the only instance of the root *abaq* (awbaq). Though wrestling does not figure directly in Apollonius' *Argonautica*, it is associated with several Greek heroes, especially Odysseus (e.g., *Iliad* 23.700–39). His defeat of Philomeleides, king of Lesbos, who compels guests to wrestle (*Odyssey* 4.342–44 = 17.133–35), corresponds closely to the Argonautic episode in which Amykus, king of the Bebrykians, compels visitors to box with him (2.1–163). But the closest match for Jacob at Jabbok is the *Odyssey*'s account of Menelaus wrestling the god Proteus at the seashore (*Odyssey* 4.351–586). As in Genesis 32:24–32, the focus is both on Menelaus not loosening his grip on his divine opponent (4.419, 4.454–55) and on the blessing and prophecy that he subsequently receives (4.468–570). Because the *Odyssey* uses Menelaus wrestling Proteus as part of a larger thematic correspondence to Odysseus' own *nostos*, Jacob's wrestling episode again evokes Odysseus.[57]

Eros between Jacob and Rachel plays a larger role than is typical of Genesis patriarchs and their wives. The difference is particularly marked if we juxtapose Alter's three betrothal type scenes (Gen 24:10–61, 29:1–20; and Exod 2:15b–21).[58] Jacob impulsively kisses Rachel on first seeing her, then bursts into tears (Gen 29:11). It is near impossible to imagine Isaac's servant doing so with Rebecca, or Moses with Zipporah. Aphrodite's prominence in Mimnermus' fragments suggests a strong erotic element is present early on in Argonautic myth. Rachel's sexual or procreative jealousy (Gen 30:1–24) also corresponds to Medea's in pre-Apollonius versions of the myth, as is evident in Euripides' tragedy.[59]

Laban's deviousness aligns him, not only with Aietes but also with several other fathers in Greek myth who violate agreements with foreign heroes. From Laomedon, cheating Herakles out of the promised horses, reward for saving Hesione (a close equivalent of Laban's attempted shortchanging of Jacob's flocks), to Minos' dealings with Theseus, and losing Ariadne, and King Antiochus in *Apollonius, King of Tyre*, this is a recurring character type in Greek myth.

Rachel's impulsiveness, not only in leaving her father but also betraying him, is paralleled in Greek myth not only by Medea but also by Ariadne. Rachel's mother, Rebecca, offers some of the strongest evidence of an earlier Greek version of the myth because she corresponds to Hera not only in Argonautic myth but also parallels Hera's role in the *Iliad*'s account (19.96–133) of how she deceived Zeus to advance Eurystheus over Herakles, as Rebecca does Jacob over Esau.[60] This sustained correspondence, Rebecca paralleling Hera's roles from two separate myths, suggests that Israelite culture euhemerized aspects of or acts by the Greek goddess, for this key Genesis matriarch. Similarly, Esau reflects Herakles not only in being cheated out of his birthright and blessing but also in his friction with Jacob before most of the journey to the East has yet taken place.

Magic as a plot element is much more at home in Greek myth than in the Hebrew Bible. From the earliest authors, including Hesiod's prominent treatment of Hekate, the goddess of magic, in the *Theogony* (411–52), to Circe's key role in the *Odyssey*, magic is conspicuous in Greek myth. For Medea, this is an established facet of her character in all other versions of her myth, including Euripides' play.[61] Rachel's use of the mandrake to cure her childlessness is an area of expertise Euripides' *Medea* also shares.[62]

While the correspondences are many, differences between the Israelite and Greek reflexes of this same mythic type make the most sense if we understand some of them as intentional. Any time it imports a myth from another culture, the Genesis tradition transforms the myth to reflect its own cultural preferences and different agenda. This is immediately evident in having a different character type as protagonist. Argonautic saga employs Greek myth's favored type of protagonist, the hero, whereas Genesis, though Jacob retains several heroic capabilities, largely converts him to a pastoralist patriarch, the pattern first established in Abraham.[63] We have already noted, in other chapters of this study as well, the necessary euhemerization of divine characters to mortal, as here Hera to Rebecca. A similar difference extends to the transformation of individual motifs. Thus, where Jason sails across the Aegean and Black Seas, Jacob travels by land, on foot, even. Where Jason sews and harvests a crop of warrior men from the teeth of a dragon, Jacob harvests speckled and spotted goats. Israelite culture modifies the stereotypically heroic motifs of Argonautic myth to make them appropriate to the Genesis pastoralists.

On the other hand, Israelite adaptation, through its different emphases, can also be understood as intended commentary on and criticism of the Greek culture from which the prototype derives. This is particularly evident in Jacob's triumph over Esau in securing his birthright and Isaac's blessing. Esau is cast in conventionally heroic tones, perhaps the only Israelite specifically figured as a hunter (Gen 25:27, 27:3–30).[64] Like Herakles, he uses the bow (Gen 27:3), is so hairy that Jacob must wear animal skins to resemble him (Gen 25:25, 27:11–24), and is known for his appetite (Gen 25:29–34). Jacob's defeat of Esau, and that he does so as a trickster, over a more conventionally heroic figure, reflects a broader cultural preference evident throughout Genesis. But if we are correct in seeing Esau as a displaced Herakles figure, can we assume that at least some members of the ancient audience would recognize this? If so, Jacob's victory is also a commentary on Greek culture, both through implied criticism of its values and, more emphatically, through defeat, if by proxy, of its own mythic protagonists, the ancient embodiments and foundation of its culture. This interpretation receives support, again, in the repeated correspondence between Hera and Rebecca, where the same figure works to defeat Herakles/Esau. Isaac's deception would thus also serve a Yahwist argument. Replacing Zeus with a blind man in his dotage is a parodic lampooning of the main god of Greek culture.

Carr argues that Jacob's myth "show signs of once having existed independently" (1996: 257; cf. 258, 264, 269, 270–71). Carr thus argues that it has undergone extensive adaptation to fit its present location, with several details later added to link it to prior and subsequent sections of Genesis. Signs of the myth's original independence include its broad polytheism, as in Laban's household gods,[65] and the relative scarcity of several definitive motifs elsewhere in the Hebrew Bible, as noted previously. If Carr is correct, an earlier independence of Jacob's myth strengthens the possibility that it has origins outside of Israelite culture.

Lastly, for those concerned that Apollonius' *Argonautika* is unreliably late to be consulted for a study such as this, we have noted that several of the motifs indicate Jacob's myth responds to an earlier version than Apollonius: "The Dispute over Inheritance," "The Hero Executes His Labors Aided by Magic," "The Bride Steals Her Father's Sacred Article (The Fleece, Household Gods)," "The Hero Sneaks off in the Night with His Wife, His Entourage, and the Sacred Article; the Father-in-Law Pursues with a Band," and "The Fathers-in-Laws' Bands Overtake Them and Negotiate a Settlement." No doubt Apollonius has considerably changed aspects of the myth, having a dragon guard the Fleece, for instance. But I suggest the larger outlines of the myth, including Medea's role, and those episodes for which we find correspondence in Jacob's myth, are close enough to earlier versions that we need not be anxious that Apollonius' Hellenistic distillation of the myth renders his version entirely off limits.

What form of the myth did Genesis authors consult? We will probably never know, but it is safe to consider that they had access an oral version. Even safer, perhaps, to assume that such a well-known myth was known from a variety of means, not only the late sections of Hesiod's *Theogony* but also Mimnermus' treatment, Eumelus' *Korinthiaka* the *Naupaktia*, all of which would have circulated in *complete* form, not just the scant excerpts we have. If Pindar's *Fourth Pythian* and the multiple mentions in Herodotus are not too late, there were several Greek tragedies also offering treatments of parts of the myth, not just Euripides' *Medea*. In our time zone, Medea, owing to Euripides' tragedy, is perhaps best known for slaying her children – impossible to conceive of Rachel doing so. Yet, as Huxley demonstrates (65), this act was not present in Eumelus' account, where her children by Jason apparently died of natural, or unexplained, causes in Hera's temple in Corinth. Argonautic myth was particularly popular in and variously associated with Miletus.[66] Moreover, Miletus' proximity to Ephesus, makes for relatively easy transmission of the tale to parts east and south.

Notes

1 Though cf. Wajdenbaum, *passim*, and Louden 2011a: 135–63.
2 E.g., West 2005, Braswell 1988, Louden 2011a: 135–63.
3 On which see Louden 2018.
4 See again, Louden 2011a: 135–63 and West 2005.
5 West 2003: 158–59.
6 Huxley (1969: 62) dates Eumelus to "the second half of the eighth century B.C."

7   Perhaps Pegasus can be seen to serve some of the functions, supernatural aid that enables the hero to accomplish the otherwise lethal task, each myth concluding with a similarly miserable ending for the hero.

8   Cf. Green 2007: 430–31.

9   Ibid.

10 On the possibility that the *Odyssey*'s depiction of Odysseus with Nausikaa draws on an Argonautic Medea, see Louden 2011a: 135–36, 143–44, 153–63.

11 For discussion of the "mentor god" in epic, see Louden 2005: 95–96.

12 Cf. Gantz (1993: 342), "Hera's partisanship of Iason in Apollonios derives partly, of course, from his act of kindness toward her, but earlier in the poem we also learn that Pelias … has ignored her in his sacrifices (1.12–14); thus the voyage of the Argo becomes an elaborate means of bringing about his punishment." Pelias also slays his stepmother at Hera's altar (Green 2007: 23).

13 See further discussion in Louden 2011a: 98–99.

14 Cf. Hunter 1993: 15: "Jason's story is one of a number of Greek myths concerning young heroes who undergo terrible ordeals before claiming their rightful place in adult society; generational passage is secured by the successful accomplishment of difficult tasks"; (16): "The central challenges of the expedition are presented in ways which make their initiatory aspects clear … his preparations for the contest (3.1256–64) recall the *pyrrhiche*, the armed dance particularly associated with young men in their training for war"; (83): "the presentation of the Argonauts as a group of young men undergoing a kind of initiation."

15 See Davidson (1979: 145–47) and Speiser (1962: 219–20) for specifics on which verses are E and which are J.

16 Additional details of the incident are discussed in the section "The Heroes Establish Cultic Etiologies."

17 For full discussion of the many parallels between the two episodes, see Louden 2011a: 113–23.

18 Cf. also how Isaiah 51:1–2 figures Abraham as a stone from which Israel is descended.

19 I see something like an ethnic joke here, a clear dig at the ancestry of the Moabites and Ammonites by ascribing their origins to an incestuous coupling. Closest to such a view is Davidson: "The Hebrews may have reshaped the tradition to stress the somewhat dubious origins of the Moabites and Ammonites." Cf. Alter 2004: 96: "Moab [which probably means 'desired place'] is construed as *me-'ab*, 'from the father.'"

20 For discussion of both types of theoxeny in Genesis, the *Odyssey*, and Ovid, see Louden 2011a: ch. 2.

21 On the episode as an instance of hospitality, cf. Green 2007: 353: "who offers them both hospitality and a clod of Libyan soil, which Euphemos (himself a son of Poseidon [1.180]) accepts, thus laying claim to sovereignty over the territory it symbolizes."

22 See ibid.: 225–26, for a summary of different perspectives on etiologies in Apollonius and Callimachos.

23 E.g., ibid.: 225, on 1.1070–77: "Ap.'s first example … of an *aition*, or aetiologizing explanation, of some current traditional custom … This quintessentially Hellenistic preoccupation is most closely associated with Kallimachos."

24 On the episode as an etiology, see Westermann 1976: 85: "One might call this narrative an etiology." On the ancient audience's familiarity with the site, see

Carr 1996: 265: "[T]he focus on the Bethel sanctuary found in Gen. 28:10–22 presupposes that this sanctuary was a reality for the audience of his text." The scholarly consensus is that Israelite culture, in fact, appropriated a preexisting site. See, e.g., Speiser: 220: "Actually, Bethel was an old center (cf. xii 8, xiii 3f.), which managed to retain its religious influence until late in the seventh century, when the holy place was destroyed by Josiah (II Kings xxiii 15)."

25 Other analogous figures include Oinomaus, as Hunter (1989: 58) notes, "Like Aietes, Oinomaus ... his evil plans are thwarted by his daughter's love for a stranger." Cf. Minos, though Theseus and Ariadne do not marry, and King Antiochus in *Apollonius, King of Tyre*. Huxley (1969: 69) notes that the *Naupaktia* was recited at a festival of Ariadne.

26 *Atasthalos* serves as a moral term in Homeric epic, "denoting behavior ... that goes against the gods' designs, much like 'sin'" (Louden 2006: 228).

27 Cf. Hunter 1989: 143: "both Aietes and Pelias set Jason tasks which they have no expectation he will survive;" (145): "Aietes conceals his desire to destroy Jason behind the mask of a high 'heroic code.'"

28 On the test as lethal, cf. Gantz 1993: 341: "Perhaps in some versions that tasks set Jason-harnessing of bulls, fighting sown men-were as in so many other tasks designed to test (or destroy) prospective suitors."

29 Cf. Alter's comment on the episode's heroic or epic modality (2004: 153): "The 'Homeric' feat of strength in rolling away the huge stone single-handedly."

30 Medea originally advises him to hurl a stone (3.1057: λᾶαν ... στιβαρώτερον); presumably Apollonius changes this to *solos* to enable him to allude to the athletic games in *Iliad* 23.

31 Cf. Speiser: 231; Alter 2004: 160: "The aphrodisiac association is reinforced in the Hebrew by a similarity of sound (exploited in the Song of Songs) between *duda'im*, 'mandrakes,' and *dodim*, 'lovemaking.'"

32 Cf. νεοτμήτῳ ... ῥίζα: 3.857; δυσπαλέας ῥίζας: 4.52; ἀρκεύθοιο νέον τετμηότι θαλλῷ 4.156, and Sophocles' play, the *Rhizotomoi, The Root Cutters*, which according to Gantz (1993: 366), focused on Medea tricking Pelias' daughters into slaying him. A surviving fragment again juxtaposes the two terms, κίσται ῥιζῶν κρύπτουσι τομάς, "boxes conceal the cuttings of the roots" (Lloyd-Jones 1996: frag. 534). The same belief that magic lies in cut roots underlies the episode of Hermes and the black root of the moly drug (10.276–306). *Moly* may be cognate with Sanskrit *mûlam*, "root" (Heubeck 1989: 60).

33 Cf. Green (2007: 274) adduces additional authors assuming mandrake is meant, though he argues no actual plant is meant but sees a Homeric precedent in *moly*.

34 Cf. ibid.: 275.

35 Cf. Carr 1996: 270: "Jacob's use of magical means to cause Laban's flock to produce more speckled and spotted goats ... and black sheep ... for himself."

36 Pindar also associates Jason with magic in his account, *Pythian* 4.216–17.

37 See West 2003: 240–41.

38 Cf. Hunter 1989: 253 on 3.1386–91.

39 Discussion in Louden 2006: 183–86; cf. Augeias with Herakles.

40 See Carr (1996: 261), on the discrepancy between Jacob "ten times" and the three instances depicted in Genesis.

41 See ibid. (262), on some of the narrative motives for the theft.

42 Cf. Green 2007: 40: "the Fleece itself, the raison d'être of this entire epic gests remains a complete (and highly numinous) mystery. The full reason for its

Grail-like desirability, which can send a shipload of the brightest and best to Kolchis and back, is never explained. This Fleece was a magical symbol: of supernatural power, of entitlement, above all of kingship." From the perspective of plotting, the Fleece is one of Alfred Hitchcock's MacGuffins.

43 Cf. Speiser 1962: 250: "According to the Nuzi documents, which have been found to reflect ... the social customs of Haran ... possession of the household gods could signify legal title to a given estate."

44 Discussion in Louden 2011a: 111–13.

45 As McCarter notes (1985: 326), "Saul's daughter shows greater loyalty to her husband than to her father."

46 Cf. Hall (2012: xxix–xxx), on the story, part of Euripides' *Iphigenia in Tauris*, of the cult image of Artemis coming to Athens.

47 See West 2003: 280–81, and Huxley 1969: 71.

48 Cf. how Agenor, father of Kadmos (and Phineus' grandfather!), orders his sons not to return home without Europa (Apollodorus 3.1).

49 Cf. Alter (2004: 169), "In heading for Canaan with his wives, children, and flocks, Jacob is actually taking what is rightly his ... but he has good reason to fear that the grasping Laban will renege on their agreement, and so he feels compelled to flee in stealth."

50 I thank Jackie Murray for pointing this out to me. Circe may allude to such a version at 4.740–42.

51 Cf. Alter's comment on Laban's sons (2004: 166), "Here they are used to dramatize in a single quick stroke the atmosphere of suspicion and jealousy in Laban's household: they make the extravagant claim that the visibly prospering Jacob 'has taken everything of our father's,' thus leaving them nothing. The anonymous sons would presumably be members of the pursuit party Laban forms to go after the fleeing Jacob."

52 Cf. Alter on Genesis 31:43, "Laban begins his response by refusing to yield an inch in point of legal prerogative."

53 Also, he gives the mound an Aramaic name (Alter 2004: 174). See Smith 2008: 103–7 for further discussion of this dimension of the encounter.

54 Alter 2004: 179: "The image of wrestling has been implicit throughout the Jacob story."

55 Cf. ibid.: 130: "the etymology is transparent: *Ya' aqob*, 'Jacob,' and *'aqeb*, 'heel.'"

56 Cf. Herakles also as a wrestler against the giant Antaeus, and the god Thanatos.

57 For further discussion of both episodes, see Louden 2011a: 113–23.

58 See Alter 1981: 52.

59 See Mastronarde (2002: 16–17), on this aspect of Medea's character in Euripides' play.

60 See further discussion in Louden 2011a: 98–99, 145, 316.

61 E.g., Mastronarde 2002: 25: "The term φάρμακα appears six times in the play."

62 Cf. ibid.: 35: "and she is the mistress of φάρμακα ... 718, of the drugs used to cure Aegeus' childlessness."

63 Cf. Pittard 1998: 34: "The ancestral tales of Genesis 12–50 depict four generations of pastoralists whose primary grazing lands lay in the land of Canaan."

64 But see Genesis 21:15–16, in figuring Ishmael as an archer, as discussed in Chapter 2.

65 The same should be noted of David's household gods at 1 Samuel 19:13–16.

66 See Huxley 1969: 69.

4 Euripides' *Hecuba* and Jael (Judg 4–5)

Dating of the book of Judges is undergoing considerable revision. Several European scholars are moving for a date within the Hellenistic period (e.g., Spronk 2015: 271). Spronk elsewhere (2010: 15–19) gives an intriguing overview of various arguments for dating Judges, noting Graeme Auld's theory concerning the larger formation of the Hebrew Bible (which we noted Chapter 1), the theory of the "Book of Two Houses." This argument posits 1 Samuel through 2 Kings as the *earliest* part of the Hebrew Bible, in terms of composition and formation – the account of the house of David and the account of Solomon (the house of the God of Israel) are "the root-work that supports the whole tree of Genesis–Kings."[1] Auld posits that Deuteronomy–Judges was composed next and, only after that, Genesis–Numbers, a backstory for the entire saga.[2] In several ways, accordingly, Judges was intended to serve as a transition between the two largest narrative sections. I find Auld's argument attractive for my larger argument, having concluded that parts of Judges are late on independent grounds (discussed in the following text).

In a specific example of his argument, Auld analyzes Judges 6–8 in "Gideon: Hacking at the Heart of the Old Testament."[3] Noting its many links with other biblical episodes (63, 69), that Gideon is not mentioned anywhere else in the Hebrew Bible except by his *other* name: Jerubbaal, and that the narrative employs a Hebrew expression elsewhere occurring only in late passages (68), he concludes (67), "[T]he Gideon story is an example of late biblical narrative." Its many allusions to other biblical episodes demonstrate that the Gideon narrative postdates them. In additional signs of lateness, Auld, noting that many commentators agree that Judges 17–21 are supplemental to the earlier chapters, argues (70), "Judg. 6–8 represent a further supplement to the Judges' traditions to the already supplementary chapter 17–21." He notes that in a Dead Sea fragment the narrative of Judges 6 goes from our 6:3–6 immediately to 6:11–13, leaving the obvious implication that 6:7–10 are an even later addition to the Gideon story. He additionally observes that Judges 3:7–11, the brief story of Othniel and Cushan-Rishathaim, "is a late piece deliberately contrived as an introduction to the tales of the deliverers" (64). As we have considered in the previous three chapters, I will argue that the scribal tradition turned to well-known examples from Greek myth as rubrics for some of the narratives in Judges.

Much of Judges has a more overtly heroic modality than is typical of most the Hebrew Bible, with several episodes suggesting the feel of Greek myth, seeming to function as brief pericopes of a largely effaced epic tradition.[4] Some, in their interplay between mortal and divine characters, have a distinctly epic modality.[5] As ancient Israel's scribal culture used sources and cultural paradigms from Ugarite, Egypt, and Mesopotamia, so it also had as sources and paradigms the narratives of ancient Greek culture. In the larger Trojan War saga, the scribes saw paradigms for depicting forms of heroism and interactions between heroes and kings that could easily be adapted for an Israelite audience. Scholars have noted the close parallels between David's duel with the Philistine Goliath and Hector's with Aias in *Iliad* 7 (Yadin 2004; Louden 2006: 173–78), with Yadin arguing that the redactors of 1 Samuel consciously employ the Homeric account as an intertext. I have elsewhere argued (in addition to the three previous chapters) that the recognition scenes in Joseph's myth are modeled on those in the *Odyssey*,[6] that Exodus 32 reworks *Odyssey* 12,[7] that Rahab sheltering the two nameless spies in Joshua 2 is modeled on Helen saving the disguised Odysseus in *Odyssey* 4,[8] and that aspects of Saul's fractious relation with Samuel respond to the *Iliad*'s depictions of Agamemnon's quarrels with Calchas and Chryseis,[9] among other such intersections.

Within Judges, it has been widely accepted that Judges 11, Jephthah's sacrifice of his daughter, is an adaptation of the Greek myth of Agamemnon sacrificing Iphigenia.[10] Römer (1998) argues that Judges 11 is reacting to Euripides in particular (34), "[T]he author of the tale of Jephthah's daughter did know the Iphigenia tradition, especially as it appears in Euripides." If we say *which* of Euripides' two plays that portray the myth, *Iphigenia in Tauris* or *Iphigenia in Aulis*, Römer, in fact, says both (35): "The author would have known both endings of the Iphigenia myth and tried to bring them together." He argues that there was a general awareness of Greek culture within some sectors of Israelite culture (36), "the Greek 'canon' to which Aeschylus and Euripides belonged fascinated part of the Jewish intelligentsia, especially those of Alexandria." Accordingly, he argues (36), "[T]he author of Judg 11.30–40 ... wanted to present Jephthah's daughter as the Hebrew Iphigenia." If we accept his argument, we must clearly assume a relatively late, perhaps Hellenistic date, for the relevant portions of Judges. We will reconsider in the following text a further possibility of presenting a Hebrew version of a Greek character.

I will argue first that the Jael narratives are the same genre of myth as Euripides' account of Hecuba's revenge on Polymestor. I will then argue that because many of the motifs seem more at home in Greek culture than in Israelite, and that the characters have more understandable motivations in *Hecuba* than in Judges 4–5, that the Judges redactors, as part of their larger awareness of the Trojan War cycle, *adapt* select parts of Euripides' *Hecuba*. As for the issue of Judges' historicity, I agree with Coogan's assessment of the book most like Judges, Joshua, "In my understanding the book of Joshua is historical-theological fiction. The primary purpose of its authors was to present a theological construct."

In Euripides' popular and well-known tragedy, Hecuba, having invited the Thracian king Polymestor and his sons into her tent, blinds the former and slays the latter aided by a group of Trojan women. Though there are key differences, these episodes from Euripides' *Hecuba* offer significant correspondences with Judges' account of Jael slaying Sisera after inviting him into her tent (Judg 4:2–5:31). Jael's tale is told twice, a prose account (4:4–24) featuring interaction and dialogue between Jael and Sisera. A verse account follows (5:2–31), presenting itself as a song sung by the prophetess Deborah, with no speech attributed to Jael or Sisera, but concluding with lines by the latter's mother, ironically assuming her son's "great victory," imagining the embroidered spoils, and potential concubines, he has won. Though the verse account, the "Song of Deborah," is often regarded as one of the oldest passages in the Bible (e.g., Boling 1975: 117; Niditch 2008: 76),[11] and the prose version of largely the same events in 4:15–22 is often thought to be considerably later,[12] I follow some recent commentators, including Levin, in viewing the verse account as later than the prose.

There are sustained homologies between the four principal characters: Hecuba, Jael; Polymestor: Sisera; Agamemnon: Barak; Deborah: chorus. Viewing Jael's myth through the lens of Euripides' *Hecuba* brings several details into clearer focus and makes unusual actions more intelligible. Hecuba and Polymestor, for instance, will be seen to have clear, compelling reasons for acting as they do, whereas Jael and Sisera do not. Jael's acts are made intelligible only within the theological framework imposed by the larger Deuteronomist agenda.

Both narratives are set in the larger context of each culture's most heroic war saga, immediately after a main battle has already concluded

Hecuba unfolds in the immediate aftermath of the Greek victory at Troy, the ruins of which are still smoldering in the background. Jael's tale is set immediately after the Israelites have defeated Sisera, the general for the Canaanite king Jabin. The account is given a distinct epic modality through the description of Jabin, who "had nine hundred iron chariots and he had oppressed the Israelites mightily for twenty years" (4:3).

The myths begin with a prophecy by another character, Polydorus, Deborah

Hecuba opens with the ghost of Polydorus, her slain son, prophesying several events later to unfold. Jael's myth begins with an extended focus on the unusual figure of Deborah, who, from the *Hecuba*'s perspective, combines the functions of several characters: Polydorus, Hecuba (esp. at 798–803), but, most of all, Euripides' chorus of Trojan women. Polydorus as, the ghost of a recently slain man, is an adapted form of the *deus ex machina*, a favorite technique for Euripides to begin a play, as we have already seen in Chapter 3 with Hermes in the *Ion* and will again see in Chapter 7 with Apollo in the *Alcestis*. Polydorus predicts Hecuba will discover his corpse and see that he receives burial, which will prompt her to seek revenge (42–51), though he does not specify her vengeance.[13] Deborah also prophesies about the corresponding figure, Jael, and her triumph over Sisera, though without naming her (4:9): "for in the hand of a woman the Lord will deliver Sisera." In a larger structural sense, Polydorus corresponds to Deborah not only in prophesying subsequent events in which Hecuba/Jael play a role but also in being the first speaking character and initial focal point of the myth, as Deborah is (in the verse account), and in having a role that is primarily verbal, as Deborah. Both characters also can be seen as standing in for God, in a sense.

Hecuba also "prophesies." As she invites Polymestor to come inside her tent (discussed in the following text), she leads him to think that, after having met with her, he will safely return home with his sons. But her remark ironically describes how he will fare after she has taken her revenge upon him. As Gregory (167) notes (1021–22), "Her prophecy will find an unexpected fulfillment." Hecuba's prediction of her triumph over Polymestor corresponds to Deborah's specific foretelling of Sisera's defeat (4:9), "for in the hand of a woman the Lord will deliver Sisera."

Both myths feature unusually prominent female agency, not only Hecuba and Jael but also the chorus and Deborah. Though commentators sometimes align Deborah's Song with earlier Near Eastern victory hymns,[14] in their five choral songs *Hecuba*'s chorus offer sustained correspondences with the Song of Deborah in Judges 5. While there are differences in tone (the Song of Deborah is triumphant, identifying with the victors, for the most part; the choral songs of the *Hecuba* identify with the conquered and defeated), there are nonetheless close correspondences between the Song of Deborah and choral songs from Greek tragedy in general (which to my knowledge have not previously been noted) and specific correspondences with those of the songs of the chorus in the *Hecuba* in particular (98–153, 444–83, 629–57, 905–52, 1023–34). I briefly note here some common tropes, *topoi*, and techniques.

- Deborah and *Hecuba*'s chorus both prophecy, the latter that Hecuba shall see the corpse of Polyxena (149–53).
- Both use geography as an organizing principal in parts of their songs.

Deborah employs both a geographic and ethnographic spread: 5:15–18, 23, of which Niditch notes (79): "This section is a traditional-style catalogue of the Israelite forces, to be compared with *Iliad* 3.160–244 [*sic*]." In the *Hecuba*, Gregory (1999: 97) notes that the organizing principle of the First Stasimon (444–83) is geographical.

- Both use apostrophes.

Judges 5:7 is an apostrophe to Deborah, Judges 5:12 to Barak. *Hecuba*'s chorus (475–79) apostrophizes their children, mothers, fathers, and city.

- Both ask rhetorical questions, Deborah at 5:16; Hecuba's chorus wonders where they will now be taken (448–67).
- Both give an account of the earlier war or battle.

Judges 5:24–27 give the song's account of Jael's triumph; *Hecuba* 629–47, 913–52 (3rd Stasimon),[15] and chorus sings its final song (4th Stasimon: 1023–34) while she defeats Polymestor.

- Both Hecuba's chorus and Song of Deborah identify with enemy women.

See Judges 5:28–30 and Hecuba 649–55, specifically of a foreign woman mourning in her house grieving by the wide Eurotas (650) for the death of her son (651).[16] This is more typically a feature of Greek myth than of Israelite, prominent in the *Iliad*: A Greek audience sympathizes with Andromache, Hecuba, and others.[17]

- The chorus and Deborah both act as co-agents with Hecuba and Jael.

In Judges this is emphasized in both the address to Deborah 5:7, 5:12, and especially her account of Jael 5:24–27. In *Hecuba* this is highlighted at 1023–34, 1041 (see Gregory 168–69).

- Right before learning of the horrible reversals that await them, Sisera's mother and Hecuba's chorus engage in similar acts of gazing.

Deborah's portrayal of the mother looking out the window (5.28–30), ignorant of the horrible news that awaits her, corresponds to the Trojan woman looking in the mirror in a choral song (925: χρυσέων ἐνόπτρων λεύσσους') as Troy is about to be sacked.[18]

Deborah and the chorus are associated with a sacred, oracular palm tree

Judges 4 features a unique palm tree, not mentioned anywhere else in the Bible. Deborah, according to Judges 4:5, "would sit under the Palm of Deborah … and Israelites would come up to her for Judgment." Boling connects this with prophesy (95), "That she had a tree named after her suggests a setting in which she was responsible for Yahwist oracular inquiry,"[19] but assumes the tree is not real (99), "the palm tree at that altitude may be explained meta-phorically." Niditch, however, notes the correspondence with larger Greek traditions (65), "Thus her countrymen come to her at the site of a special tree, as in the case of Greek oracles."

The *Hecuba* also features a sacred palm, but one known throughout Greek literature, referred to in the *Odyssey*; other literature from the Archaic period; as well as two other tragedies by Euripides. In *Hecuba*, the chorus wonder if in the future they will serve in Delos, where the sacred palm tree is, the first-ever palm tree (458–59: πρωτόγονός τε φοῖνιξ), according to Greek myth. Euripides references the sacred palm in two other plays, the *Ion* (919–20) and the *Iphigenia in Tauris* (1099), a play that Römer, as earlier noted, argues was known to the Judges redactors.[20]

Deborah exhibits further correspondences with the larger tradition of Greek female prophets and priestesses. Pindar, in his *4th Pythian*, the one that presents a lengthy account of the Argonautic myth, refers to the Pythia as the Delphic bee, "χρησμὸς ὤρθωσεν μελίσσας Δελφίδος αὐτομάτῳ κελάδῳ" (4.60). In the *Homeric Hymn to Hermes* (552–63), Apollo tells Hermes of three maidens who taught him how to prophesy; they do so after eating honey. Richardson offers a useful account of the passage (219),

> The poet appears to be describing a triad of three virgin sisters, who … taught him their mantic art … they are like bees, for they feed on honey, which gives them inspiration … they are most probably envisaged as nymphs with bee-like characteristics.

The name Deborah means "bee" (Sasson 2014: 254). As seemingly the only female prophet in the Hebrew Bible, whereas women prophets and priestesses are common in Greek myth, some of the *topoi* used to depict her are likely influenced by Greek traditions, particularly figuring her as associated with bees and with the palm tree, both far more prominent in Greek prophetic traditions.

Hecuba and Jael, though on the opposite side from those victorious in the war, form a temporary alliance with the victors

Through her marriage to the Kenite man, Heber (4:17), Judges implies that Jael is a Kenite, a non-Israelite group. As Niditch notes (65–66), the Hebrew Bible has multiple traditions about the Kenites, some passages listing them as a conquered people, some as enemies, and others, as Judges 4–5, suggesting neutrality.[21] Hecuba is unequivocally non-Greek, a Trojan, a member of the defeated party in the conflict that has just concluded, the Trojan War. Near the end of the play Agamemnon characterizes what she has done to Polymestor and his sons as τὸ βάρβαρον (*to barbaron*: 1129), what a non-Greek might do.

Both women are associated with an animal

Hecuba hears Polymestor's prophecy that she will be transformed into a dog (1265–71). Jael's name, unique in the Bible, means "mountain/wild goat."[22]

Hecuba's coming metamorphosis into a dog becomes a key part of her myth (Vergil, *Aeneid* 3.22 ff; Ovid, *Metamorphoses* 13.404–571). Before he prophesies her transformation, Polymestor earlier associates Hecuba, and the other Trojan women who assault him, with hounds or, conceivably, bitches (1173: τὰς μιαιφόνους κύνας).

Hecuba's coming metamorphosis does not necessarily correlate here with our "bitch," as it can elsewhere in Greek literature.[23] Gregory argues (xxxiv–xxxv) that it "should not be interpreted as a judgment … In the case of an older woman, the dog seems to be emblematic of the maternal impulse." She adduces the well-known simile from the *Odyssey* that compares Odysseus, as he observes the suitors' abuses, to a mother dog, defending her puppies (20.14–15).

Jael's thematic connection with goats, as suggested by her name, seems largely unexplored as a source of potential meaning in her myth, though I consider it in the following text, in connection with the possible meaning of Sisera's name. We note that, as with Hecuba's association with a dog, because the goat, classified as a clean animal (Deut 14:4), has a positive position in larger Israelite culture, Jael's association with it also seems positive.

Each woman enters into an agreement with the general of the victorious people (Agamemnon, Barak)

To take revenge on Polymestor, after learning how he slew Polydorus, Hecuba sends for Agamemnon, persuading him to let her proceed with her plot (726–904). Meeting with him alone, in her supplication (752: ἱκετεύω σε τῶνδε γουνάτων) Hecuba's appeal to *nomos* (799–96: νόμος), a law of right and wrong that governs the universe, men, and gods proves decisive in persuading him.[24] When the Greek general, though moved by the extent of Hecuba's suffering (782), hesitates because he considers Polymestor an ally (858: φίλος) of the Greek army (as Polymestor later declares: 982–83), Hecuba asks only for his passive acquiescence: she and the Trojan women will incapacitate Polymestor; he need not take part. When he expresses skepticism that *women* could do such a thing, she cites two Greek myths in which women slew groups of men (886–87: the slaying of Aegyptus' sons and the Lemnian women and their husbands, which is also part of the backstory of Argonautic myth).[25] Persuaded, Agamemnon wishes her luck (902), asserting that individuals and states both require a system of just retribution. He further notes (898–901) that if the Greeks were now able to sail away, he could not grant her request, but he can support her because absence of wind prevents them. As Gregory argues (xxix–xxxi), because favoring winds do arise at play's end (1289–90), where none are present before, the gods implicitly support Hecuba's course of action.

While Deborah earlier sends for and meets with the Israelite general Barak, exhorting him to defeat Sisera on the battlefield (4:6–10), Jael meets with him alone to show him what she has done to Sisera (Judg 4:22), "And look Barak was pursuing Sisera, and Jael went out to meet him." Unlike in Hecuba's case, this is *after* she has slain Sisera. Neither general thus takes part in the violence, which is enacted solely by the women.

Each woman invites her intended victim into her tent, under false pretenses

Hecuba claims to Polymestor that she has a hoard of jewels in her tent (1011–15, 1149), knowing he slew her son for the gold he was supposed to safeguard. She thus counters his false claims (he addresses her with feigned sincerity about her many losses)[26] with one of her own. Emphasizing her own helplessness, she asks him to dismiss his men and to meet with her in her tent in private.

Jael twice invites Sisera, having fled his disastrous battle, to come into her tent (Judg 4:18), "Turn aside, my lord, turn aside to me, do not fear." As Niditch points out (66), "Jael lures Sisera into her tent with language to calm fear."

Polymestor and Sisera reason they will be safe in her tent because no other men are present

Polymestor dismisses his men, asserting he is safe (981). In addition to promising she will reveal another cache of Priam's gold, Hecuba lures him into her tent alleging she has smuggled a horde of jewels out of Troy (1012–16), emphasizing that no men will be present, only women (1017–18). Polymestor's name is ironic in view of his credulity and larger character traits. A compound of μήστωρ (*mêstôr*), "adviser, counselor," and πολύ (*poly*), "many," his name should denote a wise, intelligent figure, whereas he is instead unable to control his own greed.[27] His coming blinding concretizes his lack of moral intelligence.

Judges 4:20 features a different form of irony addressing the same issue. When Sisera has entered Jael's tent, he gives her specific instructions, "Stand at the opening of the tent, and then, should a man come and ask you, 'Is there a man here?,' you shall say there is not," unknowingly affirming his own emasculation at Jael's hands. Sasson notes the careful calculation behind the particular form of address Jael uses with Sisera (265),

> [T]he plot requires the tent to be off-limits to men if we are to accept Sisera's request of 4:20 ... We are told that Jael went out to meet Sisera ... she certainly spied him running toward her husband's camp ... *'adoni* is used by women when stroking the ego of a man ... but most often when they are speaking to superiors.

Polymestor and Sisera both reveal themselves to be cowards and end up isolated, cut off from their own people.

The women simulate a maternal air to allay any suspicions from their intended victims

Hecuba emphasizes to Polymestor how her feminine gender assigns her a lower position in their culture (974–75), her initial move in employing and manipulating gender stereotypes against him. In his retelling, when he enters the tent, Hecuba and the Trojan women present an image of domestic femininity, fussing over his woven garments (1152–56: discussed in "A Woven Item (Robe or Blanket) Figures in How the Women Put Their Victims Off Guard"),[28] and his young sons (1157–59).

Jael, having entreated Sisera to enter her tent, covers him with a blanket or covering (in "A Woven Item (Robe or Blanket) Figures in How the Women Put Their Victims Off Guard"), though we are not told that he is cold (in Niditch's rendering she "hides" him with it). When he asks for water, she offers him a beverage with more maternal associations, milk (4:19, 5:25), and apparently readjusts his covering (Alter 2013: 129). In so doing, she is clearly "acting like a solicitous mother," as Niditch (66) argues, like Hecuba and her accomplices, to render Sisera more vulnerable to her subsequent assault.[29] There is a larger key difference in how this motif plays out in the two myths (discussed in the following text): Hecuba's iconic status as a mother and the tragic deaths of so many of her children are central to her myth, whereas Judges makes no mention of any children of Jael.

A woven item (robe or blanket) figures in how the women put their victims off guard

In both myths, at the same point in their larger sequence (right before the women assault their victims), a distinctive textile features in how the women begin to disable the men. As he recounts what happened, Polymestor underscores how the women made much of his woven robes (*peplous*), "[T]hey were praising the Thracian weaving, inspecting my robes under the light" (1152–54).

As already noted, Jael, without being asked, covers Sisera with *something* (4:18, 19), "a blanket," in Alter's rendering. The meaning of the Hebrew word at issue is far from certain, however.[30] Niditch explains (63),

> The term *semika* is difficult to translate … One wanders if the text reflects confusion with terms such as *masseka* from *nsk*, "to weave," i.e. "woven stuff, covering," and *masak*, "covering screen," from the root *s/skk*, "to cover, overshadow," or "to weave together."

In the prose account, the verb "cover," describing what Jael does to Sisera with the item, occurs twice. In the verse account, Jael is not depicted covering him with anything, but in the conclusion, when Sisera's mother wonders why he is delayed, her "wisest attendant" answers that he must be seeking add-itional spoils (5:30),

> Spoil of dyed stuff for Sisera,
>> spoil of dyed stuff,
> dyed needlework,
>> needlework pairs for every neck.

In the Septuagint, the dyed needlework spoils delineated here are explicitly for Sisera's own neck (τῷ τραχήλῳ αὐτοῦ), closest to the version of the motif in the *Hecuba*. The irony in "wisest attendant" (Αἱ σοφαὶ in the Sept.) forms an intriguing counterpart to that in Polymestor's name.

We now consider how the meaning of Jael's name, *Mountain Goat*, may have thematic functions in her myth. We begin with Patch's observation (*ISBE* vol. II, 1249–50),

> The word for she-goat is used elliptically to mean "goats' hair" ... Goats' hair was probably used in the Midianite and Israelitish camps in much the same way as in the Bedouin camps today ... The tents, tent ropes and rugs are made of spun goats' hair.

Day (*ISBE* vol. II, 1249) adds, in a broad discussion of goats in the Hebrew Bible, "the 'wild goat' (*ya'el*) ... Their milk is drunk ... Their hair is woven into tents (Cant 1:5)." Tents, milk, and the item Jael places on Sisera, three key objects in Jael's myth, may all be *goat* products. There may be further reasons behind individual items. Boling, for instance, accepting the observation of Burney, assumes it is *goat* milk that Jael serves to Sisera, particularly because (97–98) "certain goat milk products have a strongly soporific effect." The item Jael places on Sisera, whether garment, blanket, or other, is also likely woven from goat hair. We know from Exodus 26:7 and 36:14 that woven, goat-hair artifacts could be used for decorative purposes, as is the case in the taber-nacle, where such products serve as curtains.[31] Taken together, the three goat products, especially that with which Jael covers him, strongly suggest that "the wild goat" defeats Sisera.

The name "Sisera" is generally thought to be non-Hebrew (Boling: 100, 118; Niditch 64). There are few, if any, rules for gauging and ascertaining borrowings across linguistic boundaries as different as those between Greek and Hebrew. Several commentators argue that he should be thought of as one of the Sea Peoples (e.g., Boling 94, 100; Lindars 157, 166, 177; Sasson 254),[32] which, if so, would allow him even to be a Philistine, and thus a delib-erate intersection with Greek culture. With no consensus as to the name's etymology, I propose Greek σισύρα (*sisura*), for which Montari has "goatskin, goathide, used as a garment or blanket,"[33] common in the classical period (including three of Aristophanes' plays), as a possibility. If correct, a Greek origin[34] for the name Sisera not only embodies multiple correspondences within Jael's narrative, including the item with which she covers Sisera (Judg 4:18, 19) and adds further irony to his defeat, but also strengthens the myth's likely connection with Hellenic culture. It would also imply that the authors or redactors know Greek and that the name serves as a *calque*.

Inside their tents, the women incapacitate their enemy, striking him in the head with a sharp implement used in daily life

Both women, female civilians, noncombatants who take events into their own hands, use objects that are at hand, not normally intended for violent acts. Hecuba and the Trojan women use dress pins, *porpas* (1170: πόρπας), to stab Polymestor in the eyes, blinding him. While there are other incidents in Greek literature where dress pins are similarly used,[35] here it strengthens their manipulation of gender stereotypes against him and the irony of his assuming he is safe among women. He is blinded rather than slain, a typically Greek punishment, if one considers Polyphemus in *Odyssey* 9[36] and Oedipus, among others, whereas this seems rare in the Hebrew Bible.[37] Polymestor's blinding is more tragic than Sisera's slaying because, as Gregory notes (170), "it disables him while allowing him to suffer." It also serves as a form of poetic justice and furthers the ironic application of his name. Jael slays Sisera by hammering a tent peg through his temple, while he sleeps, in the account in 4:21,

> And Jael wife of Heber took the tent-peg and put a mallet in her hand, and came to him stealthily and drove the peg through his temple and it sunk into the ground – as for him, he had been asleep, exhausted – and he died.

For what Alter here renders as "exhausted," the Septuagint has ἐσκοτώθη, *eskotôthê*, literally, "became dark." While this reading is usually rendered idiomatically as "lose consciousness, faint," it also means "go blind," as at Sophocles, *Ajax* 85, or "to be metaphorically blind," as several times in Plato. Niditch (61) notes the Codex Vaticanus reading has "was suffused in darkness." Both readings bring Jael's act considerably closer to the *Hecuba*'s account of the blinding of Polymestor.[38]

While in 4:21 Jael hammers her tent peg into a sleeping Sisera, in 5:26–27 he is in a more upright position and awake because he is first kneeling, then falls. Differences between the conceptions of what Jael does in 4:21, as compared to the version in 5:26–27, thus highlight how confused the textual tradition may be for the Hebrew text at 4:21, where Boling has "he twitched convulsively." As Martin points out (75),

> While verse 26 is in agreement with ch. 4 as to the method whereby Sisera was killed, verse 27 seems to suggest a slightly different method … Verses 26 and 27 may, therefore, reflect two variant traditions regarding the death of Sisera.

The two myths differ in the sequence of how they narrate the women's assaults. It would violate accepted decorum of Greek tragedy to depict onstage an incident such as Hecuba's blinding of Polymestor. A messenger, or other character, must narrate the events after they have occurred.[39] Having Polymestor do so increases his tragic circumstances and furthers the irony of his having been metaphorically blind to the meaning of hospitality, as well as lusting after more gold.

In assaulting him, after inviting him into their tents, both women violate the sanctity of hospitality

Because hospitality is sacred in both cultures[40] its intentional violation by the women is shocking, though this rarely occasions comment in Jael's case.[41] In *Hecuba*, intentional violation of hospitality is a central thematic, running throughout the tragedy, foregrounded in Polydorus' introductory monologue (7, 19, 26), and regularly recurring (82, 710, 715, 790, 794, 803–4, 852, 890, 1216, 1247). Polymestor's own violation of hospitality, having slain Polydorus while his guest, aligns him with actual monsters such as Polyphemus.[42] Hecuba, therefore, has real reasons for violating hospitality; it constitutes a form of poetic justice:[43] the man who slew her son while his guest, who had formerly been her guest, suffers a corresponding fate at her hands. Because hospitality enters host and guest into obligatory reciprocity, Polymestor's blinding by Hecuba has considerable meaning, and can perhaps be understood as a necessary form of reciprocity, even to her specific act of slaying his sons.

By contrast, Jael's violation of it does not. Sasson (307) notes how the presentation seems designed to emphasize her violence, "With no transition, a gracious scene turns murderous ... the poet seems less concerned with choreographing the attack than with displaying its savagery ... the consequences of one murderous blow." As Martin notes (60–61), it is Jael who takes the initiative in bestowing hospitality, which thus places Sisera under her sanctuary. Quite unlike Polymestor, Sisera has no backstory with Jael, no vicious violations of her children (she apparently has none); he has committed no previous wrongs against her. Therefore, as Martin reasons (61), "Having received the gift of hospitality, Sisera can now happily demand sanctuary and protection, secure in the knowledge that the laws of hospitality cannot be violated." Schenk states the case more forcefully (1557–58), "[T]he fact remains that he was her guest, was in the sanctuary of her home, and protected by the laws of hospitality ... It is really impossible to justify Jael's act."

Most commentators, however, appear to assume quite the opposite, as Martin conjectures (61),

> Inviolable as these laws of hospitality were, God's overriding plan for his people takes precedence. The early Israelite reader would not feel that Jael was morally in the wrong in killing her guest.

Milton, however, well captures the ambiguity of her act in *Samson Agonistes* (989–90), "Jael, who with inhospitable guile, / Smote Sisera sleeping, through the temples nailed." His "inhospitable guile" could also serve as a handle for Hecuba. Milton was more than familiar with Euripides' play, his emendation at line 1151 widely accepted.[44]

The slaying of Polymestor's sons corresponds to the slaughter of Sisera's troops

Hecuba and the Trojan women, after blinding Polymestor, slay his young sons. Although the numbers are in no way equivalent, and the acts are performed by very different agents, in a broad sense his sons' deaths correspond to Sisera's loss of all his troops (4:16): "and all the camp of Sisera fell by the edge of the sword, not one remained." Unlike in the blinding of Polymestor, where implements of daily use were used, the women slay his sons with swords (1161: φάσγαν'), increasing the distinction between the blinding and slaying. Both male villains are thus correspondingly victimized in additional ways beyond their wounds by the protagonists.

Polymestor's blinding and his sons' slaughter, though offstage, are tragic. Sisera's slaying is onstage, but all pathos is denied him. While both men are ludicrous in part, Sisera dies absurdly, almost surrealistically. His being asleep (in the version at 4:21) makes his death utterly unheroic, void of any suffering, whereas Hecuba intends that Polymestor suffer. Jael's story serves as part of a larger polemic. Sisera is presented as an enemy of God (5:31); the narrative has no interest in considering him as a human being for whom the audience has sympathy. The *Hecuba* is considerably more nuanced.

Both women take credit for incapacitating their opponent before the commanding general of the victors (who has no part in their actions)

Agamemnon, who had gone to the Greek camp after Hecuba persuaded him to allow her to proceed with her plan (904), returns when he hears Polymestor's cries echoing through the Greek camp (ἀνὰ στρατὸν: 1108–14). Seeing his battered eyes and slain sons, he pretends not to know who did this to him (1117–20). An *agon* develops[45] in which Agamemnon is asked to arbitrate between the competing claims to justice made by Polymestor and Hecuba.

Polymestor's claim for why he was just in murdering Polydorus is transparent sophistry: the Greeks, learning of him, a presumed enemy of Greece (1138), would raise a second expedition against Troy (1137–45, also 1176–77, 1196–205). His misogynist conclusion (1179–83) that *all* women, based on his experience from Hecuba, are monsters forms a climax to his sophistry.[46] Hecuba, easily dismantling Polymestor's specious claims, asserts Agamemnon must rule against him because he violated sacred laws of gods and men (1233–36). Agamemnon agrees, citing Polymestor's desecration of the sanctity of hospitality in slaying Polydorus (1240–52).[47]

Barak meets with Jael only in the prose account (Judg 4:22). No previous meeting with her is mentioned; he comes to her tent as he pursues Sisera (4:22). Unbidden, she comes forth from her tent, saying, "Come, that I may show you the man you seek" (4:22). Because our narrative depicts no earlier meeting, the audience must supply her motivation for going out to meet him and to assume that Barak is pursuing Sisera. Sisera already slain, Barak has no interaction with him, nor does the narrative record his response to seeing his corpse.

Each woman gives her name in memorial to a feature of the local landscape

While Hecuba's tomb (see "Both Women Are Associated with an Animal") will become a landmark for sailors (1272–74), Deborah's palm ("Deborah and the Chorus Are Associated with a Sacred, Oracular Palm Tree"), in which Jael's myth again employs with *Deborah* a motif associated with Hecuba in her myth, features in the immediate backstory of Jael's myth, "And she [Deborah] would sit under the palm of Deborah … and the Israelites would come up to her for judgment." Deborah's palm only occurs in the prose account. Both eponymous memorials are associated with prophecy. In each myth, others come to consult the memorials. The memorials function as boundary markers for the respective myths, Hecuba's concludes her myth (1265–74), while Deborah's begins hers (Judg 4:5).

How do we interpret the correspondences between the two myths? Several of the motifs are unusual, far from common in the larger bodies of Greek and Hebrew myth. Taken together, the concatenation of the 15 motifs comprises a whole that is even more unique. Gender underscores and cements the most potent parallels. Women protagonists, neither members of a warrior group, such as the Amazons, nor witches, such as Medea, unexpectedly overpower and victimize high-status men in leadership positions, a king and a general. Most strikingly, they perform the violent act that incapacitates their high-status male opponents.

Because the correspondences the myths exhibit with each other seem too many to ascribe to coincidence, I thus argue that Judges 4–5 are a response to Euripides' *Hecuba*. Jael's myth is a *pericope* of relevant portions of it, as Judges 11 is of Agamemnon's sacrifice of Iphigenia. If we consider the narratives as existing in this relationship, if we read *through* Euripides' *Hecuba* to Judges 4–5, several principal details and acts in Jael's myth have better motivations, we can resolve a few interpretive problems and the larger narrative becomes more intelligible. For instance, the principal characters in Judges 4–5, Jael, Deborah, and Barak, exist only in these passages. They have no independent existence, no roles elsewhere in the Hebrew Bible, and no links with characters that have any existence outside of these passages.

No parents or children are mentioned for either Jael or Deborah, contrary to the usual practice of the Hebrew Bible. Jael's only link with another character is as the wife of Heber the Kenite (Judg 4:17). Deborah too is given a husband, though neither plays a role in the narratives, and almost nothing is said of them.

Hecuba, however, is not only a fully developed character, with deep roots and a substantial tradition in Greek myth, but also she has numerous children, many of whom are fully developed characters. We know her parents, background, and husband. For centuries before Euripides' tragedy, she is a fully realized character in the *Iliad* (especially in books 6, 22, and 24), in lyric poetry as early as Stesichorus,[48] and in Pindar (*Paean* 8.8) and Simonides.[49] Originally Phrygian, she is depicted in multiple roles, but particularly figured as a mourning mother.[50] The same applies, *mutatis mutandis*, for Agamemnon, as opposed to Barak.

Quite unlike Hecuba, Jael has suffered no personal loss at the hands of Sisera and has not previously been impacted by him in any way. Hecuba has considerable reason and motivation for the violent acts she performs against Polymestor and his sons. Her earlier losses, a queen become slave and a mother who endures the loss of child after child, capped by two more during the play – even after the war has essentially concluded – make her the epitome and paradigm of human suffering, as Shakespeare understands her in his many references.[51] Her blinding of Polymestor and slaying of his sons is thus fully motivated where Jael's slaying of Sisera is not. Jael is given no reason whatsoever to violate hospitality, brutally slaying a man who has done her no wrong, nor her people.

Polymestor as well has very credible motivation for entering Hecuba's tent. His greed is his defining characteristic. His previous acquaintance with Hecuba allows her to easily manipulate him, without provoking his suspicions. Sisera, though fleeing from a disastrous defeat, is given far less reason for entering the tent of an unknown woman, much less for completely entrusting himself to her. His doing so has an almost surreal air, by comparison. Both men are shown to be credulous fools, ready to suffer at a woman's hands, but Polymestor's actions are credible and consistent.

The changing status of the winds implies the gods' support for Hecuba's vengeance against Polymestor. The motif is also evident in *Odyssey* 4 when Menelaus recounts how he was stranded on the island of Pharos for 20 days, trapped by an absence of favorable winds. After he performs a sacrifice to Zeus and the other gods, the winds allow him to finish his journey (4.360–586). In the *Hecuba*, the Greeks are unable to sail away for most of the play – a situation that changes right after Hecuba blinds Polymestor, as Gregory notes (xxxi),

> The winds turn favorable again after Hecuba has blinded Polymestor and murdered his sons … The gods who disapproved of the Greeks' sacrificial offering seem to take a positive view of the Trojan queen's revenge.[52]

The gods' support of Hecuba, as revealed in the winds, is a subtler version of the much more explicit divine validation Jael receives in Judges 4–5.

Hecuba achieves her vengeance by, at least temporarily, operating as a *neutral* regarding the war. To do so, she must make arrangements with the very general in command of the army that has slain so many of her children. Jael's apparent neutrality renders her slaying of Sisera and interactions with Barak less intelligible. Sasson, for example, notes (274), "Jael is not of Israel, and her motivation for murdering Sisera can be endlessly debated."[53] Her husband's identity as a Kenite establishes her seeming neutrality in this conflict between the Israelites and Canaanites. The nomadic Kenites are malleable chameleons, with one characteristic in one passage, but a different one in another (Gen 15:19, Exod 3:1, 1 Sam 15:16, etc.), lacking a definitive identity. In short, they are a *convenient* entity to attach to a minor character. But is Jael originally a Kenite or only so by marriage? We do not know. Euripides' play presents a more intelligible account of Hecuba's independent agency.

Barak, the Israelite general, lacks both any engagement with Sisera and any prior arrangement with Jael. Though her narrative clearly seeks to maximize Jael's own agency, his lack of interaction with Sisera while he is alive and, perhaps even more mysterious, his lack of prior arrangement or interaction with Jael are far less intelligible than the relations and agreements made in Euripides' play. The *Hecuba* presents a full account of why Agamemnon takes no part in the violence against Polymestor and his sons, and how he agrees ahead of time that Hecuba may proceed against him. Further, the Greek general interacts with Polymestor after Hecuba accomplishes her revenge, where Barak merely sees a corpse. In Judges 4, a sleeping Sisera is completely unaware that he is even being slain, whereas Polymestor not only knows why Hecuba acts as she does but also hears Agamemnon agree that she did so with a larger sense of justice.

A few of the key motifs and characters seem more at home in Greek culture than in Hebrew. Greek myth offers more relevant instances both of a woman acting as an independent agent and as performing a violent act against a man. Other works by the same author, Euripides, including the *Medea*, constitute the most obvious examples. If we accept Römer's argument that in Judges 11 the redactors refer to *both* of Euripides' Iphigenia plays, this suggests their broader familiarity with Euripides in particular. Moreover, we have argued in Chapter 2 that the same is true of the Genesis tradition. Women acting in concert to slay men is also a recurring motif in Greek myth, as Hecuba is aware (886–88). Polymestor's lament that he was defeated by a woman (1252: γυναικός ... ἡσσώμενος), seems almost answered by Deborah's prophesy at Judges 4:9: "for in the hand of a woman the Lord will deliver Sisera." The oracular palm tree, so central and well known in Greek myth where Deborah's is atypical, even unique in the Hebrew Bible, can serve as the clearest example of the larger tendency.

My suggested derivation of Sisera's name from σισύρα (*sisura*), if accepted as plausible, would constitute a further sign of the interaction of Jael's myth with Greek culture, its dependence on Hecuba's myth, and on the ability of the Judges redactors to adapt it for a new, different audience. I find general support for my larger argument in Spronk's recent conclusion (2015: 271), "We may conclude that it is not only possible to read the book of Judges against a Hellenistic background, but also plausible that this book was written and edited by someone living in the early Hellenistic period and familiar with Greek literature."

I need briefly address the majority view on the dating of the Song of Deborah, that it is often regarded as one of the *oldest* passages in the Hebrew Bible, because this will present a significant impediment for some for accepting my argument. Some linguistic features are present in Judges 5 that are often regarded as very early Hebraic forms, some, based on their presence in other passages, such as Psalm 68, also thought to be early. However, Sasson offers a reasonable caveat on dating passages based on the *assumed* dates of other passages that share some linguistic or structural correspondences (319), "There is a tacit assumption that stylistic (or ideological) resemblance is temporal correspondence. This inference is not warranted." The Homeric "dialect" may offer a relevant lens for considering the presence of some earlier forms in Judges 5. A few Homeric formulae are thought to descend even from Indo-European traditions, a few to go back to Mycenaean (or *Philistine*) times, others scan only if the digamma is restored; yet the whole is an artificial amalgamation that can, following Janko, be dated to the later eighth century BCE.[54] I suggest that Judges 5 is not early but composed in an archaizing style that intentionally employs early elements to seem appropriate to the time the redactors of Judges intend it to have taken place.[55] Christoph Levin, in a study of all the inset poetic narratives in the Hebrew Bible, argues that Deborah's song is the *latest* of them, its seemingly early elements in fact quoted from Psalm 68.

Jael's acts, and especially Deborah's perspective on her fame, seem far more intelligible if understood as exemplifying the much later Deuteronomist agenda. If Judges intends Jael as a model to be emulated, a distillation of Hecuba's revenge, with the queen a member of the losing side in the war, it better fits later periods, Israelite subjugation under various empires, including that of the Greeks. In this particular light, an Israelite Hecuba serves as a way of projecting or fantasizing a positive response, at the level of the individual, against foreign hegemony, a model to maintain independence of belief against foreign domination with overwhelming military superiority.

In an additional sign of likely lateness, Mobley (2005: 242) notes correspondences between the episode we focus on here, Judges 4–5, and the Hellenistic-era Judith, "Like Jael in Judges 4–5, the heroine Judith kills an unsuspecting male foreign oppressor in a domestic context." Does this suggest that this narrative type was more popular in the Hellenistic period?

As the ancient scribal tradition behind the Hebrew Bible drew on Mesopotamian narratives and rubrics to present its own version of Creation and primeval narratives, so, I argue, they drew on the larger Trojan War saga as rubrics for depicting their own heroic phase. Of the six methods Van der Toorn (110) considers by which ancient scribes produced written texts, perhaps most relevant is his fifth adaptation (133), which he defines as "Adaptation ... is a mode of text production that requires an anterior text. The scribe will use that text as a model for his own; instead of writing a text, he will be rewriting one." He goes on to note that adaptation includes translation of an anterior narrative from a different language,

> His adaptation can take several forms. It may be a mere translation from the one language into the other; the translation may transform the text substantially by appropriating it for an audience with different religious loyalties.

For episodes and contexts from Joshua through 2 Kings, Greek myth provides innumerable relevant heroic examples and paradigms.

Notes

1 Auld 2004: 24.
2 "The royal davidic story was first anticipated in the Deuteronomistic story from Moses to the Judges, and then a fresh and still 'earlier' preface supplied in the groundwork of Genesis-Numbers." Ibid.
3 Ibid.: 63–70.
4 Louden 2006: 162: "The heroic tales in Judges suggest the same raw stuff from which the *Iliad* must have derived ... but in Judges the myths are stated quickly and simply without the elaboration with which the *Iliad* develops its scenes and type-scenes." See also Spronk 2010 for a brief survey of episodes and motifs in Judges that find correspondences with a variety of Greek narratives. See Mobley (2005: 227–29) on Judges' essentially heroic modality.
5 See, for instance, discussion of Samson at Louden 2006: 169, 171.
6 Louden 2011a: 92–96.
7 Ibid.: 222–43.
8 Ibid.: 105–13.
9 Louden 2006: 158–63.
10 See Arieti (2017: 150–56) for a useful study of the two myths' correspondences and divergences, though he does not consider the possibility of Judges 11 as influenced by the Iphigenia myth.
11 However, it is surely wise to keep in mind Sasson's caveat (2014: 319), "A good many scholars seem content to establish a relative dating for the confection of the poem, setting its production before, at, or after other Hb poetry thought to be of deep antiquity ... There is a tacit assumption that stylistic (or ideological) resemblance is temporal correspondence. This inference is not warranted."
12 There is no consensus, however. Ibid. (312–15), notes seven different positions scholars have argued on their possible relationship, "1. The accounts are independent of each other ... 2. The accounts have a single author ... 3. The accounts complement each other ... 4. The poetry influences the prose ... 5. The prose influences the poetry. 6. Both versions communicate the same chain of events, inherited from a common source or shared memory ... 7. The versions have differing inspirations." My own view is that the song is later (!) because it includes more unexpected correspondences with the *Hecuba* and the particular form of irony used of Sisera's mother and her ladies has a touch of the satiric.

13 Cf. Gregory's assessment of his monologue (1999: 40): "a partial glimpse of developments to follow ... He also touches on the future (42–52), predicting Polyxena's death and his own burial, but not Hecuba's revenge."

14 E.g., Boling 1975: 117; Niditch 2008: 76–77. Cf. also within the Hebrew Bible, Exodus 15; 1 Samuel 18; Psalm 68, and Ecclesiastes 12.

15 On the latter, see discussion at Gregory 1999: 153.

16 See discussion in ibid.: 125.

17 Cf. Niditch 2008: 82: "What is so special here, however, is the composer's capacity to identify with the enemy, to assume the voice of the Canaanite women much as Homer assumes that of the Trojan women."

18 Consider Wohl's description (2015: 57), "The ode takes us into the bedroom of a Trojan woman as she combs her hair and prepares to join her husband in bed. This intimate domestic scene is ruptured by the war cry of the Greeks ... the pathos of her unanswered prayers to Artemis anticipates her pathetic future: her husband dead, she is led away, over the sea, gazing back upon her receding homeland. The ode solicits the listener's pity ... focalizes the events thru the woman's eyes."

19 Cf. Boling 1975: 99: "a little oracular oasis; the palm tree at that altitude may be growing metaphorically" and Niditch 2008: 62: "OL [Old Latin version] reads 'under a palm,' thereby reducing the more cultic image of D as an oracle associated with a sacred tree or space."

20 For further on the palm tree in Greek myth, see Gregory 1999: 100.

21 Niditch 2008: 65–66: "some traditions include the Kenites among formulaic lists of conquered peoples (e.g. Gen 15:19) or mention them as enemies (e.g., 1 Sam 27:10), others suggest a positive relationship through affinal kinship or military neutrality (Judg 1:16, 4:11; 1 Sam 15:6)."

22 Schenk 1939: 1557.

23 As in Helen referring to herself as a bitch, *Iliad* 6.344.

24 Though see Turkeltaub 2017 on significant problems in her position.

25 Discussion in Gregory 1999: 150.

26 See ibid. (160), quoting Mastronarde on his "consciously artificial" greeting.

27 Cf. ibid.: 42: "can be etymologized as 'much-counseling' ... The appellation is most likely ironic since Polymestor murders his young charge with thoughtless greed, takes minimal care in disposing of the body, and despite his initial suspicions ... allows himself to be lured by Hecuba into Agamemnon's tent."

28 Cf. ibid.: 181: "This display of a distinctively feminine interest and expertise ... is calculated to reassure Polymestor that they pose no danger to him."

29 See also Alter's interpretation that the prose version in Judges 4 (2013: 129): "highlights the ironic suggestion of Jael's playing a maternal role toward the man she is about to kill."

30 See Boling 1975: 97, for instance.

31 Cf. Alter's renderings of the two passages (2013), "And you shall make goat-hair panels for a tent over the Tabernacle, twelve panels you shall make them ... And they made goat-hair panels for a tent over the Tabernacle."

32 "Sisera's name is still a puzzler, and there is a tendency to explain it via languages and ethnic groups (once Hurrian, now mostly Luwian, Lycian, Illyrian, but also Cretan and Sardinian) that are not always fully recovered or understood, with the aim of vaguely attaching him to one of the Philistine tribes that had recently settled in the region ... In later traditions (Josephus ... esp. in Rabbinic lore, S was made into a world conqueror, rivaling Alexander in prestige and achievement."

33 Cf. Liddel, Scott, and Jones: "goat's-hair cloak, used as a garment by day and a coverlet by night."

34 Apparently only Bern Diener (1995: 116–19) has previously made this suggestion.

35 Gregory: 183: "Their dangerous potential is realized in Sophocles *OT* (1268–70) when Oedipus blinds himself with Jocasta's dress-pins."

36 In the combat motif, the ancient hero usually slays his monster, as Gilgamesh Humbaba, where Odysseus instead blinds Polyphemos, partially incapacitating him.

37 The only incidents appear to be Judges 16:21 (Philistines to Samson); 1 Samuel 11:2 (Nahash the Ammonite threatens Israelites with); 2 Kings 25:7 (the Chaldeans to Zedekiah). For a further Greco-Roman example of a woman blinding rather than killing a man who wronged her, see Charite to Thrasyllus in Apuleius, *The Golden Ass*, bk. 8.

38 Cf. also *Hecuba* 1035: τυφλοῦμαι φέγγος ὀμμάτων τάλας.

39 See Gregory (1999: 179) and Lloyd (1992: 97) on how Polymestor's account resembles a messenger's speech.

40 For hospitality as sacred in the Hebrew Bible, see especially Genesis 18–19, for Greek myth, the *Odyssey*. For discussion of parallels between Genesis 18–19 and the *Odyssey*, see Louden 2011a: 30–56.

41 But see Schenk (*ISBE* vol. III, 1939: 1557), and Martin (1975: 60–61), for exceptions.

42 Cf. Gregory 1999: 138.

43 See Wohl (49) on the play as regarding her revenge as a form of justice.

44 See Gregory: 181.

45 On the *agon* in Euripides in general, see Lloyd (1992, and 94–99 in particular) for discussion of the *agon* in *Hecuba*.

46 Cf. Gregory's comment that his assertions (184), "characterize the speaker as deficient in logic and insight."

47 Though again, see Turkeltaub on dissonance in the respective arguments.

48 Frag. 198 in Campbell 1991.

49 Frag. 559, ibid.

50 Roisman (2011: 334–35) in Finkelberg, Vol. II. See Gregory: xix, 193–94 on other lyric antecedents to Hecuba's depiction in Euripides' tragedy.

51 Throughout his career he is deeply interested in the character of Hecuba, in a narrative poem at the beginning, *The Rape of Lucrece* 1366–72 [1447–56], 1447–49), in an early play, *Titus Andronicus* (1.1.136–38; 4.1.20–21), in middle plays, *Hamlet* (2.2.551–55), and *Troilus and Cressida* (5.3.51–55, 83–86), in a late tragedy, *Coriolanus* (1.3.39–43), and a romance, *Cymbeline* (4.3.314–15).

52 For a full analysis of how the winds figure in the *Hecuba*, see Gregory: xxix–xxxiii. The motif may be present in Sophocles' *Antigone*, when the title character is accompanied by a dust storm when she strews handfuls of dust on Polyneices' corpse (415–22).

53 See Niditch (2008: 81), for instance, on the conjecture that Jael is a "Kenite priestess, her tent a sacred locus." This would, of course, provide motivation for Sisera to seek refuge with her in specific, but the text offers no evidence for this and seems to me to be reading far too much into the myth.

54 Cf. Spenser's curious, composite of archaic English developed for the *Fairie Queene*.

55 Cf. Janko (2011: 32–33) on "false archaism" in the *Homeric Hymns* to *Hermes*, *Demeter*, and *Pythian Apollo*.

Part II
New Testament

5   The oath that cannot be taken back

Ovid's *Metamorphoses* 1.751–2.400,
Mark 6, and Matthew 14
(cf. *Iliad* 19; Gen 27)

A rash, impetuous child, who has a closer relationship with its mother than with its imperial, occupied-by-his-duties father, wishes to win proof of his affection. The father, too eagerly swears ahead of time, recklessly expansive in his regal setting, to grant *anything* his child should wish. What the child demands of the father not only violates propriety but also the natural order of human existence. But the father, lest he break the oath, sworn before witnesses, grants the wish with great reluctance. Tragic consequences result, including a death; each father tarnished by his recklessness.

For a classicist, this synopsis will summon Ovid's account of Phaethon and the Sun, while within the New Testament it points to Mark's and Matthew's accounts of Herod and his unnamed daughter or niece. Is the resemblance a coincidence? In this chapter I will argue that Ovid's well-known account serves as a rubric for the Gospels' narratives, with significant details altered to serve their different narrative agendas. In Chapter 9 I will further argue that the same episode, *Metamorphoses* 2.1–18 in specific, also serves as a rubric for Revelation 4.

At the outset it is worth considering some unusual details in Mark's and Matthew's accounts. As Mann (1986: 296–97) demonstrates, there are significant problems for those who assume this Gospel narrative reflects a historical account.[1] Mark and Josephus contradict each other on several points, for instance. Is Philip the first husband of Herodias, as Mark has it, or the husband of Salome, as Josephus asserts? Who orders John's slaying? Herod, according to Josephus, but Herodias according to Mark. What was the motivation? Herodias' hatred, according to Mark, but Herod's fear of John, according to Josephus. Where does it take place? Tiberias, according to Mark, Machaerus says Josephus. Is the girl Herod's grandniece or his daughter? Could her dance, as characterized by Mark, even have taken place in such a setting? Mann argues no (297),

> There is a difficulty ... having to do with the historicity of an account suggesting that a Herodian princess should have danced before Antipas' court. The undoubted implication of the text is that the dancing was sensual and lascivious, and there is an obvious question as to whether

a member of Herod's family would have been allowed to perform in the presence of strangers.

He further suggests that the narrative responds to and builds on the Book of Esther (297): "It is highly probable that the text of Esther has influenced the text ... This is not to say that the whole story before us is fabrication." Mann also notes (295) a larger anomaly, "[T]he execution of John is in Mark the only narrative which is not about Jesus." Therefore, notes Mann (295), "it has been customary to use the word 'legend' to describe the account." In Matthew's version Jesus is only mentioned in the final verse: "Then John's disciples came and took away the body, and buried it; and they went and told Jesus." This gives one the impression that the verse has been added merely to connect a rather independent narrative about Herod's daughter to the rest of the Gospel.

The two accounts exhibit several additional oddities from a general narrative perspective. They are presented retrospectively. When Herod first hears of Jesus' disciples casting demons out of people, and healing others by anointing them with oil, he declares, apparently without sarcasm, that John the Baptist has risen from the dead (Mark 6:12–14; Matt 14:1–2). In both Mark and Matthew this provides the impetus for the narrative of Herod and his daughter, to recount, retrospectively, the circumstances of the Baptist's death. The Baptist, however, until his decapitated head is produced, remains offstage for the entire narratives, maximizing the focus on Herod and his daughter.

The inconsistencies regarding historical individuals,[2] the disruption of narrative chronology, and the unique instance of a narrative in which Jesus does not figure, collectively suggest that this is an originally independent narrative inserted into its present contexts. We can firm up this thesis by recognizing that the narratives conform to a genre of myth earlier considered, which we might designate as *The naïve Father swears a reckless oath that cannot be taken back*. We considered two relevant examples in Chapter 3 in *Iliad* 19.91–133 and Genesis 27. The authors of Mark and Matthew would, of course, certainly be familiar with Genesis 27, likely with *Iliad* 19.

However, in several particulars, the Herod narratives are closer to Ovid's account of Phaethon than to these earlier examples. *Iliad* 19 and Genesis 27 lack the gruesome loss of life that are not only common to both Ovid and the Herod narratives but also form their respective climaxes. Indeed, the larger function of the Herod narratives is to provide an account for the death of John the Baptist. In another significant difference, in *Iliad* 19 and Genesis it is the father who initiates the fateful encounter, not the child as in Ovid and the Herod narratives. Herakles, in fact, is not yet born. These significant departures from *Iliad* 19 and Genesis 27 only further emphasize the closeness of Ovid's account and the Herod narratives.

In a key difference, however, Ovid's Phaethon performs the functions of what are, in Herod's narratives, two separate characters, the "daughter" and John the Baptist. As a result, he has a much larger role than she does. I will argue that Mark, or some intervening tradition on which he draws, has bifurcated Phaethon's character functions into the two separate characters. Bifurcation, a technique by which the functions of one character are split into two separate characters, is a regular feature of Homeric epic and other mythic traditions.[3] In the *Odyssey*, for instance, the full set of character functions that Penelope displays on Ithaca are, on Skheria, distributed between the daughter Nausikaa and mother Arete. Similarly, we will observe that Phaethon's character functions in Ovid are in Mark distributed between Herod's daughter and John the Baptist.

Why would Mark do this? In Ovid's tale of Phaethon, he would have ready to hand a gripping vehicle for depicting a tragic, unnecessary death – exactly what would serve his larger narrative purpose for John the Baptist. Ovid's rash Sun, purple-robed, gleaming with emeralds, similarly provides him with an iconic rubric for his own depiction of Herod. But to make a far more negative figure than Ovid's Sun and darken him to villainous depths, Mark taps into the considerably greater potential intrigue available between a father and daughter rather than between father and son. Let alone that he will bestow half his kingdom on a daughter rather than a son, the hint of eroticism in the daughter's dance, with its implicit layer of incest, further undercuts Herod, and increases the cruel senselessness of John's death.

If we consider some of the broader characteristics of the Gospel of Mark, its treatment of the Baptist's death comes into clearer focus. As White observes (106–7),

> Mark ... has often been called "a Passion narrative with an extended introduction" ... much of the first two thirds of the Markan story anticipates the fact of Jesus' death. The story telegraphs the ending not only by having Jesus predict it on three occasions (8:30–31; 9:30–32; 10:33–34), but also by various allusions to the crucifixion throughout the story.

Implicitly, then, the focus on John's death is part of the Markan author's extended thematic treatment of the Passion. The audience is to see the Baptist's death as prefiguring Christ's, given the interconnected trajectories of the two: the particular caprice and cruelty of the former, foreshadowing the injustice of the latter.

Let us then consider the lengthy series of corresponding motifs between the Phaethon and Herod narratives, noting how the correspondences suggest that the Gospels' narratives can be seen as responding to Ovid's account.

The child of a regal father brings about a confrontational meeting with him

Phaethon, having never seen his father, and prompted to doubt his paternity by an acquaintance (1.751–56),[4] seeks reassurance from his mother, Clymene, who encourages him to seek out his father (1.765–79). The son reveals himself as impetuous, given to extravagant urges, when he begs Clymene, by his own life, to help him do this (1.762–64). Mark and Matthew provide no background on Herod's "daughter" before she dances before him. She will reveal herself to have a similar emotional makeup as Phaethon, as we discuss in subsequent motifs. As in Ovid, the high-stakes encounter with her father is in part her mother's idea.

The child is much closer to its mother than its father

Phaethon has lived exclusively with his mother, knowing nothing of his father, save what she has told him.[5] He is highly emotional in his scene with her – hints that he is a somewhat feminized male. In Mark (but not Matthew), the daughter clearly is closer to her mother, and goes to her for advice (6:24–28). Phaethon and Herod's daughter appear to be approximately the same age, adolescents.

The motif is not present in *Iliad* 19 but is with Jacob and Rebecca in Genesis 27, though, Jacob lacks the rash, impetuous nature shared by Phaethon and Herod's daughter.

The child's high-status mother encourages the child to make a demand of its father

In Ovid two characters prompt Phaethon, first Epaphus, and then Clymene. Epaphus' taunt (1.753–54), a motif also present in *Oedipus Rex* (779–80), first spurs Phaethon to desire proof as to his father. Clymene, as wife of the Sun, has a significant, if unspecified, status hinted at when she lifts her arms to the heavens (1.767) to affirm by oath that Phaethon's father is the Sun.[6] To reassure him, she supports his going to confront his father in his temple (1.765–75, esp. 1.775: *si modo fert animus, gradere et scitabere ab ipso*). Her phrasing (*fert animus*) hints at the later tragedy, that Phaethon is rash. In the two Gospels, Herodias fulfills both character functions, those of Epaphus and Clymene. Mark casts Herodias as a vengeful, behind-the-scenes villain (again suggesting a fictional rather than historical approach to character and motivation), both prompting the Baptist's arrest and coaching her daughter to ask for his head.[7] Clymene has no such ulterior motives. Epaphus anticipates, in a lesser degree, some of the meanness of Herodias' character.

This motif is not present in *Iliad* 19 but is in slightly altered form in Genesis 27.

The father is surrounded by a throng of important individuals

When Phaethon approaches his father (2.25–31), he finds him attended by a great many celestial beings,[8] all of whom suggest instantiations of various aspects of the Sun in his role of marking time, hours, days, the week, month, and seasons. As Anderson suggests (1997: 233), "Like a king attended by his courtiers, the Sun is flanked by the 'nobility of time.'"[9] Anderson notes how influential this passage is for later traditions (ibid.), "In this passage, as in the description of the wind Notus in 1.265 ff. and in many later passages of this poem, Ovid is a major poetic inspiration of later allegory [cf. 15.199–213]." Mark specifies as present at Herod's birthday party (6:21), τοῖς γενεσίοις αὐτοῦ δεῖπνον ἐποίησεν τοῖς μεγιστᾶσιν αὐτοῦ καὶ τοῖς χιλιάρχος καὶ τοῖς πρώτοις τῆς Γαλιλαίας, "on his birthday, he held a banquet for his chief officials and for the commanders and for the foremost men in Galilee," which can be seen, *mutatis mutandis*, as corresponding both in rank and approximate number to the Sun's attendants – a euhemerized version of the same essential entourage.

This motif is not present in Genesis 27 but is in *Iliad* 19 where Zeus presides over a full divine council.

In his regal setting, the father proclaims his reckless oath to his rash child

Ovid foregrounds how important oaths are in his narrative by earlier having Clymene swear by the Sun (1.765–72) that Phaethon is his son, *Sole satum* (1.771). As Phaethon approaches him, the Sun is stereotypically regal, wearing a purple robe (2.23: *purpurea velatus veste sedebat*), and attended by several dozen divine attendants.[10] Initially, Phaethon cannot endure to behold his father's radiance (2.22–23). His failure in *even this capacity* highlights how profoundly inappropriate his wish will be, his mortality highlighted against his father's immortality. Eager to assuage his son's anxiety over his paternity, the Sun offers an open-ended gift (2.44–46: *Quodvis pete munus, ut illud / me tribuente feras! Promissi testis adesto / dis iuranda palus, oculis incognita nostris!* As is the custom, attested in Hesiod's *Theogony* (397–401),[11] he swears an oath by the river Styx (2.46: *Dis iuranda palus*), later articulated more clearly, *Stygias iuravimus undas* (2.101).

The dance of Herod's daughter is the vehicle by which she obtains Herod's correspondingly reckless oath. We are given no backstory for why she dances, other than that it is Herod's birthday. In a sense, for Ovid's Sun every day might be understood as his birthday (including the day Phaethon confronts him). Her dance (Mark 6:22) is clearly improper[12] (ἤρεσεν τῷ Ἡρῴδῃ καὶ τοῖς συνανακειμένοις),[13] "it pleased Herod and his guests." Though commentators have argued that it would not be right for her to perform such a dance before outsiders (e.g., Mann 297), I suggest, if we are correct in seeing the dance as erotic, it would have *also been improper to do so before her own father*. Several issues should be raised. Because the daughter would have been instructed by her mother to dance as she does, this means Herod's wife would knowingly be using her to arouse him. If so, there is a hint of incest in her erotic dance before her own father, a motif present in villainous characters in ancient Romances, as between King Antiochus and his daughter in the *Apollonius Romance* (1–4). Herod's oath is quite close to the Sun's in its open-endedness (Mark 6:22–23: Αἴτησόν με ὃ ἐὰν θέλῃς, καὶ δώσω σοι. καὶ ὤμοσεν αὐτῇ ὅτι Ὃ ἐάν με αἰτήσῃς δώσω σοι ἕως ἡμίσους τῆς βασιλεάς μου), " 'Ask me for anything you wish, and I will grant it to you.' And he swore to her, 'Whatever you ask I will give you up to half of my kingdom.' "[14]

In *Iliad* 19 and Genesis 27 the child does not make any request. It is entirely the father's idea to proclaim his oath. The fathers, in turn, have very specific outcomes in mind in their blessings/oaths. They do not utter open-ended blank checks, as do the Sun and Herod, though both end up, nonetheless, bestowing their blessings on the wrong offspring. In her behind-the-scenes manipulation, however, Herodias acts in ways that closely correspond to Hera in *Iliad* 19, who elsewhere seduces her husband to manipulate him (*Iliad* 14.153–351), and Rebecca, who utterly manipulates Isaac in Genesis 27. By contrast, Clymene, though supportive and encouraging Phaethon, pursues no other agenda nor seeks to manipulate the Sun.

However, on hearing his child's request, he grieves, regretting his sworn oath

Both fathers are naïve as to how intractable their children will be and, through their actions, reveal themselves as unworthy of their lofty positions. The Sun, hearing Phaethon's demand, regrets his oath and shakes his head over and over (2.49–52: *paenituit iurasse patrem qui terque quaterque / concutiens inlustre caput ... utinam promissa liceret / non dare*).[15] In Mark and Matthew, Herod grieves (Mark 6:26: καὶ περίλυπος γενόμενος ὁ βασιλεὺς; Matt 14:9: καὶ λυπηθεὶς ὁ βασιλεύς), and in both, his having sworn an oath before witnesses, exacerbates his anguish (Mark: διὰ τοὺς ὅρκους καὶ τοὺς ἀνακειμένους οὐκ ἠθέλησεν ἀθετῆσαι αὐτήν; Matt: διὰ τοὺς ὅρκους συνανακειμένους ἐκέλευσεν δοθῆναι).

The father's regret is also a motif in *Iliad* 19 and Genesis 27.

The child's request causes a death and violates the laws or boundaries of mortal existence

The Sun goes on at length (2.54–102) to explain how Phaethon's request, to drive his special chariot for a day (2.47–48), is not only improper but also contrary to the lot of mortals. In effect, he declares, Phaethon is not asking for a gift but for a horrible punishment (99: *poenam, Phaethon, pro munere poscis!*).[16] Matthew has Herod as having earlier desired the Baptist's death (14:5), but Mark has it quite opposite: Herod likes, respects, and helps protect him (Mark 6:20). Implicit in how criminal Herod's taking of John's life is, the Baptist receives no trial, death by decapitation resembling battlefield atrocity more than a criminal justice system. The added specific, the most iconic detail from the narratives, that his decapitated head be placed on a plate, constitutes an ever-greater, more outrageous violation of human norms for the treatment of the dead.

This motif is not present in *Iliad* 19 and Genesis 27.

The father knowingly enables a tragic act; horrible consequences result

The Sun knows full well what will happen when his impetuous, incapable son attempts to drive the solar chariot (2.60–87). As his failed attempt quickly proves catastrophic, Phaethon wishes he had not made his request (2.182). Shortly after, whole cities and nations are destroyed (2.214), Phaethon hurled from the chariot, leading the Sun in his grief and self-pity to cause an eclipse (2.329–31: *Nam pater obductos luctu miserabilis aegro / condiderat vultus, et, si modo credimus, unum / isse diem sine sole ferunt*; cf. 2.381–85).[17]

Herod is implicitly painted in even more negative terms. With naiveté equal to the Sun's, his ordering the slaying of the Baptist, perhaps having been sexually aroused by his "daughter," makes him more like a murderer than a ruler. Unlike for Phaethon, whatever suffering John may have experienced is omitted from the narratives. The tragedy exists more in who he was and in the callousness and cruelty of all three members of Herod's family to bring about his death.

This motif is not present in Genesis 27 and *Iliad* 19.

Each account provides a larger etiology for related events

Phaethon's disastrous chariot drive leads to several metamorphoses, as in each of Ovid's tales, that provide etiologies for larger aspects of geography, natural history, and even the racial composition of humanity (2.235–71). Anderson sums up the effect of these larger consequences (1997: 227): "a tour de force of metamorphoses as the earth reacts geologically and anthropologically to the unusual proximity of the scorching sun." A second round of metamorphoses involving Phaethon's relatives follows at 2.346–80. John's death impacts Jesus, providing the reason for two significant points in his mission: why he must now go into seclusion (Matt 14:13; Mark 6:30–31) and the termination of the Judean ministry, which he had received from John.[18] As John and Jesus are linked and paralleled in so many ways: Herod's characterization and acts predict those of Pontius Pilate; John's violent end at the hands of authorities predicts Jesus' own. Herod assumes the strongest link between them, even if his assumption is misguided: Ὃν ἐγὼ ἀπεκεφάλισα Ἰωάννην, αὐτὸς ἠγέρθη (Mark 6:16; cf. Matt 14:2). However, as a corollary of the link he perceives, Herod here ironically, unknowingly, predicts Jesus' own resurrection.

This etiological function is present in all four instances of the mythic type, a prominent part of *Iliad* 19 and Genesis 27. Herakles, now subordinated under Eurystheus, will be required to perform his series of labors, instead of serving as the ruler Zeus intended, as Jacob now receives the blessing Isaac intended for Esau, without which he could not become the patriarch he now will.

The corpse is retrieved and given burial rituals by nonfamily members

His body thrown from the chariot, Naiads retrieve Phaethon's corpse, place it in a tomb, and erect an epitaph over it (2.325–26: *Naides Hesperae trifidia fumantia flamma corpora dant tumulo, signant quoque carmine saxum*). In Herod's narratives, the disciples take on this function (Mark 6:29: Καὶ ἀκούσαντες οἱ μαθηταὶ αὐτοῦ ἦλθον καὶ ἦραν τὸ πτῶμα αὐτοῦ, καὶ ἔθηκαν αὐτὸ ἐν μνημείῳ; cf., Matt 14:12: Καὶ προσελθόντες οἱ μαθηταὶ αὐτοῦ ἦραν τὸ πτῶμα, λαὶ ἔθαψαν αὐτόν· καὶ ἐλθόντες ἀπήγγειλαν τῷ Ἰησοῦ). In both myths this is unusual because this a duty typically performed by family members. In Phaethon's case it is more understandable, perhaps, in the considerable geographical distance separating his corpse from his family. Because we know of some of John's relatives (both parents have speaking parts in Luke 1), their not taking part here seems remarkable. It seems likely, therefore, that the Gospels are innovating by having the disciples perform this function – with considerable correspondence to the Naiads – as the transition and connection between the Herod narratives and the larger myth of Christ, deliberate insertion into the larger Christ story.

This motif cannot be present in *Iliad* 19 and Genesis 27.

Part of the corpse is handed over to the child's mother

Clymene, who does not yet know of the tomb the Naiads built, first searches the earth for Phaethon's limbs, then, unsuccessful, his bones (2.333–36). Her doing so resembles episodes in Euripidean tragedy, Pentheus' dismemberment in the *Bacchae*, and Agave's role in his body's recovery, Hippolytus' in his eponymous tragedy, and the lost *Phaethon*.[19] Coming upon the tomb, Clymene weeps profusely over it, then presses her bared breast against her son's name in the epitaph (2.338–39). Though she does not come into contact with his limbs or bones, because this was explicitly her own goal (2.334–37), and vicariously clutches him, the motif is present, if in an altered form.

In the Gospels[20] Herodias receiving John's head on a serving plate has become the tale's iconic center for modern audiences. Two key distinctions are present, of course. The Baptist's head is not that of her own child. Quite unlike Clymene, she exults, we are to assume, in receiving it. On the former, because her daughter uttered the specific request for his head, and is inextricably involved in the motif, and Herodias the sole mother present in the narrative, the motif is recognizably present, if in altered form.

We have demonstrated that Mark's and Matthew's versions of the narrative of Herod's daughter displays affinities with three other narratives, Ovid's Phaethon in particular, but also *Iliad* 19 and Genesis 17, such that they may all be regarded as instances of the same genre of myth. Perhaps surprisingly, however, of the 11 motifs we have traced that the narrative of Herod's daughter shares with Ovid's Phaethon, about two-thirds are *not* present in

Genesis 27: 1, 4–5, 7–8, 10–11.[21] This rather clearly demonstrates that Mark, though certainly aware of that account, is not using Genesis 27 as his primary model or rubric.

While each of the four myths features the naïve father who recklessly utters a speech act, Genesis 27 lacks the other specific details pertaining to him, his oath, sworn before witnesses, details present in both the Phaethon account and *Iliad* 19. Nor does Genesis 27 depict dignitaries present for his interactions with his child. What sets Ovid and the accounts of Herod's daughter apart from Genesis 27 even more is the child's outrageous behavior. Phaethon and Herod's "daughter" both act as spoiled, mother's favorites, who, in their impetuous natures, see nothing wrong in making outrageous demands that violate mortal relations. Because of its rash nature, the child causes a death, resulting in a gruesome dismemberment of the victim, even specified before-hand in Herod's daughter's case.

I thus argue that the author of Mark was not only aware of Ovid's account of Phaethon but also found it relevant for how he wanted to depict the death of John the Baptist. To do so, he interrupts, only here, his sustained focus on Christ. In both Mark and Matthew, right before this, Jesus is in Nazareth, where a prophet has no honor. After the Baptist's death, both Gospels proceed with the miracle of the loaves and fishes. Ovid's Phaethon account offers Mark a rubric for depicting the Baptist's death as caused by cruelty and caprice. Mark's depiction of Herod, building in many ways on the key characteristics Ovid endows his Sun with, also looks *ahead* to Mark's characterization and depiction of Pontius Pilate, which seems similarly shaped by nonhistorical concerns.

Mark uses Phaethon's tale as a model, a paradigm of sorts. But for those among his audience who could be aware that he draws on Ovid's text, he may intend additional meaning in the contrasts he develops. For a reader aware that Herod is modeled on Ovid's Sun, Mark would be consciously employing a form of euhemerization, which we know was embraced by early Christian apologists.[22] Whenever a myth from a polytheistic culture is adapted into monotheism, forms of euhemerization are necessary, in that the functions and characteristics of any god will now be reset in a mortal character. Mark could intend possible oblique comment, even satire, on the Sun, by having a euhemerized Herod correspond in such a nasty way.

If we further compare John and Phaethon, the former is killed for speaking the truth, the latter because of youthful hubris. The parallel, with the contrast, amplifies the pathos of John's murder.

As perhaps an indication of the Markan author's Latinity (and, therefore, access to Ovid), we should note the presence at Mark 6:27 of σπεκουλάτορα, a *Latin* loan word, occurring only here in the Gospels. The *Metamorphoses* was in wide circulation and quickly became a highly influential work, much imitated, a handbook, in some respects, for later generations. It seems high time to consider it as a key part of larger Greco-Roman culture that is reflected in the New Testament.

Notes

1 Cf. Albright and Mann 1971: 176.

2 Cf. Mann 1986: 294: "But the account of the death of John is given no time frame, and Mark is no more familiar with any historical detail than is Matthew."

3 Louden 2006: 3. Cf. Louden 1999: 7; 2006: 80–81, 103, 120–21, 129; 2011a: 153.

4 Because the Hurro-Hittite *Song of Silver* has some of these same motifs (Bachvarova 2016: 27), Phaethon's myth appears to have very deep and ancient roots.

5 Cf. Anderson 1997: 222: "Phaethon's dependency on his mother at this stage seems obvious."

6 Cf., Anderson 1997: 223: "Clymene's gesture of lifting her arms to the sky … is particularly relevant … she swears that the witnessing Sun is the father Phaethon seeks."

7 Note Mann (297) on Mark 6.24–25: "The account suggests an arrangement already made between mother and daughter, which the daughter merely wishes to have confirmed." And again, (297), "The whole reply in the latter part of v. 25 has an air of impertinence about it, as though the girl is fully aware that she has pleased a besotted king who will deny her nothing."

8 As noted previously, we will focus more specifically on the Sun's divine attendants in Chapter 10.

9 Cf. Feldherr 2016: 35: "The Sun sits in the middle of an allegorical depiction of temporal units: days, months, ages, and ultimately Horae."

10 We return to a more detailed discussion of the Sun's temple and his divine attendants in Chapter 10.

11 Cf. *Odyssey* 5.184–86; *Homeric Hymn to Hermes* 518–20.

12 See again Mann: 297: "The undoubted implication of the text is that the dancing was sensual and lascivious."

13 Matthew 14:7 also has ἤρεσεν τῷ Ἡρῴδῃ.

14 Cf. Matthew 14:7: ὅθεν μεθ' ὅρκον ὡμολόγησεν αὐτῇ δοῦναι ὃ ἐὰν αἰτήσηται. In Esther 5:3, 6, the king makes the same offer to her of half his kingdom. Perhaps because of this Esther is often thought to be a significant source for the Herod's daughter narratives, but we should note that it lacks the definitive motifs that it shares with Ovid's Phaethon narrative: the king's paternity has no bearing on the story; as an orphan, Esther does not act at the behest of her mother; the king's offer does not come back to haunt him; there is no tragic death that results. The vast majority of the motifs we pursue here are absent from Esther.

15 Cf. Anderson 1997: 234: "The father is trapped into giving what he knows will kill his son, who insists on having the lethal present, in spite of every effort of the Sun, too late, to dissuade him."

16 Cf. Anderson 1997: 227: "the fatal presumption that asks to do what no mortal can accomplish."

17 Again, see ibid.: 265: "The bumbling Sun, who in other versions closely attended Phaethon at death, here in Ovid can only wallow in self-pity … it was a standard gesture and sign of grief to cover the head with the robe … hiding the face in grief equals going into eclipse."

18 Cf. Mann: 294: "It was the arrest of John that had terminated the Judean ministry which Jesus inherited from the Baptizer."

19 On which see Anderson 1997: 228.

20 Mark 6:28: καὶ ἤνεγκεν τὴν κεφαλὴν αὐτοῦ ἐπὶ πίνακι καὶ ἔδωκεν αὐτὴν τῷ κορασίῳ, καὶ τὸ κοράσιον ἔδωκεν αὐτὴν τῇ μητρὶ αὐτῆς; Matthew 14:11: καὶ ἠνέχθη ἡ κεφαλὴ αὐτοῦ ἐπὶ πίνακι καὶ ἐδόθη τῷ κορασίῳ· καὶ ἤνεγκεν τῇ μητρὶ αὐτῆς.

21 And "However, on Hearing His Child's Request, He Grieves, Regretting His Sworn Oath" is only present in a significantly altered form.

22 We argued for Japheth as a euhemerized version of Iapetos in Chapter 1, Rebecca as a euhemerized Hera in Chapter 3.

6 Luke 24 and Homer

Odyssey 3, *Iliad* 24, and postponed recognition

Luke's depiction of Jesus's appearance to the disciples after his resurrection (Luke 24:15–51) is a rich, intriguing encounter that finds few correspondences in the other Gospels. Of the Gospels' startling divergence in the resurrection narratives in general, Fitzmyer observes (1985: 1534), "[T]he lack of concord in the resurrection narratives of the Gospels is noteworthy." The only parallel Burton and Goodspeed (310–14) cite in the other Synoptic Gospels for Luke 24 are Mark 16:13–14, generally agreed to be a later addition, the "Marcan appendix" (Mark 16:8b–20). Aland (1973: 502–4), in addition to the same passage from Mark, adduces John 20:19–23, though the parallels are quite slender.

We have valuable context for Luke's treatment in what Paul has to say about Jesus's postresurrection appearances. At 1 Corinthians 13:5–8, some decades before Luke is composed, Paul asserts that, after Jesus rose on the third day,

> [H]e appeared to Peter, and afterwards to the Twelve. Then he appeared to over five hundred of our brothers at once, most of them are still alive, though some have died. Then he appeared to James, and afterwards to all the apostles. Last of all he appeared to me too.

This summary is considerably at odds with those in all the Gospels' accounts, as White observes (2010: 112),

> [T]he most striking feature of Paul's account is that some of these earliest oral traditions about Jesus' death and resurrection should have been lost in later oral tradition … James and the other five hundred got dropped from the story.[1]

As White further observes (ibid.), Paul's account omits components that are prominent in the later Gospel versions: no one is said to witness the actual resurrection; no women find the empty tomb. Thus, he concludes, "[E]ach of these episodes, like the Judas character, is a later addition to the story." Differences with Paul's account establish at the outset, then, that the tradition was exceptionally fluid in the matter of the postresurrection appearances.

Differing significantly, then, from Paul (surprising, because scholars often assume that Paul is one of the Lukan author's sources), the Lukan account is a more disciple-centered version. This may reflect the Lukan author's inter-action with the larger traditions of Greek philosophy (White: 336–37, 340), his interest in depicting Jesus, in part, as like the founder of a philosophical school and showing continuity in his students and followers. But even in this respect, there are further surprises: the biggest role given to a disciple is to Cleopas, who has no existence in the New Testament outside of this episode.

But there are other ways in which the Lukan author signals his distance from Mark and Matthew, larger cultural stances. As Bonz notes (2000: 93), Luke is "writing more than twenty years after Mark, and living in a predom-inantly gentile community, now wholly separate from the synagogue." The Lukan author is writing for a largely different audience than Mark, even as some of Paul's letters are addressed to primarily non-Jewish audiences. As noted in the introduction, the author of Luke has consciously shaped his narrative to reflect larger engagement of the contemporary Greco-Roman world. As with his interest in contextualizing Jesus amid Greek philosophical traditions, the Lukan author maps Jesus onto additional cultural nodes of larger Greco-Roman culture to make it easier for his audience to follow, as I note in the following text.

Recent New Testament scholarship has also opened an additional perspec-tive and context for considering the postresurrection scenes. The transfigur-ation scenes (Mark 9:2–8; Matt 17:1–8; Luke 9:28–36), in which Jesus appears to Peter, James, and John, high on a mountain, dazzling white, accompanied by Moses and Elijah, are now interpreted as "displaced appearance" episodes.[2] Thus, the Gospel of Mark, which seems to have had no postresurrection epi-sode (accepting 16:8 as the original ending), nonetheless *prefigures* Jesus in the same mode *in the transfiguration episode*. 2 Kings 2 depicts Elijah as ascending to heaven, and Moses had undergone a busy post-Bible continuation, now depicted in Philo and elsewhere as having ascended to heaven. These contexts thus determine why they are the two depicted with Christ in the transfiguration scenes, as White observes (156), "Who better, then, to come and escort the risen Jesus to heaven than those who had gone before?" While this is a fruitful perspective, it does not shed specific light on the uniqueness of Luke 24.

If we turn to Greek myth, however, considerably more relevant examples and closer correspondences with Luke 24 easily emerge. Bonz, for instance, notes clear larger affinities between classical epic and the broader contours of Luke and Acts (191), "Luke-Acts appears to have drawn inspiration from heroic epic in the manner in which it creates its story as the fulfillment of divine prophecy and the accomplishment of a divine plan." Homeric epic in particular, both the *Odyssey* and *Iliad*, provides highly significant and informative contexts. The larger narrative of Luke 24 parallels the contours of several episodes from the *Odyssey*[3] and one from the *Iliad*. In more than a few respects, Jesus's interactions with the disciples suggest a theoxeny, a traditional, well-established genre of myth in which a god, appearing as a stranger from elsewhere, tests the hospitality of his host.[4] In other respects, the episode of the women meeting the angels at the tomb in Luke 24 recalls the ambiguous and ironic interplay between the disguised Hermes and Priam, as the Trojan king anxiously leaves Troy to recover his son's corpse in *Iliad* 24, as well as Aphrodite's earlier preservation of the corpse. From an additional perspective, Jesus, in deliberately postponing the revelation of his true identity, even among his disciples, conforms to the *Odyssey*'s very specific subtype of recognition scene, "postponed recognition," thematically paralleling Odysseus' interactions with his family and loyal servants in Books 14–24.[5] What might we make of the extensive correspondences Luke 24 demonstrates with Homeric epic? After first exploring the parallels, I will offer some possible interpretations for them.

Because, from the perspective of the *Iliad* and the *Odyssey*, Luke 24 blends three distinct mythic types' I will go through parts of it three times, once for each respective genre of myth. Our model for positive theoxeny will be that in *Odyssey* Book 3, when Nestor and his family graciously receive the disguised Athena, and the scene shortly before, at 2.260–97, when the daughter of Zeus first comes to Telemachos in the form of Mentor, as he prays by the seashore. To more fully establish the behavior and expectations of this genre of myth, we will adduce Genesis 18, also a positive theoxeny. Next, we turn to *Iliad* Book 24, when the disguised Hermes meets with Priam, for the parallels it provides on forms of ironic discourse and the key motif of the immortal character as son of the *Father*. We include brief consideration of a preceding episode in *Iliad* 23, where Aphrodite is depicted carefully preserving Hector's corpse. We will conclude with consideration of several of the *Odyssey*'s *postponed* recognition scenes, and, to more fully establish the behavior and expectations of this type scene, we will adduce parallels from Genesis 43–45, Joseph in Egypt, the only other ancient narrative that also features postponed recognition.

Theoxeny exists in two specific subtypes, both of which feature in the *Odyssey*, Genesis, and Ovid. Perhaps the more familiar is *negative* theoxeny, in which the host passes the crucial test, scrupulously demonstrating his regard for hospitality by correct reception of his unknown guest, but the surrounding community *violates* hospitality in several ways. The principal thread of the *Odyssey*'s plot that features the suitors is an extended negative theoxeny, as the disguised Athena's comments make clear early on (1.227–29). This same mythic subtype is familiar to biblical audiences from Genesis 19. The mob that would take over Lot's house serves as a surprisingly close parallel to the *Odyssey*'s depiction of the suitors.[6]

Positive theoxeny

In positive theoxeny, all the participants behave as they should, honoring and upholding the sacred institution of hospitality. Book 3 of the *Odyssey*, when Telemachos and Athena, disguised as Mentor, visit Nestor, constitutes an extended depiction of positive theoxeny. In this mythic subtype, not only does the host display exemplary hospitality but so does his entire community. This same type is familiar to biblical audiences from Genesis 18,[7] when Abraham and Sara receive their divine guests. To a considerable degree, Abraham's actions closely follow the dynamics of Nestor's reception of the disguised Athena.[8]

Luke 24, however, differs in two ways from conventional theoxenic myth. We are not told that Jesus has altered or changed his appearance or taken the guise of someone else. In the *Odyssey*'s negative theoxeny, Athena assumes the appearance of a foreign man, a Taphian (*Odyssey* 1.105). Genesis is not clear as to the visual appearance of God and the angels in Genesis 18–19, though it seems certain that they are thought to be strangers from elsewhere (cf. Jupiter and Mercury in *Metamorphoses* 8.611–724). Rather, Luke 24:16 specifies that the disciples are unable to identify him (οἱ δὲ ὀφθαλμοὶ αὐτῶν ἐκρατοῦντο τοῦ μὴ ἐπιγνῶναι αὐτόν, literally, "But their eyes were unable to recognize him"). Also, theoxeny, as a subset of hospitality myth, normally begins with a guest's entrance into a host's dwelling or their first meeting right outside the dwelling (as at *Odyssey* 1.103 & ff., 3.31 & ff., Genesis 18:1–15, 19:1–26). But here, Jesus encounters Cleopas (who does not appear elsewhere in New Testament myth) and another unnamed disciple en route to Jerusalem, still some seven miles distant (24:13). The opening of the episode is close to the first scene in Apuleius' *Golden Ass*, where different travelers come together on the same path.

However, the *Odyssey*'s positive theoxeny begins in much the same way, earlier set in motion in Book 2, when, after the unsuccessful assembly, Athena, first taking the form of Mentor, appears to a distraught Telemachos (2.267–68). Offering to become his companion, providing the necessary ship, she will escort him over the sea to Pylos, καὶ ἅμ' ἕψομαι αὐτός, "and I myself will accompany you" (2.286). The encounter does not fully transition to a theoxeny until the two are received in Pylos by Peisistratos and Nestor, some 200 lines later (3.36 & ff.). Athena's sequence of actions in Books 2–3, joining Telemachos, unrecognized, and escorting him on a journey, is much closer to those of Christ in Luke 24, than is Genesis 18's depiction of Yahweh and the angels.

Telemachos and the disciples have both just suffered frustrations and setbacks involving their association with the unrecognized immortal that now stands before them. For Telemachos, the suitors' manipulation of the assembly thwarted the advice given by yesterday's mysterious stranger, whom he later realized is a god (1.323).[9] Telemachos' isolation now at the seashore, after the failed assembly, is thematic as de Jong notes of the context at *Odyssey* 2.260 (2001: 60): "The seashore in the Homeric epics carries connotations of isolation, tension or misery." The disciples have suffered much worse, the apparent loss of their teacher and prophet, betrayed by what is the suitors' counterparts, elements in the Roman Empire and the Jewish church. As Jesus approaches them they are sad (ἐστάθησαν σκυθρωποί: 24:17) and alone. Though attempts have been made to interpret Cleopas from a historical context,[10] his main function in Luke 24 seems to be to serve as a foil, of sorts, to Jesus, which is evident in the meaning of his name (discussed in the following text).

Theoxenies feature considerable irony in the discrepancy between the external audience's awareness of the guest's actual divine nature and the other character's mistaken perception that the stranger is of mortal status. Thus, when Cleopas remarks that the stranger must be the *only* one in Jerusalem who does not know the events of the last few days (Σὺ μόνος … οὐκ ἔγνως τὰ γενόμενα; 24:18), there is remarkable irony in his assumption that his guest has limited knowledge of the events in which he was the actual protagonist. When Jesus replies, playing along, in a sense, "what sort of events" (Ποῖα), he extends the irony into an almost comic modality, which is also typical of positive theoxeny, both in *Odyssey* 3 at Pylos and Genesis 18 at Mamre.

Cleopas explains that they are all upset because Jesus of Nazareth, a prophet, whom he had hoped would be the liberator of Israel, has died, but three days later, his tomb is empty. His lack of comprehension is too much for Jesus (and note the ironic: αὐτὸν δὲ οὐκ εἶδον 24:24, in Cleopas' account of the women, "but they [the disciples] did not see him," juxtaposed with his present circumstances), who essentially says how dull-witted they are (Ὦ ἀνόητοι: 24:25) and criticizes them for being too slow to believe what the prophets had said about these events (καὶ βραδεῖς τῇ καρδίᾳ τοῦ πιστεύειν ἐπὶ πᾶσιν οἷς ἐλάλησαν οἱ προφῆται). Jesus continues by launching into an extensive summary of all the prophecies, from Moses through the later prophets, that refer to himself (τὰ περὶ ἑαυτοῦ: 24:27).

The episode finds a highly relevant precedent in Athena's correction of Telemachos in *Odyssey* 3, while Nestor's guests at Pylos. Nestor, having learned his guest is the son of Odysseus, perceptively suggests that, just as Athena was ever at his father's side, aiding him at Troy, so likewise the goddess will surely help Odysseus' son (3.218–24). But when Telemachos insists there is no way such a thing could happen (3.226–28), or "despairs of divine support," as de Jong describes his circumstances (80), the disguised Athena immediately corrects him,

Τηλέμαχε, ποῖόν σε ἔπος φύγεν ἕρκος ὀδόντων,
ῥεῖα θεός γ' ἐθέλων καὶ τηλόθεν ἄνδρα σαώσαι.
3.230–31

Telemachos, what is this word that should have not gotten past your teeth?
Easily a god, should he wish, can save a man, even from a distance.

She continues, contrasting two different types of homecoming, that like Agamemnon's, slain treacherously at his own hearth (3.234–35), and that she would prefer: to have first suffered many hardships before reaching home (3.232–33), evoking for the audience, but not naming, Odysseus. Her correction of Telemachos' limited understanding of the gods' powers and evocation of Odysseus, the poem's protagonist, has more than a little in common with Jesus's correction of Cleopas. Jesus notes that earlier prophets had emphasized how much this prophet was going to have to suffer (ταῦτα ἔδει παθεῖν: 24:26), much as Athena similarly emphasizes to Telemachos in her description of the type of homecoming she validates (ἄλγεα πολλὰ μογήσας). In so doing, she communicates directly to the audience over Telemachos' head, as Jesus does with Cleopas. Both Jesus and Athena are referring to the respective protagonists of the larger myths, but for Jesus this is himself, where for Athena it is, of course, Odysseus.

The distinction affirms how, from the perspective of the *Odyssey*, Jesus combines in one character what in Greek myth are the two separate roles of hero and god, Odysseus and Athena. However, the *Odyssey* in some later episodes displays the seeds of such an approach in its use of "virtual theoxeny," a series of episodes in which Odysseus plays the role usually taken by a God,[11] and as taken by Jesus in Luke 24, the God testing mortals' hospitality.

The positive theoxeny in Genesis 18 also features the unrecognized divine guest correcting another character's limited views on the power of god. When Sarah overhears Yahweh declare that, when he returns in a year, she will have born a son (18:10), she laughs, knowing she and her husband are both well past a child-bearing age. But the divine guest, hearing her laugh, corrects her limited understanding of his power, first, wondering why she laughed, then asserting, "Is anything impossible for the Lord?" (Septuagint: Μὴ ἀδυνατήσει παρὰ τῷ Θεῷ ῥῆμα). An embarrassed and flummoxed Sarah then dishonestly denies that she had laughed. As Athena in the *Odyssey*, here the divine guest corrects a *relative* of the main character. The main characters (Odysseus, Nestor as well, Abraham) would not have needed the correction.

Back to Luke 24: Jesus's correction of Cleopas' lack of sufficient faith in the prophets is thus a typological equivalent to Athena's correction of Telemachos' doubting the Homeric gods, and Yahweh doing the same with Sarah. But Jesus gives a greatly expanded version of the motif. Here the immortal guest goes the farthest, not only correcting but also criticizing, almost insulting, the unperceiving mortal: "You fools, how slow you are to believe." His correcting Cleopas' insufficient faith incorporates a brief over-view of references to the Messiah, from Moses through the prophets of the Hebrew Bible.

I suggested earlier the possibility of some humor here at Cleopas' expense. In both *Odyssey* 3 and Genesis 18, at this same stage of interaction, the disguised gods participate in wordplays on a character's name, Telemachos, and the as-yet unborn Isaac.[12] When Athena says, "Even *from a distance*," she repeats the first element of *Tele*-machos' name, literally, "fighter *from a distance*." In Genesis 18, the son that will be born to the unbelieving Sara will be named Isaac, the name that echoes the Hebrew word just used to describe her laughter, *yishaq*. Similar wordplay also occurs in New Testament myth, as in the well-known example in Matthew 16:18: "[Y]ou are Peter, and upon this *Rock* I will build my church" (σὺ εἶ Πέτρος, καὶ ἐπὶ ταύτῃ τῇ πέτρᾳ οἰκοδομήσω μοι τὴν ἐκκλησίαν). In Luke 24 the literal meaning of the name Cleopas offers further evidence that he functions much as a *foil* for Jesus. "Cleopas" is clearly a truncated version of the very common Greek name Cleopatras,[13] which even occurs in the *Iliad*, but with the components reversed, for Achilles' boon companion, Patroclos. Such compound proper names are often possessive, that is, "Having a Famous Father," or even "The Father's Glory," the meaning I propose "Cleopas" denotes in Luke 24.[14]

The character called Barábbas, who appears in all four of the Gospels (Matt 27:15–26; Mark 15:6–15; Luke 23:13–25; John 18:38–19:16), in his interactions with Jesus provides relevant contexts for understanding Jesus's interactions here with Cleopas. In the case of the insurrectionary, "Barábbas" literally means, in Aramaic, "Son of the Father." I have argued elsewhere[15] that Barábbas functions as a parodic counterpart to Jesus, much as the beggar Iros does to Odysseus in Book 17 of the *Odyssey*.[16] Iros is also an epithet or nickname for the character, a beggar, whose actual name is Arnaios, whose presence the suitors tolerate, until he loses to the disguised Odysseus, who replaces him as the sole beggar allowed at the suitors' feasts. Ironically, then, Jesus, the true *Son of the Father*, in the Gospels, before Pilate loses to his parodic counterpart, Barábbas, Son of the Father, who has the crowd's favor.

Cleopas also has a "speaking name," as is typical of many characters in myth.[17] "The Father's Glory" is a central notion in New Testament myth, at one level perhaps referring to the visual quality of the heavens, where God is thought to reside, in other ways it expresses the ineffable that is God. Because the Gospels use δόξα for "glory" instead of the older, and very Homeric, κλέος,[18] the *kleos* in Cleopas may be a deliberate archaism, another typical tendency of myth. The Gospels repeatedly associate the Father's Glory with Jesus. In Matthew and in Mark, Jesus declares that the Son of Man will come in the glory of God (Matt 16:27; Mark 8:38), attended by angels. In John, Jesus declares that through his raising of Lazarus, God's glory will be revealed and he will be glorified (John 11:4: δοξασθῇ. In Matthew, Jesus declares that in the world that is to come, "The Son of Man will be seated on his throne of glory" (ἐπὶ θρόνου δόξης: Matt 19:28). When he corrects Cleopas in Luke 24, the unrecognized Jesus emphasizes that the Christ was destined to suffer before "entering into his glory" (εἰσελθεῖν τὴν δόξαν αὐτοῦ: 24:26).

In Luke 24, then, at the same point as in the theoxenies in *Odyssey* 3 and Genesis 18, when wordplays occur on the names of Telemachos and Isaac, the sons of the respective protagonists, Odysseus and Abraham, Jesus corrects and lectures Cleopas, "The Glory of the Father," on how Christ attains the *glory of the Father*. Cleopas' name externalizes and nominally instantiates the divine attribute that Jesus as the risen Messiah now embodies. As Fitzmyer notes, when Christ appears to his disciples and when he again disappears, "glory" can be thought of as the term for the *place* that he now comes from, and to which he retires when he leaves the earthly plane (1985: 1539): "In other words, it is from 'glory,' i.e. from his Father's presence, that the risen Christ appears to his disciples."[19]

Hermes with Priam in *Iliad* 24

The episode at *Iliad* 24.152–468, between the disguised Hermes and Priam, often considered one of the *Iliad*'s most Odyssean episodes,[20] also provides an important context for studying Jesus's meeting with Cleopas in Luke 24. Again, the episode features a similar focus on the unrecognized immortal (in this case Hermes) as the son of the Father. Despite significant differences in conception (e.g., the Gospels offer no depiction of Heaven or God, whereas Homeric epic depicts Olympos, Zeus, and the other gods),[21] the episode characterizes Hermes in ways that are quite relevant to the overall depiction of Christ in New Testament myth.

Zeus sends his son Hermes down (οἱ πομπὸν ὀπάσσομεν Ἀργειφόντην: *Iliad* 24.153; cf. βάσκ' ἴθι, καὶ Πρίαμον κοίλας ἐπὶ νῆας Ἀχαιῶν / ὡς ἄγαγ': 24.336–37) to meet with and escort Priam as the elderly Trojan king undertakes his hazardous mission to pass through Greek lines and ransom his son's corpse. As Zeus for Hermes in *Iliad* 24, in the Gospels Jesus often declares that the Father has sent him; such a saying is formulaic in John (ὁ Πατήρ με ἀπέσταλκεν: John 5:36, καὶ ὁ πέψας με Πατήρ: 5:37 = 12:49; 6:57; 10:36; cf. Luke 2:49; 10:22; 22:29).

Immediately before, the narrator has described Hermes as Zeus' beloved son (Ἑρμείαν, υἱὸν φίλον: 24.333). Zeus further characterizes Hermes as the god who most likes to associate with mortals, σοὶ γάρ τε μάλιστά γε φίλτατόν ἐστιν / ἀνδρὶ ἑταιρίσσαι (24.334–35), a characterization utterly unique within Homeric epic. Milton, showing, in a sense, the conception's compatibility with Christianity, echoes the line in his description of Raphael at *Paradise Lost* 5.221.[22] In the *Odyssey*, Hermes is designated "Son of Zeus, the Runner, Giver of Good Things," Ἑρμεία, Διὸς υἱέ, διάκτορε, δῶτορ ἑάων (8.335), again a divine characterization utterly unique in Homeric epic.[23] In his analysis of the episode, Richardson (307) adduces Aristophanes' description at *Pax*, 392–94: ὦ φιλανθρωπότατε καὶ μεγαλοδωρότατε δαιμόνων. Taken together, Hermes, Zeus' dear son, the god who "most likes to consort with humans, a giver of good things, the most philanthropic and greatest giver of gifts," offers considerable overlap with the ways in which much New Testament myth characterizes Jesus.

When Hermes, having taken the form of a princely young man (κούρῳ αἰσυμντῆρι ἐοικώς / πρῶτον ὑπηνήτῃ, τοῦ περ χαριεστάτη ἥβη: 24.347–48), meets with Priam, much of their dialogue involves ambiguities concerning the status of the "young man" as the son of an important father. Priam addresses him as dear child (24.373), asserting that he is surely the offspring of *blessed parents* (μακάρων … τοκήων), using the same word that Christianity will later use for its saints (*makarios*). The disguised Hermes replies that his father is Polyktor, literally "Mr. Having Many Things," later adding that *his father sent him* to be an escort for Priam (24.437, 461).

Hermes' encounter with Priam also provides contexts for understanding episodes at the beginning of Luke 24. In the immediate background, for both episodes, is the death of the character most important to the human whom the unrecognized immortal has come to escort. Hector, Priam's most important son, prince of Troy, is its greatest warrior, whose name, literally "Upholder (of the City)," instantiates his central importance. To a smaller degree, on a smaller scale, his death offers an approximate parallel to the death of Jesus, with Priam and the Trojans roughly corresponding to Cleopas and the disciples. Because it has been some days since Achilles slew Hector, and he was last seen abusing the corpse, Hermes first allays Priam's anxieties over the state of his son's body, asserting that it lies fresh with dew, its wounds healed, cared for by the blessed (μάκαρες) immortals themselves (24.411–22). The audience knows in fact that Aphrodite and Apollo have been caring for Hector's corpse (23.184–91, 24.18–21): it is in a miraculous state of preservation.

Luke 24 begins with a focus on the women who are coming to Jesus's tomb, bringing spices (ἀρώματα) for the treatment or preservation of his corpse (23:56–24:1). But when they reach the tomb, they find the stone has been rolled away, the body not there, but two "men" in dazzling garments (24:2–4: ἐν ἐσθῆτι ἀστραπτούσῃ), who inform them that Jesus has been resurrected. The women (whom Luke later, 24:10, identifies as Mary of Magdala, Joanna, and Mary, mother of James), in addition to paralleling Priam as he would ransom Hector's corpse, suggest a parallel for the gods' preservation of Hector's corpse in *Iliad* 23–24. In Book 23 a fuller depiction is given of *Aphrodite* anointing Hector's corpse, keeping it in a miraculous state of preservation,

Διὸς θυγάτηρ Ἀφροδίτη
ἤματα καὶ νύκτας, ῥοδόεντι δὲ χρῖεν ἐλαίῳ
ἀμβροσίῳ, ἵνα μή μιν ἀποδρύφοι ἑλκυστάζων.
23.185–87

Aphrodite, daughter of Zeus
by day and by night, was anointing it with rose-scented olive oil,
ambrosial, that he (Achilles) not tear him, dragging.

The verb here used of Aphrodite anointing Hector's corpse, χρίω (*chriô*), is the same verb from which Jesus's epithet, the Christ, literally "having been anointed," derives.

Homeric epic offers additional instances that enlarge our context for understanding Aphrodite's act. In *Odyssey* 10, after Odysseus, having overcome Circe's spell – with Hermes' aid – reaches an understanding with her, she bathes and anoints him (10.364: αὐτὰρ ἐπεὶ λοῦέν τε καὶ ἔχρισεν λίπ' ἐλαίῳ), with the same essential phrase repeated, minus "ambrosial." Shortly afterward, she anoints the rest of his crew in similar formula (10.450: ἐνδυκέως λοῦσέν τε καὶ ἔχρισεν λίπ' ἐλαίῳ). Odysseus and his crew do not age for the year they remain on her isle. Later in the *Odyssey*, Penelope, thematically paralleling Circe in many respects,[24] asks her maidservants to bathe and anoint the unrecognized Odysseus (19.320: λοέσσαι τε χρῖσαί τε). To conclude our sample, back in the

Iliad, when Priam persuades Achilles to ransom Hector's corpse, the Greek hero has his own maidservants bathe and anoint the corpse with the same essential formula (24.587: τὸν δ; ἐπεὶ οὖν δμωαὶ λοῦσαν καὶ <u>χρῖσαν</u> ἐλαίῳ). In Homeric epic, then, these scenes of anointing that use the verb *chriô* convey the notion of extending life, *preserving* life, with perhaps those meanings implicit when used to treat a corpse.

In Mark, the specific connection is made, an anointing of Christ that also serves as preparing for his death, "She anointed my body ahead of time for my burial" (Mark 14:8: προέλαβεν μυρίσαι τὸ σῶμά μου εἰς τὸν ἐνταφια σμόν), though here one of the many other Greek verbs for "anointing" is used. In Matthew 2:11, the third magos' gift of myrrh may, in some respects, also be a first thematic statement of this same theme. At John 19:39, when he helps Joseph of Arimathaea recover Jesus's body, Nicodemus is said to bring myrrh and aloes. When they bind Jesus's *soma* with linens, Nicodemus' contributions are now referred to as "spices" (ἀρωμάτων: 19:40), as of the women at Luke 23:56.

I would thus argue that a literal meaning of "Christ," the anointed, is latent in the episode at the beginning of Luke 24. The women here, in their goal, if unattained, of *anointing* the body of Jesus, suggest a broad parallel for how the *Iliad* depicts Aphrodite, daughter of Zeus, anointing Hector's body, which is like, Christ's, in a similar state of miraculous preservation, though for different reasons.[25]

The two men, or angels (cf. Acts 1:10; 10:30), in dazzling garments (ἐν ἐσθῆτι ἀστραπτούσῃ), have similar interactions with the women, as Hermes with Priam. The places where they meet are thematically parallel. Priam's trip through the battlefield has often been analyzed as an adaptation of a *catabasis*, or trip to the underworld, as de Jáuregui has most recently argued. De Jáuregui notes (2011: 43), "Priam figuratively enters the realm of the dead in *Iliad* 24.349–53," signaled by his passing by the great tomb of Ilos. The women approach the tomb of Jesus. Both sets of characters, figuratively, are in the land of the dead when they meet their respective supernatural beings, Hermes and the two dazzling "men." In Homeric epic, in addition to his other functions, Hermes is the conductor of souls (*psychopomp*) to the underworld. *Odyssey* 24.1–16 depicts him conducting the souls of the slain suitors to Hades, a passage that may be reflected in Isaiah 14:9. His advising Odysseus on how to approach and resist Circe (*Odyssey* 10.277–307) on her otherworldly isle is only a slight modification of this same capacity. There, he is, specifically, "Hermes with the golden staff ... seeming like a young man when his beard first comes in, whose youth is the most graceful" (Ἑρμείας χρυσόῤῥ απις ἀντεβόλησεν ... νεηνίῃ ἀνδρὶ ἐοικὼς / πρῶτον ὑπηνήτῃ, τοῦ περ χαριεστάτη ἥβη). The formulaic expression of his youthful beard also occurs with Hermes as he approaches Priam. On first catching sight of Hermes, Priam is very afraid (δείδιε δ' αἰνῶς ... στῆ δὲ ταφών: 24.358–60). On first seeing the angels, the women are also afraid (ἐμφόβων δὲ γενομένων αὐτῶν καὶ κλινουσῶν τὰ πρόσωπα εἰς τὴν γῆν), much as Priam.

Hermes and the angels both immediately ask pointed, unsettling questions. Hermes, while asking Priam where he is going, emphasizes the danger of the location (μένεα πνείοντας), the hostility of his enemies (δυσμενέες καὶ ἀνάρσιοι), and wonders if he is not afraid (ἔδεισας: 24.362–67). In Luke "the men" tersely ask the women, "Why do you search for the living among the dead" (Τί ζητεῖτε τὸν ζῶντα μετὰ τῶν νεκρῶν: 24:5), instantiating the larger underworld association. As Fitzmyer (1985: 1545) notes, "This query is exclusive to Luke; it replaces the assurance given to the women in the other Synoptics (Mark 16:6; Mat 28:5)." As a general tendency, whenever Luke 24 most notably differs from the other Synoptic Gospels, it most resembles Homeric myth.

Hermes quickly assumes a more reassuring role, asserting he will personally protect Priam, whom he likens to his own father (24.370–71). He goes on to offer even greater reassurance as to Hector's corpse, emphasizing that it is marvelously free from corruption (μιαρός), that the immortals care for it. In Luke the angels now also calm the women, reminding them that all this was earlier prophesied, that he was to be handed over to sinful men, crucified, but resurrected on the third day (24:6–7). Their brief summary could serve as a thematic parallel to Hector's own recent fate, with the miraculous preservation of his corpse partly resembling, but falling short of, the resurrection.

To sum up, Priam's meeting with the unrecognized Hermes has several motifs in common with Luke 24, significant differences notwithstanding. From the perspective of *Iliad* 24, Christ, in Luke 24, serves the functions of the hero who has died, Hector, mourned by his community, his body now in a state of miraculous preservation, with the angels corresponding to Hermes. But in the middle of Luke 24, Jesus resembles Hermes, the immortal who meets with mortals unable to recognize him or perceive his true divine status. In a sense, the women in Luke 24, like Priam in *Iliad* 24, are coming "to ransom" the corpse. The *Iliad*'s vocabulary for ransom is also relevant, deriving from the same root as terms used for Jesus in New Testament myth, that he will serve as the *ransom* for many; λύσις, the noun, λύω, the verb, which in the middle, λύσασθαι is most often used of Priam in Book 24 (*Iliad* 24.118 = 146 = 195; 175, 237, 502, 685). Both Matthew and Mark have the noun, λύτρον, in the same formula (Mark 10:45 = Matt 20:28: δοῦναι τὴν ψυχὴν αὐτοῦ λύτρον ἀντὶ πολλῶν): "he came to give his own soul as ransom/redemption for many." Luke 24 also has the denominative verb, λυτροῦσθαι, which Cleopas employs in his summary of recent events, face to face with the unrecognized Jesus (24:21).

To resume our analysis of how Luke 24 suggests the contours of a Homeric theoxeny: the traditional *hospitality* setting required by a theoxeny soon materializes. After their peripatetic conversation with the stranger, the disciples reach their destination, the village Emmaus. They invite the stranger not only to share a meal but also to stay the night with them (Luke 24: 28–30). Here they act parallel to Telemachos and Nestor with Athena (*Odyssey* 1 and 3), but especially like Lot, who must persuade his reluctant angelic guests to come to his dwelling (Gen 19: 2–3). Jesus is also at first reluctant to stay, until they urge him (παρεβιάσαντο, also at Acts 16:15, of an insistent host).

Having entered, Jesus, the divine guest, as in so many theoxenies (*Odyssey* 1.139–43; 3.40, 65–57; Gen 18:6–8; 19:3; *Metamorphoses* 8.641–88), is given food and full hospitality (Luke 24: 29–30). But when they break bread together, it is Jesus who says the blessing (24:30: εὐλόγησεν). In Steve Reece's (1993) *schema*, this may be analyzed as either, or both, of the following motifs: "*XIV. Visitor Pronounces a Blessing on the Host*" and "*XV. Visitor Shares in a Libation or Sacrifice.*" The *Odyssey* offers the closest parallel to this.[26] In the theoxeny in Book 3, the unrecognized Athena proclaims the prayer to Poseidon, in the midst of Nestor's lavish hecatomb (*Odyssey* 3.55–61).[27] The parallel is an important one because it reiterates that Luke 24, as Athena with Nestor, is a positive theoxeny. As Reece notes (61), the theoxeny at Pylos features an unusual emphasis on prayer and ritual,

> The prevalence of religious rituals in this scene is even more striking when one observes that scenes of sacrifice and libation are functional replacements for the more usual scenes of feast preparation and consumption … here in Pylos, a long description of sacrifice, libation, and prayer intervenes … The guests are given "portions of entrails" … to taste instead of bread and meat, and the wine that is offered is designated for *libations* rather than for drinking.

As Brown (1966: 162) notes, this portion of Luke 24 clearly reflects the *later* tradition of the Eucharist.

The episode concludes with Jesus's sudden disappearance from their sight, (καὶ αὐτὸς ἄφαντος ἐγένετο ἀπ᾽ αὐτῶν; 24:31), which finds multiple parallels in Homeric theoxeny. When Athena as Mentes leaves Telemachos in Book 1 of the *Odyssey*, she vanishes just as suddenly and mysteriously (Ἡ μὲν ἄρ᾽ ὣς εἰποῦσ᾽ ἀπέβη γλαυκῶπις Ἀθήνη / ὄρνις δ᾽ ὣς ἀνοπαῖα διέπτατο: *Odyssey* 1.319–21, "having spoken the grey-eyed Athena flew away like a bird"). West suggests (116), "[W]e are surely meant to suppose that [s]he suddenly vanished and Telemachus saw instead a bird flying overhead."

Even closer to Luke 24, however, is how Athena departs from the positive theoxeny at Pylos. Initially, she does so in much the same manner, Ὣς ἄρα φωνήσασ᾽ ἀπέβη γλαυκῶπις Ἀθήνη / φήνῃ εἰδομένη (3.371–72), "having spoken the grey-eyed Athena, seeming like a vulture, flew away." But this time, Nestor, who earlier deduced that Athena *might* aid Telemachos, as she was wont to aid his father, recognizes that the bird was the daughter of Zeus, and vows a calf, with horns tipped in gold (3.375–84). West notes (183): "εἰδομένη must mean that the goddess assumes the form of a bird."[28] As to the ornithomorphic manner of Athena's departure, elsewhere in New Testament myth a similar conception of deity seems at work, particularly in connection with John's baptism of Christ. In each of the Gospels the Spirit descends like a dove (Matt 3:16: ὡσεὶ περιστεράν; Mark 1:10; ὡς περιστερὰν = Luke 3:22 = John 1:32).

Beyond our discussion of Luke 24, the basic idea or form of theoxeny is alive and well throughout the New Testament. Perhaps the fullest statement of this mythic type is Paul's command in Hebrews, τῆς φιλοξενίας μὴ ἐπιλανθάνεσθε· διὰ ταύτης γὰρ ἔλαθόν τε ξενίσαντες ἀγγέλους (Heb 13:1–2). But perhaps the most important theoxenic statement in New Testament myth comes from Jesus, when, in Matthew 25, he makes hospitality one of the litmus tests for the Day of Judgment,

> ἐπείνασα γὰρ καὶ ἐδώκατέ μοι φαγεῖν, ἐδίψησα καὶ ἐποτίσατέ με, ξένος ἤμην καὶ συνηγάγετέ με.
>
> Matt 25:35

> For when I was hungry, you gave me to eat, when thirsty, to drink, when I was a stranger, you welcomed me.

> ἐπείνασα γὰρ καὶ οὐκ ἐδώκατέ μοι φαγεῖν, ἐδίψησα καὶ οὐκ ἐποτίσατέ με, ξένος ἤμην καὶ οὐ συνηγάγετέ με.
>
> Matt 25:42–43

> For when I was hungry, you gave me nothing to eat, when thirsty, nothing to drink, when I was a stranger, you did not welcome me.

There are several other relevant passages throughout the Epistles.[29]

Postponed recognition

The climax of an ancient Romance is the *recognition* scene between the protagonist (who has been absent from home for years, often 20) and his family members or other close associates, who have long presumed him dead. Recognition scenes are thus the core and climax of the "happy ending," the central marker of the restoration of identity and cyclical movement that typifies the romance story type. There are several different subtypes of recognition scenes, depending on a few key variables. Are *both* parties ignorant of each other's identities, or just one? How long does it take before the other member learns the protagonist's identity? Based on these distinctions, recognition scenes can be classified into specific subtypes. Euripides, for instance, prefers his recognitions develop with *both* characters *unaware* of each other's true identities (*Ion, Iphigenia in Tauris*). Shakespeare also uses this same subtype exclusively (*Pericles, Cymbeline, The Winter's Tale*). Of all the many ancient Romances that survive, and feature recognition scenes, only the *Odyssey*, and Genesis' account of Joseph in Egypt (37, 39–46), employ the specific subtype of *postponed* recognition. In this type the protagonist refrains from revealing his identity, though in the presence of relatives or close associates, for quite some time. In the *Odyssey*, Athena commands Odysseus to proceed this way, so he can first test the loyalty of everyone he encounters. In the myth of Joseph in Egypt, when Joseph's brothers come to Egypt for grain, Joseph deliberately refrains from revealing his identity. The narrative does not give a specific reason, but implicitly he too wishes to test his brothers because of how they treated him 20 years earlier, and perhaps seeks revenge.

As with theoxeny, recognition scenes also employ pronounced forms of irony. In the *Odyssey*, in one of the poem's favorite themes, as the unrecognized Odysseus stands before Eumaios, Eurykleia, Penelope, or Laertes, each character is prompted to think of the long-lost, presumably absent hero, but remains unable to recognize him right beside them. So it is with Joseph's brothers in Egypt (Gen 42, where they are also prompted by their feelings of guilt regarding how they had treated him), and so it is here in Luke 24. As Jesus approaches his disciples, he hears them in heated discussion and asks what they are debating. Cleopas, in his reply to the stranger, speaks almost entirely about Jesus, unaware that that is precisely the individual he now addresses. In his decidedly ironic ignorance, Cleopas conforms to the repeated pattern of behavior, just noted, operative throughout the entire *Odyssey*. This is even true in episodes of the *Odyssey* before the hero has returned home. For instance, Odysseus' final locale before reaching Ithaka, is the island of Scheria, among the Phaiacians. For his first two days there, he does not reveal his identity. Very like Cleopas, the Phaiacian epic singer, Demodokos, performs two whole narratives (8.73–83, 8.499–521) about Odysseus, who remains unrecognized by him or by his audience while he sits among them.

But the motif becomes especially frequent after he has reached his island, with instances recurring throughout Books 14–24. In most of the *Odyssey*'s recognition scenes, while Odysseus maintains his disguise, he nonetheless talks about Odysseus in the third person, typically asserting, or "*prophesying*," that he knows "*Odysseus*" will soon return, as for instance, he asserts to his loyal swineherd, Eumaios (14.321–33). Of many instances of postponed recognition in the *Odyssey*, the most celebrated is Odysseus' interview with Penelope in Book 19.[30] From the perspective of the Gospels, in many of the *Odyssey*'s recognition scenes, Odysseus' now achieved homecoming resembles a resurrection because many assumed he is dead.

However, in many respects, the pattern for all the *Odyssey*'s postponed recognition scenes is established by Athena, when she appears to Odysseus in Book 13 (13.221–23), in the form of a shepherd, ἀνδρὶ δέμας εἰκυῖα νέῳ, ἐπιβώτορι μήλων / παναπάλῳ, οἷοί τε ἀνάκτων παῖδες ἔασι (13.222–23). Though Hoekstra in his commentary (1989: 178) quotes the *scholia*, asserting that "in Homer sons of kings and nobles guard the flocks," the juxtaposition of *herdsman* and *son of a king* is intriguing from the perspective of New Testament myth, which thematically figures Jesus in similar forms, using the same word for shepherd as the *Odyssey*, ποιμήν (Matt 26:31; John 10:11, 15; 1 Pet 5:4). This scene between Athena and Odysseus is also unexpectedly relevant to our study of Luke 24 for its central use of another motif, key to New Testament myth.

The unrecognized Jesus, in his reply to Cleopas, emphasizes that the Christ *had* to *suffer*, ἔδει παθεῖν τὸν Χριστὸν (24:26). New Testament myth repeatedly places significant emphasis on a *suffering* Messiah, Δεῖ τὸν Υἱὸν τοῦ Ἀνθρώπου <u>πολλὰ παθεῖν</u> Luke 9:22 = Mark 8:31; πολλὰ παθεῖν: Matt 16:21. However, as Fitzmyer emphasizes (1985: 1565), discussing this passage (24:26), "that the Messiah must *suffer* ... The notion of a suffering messiah is not found in the Old Testament or in *any* texts of pre-Christian Judaism" (italics mine).[31] In *Odyssey* 13, after the daughter of Zeus reveals her true identity and assumes her normal form, she outlines her agenda for how Odysseus is to proceed against the suitors, who have now taken over his palace. She specifies and emphasizes the suffering Odysseus is destined to endure (ὅσσα τοι <u>αἶσα</u> ... <u>κήδε</u>' ἀ<u>να</u>σχ<u>έσ</u>θαι: 13.306–7). She restates the theme again, now articulating it in essentially the same formula that occurs in all three synoptic Gospels, σιωπῇ / <u>πάσχειν</u> ἄλγεα <u>πολλά</u>: 13.309–10, "*to suffer many pains* in silence." The suffering of Odysseus, in fact, is thematic throughout the *Odyssey*, strongly foregrounded in the proem, <u>πολλὰ</u> ... <u>πάθεν</u> ἄλγεα <u>ὃν</u> κατὰ <u>θυμὸν</u>, "he suffered many pains in his heart" (1.4). Moreover, we already saw previously in our discussion of how Athena, in the positive theoxeny with Nestor, corrected Telemachos' limited view of the gods' powers, noting that she, though clearly referencing Odysseus, would prefer to have first *suffered many hardships* (ἄλγεα πολλὰ μογήσας) before reaching home (3.232–33). Because of its complete absence from the Hebrew Bible, I thus suggest the *Odyssey* should be considered as a possible source for this key motif in New Testament myth.[32]

In Luke 24 Jesus continues his discourse to Cleopas giving a reason for the suffering, οὐχὶ <u>ταῦτα</u> ἔδει <u>παθεῖν</u> τὸν Χριστὸν καὶ εἰσελθεῖν εἰς τὴν δόξαν αὐτοῦ (24:26: "was it not necessary that The Christ *suffer these things* to enter into his *glory*?"; emphasis mine). This is again quite close to a motif and central concern in both Homeric epics. Though Athena, in her postponed recognition scene with Odysseus in *Odyssey* 13, does not specify that he will win glory for his suffering, moments later, she does employ the same motif, but of Odysseus' son, Telemachos (ἄλγεα πάσχῃ ... <u>ἵνα κλέος ἐσθλὸν ἄροιτο</u>: 13.418–22). She also does earlier in the poem's first divine council, programmatic for the entire plot, where it is her central justification for visiting Odysseus' son, in the poem's opening theoxeny, "so that he may have noble fame among men" (ἵνα μιν κλέος ἐσθλὸν ἐν <u>ἀν</u>θρώ<u>ποισιν</u> ἔχῇσιν: 1.95). Much of what Odysseus endures is also for the purpose of winning further epic fame, κλέος, Homeric epic's key word for "glory," the same element preserved as first component in the name "Cleo-pas."

The cardinal passage that articulates Homeric epic's concern with *kleos* is *Iliad* 9.413. Here Achilles relates how his mother, the goddess Thetis, prophesied to him that if he continues to fight at Troy he will not return home, but his "fame will be imperishable" (ἀτὰρ κλέος ἄφθιτον ἔσται). In the present time of the *Odyssey*, Odysseus has already won *kleos* (9.20), and Orestes, whom several characters hold up as a potential paradigm for Telemachos, has also (1.298). Other than as a component in Cleopas' name, *kleos* elsewhere only occurs once in the New Testament (1 Pet 2:20), instead, δόξα serves in its place, as evident in the term doxology.

The *Odyssey*'s postponed recognition scenes give us a context for considering Jesus's somewhat harsh tone with Cleopas. When Christ virtually insults him (24:25: ἀνόητοί) for his inability to understand and apply the prophecies he claims to follow, he resembles how Odysseus, as he questions his wife and father, causes them to break down and cry, still withholding his true identity, still seeming to be the wanderer from afar. In Genesis, Joseph goes even further in his abuse, falsely accusing his brothers of theft, and even imprisoning his youngest brother, Benjamin. For the external Christian audience, however, Cleopas instantiates a personal form of recognition, perhaps intended as a model that individual believers will have to experience and pass through.

Why would Luke 24 have structures and motifs in common with Homeric epic? Though the positive theoxeny in Genesis 18 and the postponed recognitions in Genesis 43–45 also offer parallels to the episodes in Luke 24, those parallels visible in the *Odyssey*, especially in Books 2–3 and in *Iliad* 24, are, in each case, closer to the specific details found in Luke 24. Furthermore, as we observed, Luke 24 also exhibits parallels with the episode preceding the *Odyssey*'s positive theoxeny, Athena appearing to Telemachos (*Odyssey* 2.267–96), unrecognized by him, in the form of Mentor, a more far-reaching parallel that encompasses multiple episodes.

Recent scholarship on the Gospels (e.g., Freeman 2005: 90) suggests that their authors may have started with collections of the sayings of Jesus. To adapt and expand a collection of sayings and teachings into memorable narratives the Gospel authors generated contexts in which these sayings would take place. Suitable contexts were readily available to them in a variety of forms, from a variety of sources. Until fairly recently, scholars have tended to place episodes from the Gospels largely within Hebrew Bible contexts, and other near eastern texts, to the relative exclusion of texts from Greek myth. Homeric epic, which had never ceased being at the core of the Greco-Roman education system, as Sandnes (2009) well demonstrates, needs to be more frequently consulted as a relevant context for the Gospels.

Homeric episodes provide a context for New Testament myth, just as they do for the Hebrew Bible. Early Christian writings overwhelmingly demonstrate that Christians saw parallels between their own sacred narratives and Greek myths (Acts 17, Paul's appearance in Athens, is premised upon such resemblances), and were often troubled by such resemblances.[33] Unable to account for the similarities logically (diffusion was not considered), many embraced Justin's fantasy, dependent upon the supernatural, that the earlier Greek versions must be demonic distortions of the later Christian narratives (discussion in Taylor 2007: 156–57), essentially a bizarre version of the *ad hominem* attack. This fantastic, nonrational view, which presupposes belief in the reality of demons, still finds currency in our culture. The kinds of parallels I have noted suggest that Homeric narrative still exerted, in a broad underlying sense, an archetypal, if indirect, influence on mythical narratives in the larger Greek-speaking world. Bonz argues for this author's intentional incorporation of epic features (2000: 190): "Luke's narrative has ... incorporated with evident skill, if not real polish, a number of the stylistic and dramatic devices characteristic of Greco-Roman epic in general." More specifically, she argues that classical epic was uniquely relevant to the larger purposes and agenda of the author of Luke (189),

> Of all the literary forms that were popular in the late-first-century Greco-Roman world, only epic could truly bridge the gulf between the seriousness of high literature and the accessibility of popular lit ... heroic epics, whether historical or mythological, were serious works addressing the most profound issues of human destiny in ways that both inspired and entertained their audiences.[34]

If we use context, then, to determine the most expected and traditional components shared by each member of a group of narratives, we can focus on the less common, or even unique, elements that stand out in a specific narrative, in this case, elements unique to Luke 24. Because Cleopas does not occur elsewhere in the New Testament – it is unique to Luke 24 – this increases the likelihood that the author of the Gospel has drawn on, or been influenced by, an *external* source. I have made a case for his deriving some of the broad outlines of the only episode in which Cleopas figures from Homeric epic in the three different types of Homeric contexts we have considered. Above all, Athena's interactions with Telemachos and Nestor in *Odyssey* 2–3 repeatedly provide very specific correspondences to Luke 24, more so than any other texts. The gods' preservation of Hector's corpse in *Iliad* 23 and Hermes' subsequent interactions with Priam to help him retrieve the corpse in *Iliad* 24, as well as his interventions with Odysseus in *Odyssey* 10, provide highly relevant parallels to the women in Luke 24 as they attempt to recover, as they assume, the corpse of Christ. The extraordinary irony when Cleopas, with his decidedly Homeric name, asks the unrecognized Christ, "Are you the only person staying in Jerusalem not to have heard the news of what has happened in the last few days" (Luke 24:18), instantiates one of the *Odyssey*'s favorite scenarios. The Gospels as a group *separate* themselves from the Hebrew Bible's traditions of the messiah in their repeated emphasis on the *suffering* that he must endure. Yet as we have seen, that Jesus must do so is expressed in virtually the same formula as Athena declares of Odysseus in the *Odyssey*. We know that Luke has been shaped by patterns and events outside of its immediate narrative objectives because it is commonly held, for instance, that Luke 24 has been reshaped to reflect the chronologically later conventions of the Eucharist.[35] Whenever Luke 24 has a most noticeable departure from the other Synoptic Gospels is when it most resembles Homeric epic.

Notes

1 Cf. White 2010: 147: "The post-resurrection *appearances* to Peter and the 12, 'the five hundred,' James and the apostles, and Paul were the first and most important witnesses to the resurrection story."

2 See ibid.: 154–56, especially.

3 Throughout my treatment here, I build on Taylor's valuable discussion (2007: 128–30, 132).

4 On theoxeny in general, see Reece 1993: 47–57, 181–87. For extensive analysis of theoxeny in the *Odyssey*, see Louden 2011a: 30–56. On the Gospel of John employing the conventions of theoxenic myth (though he does not use the term), note Larsen 2008: 219: "From the outset of the narratives, Jesus appears as a stranger from heaven."

5 On the *Odyssey*'s recognition scenes in general see again Louden 2011a: 72–92. See Larsen on recognition scenes in the Gospel of John.

6 For specific comparison, see ibid.: 33–36, 43–52, 303–11. Negative theoxeny is also the mythic type Ovid uses in his depiction of Baucis and Philemon, *Metamorphoses*, 8.611–724. It is also arguably present in New Testament myth, Matthew 25:42–43.

7 And see Ovid, *Fasti* 5.493–544, when Jupiter, Neptune, and Mercury visit Hyrieus.

8 For discussion, see Louden 2011a: 36–41.

9 de Jong (2001: 60) characterizes his prayer to the unknown god that had earlier visited him as "despondent."

10 E.g., R. B. Brown (1970: 163), on the possibility that he is the brother of Joseph, Jesus's foster father, though some of the testimony on which his identification is based is quite late.

11 See discussion in Louden 2011a: 44–54.

12 See discussion in ibid.: 39

13 Orr 1976: 669; Fitzmyer 1985: 1563. Fitzmyer noted that this shortened form is also attested in Greek *ostraca* in Egypt. A relevant parallel instance is *Antipas*, also obviously shortened for *Antipatros*, as Fitzmyer observes in ibid.: 1563.

14 Ibid.: 1555, briefly raises the possibility that Luke invented his name.

15 See discussion in Louden 2011a: 274–75.

16 See ibid.: 273–74.

17 The *Odyssey* has many: Eurylochos, Antinoos, Elpenor; cf. Thersites in the *Iliad*.

18 Κλέος occurs only once in the New Testament, 1 Peter 2:20.

19 Cf. Fitzmyer (1985) on Luke 24:36–43, "In this 1st scene of the unit the risen Christ again appears from 'glory'" (1574).

20 Cf. Richardson 1993: 308–10.

21 New Testament myth only portrays Heaven in the Book of Revelation, and there, only in a highly stylized, symbolic manner.

22 "[T]he sociable Spirit, that deigned To travel with Tobias."

23 See Dee 1994: 139. Though a plural occurs, θεοὶ δωτῆρες ἐάων (*Odyssey* 8.325), Hermes is the only individual god specified by the formula.

24 See discussion at Louden 1999: 9–14, 32–35.

25 See Fitzmyer (1981: 684–87) and Louden (2011a: 269–71) for larger discussion of the New Testament scenes in which a woman anoints Jesus. See also Luke 4:18, where Christ uses ἔχρισεν of himself.

26 Though the onset of evening as a factor is also present in the negative theoxeny in Genesis 19.

27 See Reece: 61: "The incorporation of these strangers into the social group is powerfully expressed by Pisistratos' invitation to participate in the performance of religious rituals: sacrifice, libation and prayer."

28 In a further parallel with Greek myth, Fitzmyer (1985: 1568) also notes that ἄφαντος, used of Christ's sudden disappearance in Luke 24 is also used in

Euripides' *Helen* of the disappearance of the phantom Helen (βέβηκεν ἄλοχος σὴ πρὸς αἰθέρος πτυχὰς / ἀρθεῖσ' ἄφαντος· οὐρανῷ δὲ κρύπτεται: 605–6).

29   Galatians 4:14: ἀλλὰ ὡς ἄγγελον θεοῦ ἐδέξασθέ με, ὡς Χριστὸν Ἰησοῦν; Romans 12:13: ταῖς χρείαις τῶν ἁγίων κοινωνοῦντες, τὴν φιλοξενίαν διώκοντες; Titus 1:8: ἀλλὰ φιλόξενον, φιλάγαθον, σώφρονα, δίκαιον, ὅσιον, ἐγρατῆ; 1 Timothy 3:2: φιλόξενον; 1 Peter 4:9: φιλόξενοι εἰς ἀλλήλους ἄνευ γογγυσμοῦ; cf. 2 Maccabees 6:2: "the sanctuary on Mount Gerizim he was to dedicate to Zeus God of hospitality."

30   For a fuller discussion, see Louden 2011a: 78–98.

31   Cf. Mann (1986: 346), and Fitzmyer (1981: 780), "There is no suffering Son of Man figure in the OT. It has often been asked whether the notion of 'suffering' is derived from the Servant of Isa 52:13–53:12 … But the extent to which the 'suffering Son of Man' is to be related to that Isaian passage may be debated … there is no evidence that Jews in Jesus' day associated the Isaian Servant texts with the Messiah."

32   Though absent from John, the motif continues to be thematic elsewhere (Acts 3:18, 17:3; Heb 2:18, 5:8, 9:26, 13:12; 1 Pet 2:21, 2:23, 4:1.

33   See discussion in Taylor: 137–43.

34   Cf. Bonz 2000: 190: "If, therefore, Luke was seeking an effective and widely appealing literary means of presenting the profound significance of the Christian kerygma and its connection with the creation of a newly constituted people in the furtherance of God's plan for a universal human destiny, then a Christian prose adaptation of heroic epic, in the form of a response to its most famous Roman imperial example, may have presented itself as a uniquely promising form of proclamation." Though her own argument is the Lukan author consciously applies forms of organization derived the *Aeneid* in particular

35   E.g., Brown: 162: "[B]efore this tradition [24] reached Luke, it had been modified by the Eucharistic liturgy; it follows the sequence of the latter: a reading and explanation of Scripture (vv. 25–27) and the breaking of bread (v. 30)."

7 Euripides' *Alcestis* and John's Lazarus (John 11:1–44, 12:1–8)

Along with its incompatible chronology, of the many differences between John and the Synoptic Gospels, as White reminds us (2010: x, 166, 208), perhaps most striking is that here Jesus' raising of Lazarus is the immediate cause for his execution, where the cleansing of the Temple is in the others.[1] Not only does the Lazarus myth only have this key function in John but also the episode does not even appear in the Synoptics. This is in keeping with larger tendencies of the fourth Gospel, which generally treats Christ's miracles differently than the other three. It has the fewest miracles of any of the Gospels. Of its seven, only two have clear parallels with the other three accounts.[2]

John clearly reflects a stronger break, in many respects, with larger Jewish tradition.[3] Instead, we have strong indications, as with Luke, of greater affinity with Greek ideas and cultural paradigms.[4] One of these is the broadly Greek idea of the "divine man," a lens through which historical figures such as Pythagoras and Empedocles were later seen, and perhaps less historical personages such as Asclepius.

Stepping back a bit, we can note that at the core of much ancient Mediterranean mythology is the figure who can transcend the boundaries of mortality. Far more common in Greek than in Israelite myth are characters who do so in a heroic mode, from Odysseus, who brings his crew back from Hades (and from Polyphemos' cave), to the only partially successful Theseus, who, in the middle of his own journey, becomes imprisoned in the underworld, needing another hero to win his release. Greek myth also has figures who transcend mortality by nonheroic means. Orpheus, who, having descended to the underworld, persuades Hades and Persephone to allow his wife to return to the surface, is perhaps the best known in our era. But we can also include the slippery Sisyphus, who does so through sheer cunning, though his triumph proves short-lived. Of all such Greek heroes, however, none is more closely associated with a triumph over death than Heracles, the special son of Zeus, who does so thematically in several of his 12 labors, most emphatically in his successfully retrieving Cerberus from Hades, and rescues Theseus while he is trapped in the realm of the Dead. His horrible suffering at his death and subsequent translation to divine status also have more than a little in common with matters at the core of Christian myth.

But more like Christ, in other respects, is Asclepius, son of Apollo. He transcends death through another means: he inherits his father's supernatural powers of healing. The miraculous healer brings not only Hippolytus back to life but also scores of others, according to the ancient testimonies.[5] Of special note, in addition to these key correspondences, he is slain for bringing a man back to life. Both saviors, Heracles and Asclepius, as well as Orpheus, figure in Euripides' *Alcestis*,[6] which climaxes in the title character's return from death.[7] Perhaps no other episode in the Gospels better illustrates Christ as the savior who can bring someone back from the dead than the story of Lazarus in John (11:1–44, 12:1–8).

The myths of Alcestis and Lazarus contain several parallels, some generic, others highly specific. Comparison of the two myths can serve several purposes. Highlighting the parallels brings a new perspective and greater understanding to each narrative because each can now provide a context for the other, allowing closer examination of the series of motifs common to both. Comparison also suggests that both narratives might be seen as separate, distinct instances of a specific genre of myth. But comparison also raises the possibility of diffusion or influence: the much older, well-known myth of Alcestis serves as a possible source for John's account of Lazarus. Though the Synoptics' accounts of Christ healing Jairus' daughter (Matt 9:18–26; Mark 5:21–43; Luke 8:41–56) offer some correspondences (as we note in the following text), the *Alcestis* and John 11–12 have significantly more in common with each other than with these accounts.

Let us first note some significant differences, which have hindered recognition of the more important similarities. First, differences between polytheistic and monotheistic myth impact some events. Euripides' play, for instance, has two gods onstage, Apollo and Thanatos, which is impossible for Hebrew Bible myth. The extremely complex backstory also includes other gods, one of whom, Zeus, the sky father, corresponds to the Father in the New Testament. Lazarus simply cannot become ill through any means resembling the intricate series of interconnected events that causes Alcestis' death.

Another difference is perspective. Lazarus' myth is told from the point of view of Christ, who is the protagonist, whereas the *Alcestis* is told from the perspective of Admetus, not Heracles, the figure corresponding to Christ. Admetus has a significant role, but is not the protagonist. Functionally correspondent to Admetus, however, is Lazarus' sister, Mary. Furthermore, Jesus is specifically depicted as a healer, whereas Heracles will be a savior through more traditionally heroic means. But the *Alcestis*, in its several references to the miraculous healer Asclepius (4, 122–29, 966–71), evokes a tone and conception similar to Christ's own means with Lazarus.[8] Early Christians were aware of Christ's close similarities to Asclepius, as Edelstein and Edelstein demonstrate. Their citation of Justinus is representative (1998: 48–49),

When we say that He [Jesus] made well the lame and the paralytic and those who were feeble from birth and that he resurrected the dead, we shall seem to be mentioning the deeds similar to and even identical with those which were said to have been performed by Asclepius.[9]

As White observes (56), "The hero-god Asclepius ... was commonly called savior." However, bringing mortals back to life is more complicated in the *Alcestis* than in John, because of the fully polytheistic cosmos in which the myth is set. In the *Alcestis*' backstory Apollo narrates how Asclepius, the miraculous healer and his own son, is slain at Zeus' insistence (3–4), precisely because *he brought Hippolytus back to life*. Zeus, however, will validate having *his* son Heracles bring Alcestis back to life, though he did not support Asclepius having done so for Hippolytus. In John 11–12, the Father implicitly supports Jesus' restoration of Lazarus throughout. Because the episode is presented as glorifying Christ, in the monotheistic New Testament there are no multiple divine perspectives that could conflict with one another, as we find between Zeus, Apollo, and Thanatos in the *Alcestis*.

There are also significant differences in tone. Greek myth tends to focus on heroes and royalty, whereas New Testament myth, for the most part, depicts Christ's interactions with more common folk. Thus, Alcestis is a queen, Lazarus apparently a common man, whose position and vocation are never even specified. Furthermore, Lazarus is a *silent* character, a cipher, whose speech and thoughts are never depicted (nor is the cause or type of his illness). Everything about him remains generic. Alcestis, however, is fully individuated as a character, given specific character motivations to a considerable degree, speaking at length in the opening scenes, though assuming a Lazarus-like silence at the end. Lazarus has no active role in his myth, other than to be brought back from death, whereas Alcestis is articulate, makes demands that affect the plot and, with Euripidean realism, comments on her dilemma. Euripides also employs several comedic elements in his plot, elements largely alien to John's narrative techniques, though we will discern a few seemingly comic touches. These largely culture-specific differences notwithstanding, the larger structure and specific events of the two narratives not only have at least 12 common motifs, but perhaps more important, their larger concatenation corresponds closely, as we now consider.

Jesus and Heracles are both linked by friendship and hospitality to the mortal they will bring back from death

Hospitality is Admetus' defining characteristic in the *Alcestis* (8, 68, 538–605, 747–50, 809, 830, 858, 1120, 1148, 1151).[10] In both Greek and biblical myth, hospitality is *sacred*; those who uphold it demonstrate their exemplary piety and morality.[11] Characters who correctly uphold the institution, which in Greek myth is watched over by Zeus (*Odyssey* 9.270–71, 14.283–84; *Iliad* 13.624–25), are rewarded. In the Hebrew Bible, Abraham's son Isaac is depicted as a miraculous gift from God after his and Sara's hospitable reception of their mysterious guests (Gen 18). Her subsequent conception is implicitly a miracle because Abraham and Sara are both in their 90s.[12] The episode underscores the rewards given those who display hospitality because, without legitimate male offspring, not only can Abraham not become the patriarch he has been prophesied but also the Hebrew Bible and Judaism would not exist unless he has this son. In the New Testament, Matthew makes hospitality the basis of the determination between eternal salvation and condemnation: "When I was a stranger, you took me into your home" (Matt 25:35).[13]

In the *Alcestis* Admetus' exemplary hospitality to Heracles resolves his crisis. Zeus' son brings Alcestis back from the dead explicitly because of the hospitality and friendship Admetus has shown him (830–31, 842, and especially 854–59). Much as Heracles to Admetus, Jesus is repeatedly depicted as Lazarus' friend (ὃν φιλεῖς: 11:3; ὁ φίλος ημῶν: 11:11; πῶς ἐφίλει αὐτόν: 11:36), and, as with Heracles, Christ's friendship is a key motive for his saving intervention, though in John the intervention is also ascribed to the desire to glorify Christ and God's will (John 11:4, 40). Both Heracles and Jesus receive lavish hospitality from the households of the mortals whom they will save. Admetus and his servants go out of their way to receive Heracles into the palace, even at a most difficult time for the host. In John, the household's hospitality is depicted *after* Christ has saved Lazarus. A feast is held specifically for Jesus (12:2) with Martha presiding and Lazarus also present. At the feast Maria anoints Jesus' feet (12:3), a motif often present in hospitality myths (*Odyssey* 19.317–92, esp. 19.320: χρῖσαι; Gen 18:4, 19:2; cf. *Odyssey* 1.310, 4.252).[14]

But both Heracles and Christ have closer ties to a relative of the mortal who is to be saved

As noted, Heracles is a close friend to Admetus but will save his wife Alcestis. He comes to Admetus' house specifically to visit his dear friend,[15] remaining unaware of Alcestis' actual status until much later, nor is he ever depicted in conversation with her. Jesus is similarly depicted as much closer to Mary (John 11:1–2, 12:3) and Martha, whom he is also said to love (11:5 ἠγάπα), than to their brother Lazarus. He converses and interacts with both sisters (11:20–28, 32–33, 39–40; 12:3–7), whereas, even after his revival, Lazarus' only interaction with Christ is reclining at the same table at the feast. In both myths the relatives to whom the saviors are close are the opposite gender of the mortal who is saved.

Each myth contains an earlier prediction that the hero will bring the mortal back from death (Alcestis 68–70; John 11:11, 11:23; cf. 11: 4)

It is a common feature in heroic myths that the hero's accomplishments confirm earlier prophecies. The *Odyssey* repeatedly depicts Odysseus in this light (first at 2.171–76). In the *Alcestis*, the god Apollo declares that Heracles will restore Alcestis to life, which, by virtue of his divine prophetic powers, makes the utterance a speech act.[16] In John, the earlier prophecies are more connected with the myth's explicit agenda of glorifying God (as at John 11:4).[17]

Both episodes are set in the context of the hero's larger struggle and calling as the special Son of God

When he arrives at Admetus' palace, Heracles is in the middle of accomplishing his 12 labors (*Alcestis* 66–68, 481–504) on his way to defeat the man-eating mares of Diomedes (483–504), eighth of the 12 labors, an episode that will also center on hospitality. Heracles associates his rescue of Alcestis both with his next labor (1020–22) and with his larger mission and identity as Zeus' son.[18] In John, the situation is tense before and after Jesus resurrects Lazarus. He risks being stoned if he returns to Judaea (11:8). The danger is emphasized even more near the end of the episode, where his saving Lazarus is, only in John (Brown 428–29), what prompts the Pharisees to decide to have him slain (11:45–57). But Jesus proclaims the episode's purpose is to glorify God and the Son of God (ὑπὲρ τῆς δόξης τοῦ θεοῦ, ἵνα δοξασθῇ ὁ Υἱὸς τοῦ Θεοῦ δι' αὐτῆς: 11:4; cf. 11:40: τὴν δόξαν τοῦ θεοῦ). The *Alcestis* offers an anticipation of this motif, the glorification of the Father, in two passages, Admetus' expression of gratitude, "Oh well-born son of Zeus the highest, may you fare well, may the father who sired you keep you safe" (1136–38). Earlier, when Heracles resolves to bring Alcestis back from the dead he declares, "O my heart and hand, which have endured so much, show now what sort of child Tirynthian Alcmene, daughter of Electryon, bore to Zeus" (837–39), a lesser, implicit version of the concern present in John for glorifying the Son and the Father.

The house to which they come is overcome by mourners and mourning

Much of the first half of the *Alcestis* depicts Admetus' palace in mourning (77–475), as the household prepares for Alcestis' imminent death. After she dies, the mourning reaches a climax when Admetus and the chorus perform the play's *kommos* (861–961), a ritual song of lament.[19] John repeatedly depicts Lazarus' sisters and friends mourning him at his house and elsewhere (11:19–20, 31–33). Brown notes that the description of Mary conforms to other biblical accounts of women's roles in mourning (424): "Women in mourning sat on the floor of the house." In a difference, Jesus knows ahead of time that the house mourns, whereas Heracles comes unawares, and even then, the household, at Admetus' behest, keeps the identity of the deceased secret from him.

Both initially fail to respond or do so with such incongruous leisure that others misunderstand them

When Heracles arrives, Admetus, fearing he will not accept his hospitality if he learns it is his wife who has died, encourages him to believe the deceased is a woman outside of his family. In an ancient version of *"mi casa es tu casa,*" Heracles is urged to make himself at home. For the larger-than-life hero, however, his doing so entails considerable consumption of wine, getting drunk, scandalously unaware that the household mourns the death of its mistress. These tendencies climax in the complaints of the servant in charge of providing hospitality for Heracles (747–72) and his subsequent encounter with his now intoxicated guest (773–860). Unaware that his guest does not know Alcestis has died, he repeatedly criticizes his seemingly inappropriate behavior.[20] John offers unexpected parallels, if in smaller degree and in different modality. Culpepper notes a thematic tendency throughout John's depiction of Jesus (110), "he moves at his own time and initiative," more than a little suggestive of Heracles in the *Alcestis*. Having learned Lazarus is seriously ill (11:3), Jesus responds at a very leisurely pace, remaining where he is for two days (11:6). Culpepper summarizes his response in ways that offer unexpected parallels to Heracles' behavior (110–11),

> Jesus loves Martha, Mary and Lazarus (11:3, 5, 36), but delays before responding to their call for help ... he rejoices when Lazarus dies, because his death provides an opportunity for the disciples to believe.

When Jesus mentions returning to Judaea, he refers to Lazarus as having fallen asleep, and that he shall go waken him (11:11: κεκοίμηται ... ἐξυπνίσω). The disciples do not understand his reference.[21] This functions as a milder version of the lighthearted, comedic tone used of Heracles before he learns it is Alcestis who has perished. Translations of John often obscure the fact that at the subsequent feast, the guests, Jesus included, are depicted as reclining (12:2: ἀνακειμένων) at the table, in Greek banquet style, just as Heracles in the *Alcestis*. John elsewhere depicts Christ as closely associated with wine in the miracle at Galilee (2:1–11), an incident that, as with the entire Lazarus episode, is also absent from the other gospels.

A family member criticizes the hero, complaining that he is responsible for the death, that he allowed him or her to die

In John, both of Lazarus' sisters, Martha and Mary, make the same charge: "Lord, if you had been here, my brother would not have died" (11:21 = 32) (Κύριε, εἰ ἦς ὧδε, οὐκ ἀπέθανεν ὁ ἀδελφός). The motif is repeated a third time when anonymous Jews, before Jesus has saved Lazarus, assert that he healed a blind man but did nothing for his friend (11:37). These reactions are in keeping with John's thematic tendency to have secondary characters misunderstand Jesus.[22] In the *Alcestis*, this motif is also applied to the healer Asclepius: "If the son of Phoebus [Asclepius] were seeing this light with his eyes, she, having left the abode of Hades and its dark gates, would have returned" (121–26). The motif is not only implicit in Heracles' dilatory response but also in the nasty scene between Admetus and his father (606–740): Pheres three times charges *Admetus* with being responsible for Alcestis' death (695, 700–1,

730). Their bitter recriminations find a thematic correspondence in the some-what acrimonious exchange when Judas interrupts the banquet to criticize Mary for anointing Christ's feet with a costly ointment (12:4–8).

Heracles and Christ are both deeply moved immediately before they intervene to save the mortal who has died

Informed by a servant that it is Alcestis who has perished not a foreign woman (*Alcestis* 812–25), Heracles berates himself for not having realized earlier and for partying in the palace under such inappropriate circumstances. He immediately resolves to save her, to repay Admetus for his hospitality and friendship (826–60).[23] When Jesus sees Mary and the others who accompany her, weeping over Lazarus' death, he is strongly moved (ἐνεβριμήσατο τῷ πνεύματι καὶ ἐτάραξεν ἑαυτὸν: 11:33).[24] The motif is repeated when he approaches Lazarus' tomb (πάλιν ἐμβριμώμενος: 11:38).

Each asks where the deceased has been buried and proceeds directly to the place of burial

Disabused over the identity of the deceased, Heracles asks the servant where Alcestis' tomb and memorial are and immediately rushes there (834–60). In John, after Mary and her friends come to meet Jesus outside of their village, he asks where they have placed Lazarus (Ποῦ τεθείκατε αὐτόν: 11:34) and imme-diately follows them to the location, specifically a tomb in both narratives (*Alcestis* 836; John 11:38).

Both narratives climax in the Son of God's resurrection of the deceased: Alcestis and Lazarus

In both myths the miracle occurs offstage, though through very different means. Heracles, founder of the Olympics, exemplar of Greek (and subse-quent Western) conceptions of athletics, saves Alcestis as an athlete, by wrest-ling Thanatos (847–49). When he restores her to Admetus he claims he won her as a prize in some athletic games (1025–33). His actual retrieval of her, however, is not depicted but occurs offstage during the previous choral song, in keeping with the conventions of Greek tragedy. In John, Lazarus has been buried in a cave, covered with a stone (11:38). In Greek myth and in Plato's *Allegory of the Cave* in Book 7 of the *Republic*, a cave often serves as a version of the underworld (e.g., those of Polyphemos in *Odyssey* 9, and Cacus in *Aeneid* 8).[25] A similar conception is operative in John 11. When Jesus tells them to remove the stone and commands Lazarus to emerge a bandaged Lazarus does so, but the actual resurrection takes place unseen within the cave, a close correspondence to Heracles wrestling Thanatos in the under-world. The narrative associates the act with other instances of miraculous healing in its link with Christ's restoration of sight to the blind man (9:1–7).

In similar fashion, the *Alcestis* thematically associates Heracles' restoration of Alcestis with Asclepius' miraculous acts of healing (4, 122–29, 966–71).

The resurrected mortal remains silent with a shrouded face

Heracles returns with Alcestis, who remains silent for the entire scene (*Alcestis* 1008–158). He declares she is to remain silent for three days, until rituals have satisfied the underworld deities (1143–46).[26] Though there are no stage directions in ancient tragic texts, events demonstrate that Alcestis is veiled until 1120, when Heracles uncovers her face (Parker: 251). In John, Lazarus' identity is never in doubt, but like Alcestis he is silent and remains so, his face covered, when he emerges from his tomb (11:44).

Heracles' and Jesus' restoration of the mortal points to their own coming translation to divine status

It is typical of myth to be so structured that a particular episode functions as a miniature of the larger, entire myth. Both Heracles and Jesus are referred to as saviors, forms of the same Greek word, in fact, used of each, σωτήρ (*Alcestis* 1138: σῴζοι; John 4:42). The connections are more explicit in John, and it is standard in biblical commentary to draw parallels between Christ's restoration of life to Lazarus and his own coming resurrection. Thompson (190) offers a succinct equation: "Jesus, who raises Lazarus from the dead and is himself the resurrection and life."[27] Culpepper notes both correspondences among additional details (198), "Lazarus' tomb and grave wrappings (cf. 11:44; 20:7) and the anointing of Jesus point ahead to Jesus's death, royal burial, and resurrection," as well as the larger parallels (141), "the raising of Lazarus is the final offence which sets in motion the plot to kill Jesus – and he was well aware that it would be (11:7, 8, 16) – Jesus actually lays down his life for a friend by returning to bring life to Lazarus." Some commentators see parallels in the four days Lazarus has been in his tomb (11:17, 39) and the three days between Jesus' own death and resurrection (Brown: 423 [1 Cor 15: 4]). The *Alcestis* features the three-days-of-death motif in the three days the title character must remain silent (1146), of which Parker (281) notes, "The standard magic number." Brown (427) also calls our attention to the fact that Jesus' head is wrapped in a separate bandage when he has been resurrected (20:7), as was Lazarus. While the *Alcestis* makes no specific reference to Heracles' own translation, occasional oblique references may do so (e.g., 499–500). Parker well captures the overall tone (280): "Now, by bringing her back, Heracles has become his one and only saviour."

Heracles' retrieval of Alcestis from the underworld has enough motifs in common with John's depiction of Christ resurrecting Lazarus that we should regard them as interrelated in either of two ways. They are separate instances of the same genre of myth, which we might designate: *The Son of God, in the midst of his own heroic trials, resurrects a mortal, to whom he was tied by hospitality, prefiguring his own coming translation to divine status.* But how *separate*, ultimately, are the two narratives? We should also consider an instance of diffusion, that the John tradition has encountered the ancient Greek myth of Alcestis.

Let us first adduce the narrative of Jairus' daughter (Matt 9:18–26; Mark 5:21–43; Luke 8:41–56), which has several motifs in common with John's account of Lazarus. Could they serve as source material for John 11–12:8? Here Jesus, the man who had a legion of demons just dispossessed, is approached by the president of a synagogue, who begs him to save his dying daughter. Followed by a crowd, as Jesus proceeds to the house a long-ill woman touches his clothes and is instantly healed, though Jesus did not consciously heal her. Reaching the house, he finds it full of mourners and wailing. Inside, with Peter, John, James, Jairus, and his wife, when Jesus declares she is not dead but asleep, they laugh at him (καὶ κατεγέλων αὐτοῦ: Matt 9:24 = Mark 5:40 = Luke 8:53).

Of the 12 corresponding motifs we have traced between the *Alcestis* and John 11–12, the Jairus narratives contain: 4 (implicitly), 5, 10, and 12. However, the following motifs common to the *Alcestis* and John are not present in the Jairus narratives: 1, 2, 3, 6, 7, 8, and 9. One, number 11, is partially present: the daughter remains silent, but her face is not shrouded. Because the Jairus narratives lack all the motifs that most closely link the *Alcestis* and the Lazarus myth – everything having to do with hospitality, the leisurely pace, Heracles' and Christ's personal ties with the deceased, and the bitterness temporarily projected against them – it does not seem reasonable to see them as a key source for John's Lazarus. However, they may still serve as some sort of indirect, intermediate, or transitional source between the *Alcestis* and John's Lazarus because they share one feature with the *Alcestis* we have not mentioned: the deceased is the same gender as in the *Alcestis*. Also, the narratives are part of a series of miraculous healing stories,[28] rather like the position of *Alcestis* within Heracles' labors. We should note Mark 5:35 depicts the Christ as overhearing the message, relayed to Jairus, that his daughter has died, which broadly corresponds to the servant informing Heracles that it is Alcestis whom the house mourns. Furthermore, Mark 5:41, which quotes what Jesus says to the daughter in Aramaic, emphasizes that he speaks in a different language and can perhaps be seen to correspond to Heracles' off-key singing, about which the servant complains (760–62). Thus, the Jairus narratives may reflect some influence of Euripides' play.

The Lazarus episode is missing from all the Synoptic Gospels,[29] its Martha and Mary elsewhere mentioned only at Luke 10:38–42 (though it is not certain that these are, in fact, the same individuals). Only in John does the episode prompt the Pharisees to have Christ slain (a similar tension to that in Heracles rescuing Alcestis during his 12 labors). As a result, some scholars have argued that the Lazarus tale may have originally existed in an independent form (e.g., Brown: 427: "chs. xi–xii were a later addition to the plan of the Gospel").[30] The New Testament elsewhere openly draws on works of Greek literature. Paul, for instance, does so at least twice in his letters (1 Cor 15:33 "evil communications corrupt good manners" = Menander, *Thais* [fr. 187 Koerte]; Titus 1:12 "The Cretans are always liars, evil beasts, slow bellies" = Epimenides, *De oraculis*). The Book of Acts also does so at least once (17:28 "for we are also his offspring" = Aratus, *Phaenomena* 5).[31]

The considerable number of parallels, some quite specific, present us with the likelihood that the myth of Alcestis serves as the source for John's account of Lazarus, which depicts Christ in ways the other Gospels do not. In the complex backstory of Euripides' play, the figure of Asclepius provides the prompt for the entire plot. Zeus had him slain for bringing a mortal back to life (3 ff.). Here we may have the clinching link between the two works. In a highly specific, perhaps otherwise unique, motif, the miraculous healers Asclepius and Christ are both put to death precisely because they have brought a mortal back to life. The Gospel of John is thus not only using the *Alcestis* but also like Euripides' play may look through it to the example of Asclepius.

The *Alcestis* thus provides a rubric both for Lazarus' miraculous restoration to life and for how the Johannine author wanted the miracle to function in his larger narrative: to prompt the death of the miraculous healer.

Not only is Euripides' play more than five centuries older (438 BCE) than the Gospel of John, the myth is well known beyond Euripides, well before his version. *The Iliad* demonstrates awareness of the larger myth in its several references to Eumelos, Admetus' son, and his fabulous horses. Eumelos has such splendid horses because of Apollo's divine tendance (2.713–15, 763–67, 23.288–89, 532–38). This presupposes a version of the myth in circulation several centuries before Euripides' retelling. Hesiod, in the *Catalogue of Women*, recounts some of the story of Apollo being sentenced to work for Admetus.[32] Thus the two authors, who constitute the bedrock of the Greek educational system for centuries, guarantee broad familiarity with some version of the myth throughout the Greek-speaking world.

The early Greek tragedian Phrynichus also wrote an *Alcestis*, which, though not extant in our time zone, would have been several decades earlier than Euripides'.[33] Aeschylus twice alludes to particulars of the myth in his extant works (*Suppliants* 214, the *Eumenides* 723–28). Plato's *Symposium* makes prominent use of a slight variant of the myth in Phaedrus' speech (179b). These multiple allusions over a range of centuries attest to how well known the myth was, alive over several phases of Greek culture, all of which remain prominent and easily accessed in the first century CE.

To state the obvious, Euripides' *Alcestis* is also written in largely the same language as John, Greek having become, since the conquests of Alexander the Great, the international language of the Mediterranean, a key language of educated Jews, as evidenced in the New Testament's own use of it. It is perhaps less often realized by modern audiences that the authors of the Gospels *only* know the Hebrew Bible in the Greek Septuagint, the source of all New Testament citations.

The Son of God restores to life a close friend who had perished. Doing so at a surprisingly leisurely pace, he is criticized by associates of the deceased. He receives exemplary hospitality from the deceased's household. He is deeply moved at the moment before he retrieves the deceased mortal. It was earlier prophesied that he would save the deceased mortal. Though the basic motif of a special hero or healer who restores to life someone who had perished is common, several of these other motifs are considerably more specific. Furthermore, the concatenation of all 12 motifs noted in the preceding text is, to my knowledge, *exclusive* to these two narratives. The parallels thus suggest some form of interrelationship between the two myths. The likeliest explanation is that John's account of Lazarus is influenced, whether directly or indirectly, by some version of the myth of Alcestis, Euripides' account being the only complete one we have. Given how widespread the tale of Alcestis was – from the *Iliad* to Plato's *Symposium*, from Aeschylus to Euripides – and given how widespread Greek language and culture was at the time (so that at the feast for Jesus, at the house of Mary, Martha, and Lazarus, the guests are depicted as reclining in the Hellenistic fashion: John 12:2, ἀνακειμένων), actual influence, diffusion of some form of the myth of Alcestis, seems the likelier explanation.[34]

Notes

1 This chapter is an expanded version of Louden 2007.
2 White 2010: 351.
3 On this, see, for instance, ibid.: 360: "The Gospel of John thus represents a social situation of much greater separation of the Christian community from its Jewish neighbors."
4 Cf. Larsen 2008: 7–8: "[T]he notion of an insurmountable divide between Judaism and Hellenism has been progressively deconstructed, resulting in a new understanding of Hellenism as an overall descriptive concept under which both the Judaisms and the Christianities of the period appear as subsets. This development requires that we see the New Testament texts, including the Fourth Gospel, as inherent players in a larger Panhellenistic literary *koinê*, both with regard to content and form."
5 For a basic account see Apollodorus, *The Library*, 3.10.3–4; cf., Pindar, *Pythia* 3; Ovid, *Metamorphoses*, 15.620–744. For the full *testimonia*, see Edelstein and Edelstein 1998.
6 See Larsen's discussion (9–16) of several previous commentators who have traced common ground between the Gospel of John and Greek tragedy in general, particularly with regard to recognition, *anagnôrisis.*
7 I have elsewhere argued (Louden 2011a: 259–60) that the Gospels' overall depiction of Christ may be understood, from the perspective of earlier myth, as a synthesis of five traditional types of mythical figures: (1) The prophet who can perform miracles (Melampous; Elijah and Elishah); (2) The prophet who predicts the coming apocalypse (Theoclymenos; many Hebrew Bible prophets); (3) The healer who can bring mortals back from death (Asclepius); (4) The hero who can bring mortals back from death (Heracles); and (5) A god, the son of god, who founds a new religion, but is mocked and thrown into prison while doing so (Dionysus).
8 Asclepius and Heracles also evince an association in several other myths; see Edelstein: 46–48.
9 Justinus, *Apologia*, 22.6.
10 Louden 2007:10.
11 Cf. Race 1993: 82, and Bolin 2004: 48.

12 For additional Hebrew Bible narratives depicting the sanctity of hospitality, and the miraculous reward for those who uphold it, cf. the widows visited by Elijah and Elishah in 1 Kings 17:8–24 and 2 Kings 4:18–35.

13 See discussion in Louden 2011a: 312–13.

14 Culpepper (1983: 141) notes that the strength of Jesus' friendship with Lazarus is so important to the myth that several scholars have thought he was in fact the Beloved Disciple.

15 See Louden (2007: 12) on Heracles' friendship with Admetus as thematic in the play.

16 Parker (2007: 66) notes that "true to the oracular style, Apollo does not name the man, but demonstrates the clarity of his prophetic vision by some corroborative detail."

17 Hays (2006: 70) notes the general tendency in all the Gospels, "John, like Matthew, offers a number of fulfillment citations asserting that various events happened in order to fulfill scripture."

18 Cf. Parker 2007: 255, "His constant awareness of death does much to distinguish this Heracles … This Heracles can wrestle with death and win, something that no mortal man can do … Yet he sees himself as subject to death."

19 For discussion of the *kommos*, see Luschnig and Roisman 2003: 144–45, 203–4; Dale: 114–19; and Parker: 224–43.

20 Parker (2007: 210–15) offers a thorough discussion.

21 Culpepper (158) offers discussion of the incident, and (152) notes the phenomenon as part of a general tendency in John: "One of the distinctive features of the Gospel of John is the frequency with which its secondary characters misunderstand Jesus." Cf. Thompson 2006: 195.

22 In addition to Culpepper on this topic (see previously), cf. Brown 1970: cxxxv.

23 Luschnig and Roisman: 201: "[H]e finds the good in Admetus' deception (855–60) and repays it with a greater kindness."

24 Note Culpepper: 110: "There are more references to Jesus' emotions in John 11 than in any other chapter, and at this point they become particularly intense."

25 See Louden 2011a: 211–17.

26 See also Luschnig and Roisman (159), however, for discussion of whether Alcestis' silence is further connected with the number of actors that would have performed the play.

27 See also White: 166: "[T]he story's structure already has resonances to the resurrection of J himself."

28 On which see Fitzmyer (742) as to the larger sequence in Luke and how Luke's version is derived from Mark's.

29 Brown: 422; Culpepper: 132; Thompson: 184.

30 Brown (1970: 428–30) has many other pertinent observations about significant differences between John 11–12 and the rest of this Gospel, and perhaps even more noteworthy, differences between this episode and the Synoptic Gospels.

31 I thank Garth Tissol for acquainting me with these instances of New Testament dependence on classical Greek texts.

32 Merkelbach and West 1967: fragments 51–58.

33 See discussion in Dale 1954: xii–xiv.

34 An earlier version of this chapter was also given at the 2011 meeting of the Classical Association of the Middle West and South, April 8, in Grand Rapids, Michigan.

8 Hesiod's *Theogony* and the Book of Revelation 4, 12, and 19–20

The Book of Revelation instantiates a paradox at the heart of many Christian narratives. Among the newest books of the New Testament,[1] nonetheless, it structures much of its narrative using motifs and type scenes common to some of the *oldest* myths. While commentators often place Revelation in the context of episodes from the Hebrew Bible (e.g., Ford), many of the traditional structures it employs occur in other mythical traditions as well, and bears closer correspondences with them.[2] For instance, a dragon, that seeks to dominate or rule the cosmos, defeated by a victorious god corresponds to Tiamat defeated by Marduk in the *Enuma Elish* and to Typhoeus' defeat by Zeus in Hesiod's *Theogony*. A battle between different groups of gods occurs in the *Enuma Elish*, *The Baal Cycle*, and, again in the *Theogony*, between the Titans and the Olympians.

Scholars have long recognized that Hesiod's *Theogony* incorporates motifs, type scenes, or episodes found in Near Eastern myth.[3] Hesiod's version of the divine succession myth and the climactic encounter with Typhoeus both have strong affiliations with earlier myths from various cultures[4]: Mesopotamian, Egyptian, Anatolian, and Northwest Semitic (the Ugaritic texts, and their later descendants or counterparts: the Homeric Phoenicians/Sidonians, the biblical Canaanites). Scholars have also demonstrated that the Hebrew Bible shares common ground with narratives from these same four traditions. Because of these parallel patterns of cultural interaction, Hebrew Bible narratives offers several parallels with Hesiod's *Theogony*. For instance, as we noted in Chapter 1, it briefly incorporates a mythic type resembling succession myth (Deuteronomy 32:8–9),[5] where different gods draw lots to determine their portions (as at *Iliad* 15. 15.187–93), and repeatedly mentions the defeat of the great dragon, known as Leviathan and Rahab (Job 9:8, 26:12–13; Ps 74:13–14, 89:10; Isa 27:1, 51:9–10).

While connections between Hebrew Bible myth and the Near Eastern cultural traditions noted have become well known,[6] we are here concerned with tracing connections between New Testament myth and Greek mythic traditions.[7] Gunkel exposed Revelation 12's affiliation with elements of creation myth in general, arguing for close affinity with Babylonian myth in specific, in his landmark study 1895 study (now available in English translation as *Creation and Chaos in the Primeval Era and the Eschaton: A Religio-Historical Study of Genesis 1 and Revelation 12*). Perhaps most important, for my purposes here, is his documentation of how several ancient mythic traditions refashion elements from the creation myth, the defeat of a primordial Dragon that allows Creation to occur but employs them for a depiction of the Endtimes. Thus Revelation 12, as Gunkel persuasively demonstrates, unexpectedly has much in common with several episodes in Hesiod's version of the Greek creation myth. However, Gunkel downplays (138, 181–88) the likelihood of any Greek influence in Revelation.

Among the few studies noting Revelation's correspondences with Greek myth, Fontenrose (1959: 210), following Gunkel, identifies the dragon in Revelation 12 as an instance of the traditional mythic genre, the "combat myth." A. Y. Collins (1976), building on Fontenrose in particular, argued that Revelation 12's version of the combat myth does intersect with a Greek myth, that it reworks Apollo's defeat of Python. The pregnant "woman," whose offspring the dragon threatens to devour, would then correspond to Leto, about to give birth to Apollo.

While her argument has considerable merit, I will argue that Hesiod's *Theogony*, in its account of Zeus and Typhoeus, and Kronos' attempted swallowing of the infant Zeus, not only offers a version of the combat motif considerably closer to that in Revelation 12 but also provides backgrounds and contexts for other episodes, the eternally singing choir (4), the war in heaven (12), and the dragon's defeat as he is cast into the lake of fire (19–20). We have already argued in Chapter 1 that some form of Hesiod's account of the Titans, euhemerized, lies behind Genesis' account of Noah's sons, Iapetos > Japeth, and the transition into the Table of Nations. I will also demonstrate that the Hebrew Bible elsewhere suggests awareness of the *Theogony* as do two Apocryphal texts known to the Revelation authors.

Analyzing the common ground Revelation shares with the *Theogony* serves several purposes. Awareness of the parallels in both narratives helps clarify the underlying structure of each myth. Hesiod's *Theogony* functions as a sort of master text behind these several sections of Revelation, serving as a structure to be partly emulated, as a vessel to be filled with somewhat similar contents, and as a structuring and framing mechanism. However, because each myth now provides a context for the other, where Revelation diverges from the *Theogony* becomes evident and its different agenda becomes clearer. Our study will reveal Revelation to be a product of its time.[8]

Due to fundamental differences between polytheism and monotheism, and a desire to validate and privilege its own religion, Revelation significantly transforms whatever Hesiodic materials it finds useful. For instance, given monotheism's smaller cast of divine characters, in some instances Revelation must fuse and combine what are in Hesiod multiple characters into one, even fuse multiple episodes into one. For example, I will argue that Revelation finds Hesiod's accounts of both Kronos and Typhoeus useful for its own agenda but fuses these two characters into one: the dragon of Revelation 12. But because Kronos figures in two separate episodes in Hesiod (the immortal who attempts to swallow the newborn immortal destined to rule over all; the immortal who leads a group of gods who are defeated by those loyal to the newborn ruler), and Typhoeus, in another (the immortal dragon that wants to rule the cosmos), by fusing the two figures, Kronos and Typhoeus, into one, Revelation 12 transforms and combines into one what are in Hesiod three separate episodes. In another type of fusion, Revelation finds the *Theogony*'s Rhea a relevant model for its own purposes, as the figure of the goddess, queen of Heaven, whose offspring, the projected ruler of the universe, another immortal is waiting to devour. But Revelation imbues her with attributes more typical of depictions of Isis from its own era.[9] These fusions help demonstrate how the "woman" of Revelation 12 can be coherently interpreted, variously, as Mary, Israel, and/or the Church.

The Hesiodic backdrop reveals a profound syncretism at work in biblical narrative, which exists for multiple reasons. I will propose that Revelation not only draws upon the *Theogony* for material but also consciously *engages* Hesiod's narrative, intending itself as a corrective, and perhaps a parody, for its own audience, of the *Theogony*'s earlier narrative agendas.

Let us here note a few fundamental differences in technique between Revelation and the *Theogony*. As we discuss more fully in Chapter 10, Revelation frames its presentation as primarily *visual*, much of it being an extended instance of a frequently recurring genre of myth, *the vision*, which we can characterize as follows: *The protagonist is removed from the mortal plane; an otherworldly guide accompanies him, who reveals to him a larger truth, the "big picture," previously unknown to him. He is a transformed man as a result.*[10] Revelation depicts events as if they will occur in the future, employing its primal mythic motifs for eschatological concerns.[11] Whereas Hesiod's text, other than the opening interactions with the Muses, depicts the distant past and only briefly suggests a structure like *the vision*. Revelation, following the tradition of prophetic books of the Hebrew Bible such as Daniel and Isaiah, uses a symbolic, coded language for an audience in which it expects some competence in following the implied code. Hesiod's narrative seems less multi-dimensional in this respect. Revelation addresses a specific historical context, the Second Jewish Revolt and the Roman response to it (66–70 AD). Its intended audience is originally one living in that time, or in its immediate aftermath. The *Theogony* does not appear to have any such specific concern, or if it does, addresses it with less intensity and less evidence.

Lastly, we briefly note other evidence that the authors of the Hebrew Bible are aware of the *Theogony*. As we noted in Chapter 1, many observers find Genesis tapping into a Hesiodic account at 6:2–5, the passage right before the Flood Myth, and transition to it.[12] As we further argued at greater length, Genesis 9–10's account of the sons of Noah and the Table of Nations also taps into a Hesiodic tradition, evident in the curious episode of Noah drunk in his tent, Ham's punishment, and the translation of Iapetos into Japheth.[13] The following mention of Javan (10:4–5), son of Japheth, whose four sons in turn become the sea and coastal peoples, evidences the episode's deliberate intersection with Greek culture.

To these Genesis passages we may now add a few others. After David succeeds Saul, 2 Samuel 5 gives a brief account of his defeat of the Philistines. The latter are twice said to "overrun the valley of *Rephaim*," 2 Samuel 5:18 and 22. In the Septuagint, however, the version of the Hebrew Bible which New Testament authors knew and consulted, the Greek text for these verses has "valley of the *Titans*."[14] In associating the Philistines with the place name "Titans," the Septuagint translators appear to be making overt connections between them and Greek culture as we argue in the introduction for several episodes in 1 Samuel–2 Kings, and with the signature text in which the Titans appear, Hesiod's *Theogony*. In particular, a brief Titanomachy is figured here: David, corresponding to Zeus, defeats the Philistines, who, figured as Titans, embody the heroic aspects of Greek culture, as the sons of the Gods do at Genesis 6:2, 4. Such a view seems confirmed by the Septuagint's account of what follows (2 Sam 5:21): "And *they leave their gods behind* there, and David and his men took them" (Καὶ καταλιμπάνουσιν ἐκεῖ τοὺς θεοὺς αὐτῶν, καὶ ἐλάβοσαν αὐτοὺς Δαυὶδ καὶ οἱ ἄνδρες οἱ μετ' αὐτοῦ). This reading may be further confirmed by the brief account at 2 Samuel 23:13, apparently set at the same locale. On this occasion the narrative has no theomachian relevance and the Septuagint instead uses Rephaim (Ῥαφαῖν). In any case, 1 Samuel 5:18 and 22 demonstrate that New Testament authors had direct acquaintance with the term.

The apocryphal Book of Judith, perhaps dating from the second or early in the first century BCE, provides additional Hesiodic context. Judith's hymn features the following description of the death of the Assyrian as part of its priamel (16:7): "For the champion fell not by their young men, nor did the sons of the Titans strike him, not did the lofty giants set upon him" (Οὐ γὰρ ὑπέπεσεν ὁ δυνατὸς αὐτῶν ὑπὸ νεανίσκων, οὐδὲ υἱοὶ Τιτάνων ἐπάταξαν αὐτόν, οὐδὲ ὑψηλοὶ γίγαντες ἐπέθεντο αὐτῷ). Here, as in Hesiod and larger Greek tradition, the Titans and giants are clearly differentiated.[15] We return to the 2 Samuel 5 passages in the following text.

White offers a useful diachronic perspective on the development of the apocalyptic worldview in the relevant period. While the roots of apocalypticism go back into the second millennium BCE, for White the apocalyptic worldview (26–27),

> grew out of the new mood of crisis about the time that Judah came under Seleucid rule at the end of the 2nd cent BCE. Its first flourish then was directly related to the crisis of Hellenization that produced the Maccabean revolt ... Although Daniel is the best-known early reflection of this outlook ... it was neither the first nor the most influential.

The most influential work, in White's view, is the apocryphal *I Enoch* (ibid.): "The work that best characterizes the early development of apocalypticism and its abiding influence on Jewish thought is that known as *I Enoch* … it was generally accorded scriptural status among many Jews and Christians." He offers further specifics (27–28),

> The core of the work (chapters 1–36) … reinterprets the brief story from Gen 6:1–3 in the light of the Greek myth of the Titans, who rebelled against Zeus and were subsequently imprisoned in Tartarus (Hades) or, in another version, were blasted by Zeus' thunderbolt.

Though he does not mention the relevant Greek account here, it is Hesiod's *Theogony* that contains the canonical depiction of the Titan's rebellion and subsequent punishment. White goes on to state some of the larger issues involved (28), "*I Enoch* is also important because it reflects a heavy dose of Hellenistic influence, even though it seeks to instill a Jewish piety in reaction against elements of Greek culture." Consequently, we can thus regard *I Enoch*'s refiguring of elements from Hesiod's *Theogony* as an instance of Carr's formulation "a hybrid form of cultural resistance," a countercurriculum, as we discussed in the introduction. While White may very well be correct about *I Enoch* intersecting the *Theogony*, the author of Revelation, as I will show, does not depend on an indirect account of the *Theogony*, but directly engages several of its episodes in much closer correspondence than anything in *I Enoch*.

Turning back to Revelation 4, 12, and 19–20, we will trace the following series of corresponding motifs common to Hesiod's *Theogony* and Revelation:

- In an introductory scene, the narrator interacts with some of the immortal characters.
- A heavenly choir ceaselessly hymns praises of the Heavenly Father.
    - Both choirs are associated with a similar formula denoting divine knowledge.

- An immortal being waits to devour the immortal offspring of a goddess.
    - The goddess safely gives birth, taking refuge in a place prepared for her.
    - The special child, who is to rule over all, is whisked away to safety.
    - He is immediately handed over to another immortal.
- A war breaks out in heaven between two groups of immortals.
    - Earth, personified, intervenes, helping to determine the outcome.
    - The defeated group of immortals is imprisoned in the underworld.
- A multiheaded dragon that wants to rule the cosmos is defeated, imprisoned in the underworld.
    - The dragon is one of a series of monsters.
    - Even after his defeat he continues to harass mortals.
    - In his final defeat, the chief god overcomes him with superior firepower.

In both works, "In an Introductory Scene, the Narrator Interacts with Some of the Immortal Characters" and "A Heavenly Choir Ceaselessly Hymns Praises of the Heavenly Father" are part of a connected unit near the beginning of the respective narratives, whereas "An Immortal Being Waits to Devour the Immortal Offspring of a "Goddess," "A War Breaks Out in Heaven between Two Groups of Immortals," and "A Multiheaded Dragon That Wants to Rule the Cosmos Is Defeated, Imprisoned in the Underworld" are part of another connected unit occurring much later in each work.

In an introductory scene, the narrator interacts with some of the immortal characters (Theogony 20–34; Rev 1:1, 4:1 and ff.)

Each work figures the narrator as a character who has privileged relations with the gods and interacts with them. This is opposite the way of Homeric epic (one of many indications the *Theogony* should *not* be classified as epic) and helps align Hesiod's work in part with prophetic works in the Hebrew Bible and New Testament. The nature of the narrators' interactions, however, is quite distinct, in accord with cultural differences.

In the *Theogony*, the Muses appear to Hesiod while he is herding his flocks (22–34). They teach him to become a divinely inspired singer (22); he subsequently refers to himself as their servant (Μουσάων θεράπων: 100). The discourse he learns from them is privileged (ἀληθέα γηρύσασθαι: 28); he receives it directly from them (ἐνέπνευσαν δέ μοι αὐδὴν / θέσπιν: 31–32).

The narrator of Revelation is figured more as a prophet (1.3: τῆς προφητείας), whereas Hesiod is figured as an inspired singer. However, as West notes (1966: 166), in connection with Hesiod's expression, τά τ᾽ ἐσσόμενα πρό τ᾽ ἐόντα (discussed in the following text), "The phrase expresses the close connexion between poetry and prophecy which is widespread in early literature."[16]

As in Hesiod, John is directly addressed, and not named, by an immortal (Ἀνάβη ὧδε, καὶ δείξω σοι ἃ δεῖ γενέσθαι μετὰ ταῦτα: 4:1), though then transported to heaven somehow, rather than the immortal coming to him on earth, as in Hesiod. He is later commanded to write down what he sees (Γράψον, ὅτι οὗτοι οἱ λόγοι πιστοὶ καὶ ἀληθινοί εἰσιν: 21:5; cf. 1:19: γράψον οὖν ἃ εἶδες καὶ ἃ μέλλει γίνεσθαι μετὰ ταῦτα). As in Hesiod the privileged nature of the contents is emphasized, both narratives asserting so with similar diction (ἀληθέα γηρύσασθα; οἱ λόγοι πιστοὶ καὶ ἀληθινοί εἰσιν).

In each case the in-person interaction is risky and fearful for the mortal. The Muses address Hesiod in disparaging words, Ποιμένες ... κάκ᾽ ἐλέγχεα, γαστέρες οἶον, "Shepherds ... shameful, wicked things, mere bellies" (26). John faints when he first sees Jesus, "I fell before his feet like a corpse" (ἔπεσα πρὸς τοὺς πόδας αὐτοῦ ὡς νεκρός: 1:17). But the latter reassures him, again stressing the connection between what John reports, and a divine truth (1:19: ἃ μέλλει γίνεσθαι μετὰ ταῦτα).

Both works further specify that those who receive the divine guidance and instruction depicted will be fortunate or blessed, "fortunate is he, whomever the Muses love" (*Theogony*, 96: ὃ δ᾽ ὄλβιος, ὅν τινα Μοῦσαι / φίλονται);

"blessed is he who reads and those who hear the words of this prophecy" (Rev 1:3, μακάριος ὁ ἀναγινώσκων καὶ οἱ ἀκούοντες τοὺς λόγους τῆς προφητείας).

A heavenly choir ceaselessly hymns the praises of the Heavenly Father (Theogony 1–115; Rev 4:8–9)

In Hesiod, the Muses, the same immortal beings who have direct interaction with him also constitute the heavenly choir. The *Theogony* opens with an elaborate hymn to them (1–115), delineating their special attributes and functions. Their voice is immortal (43: ἄμβροτον ὄσσαν ἱεῖσαι); it flows without interruption (39: ἀκάματος ῥέει αὐδή); song is their sole concern (60–61: ἧσιν ἀοιδὴ / μέμβλεται ἐν στήθεσσιν). While they celebrate the deeds of all the immortals (66–67: πάντων τε νόμους καὶ ἤθεα κεδνὰ / ἀθανάτων κλείουσιν), they specifically sing hymns in praise of Zeus (11: ὑμνεῦσαι Δία; 36–37: ταὶ Διὶ πατρὶ / ὑμνεῦσαι τέρπουσι μέγαν νόον ἐντὸς Ὀλύμπου; cf. 51–52). They instruct Hesiod to sing of them, first and last (34: πρῶτόν τε και ὕστατον αἰὲν ἀείδειν), as they begin and end their song with Zeus, (48: ἀρχόμεναί θ' ὑμνεῦσι καὶ ἐκλήγουσαι ἀοιδῆς).

John's revelation proper begins with his description of what he sees after having been told to ascend (Ἀνάβα), in a vision, to heaven. Prominent among the strange beings John describes are the four *zoas*, with the heads of a lion, ox, human, and eagle, each having six wings, each covered with eyes (4:6–8). Though Revelation takes their basic form from Ezekiel 1:5 ff.,[17] their multiformity is also quite reminiscent of two passages in the *Theogony*, descriptions of the Chimera (319–24) and Typhoeus (824–35, discussed in the following text). The Chimera has three heads, the first, as with the *zoas*, a lion, the second and third, a goat and a serpent. John describes the *zoas'* activity,

> And they make no pause by day or by night, saying,
> "Holy, Holy, Holy is God, the Lord, the Creator of All,
> who was, who is, and who is going to be."
> καὶ ἀνάπαυσιν οὐκ ἔχουσιν ἡμέρας καὶ νυκτὸς λέγοντες,
> Ἅγιος, ἅγιος, ἅγιος Κύριος ὁ Θεὸς ὁ Παντοκράτωρ,
> ὁ ἦν καὶ ὢν καὶ ὁ ἐρχόμενος.
>
> 4:8

The text's "speaking," λέγοντες, is commonly understood to denote singing.[18] As in Hesiod, their singing is without interruption; their subject is the Supreme God. Their special epithet for him, ὁ Παντοκράτωρ, "The Creator of All Things," is similar to the epithets Hesiod's Muses use of Zeus, "The Father Both of Gods and Men" (47: θεῶν πατέρ' ἠδὲ καὶ ἀνδρῶν). In a difference that is in keeping with larger tendencies already observed, John is before the heavenly choir in heaven, whereas Hesiod depicts the Muses in like activity, but without specifying his own presence before them on Olympos. His interaction occurs earlier, on the earthly plane.

Both heavenly choirs are depicted with a similar formula denoting divine knowledge

Hesiod describes how the Muses sing on Olympus for Zeus, "singing the things that are, and those that will be, and those that were before" (38: εἰρεῦσαι τά τ᾽ ἐόντα τά τ᾽ ἐσσόμενα πρό τ᾽ ἐόντα). They have also bequeathed a similar ability to Hesiod, that he, by means of their divine inspiration (31) can similarly sing, τά τ᾽ ἐσσόμενα πρό τ᾽ ἐόντα (32), "the things that will be, and the things that were." As noted, Revelation's heavenly choir gives glory to the one, "who was, who is, and who is going to be" (ὁ ἦν καὶ ὢν καὶ ὁ ἐρχόμενος: 4:8).

The Muses (West 1997: 170) lack a counterpart in Near Eastern cultures: "The Muses are, so far as we know, purely Greek creatures, and have no counterpart in the orient." While passages in Psalms offer partial antecedents for Revelation's depiction of the four *zoas* hymning (Ps 89:5: "Let the heavens praise your wonders, Lord; let the assembly of angels exalt your faithfulness"; 113:1: Praise the Lord, you that are his servants"; 148:2: "Praise him, all his angels"; 149:1: "Sing to the Lord a new song, his praise in the assembly of his loyal servants!"),[19] they lack the specific formula the *Theogony* includes.

Both narratives employ the motifs so far considered to establish their narrators' credentials. Hesiod and John have both been in the presence of the immortal characters, and interacted with them. Each narrative now transitions to other episodes, serving divergent narrative agendas. Later, however, both again turn to a group of climactic interconnected episodes that correspond with each other. In both narratives the next cluster of motifs features first as prelude to, then an account of, a war between two different groups of immortals. Both wars are triggered by the birth of the new immortal (Zeus, Christ), destined to rule over all.

An immortal being waits to devour the immortal offspring of a "goddess" (Theogony 459–66; Rev 12:4–5)

Kronos, learning a prophecy that one of his offspring will supplant him, resolves on swallowing his children as they are born (459–62: καὶ τοὺς μὲν κατέπινε μέγας Κρόνος, 466–67: παῖδας ἑοὺς κατέπινε, cf. 479–80). Each time his Titan wife, Rhea, gives birth, he swallows (467, 473: κατέπινε) the newborn child (459–62). Immortal, they do not perish when he does so but remain alive and will later reemerge, unharmed. Zeus is the child foretold in prophecy who will be stronger than Kronos and replace him as ruler of the gods, whose birth Kronos tries to prevent.[20]

Revelation 12 begins focusing on a "woman" (γυνή) in heaven (τῷ οὐρανῷ) "wearing" (περιβεβλημένη) the sun, the moon beneath her garlanded with a corona of 12 stars and about to give birth. As the extraordinary description suggests, she is clearly *not* a woman. In perhaps the three most common interpretations, she is Israel, the Church, or Mary. In some respects, she also suggests a Mother Earth figure. From a first-century perspective and context, she is a goddess.[21] She is positioned in heaven. Particulars of her description resemble Apuleius' depiction of Isis in her theophany (*Golden Ass*, 11.3–7). A great fiery-red dragon (δράκων πυρρὸς μέγας), with seven heads and ten horns, is waiting to devour (καταφάγῃ) her offspring.

While A. Y. Collins's suggestion that the "woman" reflects Leto, pursued by Python,[22] has merit, I argue the *Theogony*'s Rhea offers more correspondences. As the daughter of Ouranos (132–35), wife of the second sky father, Kronos, and often called "the mother of the gods,"[23] Rhea is not only a "queen of Heaven" but also her special position as mother of Zeus parallels "the woman" as mother of Christ, each the central figure of their respective religions.[24] Hershbell sums up the central trajectory of the *Theogony* in ways parallel to Revelation's depiction of Christ (1970: 152): it has "the unmistakable purpose of identifying the birth and subsequent reign of Zeus as the climax of cosmic history." In these particulars, Rhea is closer in several ways to Mary's larger functions as mother of Christ[25] than is Leto. No extant version of the myth of Apollo depicts Python as specifically attempting to *swallow* Leto's offspring. Whereas this is not only a central motif in the *Theogony* but also Rhea is the only "queen of Heaven" figure whose offspring is threatened with this specific act. Revelation 12 thus would seem to appropriate Rhea's defining roles from the *Theogony* but imbue her with characteristics of Isis from its own era – a typical instance of syncretism – resulting in the composite figure of "the woman." Both Rhea and the "woman" are suffering, in pain (467: πένθος ἄλαστον; 12:2: καὶ κράζει ὠδίνουσα καὶ βασανιζομένη τεκεῖν),[26] for which Leto remains relevant.

The "goddess" safely gives birth, taking refuge in a place prepared for her

In the *Theogony*, Rhea, about to bear Zeus (468–69), is advised ahead of time by Gaia how to give birth in secret (477). Rhea goes to Lyktos on Crete, escaping detection by Kronos (479–80), safely giving birth to Zeus, her youngest child. Kronos and Revelation's dragon are both easily prevented from carrying out their attempted ingestions. The *Theogony* implies that Kronos' failure to carry out his threat results from his earlier wrongdoing (472–73: τίσαιτο δ' ἐρινῦς πατρὸς ἑοῖο / παίδων θ'), "that he requite the wrongs he did his father and children." In what seems a comic modality, Kronos swallows a boulder[27] wrapped in swaddling clothes (487), thinking it is Zeus.

In Revelation 12, the "woman" similarly escapes the dragon, fleeing into the wilderness (12:5: τὴν ἔρημον) to a place prepared for her by God (ἐκεῖ τόπον ἡτοιμασμένον ἀπὸ τοῦ Θεοῦ), paralleling the divine advice Rhea receives from Gaia and Ouranos.[28] In both myths the "goddess" gives birth in safety, despite the earlier threat of having her offspring swallowed. The "woman" is given two wings of an eagle so she can fly to her place in the wilderness, out of reach of the dragon (12:14: καὶ ἐδόθησαν τῇ γυναικὶ αἱ δύο πτέρυγες τοῦ ἀετοῦ τοῦ μεγάλου, ἵνα πέτηται εἰς τὴν ἔρημον εἰς τὸν τόπον αὐτῆς). The eagle's wings correspond to the power of movement Rhea naturally has as a goddess. Revelation 12's "woman" will be looked after for 1,260 days in the special place that was prepared for her (12:6).

The special child, who is to rule over all, is whisked away to safety

In each myth the special child whom the other immortal tries to devour is the central figure in each respective religion. Zeus is figured as a new kind of divine ruler, who rules with a larger perspective, more justly than Kronos. Rapidly reaching maturity, he first sets free his brethren (501–2), who, in gratitude, give him thunder, thunderbolt, and lightning (503–5) as his weapons. In the *Theogony*'s conclusion the other gods are eager to have him as ruler (883), as he, on Gaia's advice, establishes the respective offices and honors among the other gods, and, in contrast with Kronos, will be associated (806–903) with intelligence (μῆτις), order (εὐνομία), justice (δίκη), and peace (εἰρήνη), as he guides events in accord with a big-picture conception of fate or destiny (μοῖραι). Kronos implicitly ruled without these same principles.

Revelation 12's newborn child is destined to rule over all with an iron rod (12:5: ὃς μέλλει ποιμαίνειν πάντα τὰ ἔθνη ἐν ῥάβδῳ σιδηρᾷ). However, where the *Theogony* clearly establishes Zeus as sole ruler of the cosmos, in Revelation both the Father and the Son seem to rule over mankind, (1:6: αὐτῷ ἡ δόξα καὶ τὸ κράτος εἰς τοὺς αἰῶνας τῶν αἰώνων, 1:8: ὁ Παντοκράτωρ). In this respect, and others, Revelation employs a relatively polytheistic conception.

He is immediately handed over to another immortal

In the *Theogony*, having safely giving birth to Zeus, Rhea entrusts the newborn to *Gaia* to nourish and rear, Gaia hiding him in an inaccessible cave beneath the "sacred earth" (481–84). In Revelation 12, as soon as the special child is born he is immediately taken up by another immortal, "and her child was snatched up to God, to his throne" (12:5: καὶ ἡρπάσθη τὸ τέκνον αὐτῆς πρὸς τὸν Θεὸν καὶ πρὸς τὸν θρόνον αὐτοῦ).

A war breaks out in heaven between two groups of immortals (Theogony 617–735; Rev 12:7–9)

In both myths, as a consequence of the birth of the special son,[29] war breaks out between two groups of immortals because the new immortal is seen as a threat to the group opposing him. In both myths, the leader of the immortals hostile to the newborn ruler is the same figure that had attempted to swallow him, Kronos, and the dragon. In both myths the new immortal ruler's maturation is not depicted, but seems almost instantaneous.

In Hesiod, the war between the Olympians and the Titans develops into a major episode, starting out as a revolt of the younger Olympian gods against the elder Titans.[30] Tension builds earlier in the testy exchanges between Zeus and Prometheus (535–64, cf. 613–16), and references to Atlas and Menoitios imprisoned in the underworld (514–20), but when Hesiod segues to the *Titanomachy*, the two sides have already been at war for ten years, in a stale-mate (629–38).

Revelation 12:7–9's account of the war is so unique from the perspective of the Hebrew Bible and New Testament that commentators often assume it derives from an unknown, extrabiblical source, as Ford (205) notes,

> Vss. 6–13 seem to come from another source and to interrupt the flow of the thought between 12:5 and 12:14 ... Neither the war in heaven or Michael are mentioned elsewhere in our text ... in the NT Michael occurs only here and in Jude 9.[31]

Such an assessment supports my argument that Hesiod's *Theogony* serves as a master source for the episode in Revelation.[32]

In Revelation 12's account of the war, one-third of the angels rebel, forming Satan's faction. While no specific cause is given (Rev 12:7 simply states, Καὶ ἐγένετο πόλεμος ἐν τῷ οὐρανῷ, "And there was war in heaven"), the sequence of events demonstrates the rebellion is a consequence of the birth of Christ. Unlike in Hesiod, Revelation 12's war seems quite brief. The two sides are quickly delineated, "Michael and his angels fought against the dragon; the dragon with his angels fought back" (ὁ Μιχαὴλ καὶ οἱ ἄγγελοι αὐτοῦ τοῦ πολεμῆσαι μετὰ τοῦ δράκοντος· καὶ ὁ δράκων ἐπολέμησεν καὶ οἱ ἄγγελοι αὐτοῦ: 12:7), and the outcome of the war is immediately apparent, "but they did not prevail, and no place in heaven was found for them," καὶ οὐκ ἴσχυσαν, οὐδὲ τόπος εὑρέθη αὐτῶν ἔτι ἐν τῷ οὐρανῷ (12:8).

In both myths, other immortals are individuated, playing key roles in the outcomes of the war. In Revelation, the angel Michael is the greatest war-rior, with the immortal combatants fighting alongside him referred to as his angels (12:7). Christ is figured as the chief warrior in a later battle (19:11–21). In Hesiod, Zeus is the greatest warrior but a pivotal role is also assigned to the three figures Briareos, Kottos, and Gyges, all giants with tremendous, if unspecified powers, whom Ouranos had earlier imprisoned in the underworld (626–28). It is Gaia who decisively alters the war's earlier stalemate through her suggestion that Zeus bring Briareos, Kottos, and Gyges up from the underworld, to ensure victory for the Olympians (713–21).[33] Zeus' triumph is that of a younger god over an elder.

The defeated group of immortals is imprisoned in the underworld (*Theogony* 722–819; Rev 12:9, 19:20, 20:1–3, 10, 14)

The *Theogony* several times refers to the defeated immortals who fought against Zeus and the Olympians. Earlier episodes note those imprisoned in the under-world, the sons of Iapetos: Atlas, Prometheus, and Menoitios, all punished by Zeus, the latter confined to Erebos for unspecified acts (514–16: ὑβριστὴν

... ἀτασθαλίης τε καί ἠνορέης ὑπερόπλου). Zeus' victory in the war is signaled by the three giants, having defeated the Titans with missiles, hurling them beneath the earth, bound, and imprisoned (καὶ τοὺς μὲν ὑπὸ χθονὸς εὐρυοδείης / πέμψαν καὶ δεσμοῖσιν ἐν ἀργαλέοισιν ἔδησαν: 715–18). After the war's conclusion, the *Theogony* details the physical features of their underworld prison, the giants Briareos, Kottos, and Gyges now serving as prison guards (721–35). The episode segues into a lengthy description of various aspects of Tartaros and the goddess Styx (736–819).

As in the *Theogony*, Revelation 12's defeated immortals are hurled down from heaven, "and the great dragon was thrown down ... he was hurled down to the earth, and his angels with him" (καὶ ἐβλήθη ὁ δράκων ὁ μέγας ... ἐβλήθη εἰς τὴν γῆν, καὶ οἱ ἄγγελοι αὐτοῦ μετ' αὐτοῦ ἐβλήθησαν: 12:9–10). The motif returns in chapters 19–20 (discussed in the following text).

A multiheaded dragon that wants to rule the cosmos is defeated, imprisoned in the underworld (Theogony 820–80; Rev 12:3–17, 19:20, 20:1–3, 10, 14)

Both narratives feature corresponding climactic episodes, the defeat of a fiery, multiheaded dragon. While such a scene is traditional,[34] the dragons of the *Theogony* and Revelation match more closely than most. Both are immortal, opposed to dragons such as Tiamat, Rahab/Leviathan, and Python, all of whom are slain by their divine combatants. Typhoeus and Revelation's dragon cannot be slain, and both continue to cause problems for mortals, even after their defeat.

However, two differences in Revelations' and Hesiod's treatments of the dragon have hindered recognition of their deeper correspondences. In a structural difference noted earlier, Revelation 12 fuses into one short chapter what are three separate genres of myth in Hesiod: (1) the immortal being (Kronos) who seeks to devour the special son (Zeus), destined to rule all; (2) the war between two different groups of immortals (Olympians vs. Titans, led by Kronos); and (3) the defeat of the immortal dragon (Typhoeus). In Hesiod, Kronos is chief antagonist in the first two mythic genres, while the dragon Typhoeus, a separate character, is in the third. Revelation 12's dragon first parallels Kronos as attempting to swallow the special son (Christ), but is then simultaneously leader of the rebel forces in the war in heaven (Kronos again) and the immortal dragon who will suffer fiery defeat (Typhoeus). In a second difference, Zeus defeats Typhoeus once and for all, whereas Michael defeats Revelation's dragon in 12, but in a later conclusive encounter (20), Christ, Zeus' thematic parallel, defeats him for all time. Despite these differences, the accounts of the two dragons share several specific features.

In the *Theogony*, after Zeus, victorious over the Titans, assumes his position as king of Heaven, Gaia bears her last child, the terrible dragon, Typhoeus. Revelation's dragon and Typhoeus are both polycephalic, both thematically associated with fire (845: πυρός τ' ἀπὸ τοῖο πελώρου). Fire flashes out from the eyes of Typhoeus' one hundred heads as he glares from under his brows (825–28). Revelation 12's dragon is "great, fiery red" (12:3: πυρρὸς μέγας) and has seven heads and ten horns. Both are called by the same two terms, "dragon," δράκων (825; 12:3) and "serpent," ὄφις (825; 12:9). Both briefly threaten the sovereignty of the cosmos, explicitly so in the *Theogony*, which states, that, if not for Zeus, Typhoeus would have ruled (καί νύ κεν ... ἄναξεν: 836–37) over mortals and the gods.[35] Revelation 12 hints at this in its emphasis that the expected child, which the dragon seeks to swallow, is destined to rule all the nations (12:5). Both dragons are hurled down to earth after their defeats (858; 12:9).

Typhoeus' challenge to Zeus, the poem's climactic episode, suggests a structural correspondence with the *Theogony*'s first episode, the hymn to the Muses (Goslin 2010: 357, 361). Typhoeus' hundred heads all project voices, sounds of all kinds. His voices make sounds such as the gods make, but also those of a bellowing bull, a lion, and young animals (828–35). His voices and sounds, an unusual, inarticulate, hybrid, present a "terrifying sonic counterpoint to the Muses" (Goslin: 361). Revelation suggests a similar structural correspondence because from the perspective of Revelation 4, the *Theogony*'s Chimera (319–24) and Typhoeus, particularly his varied voices and sounds, overlap with the multiple animal forms of the four *zoas*, especially the bull and the lion.

Despite their multiple heads and mouths, both Typhoeus and Revelation 12's dragon are denied coherent speech in their respective myths. For all the power and might inherent in Typhoeus' hundred voices, he is unable to put them to any significant purpose. His monstrous potential reflects a basic incompatibility, or instability, between his constituent parts (perhaps implicitly true of the Chimera as well). As Goslin notes (362), "[T]he voices of god and beast are shown to be incompatible when combined in one and the same being." Implicitly, the same instability would apply to his potential rule of the cosmos.

Revelation's dragon, furious after the "woman" safely gives birth, also responds with a seemingly potent threat from his multiple mouths, "and the serpent from his mouth threw after the woman water like a river, so that she would be borne away by it" (12:15: Καὶ ἔβαλεν ὁ ὄφις ἐκ τοῦ στόματος αὐτοῦ ὀπίσω τῆς γυναικὸς ὕδωρ ὡς ποταμόν, ἵνα αὐτὴν ποταμοφόρητον ποιήσῃ). However, Gê, earth, intervenes: "[B]ut Earth came to the woman's aid, and earth opened her mouth and swallowed down the river which the dragon had hurled from his mouth" (12:16: καὶ ἐβοήθησεν ἡ γῆ τῇ γυναικί, καὶ ἤνοιξεν ἡ γῆ τὸ στόμα καὶ κατέπιεν τὸν ποταμὸν ὃν ἔβαλεν ὁ δράκων ἐκ τοῦ στόματος αὐτοῦ).

The dragon is part of a thematically related series of monsters

As suggested in the preceding text, Revelation's dragon also displays multiple correspondences with the *Theogony*'s Chimera, a descendant of Typhoeus.

Revelation's dragon is also linked with another monster (though not genetically), the Beast. The Chimera and Revelation 12's dragon are both described with a similar appositive phrase, ἢ δ' ὄφιος, κρατεροῖο δράκοντος: 322; ὁ δράκων ὁ μέγας, ὁ ὄφις ὁ ἀρχαῖος: 12:9. The Chimera is also fire-breathing (πνέουσαν ἀμαιμάκετον πῦρ: 319; ἀποπνείουσα πυρὸς μένος αἰθομένοιο: 324).[36] The Chimera occurs in a section of the *Theogony* known as the catalogue of monsters (*Theogony* 270–336), which also references other monsters, including the Hydra (314–18). As West notes (1966: 244), the *Enuma Elish* shares this tendency, a catalogue of monsters linked with the narrative's principal dragon. Heroes slay the *Theogony*'s other monsters: Bellerophon slays the Chimera (325), and Heracles slays the Hydra, with Athena's help (316–18). These instances provide models for why Revelation 12 first has Michael defeat the dragon,[37] but saves the climactic instance for Christ, as the *Theogony* makes Zeus' subduing of Typhoeus its climax.

Even after defeat he continues to harass mortals

Zeus defeats Typhoeus using thunder and lightning (854–57), burning all the monster's heads, the entire earth boiling with heat from the encounter. Zeus then hurls (858: ἤριπε; 868: ῥῖψε … ἐς Τάρταον εὐρύν) the defeated dragon down into Tartaros, the section of the underworld reserved for recalcitrant immortals, where the Titans are also imprisoned (cf. *Iliad* 2.780–83). However, the dragon continues to cause problems, now just for mortals: destructive winds, particularly those that cause shipwrecks, issue from him (874–80). As Goslin notes (366),

> Hesiod ends his account with the effect of the monster's defeat on the *present* day, in which he persists as a force of *disorder and trouble* for men. But if Zeus permits his enemy a circumscribed existence, this is because Typhoeus will serve as a useful negative *exemplum* of the benefits conferred by Zeus' rule on men … the lingering pockets of disorder, represented by Typhoeus' winds, are a lasting reminder that human *technê* is operable only in a cosmos under Zeus' sovereignty.[38]

According to Hesiod, then, the deadly destructive winds that plague humanity, *typhoons*, are a remnant of the dragon's destructive potential.

What is germinal in Hesiod is fully developed in Revelation. After defeat by Michael, the dragon again pursues the "woman." But when she escapes, it decides to wage war (ποιῆσαι πόλεμον) against her descendants who follow Christ (12:17). He gains allies: first going to the sea, he sees the Beast (θηρίον) emerge (13:1–2), commonly understood to signify Nero and Rome (as the *gematria* of 13:18 makes clear).[39] Another Beast emerges from the land (13:11 & ff.). The dragon with his beasts leads much of the earth astray. As Collins (1976: 29) sums up, "The dragon = Satan is defeated in heaven (vss. 8–9), but the immediate effect of that defeat is that he exercises a more direct and wrathful control over the earth."

In his final defeat, the chief god overcomes him with superior firepower

Revelation depicts a later battle (chapters 19–20), when the dragon is defeated for all time, corresponding to Hesiod's account of Typhoeus. First the Beast and his prophet are thrown into a burning lake: "the two were hurled down into the lake of fire burning in sulfur" (19:20: ἐβλήθησαν οἱ δύο εἰς τὴν λίμνην τοῦ πυρὸς τῆς καιομένης ἐν θείῳ). While the idea of a burning lake may draw on several traditions, the *Theogony* suggests the kernel of this notion in Typhoeus' defeat, and later accounts make the connection stronger in Typhoeus' association with Mount Aetna's volcanic eruptions.

Zeus' battle with Typhoeus is depicted in elemental terms and generates fire. Zeus hurls thunderbolts, striking Typhoeus repeatedly. Tremendous heat is given off, emphasized in its effect on the ocean, "heat from both of them gripped the dark-blue sea" (844: καῦμα δ᾽ ὑπ᾽ ἀμφοτέρων κάτεχεν ἰοειδέα πόντον); "and all of earth was seething, and heaven and sea" (847: ἔζεε δὲ χθὼν πᾶσα καὶ οὐρανὸς ἠδὲ θάλασσα). An elemental battle between fire and water is taking place, in which fire proves stronger. Homeric epic evidences a parallel tradition in the battle between Hephaistos and the river Xanthos (*Iliad* 21.352–67). As Zeus gains mastery of the dragon, his thunderbolts have all of Typhoeus' heads in flames (855–56: ἀμφὶ δὲ πάσας / ἔπρεσε θεσπεσίας κεφαλὰς δεινοῖο πελώρου). In his climactic defeat, a flame shoots up from the thunderstruck dragon (859: φλὸξ δὲ κεραυνωθέντος ἀπέσσυτο τοῖο ἄνακτος).

The same motifs also occur in the battle between the Olympians and the Titans, as Caldwell notes (1987: 73), "The cosmic repercussions of the battle [on ll. 839–52] duplicate in detail the description of the Titanomachy." Caldwell emphasizes (ibid.) that in both episodes, "the earth is set on fire (859–67, 693–700)." In the earlier episode as well there is an emphasis on the extreme heat's effect on the oceans: "and all the earth was seething, and Ocean's streams" (695: ἔζεε δὲ χθὼν πᾶσα καὶ Ὠκεανοῖο ῥέεθρα). As the myth develops over the next few centuries, the fire erupting from Typhoeus becomes equated with volcanic activity, with later authors locating the imprisoned Typhoeus under Mount Aetna (Aeschylus, *Prometheus* 363–68, and Pindar, *Pythian* 1.17ff).[40]

In Revelation 20, a series of acts, with motifs found in the *Theogony's* defeats of the Titans and Typhoeus, leads to the final defeat of the dragon. First in Revelation 19, the white horse and its rider take the beast, who is leading the kings of earth against him, and his prophet, throwing them into the burning lake (19:11–20). An angel, "with the keys to the abyss," then seizes the dragon, puts him in chains, and hurls him into an abyss (20:2–3: καὶ ἐκράτησεν τὸν δράκοντα … καὶ ἔβαλεν αὐτὸν εἰς τὴν ἄβυσσον, καὶ ἔκλεισεν καὶ ἐσφράγισεν ἐπάνω αὐτοῦ). This corresponds to Hesiod's depiction of Typhoeus, and earlier the Titans, hurled into Tartaros. The *Theogony* clearly expresses the notion of something along the lines of an abyss, "a great chasm, and he would not reach the floor even after a whole year" (740–41: χάσμα μέγ᾽, οὐδέ κε πάντα τελέσφορον εἰς ἐνιαυτὸν / οὖδας ἵκοιτ᾽). West (1966: 364) argues that it may be a true abyss, "or the chasm is bottomless, as in Euripides."

After having been confined in the abyss, chained for 1,000 years, the dragon is released (20:3, 7–9) and leads nations astray (πλανῆσαι) throughout the earth, mustering forces for a war. Though Typhoeus has no such direct interaction with mortals, Hesiod's account of how he is the source of dangerous winds that forever after plague humanity is a smaller, less theological, version of the same motif.

The dragon's increased degree of interaction in mortals' affairs prompts a second conflict (Rev 20:10–15). This time the dragon's defeat is even closer to Hesiod's account of Typhoeus: "And fire came down from heaven and consumed them" (καὶ κατέβη πῦρ ἐκ τοῦ οὐρανοῦ καὶ κατέφαγεν αὐτούς: 20:9) parallels Zeus defeating Typhoeus with thunderbolts prompting worldwide conflagration. "And the devil (the dragon) was hurled into the lake of fire and sulfur" (καὶ ὁ διάβολος ... ἐβλήθη εἰς τὴν λίμνην τοῦ πυρὸς καὶ θείου: 20:10). As is the case with some of the defeated Titans, the Beast, his prophet, and perhaps the dragon are to be tortured in the burning lake for all time (καὶ βασανισθήσονται ἡμέρας καὶ νυκτὸς εἰς τοὺς αἰῶνας τῶν αἰώνων: 20:10). In both Hesiod and Revelation, the dragons' defeats conclude with the same irony: each fire-breathing dragon is defeated by a superior wielder of fiery weapons.

In a final parallel, both myths feature a second instance of the motif of one immortal swallowing the offspring of another, but with a different agent, and now with the motif employed in a *positive* sense: to ensure the stability of the new divine reign. Near the end of the *Theogony*, Zeus learns from Gaia and Ouranos that his first wife, Mêtis, the goddess of cunning intelligence, is destined to give birth to wily, powerful children (886–900). Learning this only after she is pregnant, and resolved to break the chain of succession that had gone from Ouranos to Kronos, then Kronos to himself, Zeus swallows the pregnant Mêtis. As Lopéz-Ruiz notes (2010: 142), "In Hesiod the secondary reuse and elaboration of this motif ... Zeus swallows his pregnant wife ... in order to prevent the birth of a successor and always have her moral guidance." Forever after Zeus will have cunning intelligence within him.

To appreciate the swallowing motif in Revelation 12 we need to consider the surprising use of a personified *Gê*. Hesiod's Gaia, Mother Earth, has a significant role throughout the *Theogony*.[41] Her interventions, at several stages of the myth, are crucial for Zeus' ultimate victory. For instance, Gaia advises Rhea how to evade Kronos' designs to safely give birth to Zeus.[42] Hesiod's Gaia contracts to *Gê* in New Testament Greek but surprisingly maintains a corresponding role in Revelation 12. Only here, in the entire Bible,[43] is Earth personified, as in Hesiod.[44] In Revelation 12, when the dragon pursues the "woman," "after the woman the serpent threw water from his mouth like a river, so that she would be borne away by it" (12:15: Καὶ ἔβαλεν ὁ ὄφις ἐκ τοῦ στόματος αὐτοῦ ὀπίσω τῆς γυναικὸς ὕδωρ ὡς ποταμόν, ἵνα αὐτὴν ποταμοφόρητον ποιήσῃ). *Gê* intervenes to help her, "*Gê* helped the woman, *Gê* opened her mouth and swallowed down the flood that the dragon had hurled from its mouth" (12:16: καὶ ἐβοήθησεν ἡ γῆ τῇ γυναικὶ, καὶ ἤνοιξεν ἡ γῆ τὸ στόμα καὶ κατέπιεν τὸν ποταμὸν ὃν ἔβαλεν ὁ δράκων ἐκ τοῦ στόματος αὐτοῦ). As in Hesiod, where Gaia intervenes to frustrate Kronos (494), here Revelation's *Gê* intervenes to frustrate his counterpart, the dragon. While it is not exactly the same motif because what *Gê* here swallows is not offspring, it is the exact equivalent of the same Greek compound verb (Rev 12:16: κατέπιεν; *Theogony* 467, 473: κατέπινε). The author could have depicted her intervention in several other ways but has opted for having a personified Earth swallow to defeat the myth's principal antagonist, as in Hesiod.

How should we interpret these parallels? Revelation has several passages in the Hebrew Bible as models for depictions of the dragon. Psalms 74:14 briefly mentions Yahweh breaking τὰς κεφαλὰς τοῦ δράκοντος. Isaiah 27:1 depicts Yahweh smiting the dragon with his sword. Other relevant passages (Ps 18 = 2 Sam 22, Ps 89:9, Isa 51:9–10; Job 9:8, 13, 41:10–13) also refer to versions of the combat myth, but none of these passages have the specific motifs and elements we have observed. The initial focus on a heavenly choir, with whom the narrator interacts, already begins to evoke paradigms not fully at home in Hebrew Bible myth. Several other motifs, in their determined polytheism, are simply outside the Hebrew Bible's typical conception: the *goddess* about to give birth, the war in heaven, and, perhaps most unusual of all, the personification of Earth, a second goddess, acting as an agent, intervening. We know that the author of Revelation is open to employing elements from Greco-Roman culture, given the consensus that the Beast alludes to the Emperor Nero,[45] as Collins (1976: 187) notes, "The adoption of the Nero legend in Revelation 13 and 17 is a further example of the way the apocalyptist drew upon the non-Jewish culture of his environment."[46]

Hesiod's *Theogony* not only has all the same motifs, it uses them in largely the same sequence. Written in the same language as is Revelation, Hesiod's text remained well known throughout the Greco-Roman world, at the time of Revelation's composition. Early Christians were educated in a Greco-Roman rhetorical tradition: Quintilian, *Insitutio Oratoria* 10.1.52, lists Hesiod among models to be imitated. Sandnes (2009: 36, 180, 183) documents even Basil of Caesarea citing Hesiod. The New Testament authors lived in a largely Hellenic world, and knew the Hebrew Bible only in the Greek Septuagint.

At one level, then, parallels between the *Theogony* and Revelation could be indirect, part of a larger cultural background that would, consciously or unconsciously, have been absorbed by educated inhabitants of the larger Greek-speaking world. We might think of composers and songwriters who have absorbed a musical phrase, reemploying it without realizing its prominence in a previous work. However, filmmakers constantly draw on iconic scenes from, say, Hitchcock or Kubrick films, on the one hand, alluding to them, on the other, refashioning them in different guises for their own purposes. Audience members, with differing levels of competency, may or may not recognize the use of such "subtexts." To my mind, the correspondences we have traced are too specific to be indirect and suggest a relationship more like the second model, reflecting some intentionality.

But why might the *Theogony* serve as a source or model for Revelation? The series of correspondences we are considering helps explain some of the oddities of Revelation. Consider Michael's role in defeating the dragon the first time (12:7–9). As a named individual immortal, separate from God, he is unprecedented from the perspective of the Hebrew Bible and the New Testament. He instantiates the surprisingly polytheistic texture of Revelation. Comparison with the *Theogony* suggests he corresponds, in part, to Heracles, a hero whose great exploits are parallel to those of his father Zeus (as are Michael's to Christ's), in part to Athena, the immortal most concerned with executing Zeus' larger designs, and with victory in war. *Gê*'s unexpected role and intervention come into clearer focus placed in context with the *Theogony*'s treatment of Gaia.

At the core of the *Theogony* is the succession myth (cf. López-Ruiz, 2010, passim; Goslin: 354), three generations of father-to-son succession, Ouranos, to Kronos, to Zeus. Hesiod persuasively provides multiple answers to answer the question of why Zeus is the *final* sky father. López-Ruiz notes the easy adaptability of succession myths (2010: 128–29),

> [T]his kind of narrative traveled easily across neighboring ethnic and linguistic frontiers and was adapted and transformed to fit prevailing trends and interpretations of coexisting myths, whether they were "old" or "new," Greek or "foreign." The narrative schema of a succession of gods provided a "grid" into which foreign and local elements could be easily adapted to specific theological and literary ends.

At the core of Christianity, as highlighted by Revelation and its correspondences with the *Theogony*, is a succession myth (though, to my knowledge, rarely discussed as such): the center of the religion is transferred from Father to Son. Revelation presents a new version of the traditional mythic type, in which the Son not only peacefully coexists with the Father but also seems coregent with him, unlike the *Theogony* and its predecessors.

Because Christianity often positions itself as a corrective against earlier religions, I suggest that Revelation consciously appropriates structures from Hesiod's narrative, and does so with a specific agenda. In the symbolic, coded language Revelation employs, *Satan* could refer to the god of another religion, which, from a Judeo-Christian perspective, cannot be the true god. Zeus could be figured as, or equated with, Satan, as Pagels notes (11). Thus, Revelation 12's dragon, Satan, about to devour the offspring of the goddess, could also allude to Zeus' swallowing the goddess Mêtis, pregnant with Athena. Milton clearly makes a reading like this in *Paradise Lost* 2.648–870 (esp. 749–67), where Sin is depicted as a goddess, having been born from Satan's head, just as Athena from Zeus at *Theogony* 924–26 (cf. the *Homeric Hymn to Athena*, 28.4–9). In other words, Milton endows his Satan with one of Zeus' most well-known acts. In this sense, Revelation's correspondences can be interpreted as "correcting" the earlier myths that had these motifs, now showing, from a Judeo-Christian perspective, the "true" form of the several mythic types.

We are now able to briefly reconsider the episode noted previously at 2 Samuel 5, and following. It seems likely that the authors of Revelation also use it as a partial rubric, both on the strength of its own episodes and their intersection with the *Theogony*. In 2 Samuel 5, like the *Theogony* and Revelation, the Hebrew Bible presents its key instance of the succession myth. The birth of the child at Revelation 12:5, "who is destined to rule all nations," is what prompts the dragon's rebellion and war. Quite similarly, as McCarter notes of 2 Samuel 5:18 (158), "it was David's accession to the throne of Israel ... that provoked the Philistine show of force." They launch a battle in the valley of the *Titans*, in the Septuagint's rendering. When David defeats these Titan-associated Philistines, with attendant theomachian overtones, it imbues his succession with a larger dimension, central to the Hebrew Bible, as Doak well notes (2012: 114), "David's ascension to the throne of Israel must, on all symbolic levels, involve a defeat of unruly forces, of chaos, and of all disorder." Revelation's prelude to the events in chapter 12 features its only mention of the Ark (11:19), "God's sanctuary in heaven was opened, and within his sanctuary was seen the ark of his covenant." Victorious in 2 Samuel 5, David goes on to retrieve the Ark, and later have a temple built for it. Revelation culminates in a new heaven, a new earth, but especially a new Jerusalem, all corresponding to and magnifying the earlier function of the Ark in 2 Samuel.

Revelation's correspondences with the *Theogony* demonstrate the traditional nature of much of Revelation and reveal a startling syncretism at work in biblical narrative.[47] By putting it in an ancient context, its original context of Hellenized Imperial Rome, we can see that much of it is composed almost entirely of traditional motifs, many of which are so common as to be found in well-known narratives outside of the Bible. We should understand Revelation's use of Hesiod as deliberate, I suggest, meant to be perceived by some of its intended audience, who would then see Revelation as a "correction" of Hesiod's own narrative.

Notes

1 Though we lack consensus on the date, I follow Suggs: 1556: "the book in its present form probably was written during the reign of Domitian (81–96 C.E.)"; cf. A. Y. Collins 2000: 386–87.
2 See Clifford 2000 on the roots of apocalypticism, in general, in ancient Near Eastern myth.
3 Among many studies see especially West (1966, 1997) and, more recently, López-Ruiz (2010).
4 E.g., *The Enuma Elish* and *The Song of Kumarbi*.
5 See discussion in Smith 2008: 139 ff.

6 On interconnections between Ugaritic myth and the Old Testament see Smith 1990: 2001. On the essentially Babylonian character of much of Genesis, see Carr 1996.

7 Cf. also Taylor 2007, and Louden 2011a: 258–82.

8 Collins 1976: 2: "There are also certain key motifs in Revelation which ... can only be explained as adaptations of Greco-Roman mythology and political propaganda."

9 Cf. ibid.: 58: "It would seem that the author of Revelation was consciously attempting to be international by incorporating and fusing traditional elements from a variety of cultures."

10 See discussion in Louden 2009, 2011a: 204–21. Consider A. Y. Collins's characterization (2000: 387): "a description of visions and auditions of heavenly origin."

11 We discuss this tendency in Chapter 11 as an instance of *retrospective prophecy*.

12 See, e.g., Finkelberg 2005: 162–63.

13 Also noted by Milton, *Paradise Lost* 4.716–18.

14 2 Samuel 5:18: Καὶ οἱ ἀλλόφυλλοι παραγίγονται, καὶ συνέπεσαν εἰς τὴν κοιλάδα τῶν Τιτάνων, 22: Καὶ προσέθεντο ἔτι ἀλλόφυλλοι τοῦ ἀναβῆναι, καὶ συνέπεσαν εν τῇ κοιλάδι τῶν Τιτάνων.

15 On the Rephaim, giants in the Hebrew Bible, and some intersections both exhibit with Greek culture, see Doak 2012: 10–23.

16 Cf. discussion in López-Ruiz (2010: 53–54) of parallels commentators have noted between Hesiod and Moses, and other Hebrew Bible prophets.

17 See discussion in Pagels 2012: 41–43.

18 E.g., Ford 1975: 79–80: "There is a continual sound of heavenly singing both from the living creatures and the elders ... songs of praise"; cf. Liddel, Scott, and Jones, λέγω, 12: "sing."

19 Passages from the Hebrew Bible are from Suggs, *The Oxford Study Bible*.

20 See West (1966: 290–91) for discussion of some Hittite parallels in the myth of Kumarbi.

21 Cf. Collins 1976: 71–76.

22 Ibid.: 66, 75, 84, 128.

23 The *Theogony* (453–58) depicts her as mother, in addition to Zeus, of Poseidon, Hades, Hera, Demeter, and Hestia.

24 Clay 2003: 13: "The *Theogony* ... leads to the formation of a stable cosmos and ultimately achieves its *telos* under the tutelage of Zeus."

25 As Ford notes (189), the same expression Revelation 12: 2 uses to denote the "woman's" pregnancy is also used at Matthew 1:18 and 23 of Mary.

26 Cf. ibid.: 197: "her painful childbirth"; and Le Frois's translation, "and is in anguish to bring forth."

27 In a link with Apollo's myth, when Kronos later vomits up the stone, Zeus sets it in Delphi.

28 Ouranos' frequent epithet, ἀστερόεις, "starry, star-spangled" (*Theogony* 106, 463, 470, 891, and in the *Homeric Hymns* to Gê and Helios), overlaps with Revelation 12's "woman," στέφανος ἀστέρων δώδεκα.

29 Cf. 2 Samuel 5:17, "When the Philistines learnt that David had been anointed king over Israel, they came up in force to seek him out."

30 West 1966: 337.

31 Cf. Ford: 193 on 12:6–13, "Many scholars argue that the text was not originally Christian. It omits all reference to the earthly life, work, death, and resurrection of Christ, and attributes a passive and subordinate role to the Messiah: Satan is overcome by Michael, not by the Messiah."

32 Judaism developed a tradition depicting a rebellion in heaven by Satan, hinted at in the Hebrew Bible, but only fully developed in extrabiblical materials, ultimately deriving from the older Canaanite/Ugaritic account of Athtar. See Collins 1976: 129, 143.

33 See further discussion of Gaia's role at West 1966: 24.

34 For the fullest studies, see Fontenrose, and Collins 1976: 57–85.

35 For an analysis of the syntax, see Louden 1993.

36 Cf. Apollodorus, *The Library* (1.9.3, 2.3.1).

37 Athena is the Greek god with the most in common with Michael. On her role as Zeus' chief instrument in war see Louden 2006: 214–15, 253, 266–72. In Aeschylus, *Eumenides* 826–28, she is the only god who has the key to Zeus' thunderbolts.

38 Cf. Goslin: 368: "Even after his defeat Typhoeus persists as a force of disorder in the form of the destructive winds that occasionally plague men on land and sea (869–80). These rush about in the form of an indistinct whirlwind (ἀέλλη) bringing pain (πῆμα) to man … Typhoeus' winds operate as a kind of 'black hole' in Zeus' order, an ungovernable and undifferentiated force that persists even into the present time"; and (369): "The Typhonic winds … reaffirm man's fragile place in the world and dependence on Zeus' beneficial rule."

39 See our discussion in Chapter 10.

40 It is even more explicit in versions closer to the time of Revelation, such as Ovid, "*degravat Aetna caput; sub qua resupinus harenas / eiectat flammamque ferox vomit ore Typhoeus*" *Metamorphoses* 5.352–53; cf. Apollodorus, ἐξ οὗ μέχρι δεῦρό φασιν ἀπὸ τῶν βληθέντων κεραυνῶν γίνεσθαι πυρὸς ἀναφυσήματα, *The Library*, 1.6.3.

41 See Caldwell's assessment (74), "The capricious Gaia," because, while she intervenes repeatedly to aid Zeus' cause in most of the *Theogony*, she also gives birth to Typhoeus (821).

42 Gaia serves a similar role, providing guidance and prophetic advice to Prometheus, in Aeschyus' *Prometheus* 211–20.

43 There are partial parallels in Numbers 16:32, 26:10; cf. Deuteronomy 11:6, Psalms 106:16–18. But these differ in key respects, and are less similar to Gê in Revelation 12 than Gaia's usual role in Hesiod's poem, and more like *Theogony* 183–84, where Gaia receives the bloody drops that spring from Ouranos.

44 Gaia is personified, or acts as an agent, throughout the *Theogony*: 126–39, 147, 158–83, 238, 463, 469–86, 493–94, 505, 626–28, 821, [858, 861], 884, 891.

45 Cf. A. Y. Collins 1976: 174–86, A. Y. Collins 2000: 389, 395, Louden 2009, and our discussion in Chapter 10.

46 Cf. Koester 2014: 126: "Stories from Greco-Roman mythology and legend contribute to Revelation's intertextual quality."

47 Cf. Louden (2011a: 320–23), on Genesis 37, 39–46 as written in a dialogic relationship with the *Odyssey*.

9 Ovid's Palace of the Sun (*Metamorphoses* 2.1–30) and Revelation 4

When John ascends to heaven in Revelation 4, he witnesses a scene unlike any other in the Bible, though commentators have argued that Ezekiel and Exodus 28 offer precedents for some details. A gleaming throne, with a being seated on it, is surrounded by 24 additional thrones, immortal beings seated on them. Seven flaming torches are before the main throne, and four additional beings occupy the center immediately around the main throne. While there is no doubt as to the identity of the One seated on the central throne, varying suggestions have been made as to the three groups of 24, 7, and 4. It is typical of apocalyptic myth to function simultaneously on several levels. So, for instance, the woman about to give birth in Revelation 12:1–2, 13–17 is not only a queen-of-heaven figure, but she can also be, in some respects, Israel, Mary, and the Church, as we observed in Chapter 8. The same is true of the 24, the 7, and the 4: they can be understood from multiple perspectives simultaneously. In commentary on Revelation, there is perhaps the least consensus as to the identity of the 24 elders and their thrones. We here consider how these groups, and other details in Revelation 4, correspond to Ovid's description of the Palace of the Sun (*Metamorphoses* 2.1–30), when Phaethon ascends there to meet him, as also discussed in Chapter 5.

Whitaker, placing Revelation within a larger Greco-Roman context, argues that Revelation 4–5 might be understood as an instance of *ecphrasis*. I quote him at length (228),

> During the second sophistic period (70 CE onward), *ekphrasis* became a common term and a widely taught rhetorical tool, "That found its application in almost every form of oral and written communication, even in Jerusalem's inner circles."[1] Of the many possible techniques at an orator's disposal, ekphrasis is one that particularly suits the imaginative nature of apocalyptic literature ... Apocalypse is a syncretic book, bringing together both Greco-Roman and Hebrew traditions.

While Whitaker is quite correct in noting the ubiquity of ecphrasis in the period, it is unnecessary to tie or link knowledge of it to the study of rhetoric. Ecphrases are alive and well for the previous eight centuries, a standard feature in the epic tradition from Homer onward. Whitaker (234) notes the most famous example of ecphrasis in epic poetry, that depicting Achilles' shield (*Iliad* 18.478–615). Koester notes Revelation's repeated tendency to draw on preexisting narratives from classical mythology (126), "Stories from Greco-Roman mythology and legend contribute to Revelation's intertextual quality."

Having established the relevance of ecphrasis to a consideration of Revelation 4, the question one should ask at this point, then, is, do we have a particular classical instance of ecphrasis that is most relevant to Revelation 4? We have a very clear answer to this in Ovid's account of the Palace of the Sun (*Metamorphoses* 2.1–30).[2] Ovid's famous ecphrasis offers antecedent parallels for each of the items listed in the preceding text, the central throne and its occupant, the 24, the 7, and the 4, as well as for other general characteristics of Revelation 4. I repeat from Chapter 5 Anderson's observation on how influential this ecphrasis is for later traditions (233): "In this passage, as in the description of the wind Notus in 1.265 ff. and in many later passages of this poem, Ovid is a major poetic inspiration of later allegory [cf. 15.199–213]."

What might such correspondences suggest? Much as in Chapter 5, I will argue that this episode of the *Metamorphoses* serves as a model and reference for the composers of Revelation, that they are consciously reacting to it, absorbing, and building on it. A broadly similar relationship holds for Hebrew Bible scribes when they are reworking a narrative whose origin lies outside of Israel, as in the myth of the great flood. They adapt its motifs and larger contours, as necessary, to conform to a monotheistic conception, for an Israelite audience, "translation" thus in several different respects. But they are also, implicitly, intending that their resultant narrative be regarded as the *true* version of a given myth, a corrective against other, earlier, instances of a similar story. Throughout Israel's ancient history, she coexists alongside more powerful, dominant cultures against which she reacts and responds. Inevitably, in reacting to them, she is influenced by them, and defines her own existence and identity partly in response to them. The same holds for New Testament narratives, though now the dominant power is not to the east, but to the west, Greco-Roman culture in general, and the Roman Empire in particular. The Greek and Latin languages, dominant throughout the Mediterranean world, and the most influential documents composed in them, now provide significant models of sacred narrative against which emerging Christians must develop their own.

We will first trace a series of six common motifs and narrative structures to establish how Ovid's brief scene provides us with a lens, and context, for Revelation 4.

On the one hand, Ovid's depiction of the Sun's divine court serves as a template for much of Revelation 4. On the other hand, Revelation 4 can be understood as a synthesis of Ovid's account, with elements retained from the Hebrew Bible, even elements from Hesiod's *Theogony*, a classic instance of syncretism.[3]

Phaethon and John ascend to the throne room (2.19–20; 4:1)

Ovid's setting for the episode is the Sun's palace (1.1: *Regia Solis erat*). His description of how Phaethon ascends to his father's palace (*adclivi … limite … venit*: "he came by way of a steep path"), can be understood in two ways, as Anderson (1997: 232) suggests,

> This could signify that the palace, like the lordly homes of Roman nobles, was prominently situated on a commanding elevation; or possibly *the boy rose into the heavens,* where the Sun has its natural position (italics mine).

I think Anderson's second interpretation should take precedence, that, at a vague and metaphorical level, "the boy rose into the heavens, where the Sun has its natural position." We find confirmation for this reading in that the divine beings in attendance on the Sun (discussed in the following text) are better understood as being set in the heavens. Revelations 4:1 is similarly vague about the means but more specific about the location: it is set in heaven, θύρα ἠνεῳγμένη ἐν τῷ οὐρανῷ … Ἀνάβα ὧδε, "A door opened in Heaven … 'Come up here.'"

In both settings a typical ecphrasis now unfolds

As R. Brown notes (1987: 211), "[L]ike the palaces in the *Odyssey* it [the Sun's palace] is described in connection with the arrival and entrance of a visitor."[4] Revelation employs the same approach and perspective: we go with John up to the throne room and see it through his eyes. The means of his ascent is as swift as Phaethon's, and similarly metaphorical (4:2): εὐθέως ἐγενόμην ἐν Πνεύματι, "straightaway I was in the Spirit." Koester explains (2014: 359), "John's journey is a spiritual or visionary one … repeating this expression here [it occurs before at 1:10] signals a change to a heavenly setting."

The two ascents and *ecphrases* are similarly positioned within their larger works. Ovid places his right at the beginning of Book Two, out of 15 Books. In Revelation, Chapters 1–3 serve as a defined, introductory unit.[5] The beginning of Chapter 4, out of 22 total chapters, marks the beginning of the second unit or cycle.

The one seated on the throne (2.21; 4:2)

Each ascending character immediately sees God, seated on a throne. In Ovid it is the Sun, here specified by a title usually associated with Apollo (2.23–24: *sedebat / in solio Phoebus*).[6] Revelation does not specify that the figure is the deity, only that he is seated on a throne,[7] 4:2: καὶ ἰδοὺ θρόνος ἔκειτο ἐν τῷ οὐρανῷ, καὶ ἐπὶ τὸν θρόνον καθήμενος, "and behold there was a throne in Heaven, and upon it a seating one."

Is surrounded by brightness (2.22–23; 4:3)

Initially, Phaethon cannot bear to look at the Sun on his throne (*neque enim propiora ferebat / lumina*) because of the brightness. In Revelation radiance emanates from the throne and from the one seated on it (discussed with other motifs in the following text).

He is wearing a purple robe, gleaming with emeralds

Ovid's Sun is wearing a regal purple robe, gleaming with bright emeralds (2.23–24: *purpurea velatus veste … claris lucente smaragdis*). In Revelation, the one seated on the throne is ὅμοιος ὁράσει λίθῳ ἰάσπιδι καὶ σαρδίῳ, "in appearance like a precious stone, a jasper and a cornelian." While the description is only through analogy ("in appearance like"), it conveys a comparable impression as the Sun's, especially if we accept Koester's view on the colors of the two stones (360): "Jasper referred to precious stones ranging from green to blue, purple to rose. Carnelian was a reddish stone, which suggests that God's presence had a fiery radiance."[8] Though the color purple is not specified, it is perhaps implied through the combination of colors from the two stones. Revelations 4:3 continues with a more specific correspondence with Ovid: καὶ ἶρις κυκλόθεν τοῦ θρόνου ὅμοιος ὁράσει σμαραγδίνῳ, "and there was a rainbow, like an emerald, in a circle around the throne." Gleaming emeralds are closely identified with both seated gods.[9]

Among the many divine attendants is a group of 24 heavenly beings (2.25–26; 4:4)

Phaethon and John both see a throng of divine beings arrayed around, and attending, the one seated on the throne. In Ovid, the many beings are aspects of the Sun in his role as marking divisions of time on earth, as Anderson (1997: 229) notes, "a host of allegorical figures that symbolize his [the Sun's] close association with the orderly passage of time."[10] Ovid first quickly enumerates, on the Sun's right and left, four beings, Day, Month, Year, and Century (2.25–26: *A dextra laevaque Dies et Mensis et Annus / Saeculaque*). But then he slows his narrative's pace to focus on a larger group, the Hours, *et positae spatiis aequalibus Horae* (2.26), "and the Hours, positioned at equal intervals," whose number he does not need to specify, but is, in fact, 24.

In Revelations 4, first to be mentioned, in its surprisingly large cast of heavenly beings in attendance, is a group of 24, arrayed around the seated figure (4:4 Καὶ κυκλόθεν τοῦ θρόνου θρόνοι εἴκοσι τέσσαρες· καὶ ἐπὶ τοὺς θρόνους εἴκοσι τέσσαρες πρεσβυτέρους καθημένους): "and in a circle around the throne were twenty-four thrones; and upon the thrones twenty-four elders, seated." Revelation's "in a circle" neatly corresponds to Ovid's *positae spatiis aequalibus*. Throughout the respective *ecphrases*, Ovid does not specifically articulate the name of the number of the respective groups of beings, it being clear enough that the Hours are 24, the Days 7, and the Seasons 4. Whereas Revelation, with its keen employment of numerology, and *gematria*, not only specifies the number but emphatically repeats it throughout each subsection.

Koester reviews six proposals as to the identity of the 24 (360–63, 368), including what may be the majority view, that they are the 12 tribes *and* the 12 apostles.[11] But there are rarely discussed problems with this view. Revelation 4 does not say that there are *two* groups of *12*, nor do any of the either groups (the seven, the four) function as composites in this divine assemblage. If the 24 are understood as referencing the disciples, would this include Judas? Given his unique role in the Gospels, it does not seem credible to propose that Judas would be present in heaven.[12] I suggest that viewing Ovid's *ecphrasis* as a template for Revelation 4's 24, understanding the 24 as the Hours, is both more sensible and less problematic.[13] In Revelation 4:10–11, the 24 throw their στεφάνους, which Koester (365) translates as "laurel wreaths," before the one on the throne. If he is correct in choosing "laurel wreath" over "crown" as the most appropriate meaning, we have further evidence that the episode, and the 24, reference Greco-Roman culture.

Also among the divine attendants is a group of seven (2.25; 4:5)

The first individual Ovid specifies is *Dies*, Day (*a dextra laevaque Dies*). The second group specified in Revelation 4 is a group of "seven torches, burning with fire, in front of the throne, which are the spirits of God" (καὶ ἑπτα λαμπάδες πυρὸς καιόμεναι ἐνώπιον τοῦ θρόνου, ἅ εἰσιν τὰ ἑπτὰ πνεύματα τοῦ θεοῦ). As to their identity, Koester suggests (363), "These spirits are angelic beings, depicted as Flames." Although Revelation, as part of its thematic numerological program, employs the number Seven for many additional meanings, it is again sensible to view Ovid's *ecphrasis* as not only providing a rubric for virtually all of Revelation 4, but that the seven Days are here also an antecedent for the seven burning torches. In addition, the literal meaning of Day as "bright Sky" offers a relevant lens and context for the flaming torches.

A special group of four receives the longest description and closest focus, and serves a climactic function (2.27–30; 4:6–8)

Ovid's *ecphrasis* concludes with a group of four beings, who, as with the Hours and the Days, are directly dependent upon the Sun for their existence: the Seasons.[14] As throughout, Ovid does not articulate or emphasize the number four, but simply describes the Four Seasons in turn, Spring, with a flowering wreath; Summer, with gathered grain; Fall, stained with grapes; and Winter, aged with gray hair.[15] In *Metamorphoses* Book 2, in addition to being the longest individual unit, this caps Ovid's *ecphrasis*.

Revelations 4 offers a correspondence in the most unusual unit of its *ecphrasis*, the Four Zoas, "And in the middle of the throne, and in the circle of the throne, were Four *Zoas*, teeming with eyes, on front and back" (4:6).

While there is no question that here Revelation 4 is also responding to the four beings depicted at Ezekiel 1:4–10,[16] nonetheless, the larger parallels continue following the rubric Ovid's *ecphrasis* provides, in what is perhaps the fullest flowering of the syncretistic impulse. As Ovid for the Seasons, Revelation 4 continues with a brief characterization of each of the four. The first has a face like a Lion, the second an Ox, the third a Human, and the fourth an Eagle. A clear progression is implied from the undomesticated Lion, to the Ox that serves mortals, to a mortal, to an eagle capable of soaring to the heavens.[17] Ovid's progression between the four is rooted more in the world of Nature, the cycle of plant growth, from birth to death. However, he returns, in his poem's final book, with a more expanded description of the four seasons, now as instantiations of the different ages of a human life (15.199–213). He carefully arranges his section on the Four Seasons, marking each of the first three Seasons by repeating the verb "*stabat*," "(he) was standing."[18] Revelation 4 marks three of the Four Zoas with the repeated formula "the ordinal (πρῶτον / δεύτερον τρίτον τέταρον) being (ζῷον) had a face like (ὅμοιον)." Koester reviews several possibilities as to referents for the Four Zoas, including the four Gospels, the four elements, and four signs of the Zodiac.[19] If we accept my premise that Ovid's depiction of the Sun's court serves as an underlying rubric for Revelation's heavenly court, the Four Seasons provide a sensible component, perhaps as one of several different simultaneous rubrics, including Ezekiel's four beings. The unique attribute given them, γέμοντα ὀφθαλμῶν ἔμπροσθεν καὶ ὄπισθεν, which we discuss in the following text, also makes sense within the context of Ovid's ecphrasis. Ovid's celestial beings in attendance about the Sun, taken together, with all their many perspectives on time, add up to a dynamic portrayal of eternity, relevant to the larger concerns of the entire Book of Revelation.

Immediately following the description of the four Seasons, Ovid redirects his narrative's focus to the Sun, who, as he sees Phaethon before him, is characterized as all seeing: "The Sun saw the youth approach, with those eyes with which he sees all things" (2.32: *Sol oculis iuvenem, quibus adspicit omnia, vidit*).[20] In Revelation 4, it is the four Zoas who are given a form of this traditional divine attribute,[21] 4:6: γέμοντα ὀφθαλμῶν ἔμπροσθεν καὶ ὄπισθεν, a detail not present in Ezekiel 1. Correspondences with *Metamorphoses* 2 may well continue past this point because Ovid's doomed Phaethon also suggests partial parallels to Revelation's lamb with marks of sacrifice on him (5:6).

Ovid's set piece lacks any known predecessors,[22] though it is possible that there were some that have not survived. R. Brown (211) emphasizes the former and has a suggestion for the latter: "Ovid's elaborate description of the *regia Solis* (Met. 2.1–30) has no known precedent, though it is possible that Euripides's *Phaethon* contained some details about Helios' palace." The apparent uniqueness of Ovid's *ecphrasis* may increase the likelihood that the author(s) of Revelation 4 recognized it as the unique vehicle useful to his/their purposes, among the many other concepts woven together to create it.

In this instance the adaptation, even partial translation, of a Greco-Roman myth is uniquely unproblematic. No euhemerizing transformations are necessary. Because the tableau Revelation 4 presents is highly polytheistic in its traditional outline, there is an exact correspondence between the one mortal observer, Phaethon/John, on the one hand, while all the others are divine in each narrative, on the other. Nor do the Revelation authors appear to be passing judgment on the Sun that I can see. Where in other instances, for example, our argument in Chapter 3 that the elder Isaac is modeled on Zeus in *Iliad* 19, the adaptation can be thought of as making editorial judgment on the original: mocking Zeus through Isaac's blindness. In Ovid's ecphrasis of the Sun's palace and Revelation 4 we have a neutral, nonjudgmental adaptation of a dynamic structure that New Testament authors found suitable to their own purposes.

The *Metamorphoses* thus may serve as a "master text" for several New Testament authors. We have argued in Chapter 5 that Ovid's account of Apollo, Phaethon, and Clymene serves as a rubric for Mark's (and Matthew's) tale of Herod, his "daughter," John the Baptist, and Herodias. Here we have made a similar claim for his *regia Solia* and Revelations 4. Several commentators have noted correspondences between Acts 14:6–19 and Ovid's account of Baucis and Philemon (*Metamorphoses* 8.621–96).[23] There are also Ovid's narratives about Aesculapius/Asclepius, placed in something like ring compositional order over his lengthy work (2.642–48; 15.533–34, 15.622–745). Early Christians were well aware of Aesculapius' relevance to Christ, as the figure who could perform miraculous acts of healing. In Chapter 10 we will argue that the penultimate episode in the entire *Metamorphoses*, Ovid's account of the deification of Caesar (15.746–870), may serve as something of an antitype to how Revelation figures Nero. This tally, which should not be assumed to be complete, suggests that at least three separate New Testament authors, the author of Mark, the author of Luke/Acts, as well as the author of Revelation, are all not only aware of but also responding to Ovid's *Metamorphoses*.

Notes

1 Wuellner 1991: 113.
2 On Ovid's description as an ecphrasis, see Anderson 1997: 226: "First comes an epic ecphrasis or description of the palace of the Sun (1–18) and then of his attendants (days, years, seasons)." Cf. Feldherr 2016: 28.
3 We argued in Chapter 8 that Hesiod's *Theogony* serves as a greater rubric for parts of Revelation 4, 12, and 19–20.
4 On Ovid's episode as an *ecphrasis* see Anderson 1997: 226, and Brown 1987: 211, 213; on Revelation 4 as also employing the conventions of an *ecphrasis*, see Whitaker 2015.
5 See Koester (2014: 231) on Revelation 1:9–3:22 as constituting the first cycle.
6 For discussion, see Anderson 1997: 233.
7 *Theos*, "God," first occurs in the *ecphrasis* at the end of 4:5, in conjunction with the Seven flaming torches.

8 Koester (2014) goes on to compare these details to Ezekiel 1:27.

9 Some of the same precious stones are elements in Aaron's ephod and breastplate at Exodus 28, as Garth Tissol pointed out to me in a personal communication. In the Septuagint's version σμάραγδος occurs at Exodus 28:9.

10 Cf., as noted in Chapter 5, Anderson 1997: 233: "Like a king attended by his courtiers, the Sun is flanked by the 'nobility of time.'" Cf. also Brown's characterization (1987: 213) that they are "personifications of the chief divisions of time, which are structured chiefly by the sun's diurnal and annual passage," and Feldherr 2016: 35, "The Sun sits in the middle of an allegorical depiction of temporal units: days, months, ages, and ultimately Horae."

11 While Koester notes adherents of each of the six possibilities he surveys, his own view is as follows (2014: 361), "The number twenty-four can best be related to the multiples of twelve that are used for God's people."

12 Acts 1:15–26, of course, depicts Peter overseeing Matthias' selection by lot to become Judas' replacement, but the latter receives no further mention in the New Testament.

13 Koester (2014: 363) briefly considers, but dismisses, the possibility of the 24 as the Hours; he does not reference Book 2 of Ovid's *Metamorphoses*.

14 Cf. Anderson 1997: 233: "The Sun also determines the seasons of the year."

15 Verque novum stabat cinctum florente corona,

> stabat nuda Aestas et spicea serta gerebat,
> stabat et Autumnus calcatis sordidus uvis
> et glacialis Hiems canos hirsute capillos.

16 See Koester 2014: 363–64.

17 Perhaps relevant is the similar fourfold progression in the helpers Psyche receives: ants, a reed, an eagle, and Cupid (Apuleius, *The Golden Ass* 6.10–21).

18 See further Brown 1987: 214.

19 Koester: 364: "In Christian tradition the Four Creatures were often identified with the four Gospels." See also 351–53.

20 Consider the relevance of Feldherr's characterization (2016: 27): "For not only is the Sun the structural center of the episode, around which all repetitions orbit, but he also governs the cosmos described within the narrative" and (28), "who governs the world" ("qui temperat orbem," 1.770).

21 Koester 2014: 364: "The descriptions suggest that they see in all directions and keep watch continuously."

22 Though Lucretius has a likely antecedent for Ovid's treatment of the Four Seasons at *De Rerum Natura* 5.737–47.

23 See, e.g., Hollis 1970: 108–9.

10 *Retrospective prophecy* and *the vision* in *Aeneid* 6, Ovid, and Revelation

Having placed the Book of Revelation in context with Hesiod's *Theogony* in Chapter 8, and with Ovid's Palace of the Sun in Chapter 9, in our final consideration of it we place it in context with the *Aeneid,* Book Six in particular, and an additional passage from Ovid's *Metamorphoses*. Aeneas' meeting in the underworld with Anchises is the *Aeneid*'s turning point.[1] His descent to Hades frees him from uncertainty about his larger mission: what it is he will bring into being. What transforms him from a typical hero on an Odyssey of sorts to the protagonist of a foundation myth is what he *sees* when he meets with Anchises, and what his father *says it all means*. To achieve these effects Vergil has Anchises perform two traditional functions prominent in earlier myth. His father directs him to *observe* souls waiting to be reborn, a parade of future Roman heroes. I will call this structure *the vision*; Vergil closely models this on earlier instances of the same device, especially in *Odyssey* 11 and Cicero's *Somnium Scipionis*.[2] Though the *Aeneid* presents the pageant as a *prophecy* to Aeneas, everything Anchises says *has already happened*, from the perspective of the external audience of the poem. I will call this technique (sometimes known as *vaticinia ex eventu*) *retrospective prophecy*. Examples are plentiful from much earlier than the *Aeneid*, particularly in Near Eastern apocalyptic narratives but also in Greek myths Vergil knew well. Euripides, for instance, often concludes his plays with an etiological pronouncement that is, in part, a *retrospective prophecy*. Athena, as we saw in Chapter 2, closes the *Ion* prophesying the protagonist's future descendants (1575–87; cf. *Hecuba* 1259–79; *Helen* 1666–77; *Iphigenia in Tauris* 1448–74).

The book of Revelation, which also has a critical focus on Rome and the Roman Empire, employs these same two structures, *the vision* and *retrospective prophecy*, as central devices. The *Aeneid* can serve as a key for reading other texts. Understanding how Vergil uses the vision and retrospective prophecy reveals more clearly how the same structures work in other myths, including Revelation. Over the millennia, the book of Revelation in particular has attracted all manner of fantastic readings, most of which ignore everything known about the historical circumstances it depicts and the traditional elements that it employs. *Aeneid* 6 thus serves as a corrective against irresponsible readings of Revelation by providing a context into which it can be set. Brief consideration of Ovid's "Deification of the Caesars" (*Metamorphoses* 15.746–870) and the *Sibylline Oracles* expands our context for understanding elements common to both the *Aeneid* and Revelation. How the two techniques, *the vision* and *retrospective prophecy*, function will be clearer in that the *Aeneid* and Revelation deploy them to depict opposite perspectives on Rome. Vergil is the ultimate insider, creator of the ultimate Roman propaganda, whereas Revelation reflects the position of outsiders, literally demonizing Rome's emperor and empire.

Engaging Revelation by using Aeneas' spectacle in Elysium as our lens not only affirms the *Aeneid*'s foundational position in Western culture but extends its scope to subjects rarely associated with it. Modern audiences look at the *Aeneid* more objectively than at biblical narratives because they do not believe in its gods or the theology it depicts. Thus, we start there to see how these two structures function.

The vision in the Aeneid

Though *the vision* is a subgenre of myth extant in ancient narratives earlier than the *Aeneid*, we can first get a clear sense of it from its use in popular narratives such as Charles Dickens's "A Christmas Carol" and Frank Capra's film *It's a Wonderful Life*. Dickens's story is largely three consecutive instances of the structure, as the ghosts of Christmas Past, Present, and Future, respectively serve as Scrooge's guide, conducting him away from the here and now, through time and/or space, to an episode in his life. He is then a spectator, as the Ghost with supernatural powers shows Scrooge about himself, confronting him with a truth, a bigger picture of how he relates to the universe. At the end of three consecutive instances of *the vision*, Scrooge is a changed man. In *It's a Wonderful Life* protagonist George Bailey is about to commit suicide over financial irregularities at his bank (that are not his fault). The angel Clarence intervenes to show Bailey what his town, Bedford Falls, would have been like if he had never been born. Clarence's supernatural powers parallel those of Dickens's three Ghosts, as he takes George out of the here and now to an alternate reality where, without George's many selfless acts, many of which help prevent the greedy Mr. Potter from taking over the town, Bedford Falls becomes a version of the underworld: Potterville, governed by Potter's greed. Bailey now wants to return to life and family, whatever the consequences of the financial scandal.

Based on Dickens and Capra we can define *the vision* as a genre of myth[3] in which *the protagonist is removed from the mortal plane; an otherworldly guide accompanies him, who reveals to him a larger truth, the "big picture," previously unknown to him. He is a transformed man as a result.* For Capra, Clarence, Bailey's guardian angel, serves as the otherworldly guide, as do Dickens's three Ghosts for Scrooge. He, as a result of seeing the big picture, will now be generous and have a renewed sense of the meaning of life. George Bailey now wants to live and sees a greater meaning in his acts and in his interrelations with the people of his town.

Vergil employs *the vision* in *Aeneid* 6 to depict Aeneas' meeting with Anchises. The episode conforms to our definition, combining elements from two earlier instances, Odysseus' meeting with his mother Antikleia in Hades (*Odyssey* 11.84–89, 152–330) and Scipio the Younger's meeting with the Elder in the heavens (*Somnium Scipionis* 6.9–26). To receive Anchises' instructions Aeneas descends to the underworld (*the protagonist is removed from the mortal plane*). In the *Odyssey*, Odysseus does not descend but sails to the under-world[4] because the *Odyssey* adapts the more traditional heroic descent under its defining rubric of the *fantastic voyage*. Directed by Circe to consult with Teiresias, Odysseus conducts a lengthier interview with his mother, Antikleia, at the end of which she introduces the unusual Catalogue of Heroines (11.225–329). Scipio the Younger, in his dream, ascends to the heavens to meet with his ancestor (*Somnium* 6.9–26). Led by the Sibyl (who partly parallels Teireisas), Aeneas makes his way to Elysium, where, as in both model texts, the protag-onist meets with his deceased parent.

In *Odyssey* 11, when Odysseus sees his mother, unaware that she had died, he tries to embrace her three times in vain. As he wonders if she is an *eidolôn* (11.213), a phantom Persephone sent, Antikleia replies with a brief account of how the soul, after death, has no substance but flutters from the body like a dream (11.216–22). Her account is one of Vergil's models for Anchises' much-lengthier account of the nature of the soul and reincarnation (*Aeneid* 6.724–51). Antikleia concludes with the admonition that Odysseus should remember (ἴσθ') all these things to tell his wife afterward (11.223–24), the narrative trigger for the *Catalogue of Women*. In introducing the subsequent parade of mythical heroines, Antikleia becomes Odysseus' otherworldly guide. As Anchises in *Aeneid* 6, the deceased parent of the hero directs him to witness a spectacle. As soon as Antikleia concludes, the women gather, each coming before Odysseus so he can learn her story. In *Somnium Scipionis*, the spectacle that the deceased ancestor shows the Younger is the cosmos but he also briefly sees his deceased parent Paulus. Vergil clearly draws on the episode's heavenly ambience (e.g., *Somnium* 6.16, 18) for his depiction of blissful Elysium.

In *Odyssey* 11, Odysseus introduces each woman in the *Catalogue* saying "and then I saw" (11.235, 260, 266, 271, 281, 298, 306, 321, 326), using forms of the same verb Antikleia used when she initiated *the vision* (εἴδω, ἴσθ'), underscoring the episode's primarily visual nature. Cicero follows suit in the *Somnium*, employing numerous verbs of vision to depict the spectacle the Elder shows the Younger (*videsne, ostendebat* 6.11; *aspicis, vidi* 6.14; *vides* 6.15; *videbantur* 6.16; *aspicis* 6.17; *admirans* 6.18; *vides* 6.19; *cernis, cerne, vides*, 6.20). Vergil does likewise throughout Aeneas' meeting with Anchises, marking the experience as primarily a visual one for Aeneas (*imago* 6.695; *videt* 6.703; *visu* 6.710; *ostendere* 6.716; *vides* 6.760; *viden* 6.779; *aspice* 6.788; *videre* 6.818; *aspice* 6.825; *cernis* 6.826; *aspice* 6.855; *videbat* 6.860). What Aeneas sees is described by Leach (122) as "a parade of individuals embodying the future glory of his race." I present more detailed consideration of the parade in our discussion of *retrospective prophecy*.

What he sees *transforms* Aeneas, as it does Scipio, Scrooge, George Bailey, and Odysseus. The otherworldly guide initiates each protagonist into a new reality, a big picture, which, once seen, gives him a new purpose and redefines his understanding of life. Odysseus' change is the least dramatic, indicating a different sense of design and purpose in the *Odyssey*'s use of *the vision*. Vergil places his version at the very end of his larger underworld episode, and, consequently, it serves as a climax of the whole book. *Odyssey* 11, however, places its vision near the middle of the larger underworld episode, right before the *Intermezzo* (11.333–84), to which it is integrally connected. Because Odysseus' narration of the *Catalogue of Heroines* is what prompts Arete to declare the Phaiakin's hospitality and secure his homecoming, this instance of *the vision* is less climactic than its counterpart in the *Aeneid*.

Odysseus' change after seeing the vision is less dramatic because the *Odyssey* instead places the transformation, the reevaluation of the meaning of life, in another character in the underworld, Achilles. When Odysseus asserts that Thetis' son is the most honored mortal in the underworld, the latter replies that he would prefer a menial existence on the earth's surface to honors in the underworld (11.489–90). His rejection of eternal fame as the hero's ultimate goal is startling, a version of the transformation the protagonist of *the vision* undergoes, Scrooge from stingy to generous, George Bailey from suicidal to life-affirming, and a doubtful Aeneas to absolute acceptance of his mission.

Vergil earlier employs an embryonic version of the vision, when, during the Sack of Troy, Venus temporarily endows Aeneas with divine sight (2.588–623). Under her otherworldly guidance he now sees Neptune, Juno, and Minerva, dismantling Troy, forces he cannot possibly contend with. Transformed by his vision, Aeneas accepts that Troy is lost and thinks of his own family instead. As in the other instances, verbs of seeing highlight the experience (*aspice*: 2.604; *vides*: 2.610; *respice*: 2.615). Immediately afterward Venus guides him safely through the city under attack.

The vision may be set either in the underworld or in the heavens. In *Odyssey* 11 the vision unfolds right in the middle of Odysseus' larger visit to the underworld. Vergil's embryonic version with Venus during the Sack of Troy suggests a displaced version of a trip to the land of the dead, partly modeled on Vergil's own earlier depiction of Orpheus' return from Hades, as Gale argues (337–38). In "A Christmas Carol" the Ghosts of Present and Future lead Scrooge through versions of an underworld trip, as is clearly the case for Clarence and George Bailey in *It's a Wonderful Life*, where Bedford Falls is now transformed into the hellish Pottersville. Because *Scipio's Dream* sets the vision in the heavens, in *Aeneid* 6 Vergil has it both ways. Aeneas makes the traditional heroic descent to the underworld, but Vergil endows Elysium with a heavenly ambience (6.637 and ff., 703–9: *valle reducta / seclusum nemus … domos placidas*).

Cicero's protagonist wants to remain on the other plane of existence where he witnesses the vision. Vergil retains a hint of this in Aeneas' surprise at how eager the souls he sees in *the vision* are to leave Elysium and return to an earthly existence (6.719–21),[5] whereas the married Odysseus and George Bailey are only interested in returning to their wives and families.

Retrospective prophecy (*vaticinia ex eventu*)

The *Aeneid* is more concerned with the larger sweep of history than is Homeric epic. If the *Aeneid*'s present time is roughly 1200 BCE,[6] Vergil, writing from the vantage point of approximately 30–20 BCE, can have his characters, gods and prophetic mortals, refer to events over a span of almost 1,200 years, all in the past from the perspective of the author and his audience. Homeric epic's diachronic span is perhaps a third of this nor does it express as close an interest in history. Occasional passages reflect the immortals' perspective on time, which can be considerable. Thus, in the *Iliad* when Zeus or Thetis refers to battle between the gods, as at 1.393–412, 15.18–24, they are probably talking about events that took place *before* the creation of mortals.[7] But such events are outside of human history. Achilles may note the possibility of his earning eternal fame (*Iliad* 9.413), but his achieving it is not depicted within the poem. Rather, it is the *Iliad*, the resultant epic, that confers it. But neither the *Iliad* nor the *Odyssey* explicitly refers to a continuum of Hellenic culture that stretches over a millennium as the *Aeneid* does repeatedly, a consequence of Vergil writing at a much later time, still concerned with events set in the same period as Homeric epic. From Homer to Vergil, the gap between the author's own era and that of his subject matter has increased by 700 years.

Vergil can thus depict events well in the *past* for his audience, but yet to happen, set in the *future*, for his own characters. He has many ways of doing this. He uses Dido's tragic relationship with Aeneas, her curse (4.615–29), as an etiology for the Punic Wars, for example. He uses his mythic narrative to explain central historical events. In this respect, the *Aeneid* has much in common with Hebrew Bible myth, which often uses the techniques of myth to explain historical events (e.g., that a city is destroyed because an angry god leads an army against it, as at Ezek 23:25). Vergil's most emphatic technique for presenting past events as future is *retrospective prophecy*.

The *Aeneid* introduces *retrospective prophecy* in Jupiter's first extended speech (1.256–96).[8] When Venus asks her Father why Aeneas still struggles to reach his destined goal, in apparent contradiction of Jupiter's earlier promise (1.229–53), he reassures her that Aeneas and his larger enterprise have his full support (1.257–62). He goes on to declare that Aeneas will be victorious in a war in Italy (1.263–64), or what the audience will soon come to know as Books 7–12 of the *Aeneid*. But Jupiter is just getting started. He quickly moves to events beyond the end of the poem, Aeneas' death and *translation* (1.265–66), then on to the reigns of Ascanius and Romulus, where he pauses dramatically marking a geometric progression from the finite to the infinite (*his ego nec metas rerum nec tempora a pono: imperium sine fine dedi*: 1.278–79). He concludes his sweeping prophecy with a specific reference to Julius Caesar (1.286–88) and allusion to Augustus' reign (1.293–96). This retrospective prophecy, then, covers a period of some 1,150 years, from the aftermath of the Trojan War to events in the external audience's recent memory, depicting all these acts as if they were in the future.

So far it may seem as if retrospective prophecy is merely a sleight of hand, as if I were to write a story set in February 1963, in which a character predicts the assassination of John F. Kennedy. But this would be to miss its main function. Retrospective prophecy's real significance lies in the authority it confers, the divine aura it bestows on its new interpretation of history. What mortals thought of as *human history* is instead revealed to be the working out of the gods' larger designs, Providence. As Jupiter in Book 1 reassures Venus, and as Anchises demonstrates to Aeneas in Book 6, the Romans are, to use the same traditional figure used in the Hebrew Bible, *God's chosen people.*[9] Arguably, this is retrospective prophecy's principal function.

The *Aeneid* also uses a lesser form of retrospective prophecy, which looks ahead in a smaller degree, not past the end of the poem. This lesser form lacks the scope of Jupiter's sweeping speech acts in Book 1, functioning more like divine prophecies in Homeric epic that Zeus issues at divine councils, offering a sketch of the next several books (e.g., as at *Iliad* 15.54–69; *Odyssey* 5.3–43). Helenus' summary of the remainder of Aeneas' voyage (3.374–462) is the *Aeneid*'s most prominent instance prior to Book 6. Declaring that Aeneas fulfills divine will, Helenus uses terms close to our definition of *retrospective prophecy*. Because it relates to Dido some time later, this prophecy has an added degree of retrospection. The Sibyl's inspired utterance (6.83–97), linked to Helenus' earlier prophecy (3.445–60), is another lesser retrospective *prophecy*. Her prophecy sketches out much of the poem's second half, the problems marriage with Lavinia will cause, the opposition of the unnamed Turnus, and the aid the Arcadians will offer through the alliance they form with Aeneas in Book 8. Like Helenus' prophecy in Book 3, the Sibyl's does not venture past the ending of the poem.

Vergil's governing model for the use of *retrospective prophecy* is again Cicero's *Somnium Scipionis*.[10] The *Somnium* employs retrospective prophecy when Scipio the Elder prophesies the subsequent career and death of Scipio the Younger (6.11–12). He can do so with complete accuracy because the present time of *Scipio's Dream*, when Scipio the Younger holds his gathering, is 120 BCE, whereas Cicero completes his work in 51 BCE.

Retrospective prophecy implicitly divides time into three different periods:

1   The period that serves as the present for the narrative's characters (but is past time for the author and his audience);
2   The period that is in the future from the perspective of the narrative and its characters (but is still in the past for author and audience); and
3   The period that is in the future from the perspective of the author and his original audience (as well as for the narrative and its characters).

Jupiter's first prophecy largely sets itself within number 2, forecasting events that remain in the past from the perspective of the original audience circa 20 BCE. His declaration that the Roman Empire is infinite and eternal (1.278–79) briefly ventures into zone number 3 but is ironic from the vantage point of our own period.

Retrospective prophecy has deep roots in earlier mythic traditions, especially in the ancient Near East. Three recent studies of Near Eastern myths relevant to the Hebrew Bible all deal with the phenomenon. Clifford and Sparks (4) note five texts from Mesopotamia (*Text A*, the *Dynastic Prophecy*, the *Uruk Prophecy*, the *Shulgi Prophecy*, and the *Marduk Prophecy*). Foster includes complete translations of the *Shulgi Prophecy* (357–59) and the *Marduk Prophecy* (388–91). Clifford offers his comments on *Text A*, dated to seventh-century Assyria, and its "prediction" that "a prince shall arise": "The events in *Text A* took place in the twelfth century,[11] five centuries before its composition, so they are all *ex eventu* by definition" (12). He makes similar observations about the *Uruk Prophecy* (13),

> The Uruk Prophecy, possibly composed in the reign of Amel-Marduk (biblical Evil-Merodach, 561–560) ... narrates the rise of six kings. The fifth king is Nebuchadnezzar II (604–562). The genuine prediction comes in lines 16–19 ... The past "predictions" are intended to lend credibility to the last statement. The course of history has been determined by the gods: Nebuchadnezzar's son is meant to rule forever.

He offers a similar conclusion about claims in the *Marduk* and *Uruk Prophecies* (14),

> [T]he last part is the genuine prophecy, made credible by the post-factum "prophecies" preceding it ... history is seen as a sequence of kingdoms, rather than, say, the dominance of a particular city, shrine, or deity ... The *Uruk Prophecy* predicts that after Nebuchadnezzar II ... his dynasty will be established forever.

Sparks also offers a similar definition and explanation of the phenomena, but focuses on a possible motivation by the author (18),

> [T]he use of *vaticinium ex eventu* (prophecy after the fact) by many ancient authors. The writers pretended to predict events before they had occurred when, in fact, the prophecies were composed *after* the events they predict. This had the obvious effect of enhancing the prophet's reputation or message because readers interpreted the prophecies as accurate predictions of the future ... pseudo-prophecy.

He offers (241–45) an overview of the same five texts Clifford discusses, which he classifies as "Mesopotamian Pseudoprophecies." He also notes two

Egyptian instances (245–47), The Prophecy of Nefertiti, even earlier than the Mesopotamian examples, and the Demotic Chronicle, which "purports to be a commentary on an older collection of prophetic oracles ... The commentary reflects knowledge not only of events during the Persian period but also of events during the Greek era." In the *Aeneid*, Vergil thus employs a well-attested, traditional technique for representing past events as future prophecy.

When Aeneas comes upon his father in the groves of the blessed, he sees souls waiting to be reincarnated, gathered around him. Anchises' explanation to him, about how souls are reborn (6.724–51), serves as segue to the Aeneid's most developed instance of *retrospective prophecy* (6.756–853, 868–86). From Aeneas' son Silvius, to be born from Lavinia after Aeneas will have died (6.760–66), to Augustus (6.791–807), Anchises rapidly traverses the entire span available to the *Aeneid* as *past time* from the audience's perspective but *future* from the characters' vantage point.

Taking in along the way Romulus (6.777–87), the deified Julius Caesar (6.789–90, 792), even Scipio (7.842–43),[12] the episode again emphasizes how the *Somnium* serves as a key model for Vergil. As in Jupiter's far-reaching predictions in Book 1, the main purpose of this retrospective prophecy, from the perspective of the addressee, is to provide reassurance, for Venus then, for Aeneas now.

Vergil plainly builds on Homer's design in *Odyssey* 11, when Odysseus' mother introduces the *Catalogue of Heroines* their souls pass before him and then give brief narratives of their lives. Taking this basic structure, the hero's deceased parent showing him a parade of souls, Vergil overlays *retrospective prophecy* onto it by having the parade of souls set in the narrative's *future*, not the *past*, as in *Odyssey* 11. Fusing the two traditional techniques, Vergil gives Anchises' retrospective prophecy a visual form: Aeneas sees (what is for him) the future, as does Scrooge courtesy of the Ghost of Christmas Future. But not only are the two techniques traditional but also so are specific details in how Vergil uses them. For instance, Jupiter's claim in the poem's first retrospective prophecy that the Roman Empire will be eternal (1.278–79) is a traditional one, as Clifford's analysis of earlier Mesopotamian texts (13–14) shows. Clifford notes an instance of the same claim in the *Uruk Prophecy*, "Nebuchadnezzar's son is meant to rule forever ... after Nebuchadnezzar II ... his dynasty will be established forever."

The *Aeneid* continues to employ retrospective prophecy after Book 6, sometimes through nonverbal, primarily visual means. Epic hands down a specific medium for describing the visual form of a significant object, *ecphrasis*, as we noted in Chapter 9, typically a lengthy, detailed description of a thematically important item. Among the most important of the *Aeneid*'s *ecphrases*, that which relates the scene Vulcan engraves on Aeneas' divine shield (8.626–728), also serves as a large retrospective prophecy.[13] The scenes are specifically from "the age to come" (*venturi ... aevi*: 8.627), from Ascanius to Romulus and Remus, from the Sabine women to the Etruscans and Gauls, from Catiline to Cato, from Aeneas to Augustus.

The vision and retrospective prophecy in Revelation

No modern reader of the *Aeneid* will think Jupiter or Anchises is speaking of a future yet to come, but this is precisely what ancient and modern readers of Revelation tend to think, that it refers to current or future events, though it employs the same techniques as the *Aeneid*, *the vision* and *retrospective prophecy*. An understanding of how retrospective prophecy and the vision function in the *Aeneid* is a hermeneutic for *responsible* interpretation of the Book of Revelation, realizing the periods and locations to which *it* refers, its concern with the Roman Empire, and focus on a specific Emperor, all much as in the *Aeneid*.

Revelation twice declares the period to which it refers as the immediate future (1:3, 22:10). The majority of the narrative does not refer to later events at all but to the acts and aftermath of the Jewish Revolt (66–70 AD). Those parts of Revelation that most engage contemporary audiences, the Beast, with his identifying number of 666, clearly designate the Emperor Nero, as Champlin, among many others notes (18), "666, it has long been recognized, is ... the sum of the numerical equivalents for the Hebrew letters which spell the words 'Neron Caesar.'"

Three passages in Revelation are intended to serve as keys (13:8, 17:9, 17:18), establishing the identity of the Beast, the Woman associated with him, and the city with which they are both to be identified,

> This calls for skill; let anyone who has intelligence work out the number of the beast, for the number represents a man's name, and the numerical value of its letters is six hundred and sixty-six. Rev 13:18
>
> Ὧδε ἡ σοφία ἐστιν. ὁ ἔχων νοῦν ψηφισάτω τὸν ἀριθμὸν τοῦ θηρίου· ἀριθμὸς γαρ ἀνθρώπου ἐστίν. καὶ ὁ ἀριθμὸς αὐτοῦ ἑξακόσιοι ἑξήκοντα ἕξ.

Van Daalen explains the numerical equivalents involved in reaching the total of 666, given that the Hebrews, just as the Romans, used the letters of their alphabet as their numbers (which modern audiences still understand in the Romans' case), demonstrating that it designates Nero (Metzger and Coogan: 700),

> The identity of the beast is clear: it is the absolutist state as personified in the Roman Emperor Nero ... The number was arrived at by presenting Nero's Greek Name *Kaisar Nerôn* in Hebrew letters, which also function as numbers: *qsr nrwn*; q = 60, 2 = 100, r = 200, n = 50, w = 6, so *qsr nrwn* adds up to 666.[14]

The equation involves three languages, translating Nero's usual title in Latin, "Caesar Nero," into its Greek equivalent, *Kaisar Neron*, then transliterating the Greek into its Hebrew equivalent, which, because Hebrew did not mark vowels at that time (other than the long "o," Greek omega, for which an equivalent of "w" was used), gives *qsr nrwn*.[15] This numerological "kabbalistic" method is called *gematria* in Hebrew, a Grecian loanword, evidencing further connection with Greco-Roman culture.

The dragon monster of ancient myth is often multiheaded. As we noted in Chapter 8, Hesiod's Typhoeus has 100 heads (*Theogony* 824–35). Revelation's Beast has seven heads for a specific reason, as the other two passages serving as keys make all too clear,

> This calls for a mind with insight. The seven heads are seven hills on which the woman sits enthroned. 17:9

> Ὧδε ὁ νοῦς ὁ ἔχων σοφίαν. αἱ ἑπτὰ κεφαλαὶ ἑπτὰ ὄρη εἰσιν, ὅπου ἡ γυνὴ κάθηται ἐπ᾽ αὐτῶν.

> The woman you saw is the great city that holds sway over the kings of the earth. 17:18

> καὶ ἡ γυνὴ ἣν εἶδες ἔστιν ἡ πόλις ἡ μεγάλη ἡ ἔχουσα βασιλείαν ἐπὶ τῶν βασιλέων τῆς γῆς.

Given the symbolic, coded language that apocalyptic myths traditionally employ (e.g., as in Daniel, which serves as a conceptual model for certain features of Revelation; Revelation has a term for coded language, 11:8: πνευματικῶς), it would be hard to imagine a clearer reference to Rome, and basic equation of the woman with the eternal city, following the example set in Hebrew Bible apocalyptic myths in which a sinful city is figured as a whore (Ezek 16:15; Nah 3:4).

Sweet, summarizing various pieces of evidence, considers a likely date for Revelation's composition (Metzger and Coogan: 653),

> Irenaus ... dated the book of Revelation toward the end of the reign of Domitian (81–96 CE). The picture of the Antichrist reflects popular belief that Nero, who had stabbed himself in the throat, would return from the dead (13.3, 12, 14), and many scholars see Revelation as a response to the enforcement on Christians of Domitian's demand for worship as "Lord and God" ... Nero's mysterious death evoked immediate rumors that he was still alive, and would return with an army from the east; and the civil wars that followed his death (68–69 CE, the Year of the Four Emperors), coinciding with the Jewish War (66–70 CE), seem to lie behind the breakup of the Roman World depicted in chaps 6–18.

For several reasons, there was strong popular belief that Nero would return from the dead. As Champlin demonstrates (10–12), after his death in June, 68 CE there were at least three "Nero" sightings over the next two decades, around March 69, a second in 80, the third in 88 in Domitian's reign. In each case, these *Nerones* bore a physical resemblance to him, could play the lyre and sing reasonably well, and, for a time, were thought by many to be Nero. These sightings of a returned Nero, then, are another facet of the specific historical context that Revelation addresses. Champlin offers a summary of the beliefs influencing how Christians saw Nero (18–19),

> By the time of the living Nero, two separate Hellenistic Jewish beliefs had coalesced, one concerning the Anti-God (or Antichrist), a human being or human power who opposes God, and the other concerning Beliar, or Satan, a demonic power who likewise opposes God: together they allow the myth to take shape that Satan had assumed human form. To the early Christians, who were familiar with this belief, Nero was the manifest incarnation, the man who had first persecuted the Christians and who had executed both Peter and Paul, the figure who would return from hiding to harry the Roman world. To them, he becomes the Antichrist, or the precursor of the Antichrist, at the beginning of the end of the world.

Let us now note Revelation's broader correspondences with *Aeneid* 6. It employs the same techniques and structures as the *Aeneid* but with an *opposite* view toward Rome and *opposite* agenda about it. Again, a specific Roman Emperor is the focal point, depicted as pivotal in the larger history of human affairs. Again, his triumph over death is prophesied. *Retrospective prophecy* and *the vision* are again how these events are portrayed in the narrative. But where Vergil's *Aeneid* is panegyric, written by a consummate insider, for Rome's eternal glory, Revelation condemns Rome and its empire from the outside. As Vergil depicts Rome's growth through space and time, Revelation focuses on Rome's destruction of the temple in Jerusalem, and convulsions throughout its empire (Rev 6–18). Where Vergil's climactic focus is Augustus, virtually divine, ushering in a Golden Age, Revelation's pivotal emperor is now Nero, fully demonized. The *Aeneid* works a similar reversal of sympathy, if to a smaller degree, in its own refashioning of Homeric epic. That is, it uses many of the same techniques as Homeric epic, but now because of Aeneas' role in the Trojan War it uses them to depict the Greeks as the enemy, not as sympathetic protagonists.

Revelation uses the same two techniques Vergil employs in *Aeneid* 6, initiating *the vision* right at the outset, as John states that he is narrating "all that he saw" (ὅσα εἶδεν: 1:2). His declaration is quite close to Antikleia's admonition to Odysseus to "remember all that he sees" (πάντα / ἴσθ': *Odyssey* 11.223–24), as she initiates that instance. The remainder of Revelation 1–3, however, transitions to messages to the seven churches of Asia, material that for the most part is not part of *the vision. The vision*'s traditional structure resumes in Revelations 4:1,

> After this I had a vision (εἶδον): a door stood open in heaven, and the voice that I had first heard speaking to me like a trumpet, said, "Come up

here" (Ἀνάβα ὧδε), and I will show you (δείξω σοι) what must take place hereafter.

Much as *Odyssey* 11 does each time Odysseus sees a new heroine approach, Revelation repeats "I saw," when John sees a new sight. The phrase καὶ εἶδον, "and then I saw," occurs an additional 31 times, instantiating the traditional structure of *the vision* through the remainder of Revelation,[16] much as the parallel employments of verbs of vision in *Aeneid* 6, *Odyssey* 11, and the *Somnium Scipionis*.

Like *Scipio's Dream*, Revelation's vision is set in the heavens. The protagonist, summoned by an otherworldly guide, *ascends* to the heavenly realm ("Come up here," Ἀνάβα ὧδε), rather than descending, as do Odysseus, Aeneas, and George Bailey. The *otherworldly guide*, unnamed, is Christ, who speaks several times, directing the protagonist's attention (1:1; 4:1; 10:8, 11; 19:9, etc.). As with Aeneas, Revelation's use of *the vision* results in a transformation, the protagonist having witnessed the vision, the big picture, the new reality, that, once understood, leaves him with a new purpose in his life and redefines his place in the universe. But, in an extension and transformation of the motif, Revelation intends its *audience* to be transformed, "Happy is the man who takes to heart the words of prophecy contained in this book," used in ring composition around the entire book (1:3 = 22:7).

Revelation's use of *retrospective prophecy* particularly focuses on the Romans' occupation of Jerusalem during and after the Jewish Revolt of 67–70 CE, events prior to its composition. Much of Chapter 11, in particular, is concerned with the desolation and destruction resulting from the Roman suppression of the revolt and destruction of the temple. Revelations 11:2 thus "predicts" that "for forty-two months they will trample the Holy City underfoot," the duration of the suppression of the Jewish Revolt.

Though it is the events depicted in chapters 12–14 that most exercise modern audiences, again, these passages clearly depend upon *retrospective prophecy* as their organizing device or technique. Chapter 13 focuses specifically on the beast, identified by audiences as the Antichrist, and its identifying number 666. The Beast is not a being to come, as most modern audiences think, but is, through the traditional function of *retrospective prophecy*, either Rome or the Emperor Nero (as the three keys, Rev 13:18, 17:9, 17:18, show), who reigned when the Jewish Revolt began, and would have been understood as commanding its suppression (Champlin: 17). Popular beliefs, supported by accounts of the three returned *Nerones*, contributed to the expectation that he would come back. Nero, or the Antichrist, is thus figured as an opposite to Christ, who will come back from death, as a negative, destructive force, a parody of Christ's resurrection, slouching "towards Bethlehem to be born," as Yeats has it. The Romans' destruction of the temple in 70, and mandatory worship of the emperors as divine, particularly as tied to Domitian (Sweet, p. 653 in Metzger and Coogan), are what Revelation sees as outrages and is most concerned with. Revelation assumes there will be divine retribution for these offences.

Perhaps only in chapters 19–22 does Revelation refer to future events. Here Christ's victory over the Beast and episodes expected in the last judgment are figured (Suggs: 1572) but are expected in the *near* future, as Revelation emphasizes (1:3, 22:10), not hundreds or thousands of years later. Revelation climaxes in the depiction of the New Jerusalem (Rev 21–22:5) made of jewels and precious metals, the traditional conception of gods' residences (e.g., *Iliad* 13.21–2). The passage concludes by prophesying that the city's inhabitants, in accord with divine will, shall reign forever, "for the Lord God will give them light; and they shall reign forever" (Rev 22:5), the very same motif, and an extremely close parallel to Jupiter's climactic proclamation in the *Aeneid*'s first *retrospective prophecy* at 1.278–79 (*his ego metas rerum nec tempora pono: / imperium sine fine dedi*). In this respect, Revelation conforms to the pattern seen in the earlier Mesopotamian and Egyptian instances, whereby the climax of each work, the only "prophecy" that does not depict an event that has already taken place, predicts an eternal dynasty.

While the *Aeneid*'s use of *retrospective prophecy* and *the vision* help us understand how Revelation also makes use of the same techniques, the Sibylline Oracles, several of which focus on Nero, offer additional context, providing further evidence that Revelation refers to him through *retrospective prophecy*. Charlesworth (391) offers a convenient summary of Oracle 5,

> The great adversary of the end-time in Sibylline Oracles 5 is the Roman emperor Nero. Utilizing the popular legend that Nero had fled to Parthia and would one day return, the Sibyl presents him both as king of Rome (vs. 139) and as leading an attack on Rome in the eschatological time (vs. 367). It should be noted that Nero was expected to return from the Parthians, not (at least explicitly) from the dead. In verse 147 he is said to go to the Persians. In verse 363 he is said to come from the ends of the earth. He is not yet identified with Belial as he is in Sibylline Oracles 3.63–74 ... his wickedness consists, in large part, of his claim to be God (vss. 34, 139 ff.). In fact the evil of Nero has the same three dimensions as the evil of Rome: he is morally evil, he was responsible for the destruction of Jerusalem (vs. 150), since the Jewish Revolt began in his reign, and he claimed to be God.

Oracle 5 thus offers a window into a slightly earlier conception that that in Revelation. Nero will return from hiding, not from death. He is, however, already equated with evil.

A further text, the *Martyrdom and Ascension of Isaiah*, offers another piece of the emerging composite conception of Nero. As is the case with the Sibylline Oracles, this text is an amalgam, different sections composed at different times. One section that can be dated to the end of the first century CE, clearly representing a Christian perspective, identifies Nero with the demon Belial. Now Nero has been promoted to "demonic status," as Champlin (17) argues, at least within the Christian community. Revelation thus draws on these earlier traditions, combining them together, in figuring Nero as fully demonized.

The final episode in Ovid's *Metamorphoses*, the deification of the Caesars, Julius and Augustus (15.746–870), serves us as an *intermediate* text between *Aeneid* 6 and Revelation, intermediate chronologically (completed before 8 CE), and in its perspective on the deified Roman emperors. Ovid here uses retrospective prophecy to "predict" the fate of a specific emperor and employs several other traditional motifs prominent in Revelation's later treatment. Because he does so with elements of parody, his depiction is medial – between Vergil's panegyric to Augustus and Revelation's demonization of Nero – in the attitude it suggests toward the Roman emperor.

Ovid constructs his episode as a divine council, Jupiter reassuring Venus who is here concerned not over Aeneas, as in the *Aeneid*'s divine council (1.223–96), but over his and her descendant in the Julian clan, Julius Caesar. As Venus voices alarm over his *future* assassination, Ovid employs a considerable number of traditional motifs also used in Revelation, frightening omens and eerie events. Trumpets sound in the heavens to presage the assassination (15.784–85: *terribilesque tubas auditaque cornua caelo / praemonuisse nefas*), much as in the later Revelation the seven trumpets sound to mark the onset of various disasters (Rev 8:2–9:21, 11:15–19). Each episode has an earthquake (15.798; Rev 6:12, 11:13), a crime that is seen as a religious outrage (15.776–77, 800–2; Rev 13:5–6, and the destruction of the Temple), a bloodied moon (15.790; Rev 6:12), divine tablets that have a record of human events decreed by fate (15.781–82, 809–15; Rev 20:12–15), and a Caesar who transcends death (15.818, 838–50; Rev 13). In other words, Ovid's account underscores what comparison with the *Aeneid* already demonstrates, that Revelation is composed almost entirely of traditional motifs, extant in earlier narratives and mythic traditions. Ovid even mentions Lucifer in his episode (15.789), and his coded reference to Cleopatra (15.826–28) corresponds with how Revelation figures Rome as a tainted woman. Ovid concludes his account, and the whole *Metamorphoses*, with a prediction of his *own immortality* (15.871–79: *perque omnia saecula fama … vivam*), his adaptation of the motif just noted, in which a dynasty is predicted to be eternal, as later at Revelation 22:5. In appropriating the eternal dynasty motif for himself, though Ovid is being typically witty – parodying the motif and the deification of the Caesars.

When Anchises shows Aeneas the parade of Roman heroes to come, after his son has descended to the underworld to meet with him in Elysium, Vergil employs the two traditional motifs, *retrospective prophecy* and *the vision*. Readers of the *Aeneid*, whether they are consciously aware of these techniques, nonetheless understand that Vergil is referring to events that lie in Aeneas' future but not in the audience's future. Modern audiences thus have a basic competency in Vergil's craft, the ability to comprehend his intended meanings, regarding the times, places, and identities of his characters, though his design allows for considerable ambiguity. Many modern audiences of Revelation, however, not only lack familiarity with the techniques that it uses, particularly *retrospective prophecy*, but also lack a basic competency and evidence a complete disconnect with the times, places, and identities of several of its principal characters. If it is correct to see parody in Ovid's portrait of the deified Caesars, particularly in his declaration of his own eternity (ironically, the only instance of this motif that *remains true!*), Revelation, in this respect, is an extension of a process well under way in earlier texts from the previous century or more. Depiction of a deified Caesar, fully positive in Vergil, starts to receive a comic treatment in Ovid, let alone the full burlesque to which Seneca subjects Claudius in the *Apocolocyntosis*. Revelation also employs elements of comic or satiric modality in its demonized Nero, particularly in chapter 13.

Applying the *Aeneid*'s use of *retrospective prophecy* and *the vision* offers a corrective against irresponsible readings of Revelation. Like the *Aeneid*, Revelation draws on and employs the traditional components and techniques of myth, divine councils (Revelation 4 is an extended divine council), divine wraths, and the like. The same is true of much of the Bible, Hebrew Bible, and New Testament. Classicists can and should, I suggest, apply their considerable knowledge of ancient Mediterranean cultures, their knowledge of human existence in ancient times, their knowledge of ancient religions, and particularly their knowledge of ancient languages and myths, to the Bible. Like Book 6 of the *Aeneid*, and Jupiter's declarations to Venus at *Aeneid* 1.256–96, most of Revelation does not refer to the future at all, but looks back on events that have already taken place. Like the *Aeneid*, Revelation does so to propose a new interpretation of those events, that they are part of a larger divine plan for *God's chosen people*. But as far as I know, every ancient people regarded itself in much the same way. Because modern audiences read Revelation largely in a vacuum (other than relating it to other episodes within the Bible), they are at the mercy of all manner of irresponsible interpretations, including the notion that it confirms recent and ongoing events in American foreign policy.

Awareness of how traditional much of this New Testament text is, as evident in its common ground with the *Theogony*, can serve as a check against wild readings and interpretations. American audiences in particular have been fond of utterly divorcing Revelation from its ancient context.

Notes

1 A common view. See, e.g., Otis 1966: 92: "The sixth book of the *Aeneid* is the turning point."
2 On Vergil's debt to Cicero see Camps: 89, Feeney 1986: 108–9, and Leach 1999: 125. Other texts, especially Plato's *Republic*, and perhaps Parmenides opening fragments, also inform Vergil's adaptation of this traditional structure.
3 By virtue of the powers of their supernatural guides, both "A Christmas Carol" and *It's a Wonderful Life* fit my definition of myth and are sacred but not traditional: we know who the authors are.

4 See discussion in Louden 2011a, chs.7 and 9.

5 Cf. W. S. Anderson 1969: 60.

6 This approximate date of the Fall of Troy is not only suggested by some versions of the Greeks' reckoning but confirmed by the records of Ramesses II and III of their encounters with the various Sea Peoples. See, most recently, Cline, throughout.

7 For discussion of these and other related passages in the *Iliad*, see Louden 2006: 212–18.

8 Ovid parodies this speech, and its use of retrospective prophecy, in the final scene in the *Metamorphoses*, 15.807–42.

9 Cf. how Poseidon regards the Phaiakians at *Odyssey* 13.129–30; discussion in Louden 2011a: ch. 13.

10 See Feeney (108–9) on Vergil's debt to Cicero.

11 Interestingly paralleling the same gap in Homeric epic, set in thirteenth/twelfth composed/redacted in eighty/seventh century BCE.

12 See Feeney (117) for discussion.

13 By contrast the more typical *ecphrasis* describing the scenes depicted on Juno's temple at Carthage (1.456–93) look back at the Trojan War.

14 Cf. Friesen 2001: 137: "Revelation 13 ... The chapter ends with the riddle of 666 – the number of the name of the Beast. Nearly all commentators acknowledge that this number represents the sum of the numbers associated with the letters in the name Nero Caesar." Sweet (Metzger and Coogan 1993: 31): "the two beasts of Revelation 13: the beast from the sea ... the sea beast's healed wound and his number identify him as Nero, returned from the dead, the persecuting Emperor who was worshipped as a god."

15 A "w" to represent an "o" is also evident in the Hebrew Bible's sea monster Leviathan, for the earlier Ugaritic sea monster LOT. Friesen notes an alternate reading in some Revelation manuscripts (246, n. 15): "Some ancient manuscripts of Revelation use the number 616 instead, which would be the total of the Hebrew letters when transliteration is done from the Latin form of 'Nero Caesar.'" For details see Aune 1998: 769–71.

16 5:1. 6.11; 6:1, 2, 9 (7:1, 10); 8:2, 13; 9:1, 17: 10:1; 13:1; 14:1, 6, 14; 15:1, 2, 5; 16:13; 17:3; 19:11, 17, 19, 20:1, 4, 11: 21:1, 22. Cf. also the passive, ὤφθη: 12:1, 3.

Conclusion

As I hope I have demonstrated, this study has significant implications for the study and understanding of the Bible. Though commentators and readers have had good reasons for placing the Hebrew Bible in an ancient Near Eastern context, and for placing New Testament narratives in context with those of the Hebrew Bible, the ancient world was never as insular and hermetically sealed such that those could be the only relevant contexts. Greek culture, particularly Greek myth, must be taken as a far more significant component in the background, formation, and composition of the Bible than has generally been thought. Greek myth not only provides an unexpectedly germane context for both Hebrew Bible and New Testament narratives but also prompts reading the Bible in new ways, from several different perspectives. From the structural, establishing correspondences between Greek myth and both sets of narratives, to the ontological (does demonstrating that a myth is *imported* undermine its legitimacy, its claim to truth?), this study has opened several doors that need to be opened wider.

In the case of the Hebrew Bible, it is clear that ancient Israel had very early, sustained, diachronic knowledge of multiple interfaces with the various stages of Greek culture from the Mycenaean period onward. Whether one accepts a partial or complete equation of the Philistines with Mycenaean Greeks, the overlap and connections are firm, with evidence from numerous sources and perspectives. Perhaps most intriguing of all are Hittite records of interaction, over several centuries, with the Ahhijawa, or as Homer calls them, Achaians. In the Hebrew Bible, multiple Philistines bear a name that instantiates this same ancient term, Achish (1 Sam 21:11–15, 27:1–6; 1 Kings 2:39–46). Inscriptional evidence records another as having had a temple for a non-Semitic goddess constructed at Tel Miqne/Ekron.

Israel's awareness of Greek culture, starting in the second millennium BCE, does not stop, but continues into later eras. Though he is addressing the New Testament era, consider Larsen's observation (7–8), given in Chapter 7,

> [T]he notion of an insurmountable divide between Judaism and Hellenism has been progressively deconstructed, resulting in a new understanding of Hellenism as an overall descriptive concept under which both the

Judaisms and the Christianities of the period appear as subsets. This development requires that we see the New Testament texts, including the Fourth Gospel, as inherent players in a larger Panhellenistic literary *koinê*, both with regard to content and form.

The correspondences I trace here could have been unearthed a long time ago. These should not be new discoveries. There are reasons why they have not been adequately pursued before, long-standing motives behind the lack of exploration. Both Judaism, and later, to an even greater degree, Christianity regard themselves as instances of *exceptionalism*. Ancient polytheists, as we noted in the introduction, recognized their own gods in other peoples, a phenomenon we now call "divine translation." Assmann notes how ancient polytheistic cultures saw themselves as members of an international community, able to accept common ground between each other's religions. Judaism, after having fully emerged, repudiated the status quo (3),

> the emergence of the "Ancient World" as a coherent ecumene of interconnected nations. The polytheistic religions overcame the primitive ethnocentrism of tribal religions by distinguishing several deities by name, shape and function. The different peoples worshipped different gods, but nobody contested the reality of foreign gods and the legitimacy of foreign forms of worship ... The Mosaic distinction was therefore a radically new distinction ... We may call this new type of religion "counter-religion" because it rejects and repudiates everything that went before and is outside of itself as "paganism."

This distinction only works, however, for those inside the monotheistic religion. To polytheistic outsiders the differences are not so pronounced.

Traditional polytheists tended to respect other peoples' religions and their religious practices, as Freeman notes was true of the Romans (69),

> The Romans assumed that other people's gods were as important a part of the fabric of their society as their gods were of theirs, and this provides one reason why they were so easily prepared to tolerate other deities and beliefs.

Their tolerance of other cultures' religions sometimes meant Romans could rule provinces with much smaller occupying forces, as Freeman notes (57),

> In areas where there was no immediate security threat, Roman rule was comparatively light. In Judaea at the time of Pontius Pilate ... there were only 3,000 Roman troops in the whole province ... The secret of such successful administration in the long term lay in the creation of quiescent local elites that had their own interest in keeping good order ... It helped enormously that the Romans were tolerant of local deities and that these could be absorbed into the Roman pantheon

Their traditional tolerance and respect toward other peoples' beliefs notwithstanding, Judaism, in its exceptionalism, began to present a unique challenge
to Rome, again to quote Freeman (58): "Romans proved deeply ambivalent toward Judaism. While they always respected antiquity in any spiritual
belief ... the Romans felt threatened by the *exclusivity* of monotheism"
(emphasis mine).

Shortly after its inception, in the person of Paul, Christianity took the
exceptionalism that was already a traditional facet of monotheism but
developed and extended it to an unprecedented degree. In the introduction
we briefly discussed some of Paul's comments in 1 Corinthians 1–2. Thus, as
Freeman notes (5–6),

> Christianity, under the influential banner of Paul's denunciation of
> Greek philosophy, began to create the barrier between science-and
> rational thought in general-and religion that appears to be unique to
> Christianity.

Paul's position represents a radical shift away from what we can gather about
Jesus' own view of such things, as again Freeman notes (107),

> Unlike Jesus he [Paul] insisted on a dramatic break with traditional cul-
> ture, not only his own, but also that of the Greco-Roman world, and
> so he brought new challenges and tensions to Christianity as it spread
> among Gentiles.

Freeman specifically notes Paul's stance against Greek philosophy, grouping
it now with other issues he stressed that again have little or no basis in the
teachings of Christ (108): "Paul's views on idols, sexuality and Greek philosophy, issues that had not featured strongly in Jesus's teachings and often
sit uneasily with them, became embedded in the Christian tradition." Thus,
for example, when, in the fall of 2015, Senator Rubio, during his unsuccessful
quest for the Republican presidential nomination, repeatedly made comments
disparaging the study of Greek philosophy, American media failed to note
what he was really doing: speaking in code, burnishing his appeal to the
religious right.

Paul's radical exceptionalism, which became the norm within Christianity,
has remained to the present day,[1] for the most part, dominating research into
the Bible until comparatively recent times. Thus, though early Christians
recognized correspondences and similarities between their narratives and
Greek myths,[2] they accounted for them strictly through supernatural means
and agency. For instance, even as monotheists, they, according to the typical
ancient worldview, saw the world as full of supernatural agency.

From the vantage point of their exceptionalism, however, they formulated
a new understanding of many such presumed forces and agencies, as Freeman
(141–42) notes, "Far from disbelieving in the pagan gods, the Christians saw

them as demons who were very much alive." Unable to account for the similarities logically (because diffusion was not considered), many embraced something along the lines of Justin's fantasy (dependent upon the supernatural) that the earlier Greek versions must be demonic distortions of the later Christian narratives (see discussion in Taylor: 156–57), though this is essentially a bizarre variation on the *ad hominem* attack. Asclepius in particular drew vehement attacks from early Christian writers,[3] probably because the accounts of his miraculous healings and restoration to life of those who had died offered the closest parallels to so many key episodes in the Gospels.[4]

Christianity extended its exceptionalism to its use and appropriation of earlier, unrelated texts. White (2010) demonstrates the tendency in some detail in his analysis of "The Matthean Theme of Prophecy and Fulfillment." He analyzes those texts that the Matthean author asserts foretell the birth of Christ, noting their lack of connection (244),

> [I]n their original form none of these scriptures refer directly to Jesus or aspects of his birth. The flight to Egypt (2:15) is derived from Hosea 11:1, where it was originally a reference to the Exodus itself. The Matthean appropriation requires Hosea's retrospection on Israel's past to become a future prediction; the "son" shifts from Israel itself to the future messiah. The move to Nazareth (2:2) is derived from Isaiah 11:1, where it is originally a reference to the Davidic line in the days of Hezekiah ... The virginal conception (1:23) is derived from Isaiah 7:14, where it was originally about a contemporaneous event in Isaiah's own time, probably the birth of the future king Hezekiah himself. As is widely known the original wording of Isaiah 7:14 in the Hebrew reads: "a young woman is pregnant and will bear a son." The shift to the word "virgin" and the change of tenses (from present to future) both depend on the Sept, but have been further modified to fit into the Matthean structure.[5]

White (245) notes, furthermore, that Christians were not the first to appropriate scripture for their own agenda but were following the practice of contemporaneous Jewish culture: "The Matthean technique of using scriptures is not unusual; it was common in other forms of Jewish writing at the time, including the Dead Sea Scrolls."

In our own time, Christians read their own texts in the same way that the first Christians read the Hebrew Bible. That is, they tend to ignore everything we know about the historical contexts that the texts originally address, such as the Jewish Revolt and its aftermath, the well-established identity of the Beast, or Antichrist, and the Emperor Nero, even the beliefs and assumptions of the ancient authors, applying them instead to our own time in ways that would have dumbfounded and stupefied the original authors.[6] Contemporary audiences largely remain ignorant of the conventions and mechanisms that the texts employ, such as retrospective prophecy in particular.

The present work addresses these issues indirectly, but thematically, demonstrating that biblical myths in the Hebrew Bible and New Testament, do not, in fact, exhibit their assumed exceptionalism. Rather, they are, to a considerable degree, composed and constructed out of common traditional elements, many of which were circulating in Greek culture in particular.

Different periods, and perhaps members of religious communities in particular, have operated under largely different concepts of authorship than those we generally assume. Perhaps most important for this study, as we established in the introduction,[7] is that these agents felt free to import and add narratives to those in their preexisting core, generated indigenously. Thus, as the Flood myth was imported and adapted from an earlier Mesopotamian Deluge myth, so for the transition out of it (Gen 9–10) the Genesis scribal tradition, having already signposted the Hesiodic account of the Titans in Genesis 6:2–4, fashioned a euhemerized adaptation of the Greek tale of the imprisonment of the rebellion and fall of the Titans for its account of Noah's sons to serve as a bridge to the Table of Nations.

Euripides' *Ion* not only provides us a window into patriarch myth but demonstrates that the key motifs that comprise the larger Abrahamic saga and the birth story of Moses are generic, visible in other cultures. The *deus ex machina* that concludes the play, a definitive Euripidean device, should be regarded as providing a rubric for the two interventions of the angels in the Abrahamic saga (Gen 16:7–13; 21:17–20; 22:11–12, 15–18). His *Hecuba*, however, one of his most popular plays, in antiquity and through the ages, appeared attractive to the Deuteronomist's agenda. A distillation of Hecuba's revenge, the queen a member of the losing side in the war, Jael serves as a way of projecting or fantasizing a positive response (at the level of the individual) against foreign hegemony to maintain independence of belief against foreign domination with overwhelming military superiority, including the Greek. Given Römer's argument that the scribal tradition reworks elements of his two Iphigenia plays for its narrative of Jephthah's daughter in Judges 11, the scribal tradition of the Hebrew Bible seemingly made repeated use of Euripides, a relationship that extends into the New Testament in the author of John's reworking of his *Alcestis*.

For the most heroic of its patriarchs, Genesis 27–33 rewrites and adapts the saga of one of the most well-known heroes of Greek myth. Jason, Medea, Aietes, the Golden Fleece, and the requisite Labors bequeath to the scribal tradition types for all the central actors of Jacob's larger myth, with the protagonist suitably refashioned as a pastoralist. With his brother Esau clearly a refigured Heracles, in Jacob's victories over him the entire saga slyly serves as a countercurriculum against the larger thrusts of Greek culture in general, and its love of the hero protagonist, foreshadowing David's victory over Philistine Goliath.

A similar stance remains true for the Gospel authors: they clearly felt free to add new stories to the already circulating traditions to construct larger narratives about Jesus and to bring out more clearly particular qualities they wished to emphasize.[8] Thus the Johannine author, to highlight and increase the miraculous component in his conception of Christ, turned to Euripides' tale of Heracles restoring Alcestis to life as a rubric for his newly fashioned account of Christ and Lazarus. As White demonstrates, there are other signs that John feels free to alter the inherited stories to reflect other concerns he chooses to highlight. Thus John 9:1–41's account of the healing of a man born blind, as White notes (407–8), "emulates the tensions of this later period in Jewish-Christian relations ... the Johannine author has retrojected an experience from a much later time into the life of Jesus by creating this fictional story." Related to this is how Jews are depicted immediately following Christ's resurrection of Lazarus (11:45 ff.). John's unique prompt for the arrest of Jesus, Christ's raising of Lazarus, finds a model in the Alcestis' backstory of Asclepius being put to death for having resurrected a mortal but also reflects, as White demonstrates of John 9:1–44, the tensions between Christians and Jews from a much later time than Christ's own.

The Lukan author, as part of a larger strategy to engage a wider segment of Greco-Roman audience, devises a unique postresurrection story adapted largely out of elements found in Homeric epic. Mark and Matthew draw on a more recent text, but one tremendously influential in the Roman Empire, Ovid's account of Phaethon from *Metamorphoses* 1–2, to flesh out their account of the slaying of John the Baptist. In this case, Ovid's own ironic distancing from earlier conceptions of the gods better fits the earlier Gospel authors' exceptionalist agenda and framework.

When does the process of adding new narratives to the earlier traditions about Christ stop? We know that some of what are, in our times, the most popular parts of the Gospels are later additions, added even centuries later. Fox, for instance, cites the well-known example in John 8 (143),

> In our Bibles nowadays, we read Jesus's moving defense of the adulterous woman who was about to be stoned for her sins: "He that is without sin among you, let him first cast a stone at her"; "Neither do I condemn thee: go, and sin no more". The episode is missing from the surviving fourth-cent codices which underpin the rest of the New Testament text; it is not known in an early papyrus or any quotation by an early Christian author, although the subject was relevant to so much they discussed. Its style is universally held to differ from the rest of the fourth Gospel ... The verses have struck many readers as more Christian than much in Christian scripture, but an editor has plainly inserted them, and textual critics now agree that they are not the Gospel's own view.

In this sense the texts of the Gospels, at least in some respects, remained more fluid for longer than is often thought.

I intend this study, in part, as a larger argument that classicists should incorporate the Bible into their research, as a text that offers unexpectedly close, unexpectedly relevant, parallels to many Greek and Roman myths and cultural practices.[9] The tools a classicist acquires for interpreting Greek and Latin myths can and should also be applied to the Bible. Moreover, classicists can perform a great service by applying their training and skills to the study and examination of the Bible, in an objective manner. On the one hand, the New Testament is a historical product of the Roman Empire and the larger Greco-Roman culture of which that Empire was a part. On the other, it does not present historical accounts, but plugs its narratives, which derive much more from the world of myth and fiction, into key moments in history. As White notes (420–21), "[T]he one who steps into the ancient fictive world of the Gospels knowing little of their notions of history and fiction risks much … in the end, they must still be read as dramatized and idealized narratives."

The same, of course, pertains even more to Revelation. We have shown that several chapters of Revelation (especially 4, 12, 19–20) use some of the most openly mythical structures in the New Testament. Closely echoing select episodes from Hesiod's *Theogony*, while using Ovid's ecphrasis of the Temple of the Sun as an organizational rubric for Chapter 4 in particular, some of the most memorable narratives in Revelation are largely composed of elements in Greek myth. Overall, Revelation's employment of the classic structure of the vision and its clear use of retrospective prophecy closely conform to Vergil's use of the same in the *Aeneid*.

Because modern audiences read Revelation largely in a vacuum (other than relating it to other episodes within the Bible), they are at the mercy of all manner of irresponsible interpretations, including the notion that it confirms recent and ongoing events in American foreign policy. In a most unfortunate, but well-documented instance, President George W. Bush cited the Book of Revelation to win support for what has been called the worst foreign-policy decision in the history of the United States. Utterly unaware of Revelation's historical context, he referred to it when he unsuccessfully attempted to enlist the support of President Chiraq of France for his ill-fated invasion of Iraq, declaring to him, "Gog and Magog are at work in the Middle East. Biblical prophecies are being fulfilled."[10] Though the duo appear in the Hebrew Bible (Ezek 38–39), Bush would have been mainly aware of, and reacting to, their mention at Revelation 20:8 (τὸν Γὼγ καὶ Μαγώγ, συναγαγεῖν αὐτοὺς εἰς τὸν πόλεμον), entirely unaware, however, that Revelations addresses the late first century CE. The passage is part of Revelation's thematic use of retrospective prophecy.

There is an ironic consistency in method when those who ignore the text's original historical contexts assert that they address later historical contexts. This is in keeping with the approach Christianity exhibits in its use of earlier texts, ignoring the context, time, and clear intended application of a particular passage or prophesy. As this study demonstrates, the prophecies in Revelation function in the same way as those in the *Aeneid*, and in the *deus ex machina* appearances in Euripidean tragedy. Given recent events in American politics, it seems likely that the possibility that American foreign policy will be even more erroneously linked to New Testament texts will drastically increase.

Classicists could play a significant role in disabusing such readers, as well as those who may be preying upon them. The centrality of Hesiod's *Theogony*, Euripides (including plays beyond those I have treated here, his *Phaethon* and *Bacchae*, the latter clearly underlying Acts' account of Paul's escape from prison) and Ovid's *Metamorphoses*, not to mention Homer, demonstrate the larger interconnectedness of Greek myth and the Bible, and how traditional and generic many of the constituent elements are. Classicists can help dismantle the wall that Christianity, in its assumption of exceptionalism, erected between the study of both disciplines.

Notes

1 Extending even to orienting the calendar around the supposed year of Christ's birth.
2 Acts 17, Paul's appearance in Athens, is premised upon such resemblances. See discussion in Taylor 2007: 137–43.
3 See Edelstein and Edelstein 1998, vol. 2: 132–38.
4 Though there were significant differences between Asclepius and Christ (ibid.: 134–35).
5 Cf. Fox 1992: 340: "What, in fact, had they [passages in the Hebrew Bible] predicted about Jesus Christ or Christianity? The answer is extremely simple: they had predicted nothing."
6 See again, for instance, Freeman 2005: 108: "the turbulent and confused years after Jesus's death, years that Paul believed were a prelude to the imminent second coming, he could hardly have expected that they would be given the status of universal and authoritative truths and be used in contexts totally different from those in which he had written them."
7 Van der Toorn's (2007) category 5: "adaptation of an existing text for a new audience."
8 White 2010: 405: "Oral traditions and basic story forms provided a stock of components-death and resurrection, miracles and sayings-for assembling each narrative, but the storytellers were perfectly free to alter older traditions or create new stories in order to articulate a message about Jesus."
9 See Weinfeld (1993) on similarities between the *Aeneid* and the Hebrew Bible's depiction of Abraham, and Louden on parallels between the Hebrew Bible and the *Iliad* (2006: 149–230), and between the Hebrew Bible, the New Testament, and the *Odyssey* (2011a).
10 J. Smith 2008: 338–39.

Bibliography

Abusch, Tzvi. 1990. *Lingering Over Words: Studies in Ancient Near Eastern Literature in Honor of William L. Moran*, eds. Tzvi Abusch, Johnm Huehnergard, and Piotr Steinkeller. Atlanta, GA: Scholars Press.

Ackroyd, Peter R. 1977. *The Second Book of Samuel*. Cambridge: Cambridge University Press.

Agoustakis, Anthony. 2016. "Loca luminis haurit: Ovid's Recycling of Hecuba." In Fulkerson and Stover, 2016, pp. 100–25.

Aland, Kurt. 1973. *Synopsis Quattuor Evangeliorum: Locis parallelis evangeliorum apocryphorum et partum adhibitis*. Stuttgart, Germany: United Bible Societies.

Albright, W. F. and C. S. Mann. 1971. The Anchor Bible: Matthew. Introduction, Translation, and Notes. Garden City, NY: Doubleday.

Alkier, Stefan, Thomas Hieke, and Tobias Nicklas, eds. 2015. *Poetik und Intertextualität in der Apokalypse*. Tübingen, Germany: Mohr Siebeck.

Alter, Robert. 1981. *The Art of Biblical Narrative*. New York: Basic Books.

———. 1996. *Genesis: Translation and Commentary*. New York: W. W. Norton.

———. 1999. *The David Story: A Translation with Commentary of 1 and 2 Samuel*. New York: W. W. Norton.

———. 2004. *The Five Books of Moses: A Translation with Commentary*. New York: W. W. Norton.

———. 2013. *Ancient Israel: The Former Prophets: Joshua, Judges, Samuel, and Kings*. New York: W. W. Norton.

Andersen, Oivind and Dag T. T. Haug, eds. 2011. *Relative Chronology in Early Greek Epic Poetry*. Cambridge: Cambridge University Press.

Anderson, W. S. 1969. *The Art of the Aeneid*. Wauconda, IL: Bolchazy-Carducci (1989 reprint).

———. 1977. *Ovidius Metamorphoses Libri XV*. Leipzig: Teubner.

———. 1997. *Ovid's Metamorphoses: Books 1–5*. Edited, with Introduction and Commentary. Norman: University of Oklahoma Press.

Arieti, James A. 2017. *Springs of Western Civilization: A Comparative Study of Hebrew and Classical Cultures*. Lanham, MD: Lexington Books.

Assmann, Jan. 1997. *Moses the Egyptian: The Memory of Egypt in Western Monotheism*. Cambridge, MA: Harvard University Press.

Auld, Graeme. 2004. *Samuel at the Threshold: Selected Works of Graeme Auld* (SOTS Monographs). Aldershot, UK: Ashgate.

Bachvarova, Mary R. 2016. *From Hittite to Homer: The Anatolian Background of Ancient Greek Epic*. Cambridge: Cambridge University Press.

Barton, John. 1993."Isaac." In Metzger and Coogan, 1993, p. 325.

Barton, Stephen C. 2006. *The Cambridge Companion to the Gospels*. Cambridge: Cambridge University Press.

Baumgarten, Albert I. 1981. *The Phoenician History of Philo of Byblos: A Commentary*. Leiden, The Netherlands: Brill.

Beckman, Gary M., Trevor R. Bryce, and Eric H. Cline, eds. 2011. *The Ahhiyawa Texts*. Atlanta, GA: Society of Biblical Literature.

Beltz, Walter. 1983. *God and the Gods: Myths of the Bible*, trans. Peter Heinegg. London: Penguin Books.

Bogan, Zachary. 1658. *Homerus Hebraizon, sive Comparatio Homeri cum Sciptoribus Sacris quoad normam loquendi: subnectitur Hesiodus Homerizon*. Oxoniae: Excudebat H. Hall, Impensis T. Robinson.

Bolin, Thoas M. 2004. "The Role of Exchange in Ancient Mediterranean Religion and Its Implications for Reading Genesis 18–19." *Journal for the Study of the Old Testament* 29: 37–56.

Boling, Robert G. 1975. *The Anchor Bible: Judges: Introduction, Translation and Commentary*. Garden City, NJ: Doubleday.

Bonz, Marianne Palmer. 2000. *The Past as Legacy: Luke-Acts and Ancient Epic*. Minneapolis, MN: Fortress Press.

Boyd, Barbara Weiden. 2017. *Ovid's Homer: Authority, Repetition, and Reception*. Oxford: Oxford University Press.

Braswell, Bruce Karl. 1988. *A Commentary on the Fourth Pythian Ode of Pindar*. Berlin: De Gruyter.

Braund, Susanna Morton. 1997. "Virgil and the Cosmos: Religious and Philosophical Idea." In Martindale, 1997, pp. 204–21.

Brodie, Thomas L. 2001. *Genesis as Dialogue: A Literary, Historical, and Theological Commentary*. Oxford: Oxford University Press.

Brown, John Pairman. 1995. *Israel and Hellas (Beihefte zur Zeitschrift für die alttestamentliche Wissenschaft, band 231)*. Berlin: De Gruyter.

Brown, Raymond B. 1966. *The Anchor Bible: The Gospel According to John (i–xii): Introduction, Translation, and Notes*. Garden City, NY: Doubleday.

———. 1970. *The Anchor Bible: The Gospel According to John (xiii–xxi). Introduction, Translation, and Notes*. Garden City, NY: Doubleday.

Brown, Robert. 1987. "The Palace of the Sun in Ovid's Metamorphoses," pp. 210–20, in *Homo Viator: Classical Essays for John Bramble*, eds. Michael Whitby, Philip R. Hardie, and Mary Whitby. Bristol: Bristol Classical Press.

Burkert, Walter. 2004. *Babylon Memphis Persepolis: Eastern Contexts of Greek Culture*. Cambridge, MA: Harvard University Press.

Burnett, Anne Pippin. 1971. *Catastrophe Survived: Euripides' Plays of Mixed Reversal*. Oxford: Oxford University Press.

Burton, Ernest De Witt and Edgar Johnson Goodspeed. 1920. *A Harmony of the Synoptic Gospels in Greek*. Chicago: University of Chicago Press.

Burton, R. W. 1962. *Pindar's Pythian Odes: Essays in Interpretation*. Oxford: Oxford University Press.

Caldwell, Richard S. 1987. *Hesiod's Theogony: Translated, with Introduction, Commentary, and Interpretive Essay*. Cambridge, MA: Focus Classical Library.

Campbell, David A. 1991. *Greek Lyric, Volume III: Stesichorus, Ibycus, Simonides, and Others*. Loeb Classical Library. Cambridge, MA: Harvard University Press.

Carr, David M. 1996. *Reading the Fractures of Genesis: Historical and Literary Approaches*. Louisville, KY: Westminster John Knox Press.

———. 2005. *Writing on the Tablet of the Heart: Origins of Scripture and Literature*. Oxford: Oxford University Press.

Champlin, Edward. 2003. *Nero*. Cambridge, MA: Belknap Press of Harvard University Press.

Chantraine, P. 1990. *Dictionnaire etymologique de la langue grecque*. Paris: Editions Klincksieck.

Charlesworth, James H., ed. 1983. *The Old Testament Pseudepigrapha. Vol. 1: Apocalyptic Literature and Testaments*. Garden City, NY: Doubleday.

Clauss, James J. and Sarah Iles Johnston. 1997. *Medea: Essays on Medea in Myth, Literature, Philosophy, and Art*. Princeton, NJ: Princeton University Press.

Clay, Jenny Strauss. 2003. *Hesiod's Cosmos*. Cambridge: Cambridge University Press.

Clifford, Richard J., S.J. 2000. "The Roots of Apocalypticism in Near Eastern Myth." In John J. Collins, 2000, pp. 3–38.

Cline, Eric H. 2014. 1177 B. C. The Year Civilization Collapsed. Princeton, NJ: Princeton University Press.

Cogan, Mordechai. 2001. *The Anchor Bible: I Kings. A New Translation with Introduction and Commentary*. New York: Doubleday.

Collins, Adela Yarbro. 1976. The Combat Myth in the Book of Revelation. Harvard Theological Review Series. Cambridge, MA: Scholars Press.

———. 2000. "The Book of Revelation." In John J. Collins, 2000, pp. 384–414.

Collins, John J. 2000a. *The Encyclopedia of Apocalypticism. Vol. 1: The Origins of Apocalypticism in Judaism and Christianity*. New York: Continuum.

———. 2000b. "From Prophecy to Apocalypticism: The Expectation of the End." In John J. Collins, 2000, pp. 129–61.

Commager, Steele, ed. 1966. *Virgil: A Collection of Critical Essays*. Englewood Cliffs, NJ: Prentice-Hall.

Conzelmann, Hans. 1987. *The Acts of the Apostles*, trans. J. Limburg, A. T. Kraabel and D. H. Juel. Hermeneia. Philadelphia, PA: Fortress Press.

Coogan, Michael D. 1990. "Archaeology and Biblical Studies: The Book of Joshua." In Propp et al., 1990, pp. 19–32.

———. 1998. *The Oxford History of the Biblical World*. New York: Oxford University Press.

Crane, Gregory. 1987. "The *Odyssey* and Conventions of the Heroic Quest." *Classical Antiquity* 6: 11–37.

———. 1988. *Calypso: Backgrounds and Conventions of the Odyssey*. Frankfurt: Athenaums Monografien.

Culpepper, R. Alan. 1983. *Anatomy of the Fourth Gospel: A Study in Literary Design*. Philadelphia, PA: Fortress Press.

Dale, A. M. 1954. *Euripides Alcestis: Edited with Introduction and Commentary*. Oxford: Clarendon Press (1984 reprint).

Dalley, Stephanie. 1991. *Myths from Mesopotamia*. Oxford: Oxford University Press.

Davidson, Robert. 1979. *Genesis 12–50*. Cambridge: Cambridge University Press.

Day, Alfred Ely. 1976. "Goat," pp. 1248–49, in *The International Standard Bible Encyclopedia*, Vol. II, gen. ed. James Orr. Grand Rapids, MI: Eerdmans Publishing.

Dee, James H. 1994. *The Epithetic Phrases for the Homeric Gods (Epitheta Deorum apud Homerum) = Albert Bates Lord Studies in Oral Tradition (Vol. 14)*. New York and London: Garland.

de Jáuregui, Miguel Herrero. 2011. "Priam's Catabasis: Traces of the Epic Journey to Hades in *Iliad* 24." *Transactions of the American Philological Association* 141: 37–68.

de Jáuregui, Miguel Herrero, Ana Isable Jiménez San Cristóbal, Eugenio R. Luján Martinez, Raquel Martin Hernández, Marco Antonio Santamaría Alvarez, and Sofía Torallas Tovar, eds. 2011. *Tracing Orpheus: Studies of Orphic Fragments in Honour of Alberto Bernabé*. Berlin: De Gruyter.

de Jong, Irene J. F. 2001. *A Narratological Commentary on the Odyssey*. Cambridge: Cambridge University Press.

Detienne, M. 1981. "The Myth of 'Honeyed Orpheus'," pp. 95–110, in *Myth, Religion & Society: Structuralist Essays by M. Detienne, L. Gernet, J.-P. Vernant and P. Vidal-Naquet*, ed. R. L. Gordon. Cambridge: Cambridge University Press.

Diener, B.-J. 1995. "Wann sang Deborah ihr Lied? Überlegungen zu zwei der ältesten Texte des TNK (Ri 4 und 5)." *ACEBT* 14: 106–30.

Doak, Brian R. 2012. *The Last of the Rephaim: Conquest and Cataclysm in the Heroic Ages of Ancient Israel*. Boston, MA: Ilex Foundation Series.

Doherty, L. E. 1995. *Siren Songs: Gender, Audience and Narrators in the Odyssey*. Ann Arbor: University of Michigan Press.

Dunn, James D. G. 2013. *The Oral Gospel Tradition*. Grand Rapids, MI: Eerdmans Publishing.

Edelstein, M. J. and Ludwig Edelstein. 1998. *Asclepius: Collection and Interpretation of the Testimonies*. Baltimore: Johns Hopkins University Press.

Euben, J. Peter. 1986. *Greek Tragedy and Political Theory*. Berkeley: University of California Press.

Farrell, Joseph. 1997. "The Vergilian Intertext." In Martindale, 1997, pp. 222–38.

Feeney, D. C. 1986. "History and Revelation in Vergil's Underworld." *Proceedings of the Cambridge Philological Society* 32: 1–24 (reprinted in Quinn, pp. 108–22).

Feldherr, Andrew. 2016. "Nothing Like the Sun: Repetition and Representation in Ovid's Phaethon Narrative." In Fulkerson and Stover, 2016, pp. 16–46.

Finkelberg, Margalit. 2005. *Greeks and Pre-Greeks: Aegean Prehistory and Greek Heroic Tradition*. Cambridge: Cambridge University Press.

———. 2011a. *The Homer Encyclopedia*. Oxford: Wiley-Blackwell.

———. 2011b. "Iapetos." In Finkelberg 2011a, p. 309.

Finkelstein, Israel and Neil Asher Silberman. 2001. *The Bible Unearthed: Archaeology's New Vision of Ancient Israel and the Origin of Its Sacred Texts*. New York: Simon & Schuster.

Fitzmyer, Joseph A. 1981. *The Anchor Bible: The Gospel According to Luke (I–IX): Introduction, Translation and Notes*. Garden City, NY: Doubleday.

———. 1985. *The Anchor Bible: The Gospel According to Luke (X–XXIV)*. Garden City, NY: Doubleday.

Foley, John Miles. 2005. *The Blackwell Companion to Ancient Epic*. Oxford: Blackwell.

Fontenrose, Joseph. 1959. *Python: A Study of Delphic Myth and Its Origins*. Berkeley: University of California Press.

Ford, J. Massyngberde. 1975. *The Anchor Bible: Revelation: Introduction, Translation and Commentary*. Garden City, NY: Doubleday.

Foster, Benjamin R. 2005. *Before the Muses: An Anthology of Akkadian Literature*. Bethesda, MD: CDL Press.

Fox, Robin Lane. 1992. *The Unauthorized Version: Truth and Fiction in the Bible*. New York: Alfred A. Knopf.

———. 2008. *Travelling Heroes: In the Epic Age of Homer*. New York: Alfred A. Knopf.

Freedman, Rabbi Dr. H. 1992. *Midrash Rabbah Genesis Volume 1*. London: Soncino Press.

Freeman, Charles. 2005. *The Closing of the Western Mind: The Rise of Faith and the Fall of Reason*. New York: Vintage Books.

Friesen, Steven J. 2001. *Imperial Cults and the Apocalypse of John: Reading Revelation in the Ruins*. Oxford: Oxford University Press.

Frye, Northrop. 1976. *The Secular Scripture: A Study of the Structure of Romance*. Cambridge, MA: Harvard University Press.

Fulkerson, Laurel and Tim Stover. 2016. *Repeat Performances: Ovidian Repetition and the Metamorphoses*. Madison: University of Wisconsin Press.

Gale, Monica R. 2003. "Poetry and the Backward Glance in Vergil's *Georgics* and *Aeneid*." *Transaction of the American Philological Association* 133: 323–52.

Gantz, Timothy. 1993. *Early Greek Myth*. Baltimore: Johns Hopkins University Press.

Gibert, John. 1995. *Change of Mind in Greek Tragedy (Hypomnemata Untersuchungen zur Antike und zu ihrem Hachleben 108)*. Göttingen: Vandenhoeck & Ruprecht.

———. *Ion* Commentary. Forthcoming. Cambridge University Press.

Gmirkin, Russell E. 2017. *Plato and the Creation of the Hebrew Bible*. Copenhagen International Seminar. London and New York: Routledge.

Goslin, Owen. 2010. "Hesiod's Typhonomachy and the Ordering of Sound." *TAPA* 140: 351–73.

Green, Peter. 2007. *The Argonautika: Apollonius Rhodios*. Translated, with an Introduction, Commentary, and Glossary. Expanded Edition. Berkeley: University of California Press.

Greenburg, N. A. 1993. "The Attitude of Agamemnon." *Classical World* 86: 193–205.

Gregory, Justina. 1999. *Euripides: Hecuba. Introduction, Text, Commentary*. Atlanta, GA: Scholars Press.

Gunkel, Hermann. 1895. Schöpfung und Chaos in Urzeit und Endzeit: Eine religionsgeschichtliche Untersuchung über Gen 1 und Ap Joh 12. (English translation, Creation and Chaos in the Primeval Era and the Eschaton: A Religio-Historical Study of Genesis 1 and Revelation 12 [2006].) Grand Rapids, MI: Eerdmans Publishing.

Hainsworth, Bryan. 1993. *The Iliad: A Commentary, Volume III: Books 9–12*. Cambridge: Cambridge University Press.

Hall, Edith. 2012. *Adventures with Iphigenia in Tauris: A Cultural History of Euripides' Black Sea Tragedy*. Oxford: Oxford University Press.

Hard, Robin. 1998. *Apollodorus: The Library of Greek Mythology*. Translated with an Introduction and Notes. Oxford: Oxford University Press.

Hays, Richard B. 2006. "The Canonical Matrix of the Gospels," pp. 53–75, in *The Cambridge Companion to the Gospels*, ed. Stephen C. Barton. Cambridge: Cambridge University Press.

Heltzer, M. and E. Lipinski, eds. 1988. *Society and Economy in the Eastern Mediterranean (c. 1500–100 B.C.)*. Orientalis lovaniensia analecta 23. Leuven, Belgium: Uitgeverij Peeters.

Hershbell, Jackson B. 1970. "Hesiod and Empedocles." *The Classical Journal* 65: 145–61.

Heubeck, A. 1989. *"Books IX–XII": A Commentary on Homer's Odyssey*, Vol. II, eds. A. Heubeck and A. Hoekstra. Oxford: Oxford University Press.

Hoekstra, A. 1989. *"Books XIII–XVI": A Commentary on Homer's Odyssey*, Vol. II, eds. A. Heubeck and A. Hoekstra. Oxford: Oxford University Press.

Hollis, A. S. 1970. *Ovid. Metamorphoses Book VIII: Edited with an Introduction and Commentary*. Oxford: Clarendon Press.

Hunter, R. L. 1989. *Apollonius of Rhodes: Argonautika, Book III.* Cambridge: Cambridge University Press.

Hunter, Richard. 1993. *The Argonautica of Apollonius: Literary Studies*. Cambridge: Cambridge University Press.

Huxley, G. L. 1969. *Greek Epic Poetry from Eumelos to Panyassis*. Cambridge, MA: Harvard University Press.

Janko, Richard. 1982. *Homer, Hesiod and the Hymns*. Cambridge: Cambridge University Press.

———. 1992. *The Iliad: A Commentary. Vol. IV: Books 13–16*, gen. ed. G. S. Kirk. Cambridge: Cambridge University Press.

———. 2011. "πρῶτόν τε καὶ ὕστατον αἰὲν ἀείδειν." In Andersen and Haug, 2011, pp. 20–43.

Johnson, W. R. 1976. *Darkness Visible: A Study of Vergil's Aeneid*. Berkeley: University of California Press.

———. 1999. "Dis Aliter Visum: Self-Telling and Theodicy in Aeneid 2." In Perkell, 1999, pp. 50–63.

Killebrew, Ann E. and Gunnar Lehmann. 2013. *The Philistines and Other "Sea Peoples" in Text and Archaeology*. Atlanta, GA: Society of Biblical Literature.

Knox, Bernard M. W. 1979. *Word and Action: Essays on the Ancient Theater*. Baltimore: Johns Hopkins University Press.

Koester, Craig R. 2014. *Revelation: A New Translation with Introduction and Commentary*. The Anchor Yale Bible. New Haven, CT: Yale University Press.

Kugel, James. 1990. "The Case against Joseph." In Abusch, 1990, pp. 271–87.

Kullmann, Wolfgang. 2012. "Neoanalysis between Orality and Literacy: Some Remarks Concerning the Development of Greek Myths Including the Legend of the Capture of Troy." In Montari et al., 2012, pp. 13–25.

Laffineur, Robert and Robin Hägg, eds. 2001. *Potnia: Deities and Religion in the Aegean Bronze Age* (Proceedings of the 8th International Aegean Conference, Göteborg, Göteborg University, 12–15 April 2000). Austin: University of Texas at Austin.

Lamberton, Robert. 1989. *Homer the Theologian: Neoplatonist Reading and the Growth of the Epic Tradition*. Berkeley: University of California Press.

Lape, Susan. 2010. *Race and Citizen Identity in the Classical Athenian Democracy*. Cambridge: Cambridge University Press.

Larsen, Kasper Bro. 2008. *Recognizing the Stranger: Recognition Scenes in the Gospel of John*. Leiden, The Netherlands: Brill.

Leach, Eleanor Winson. 1999. "Viewing the Spectacula of Aeneid 6." In Perkell, 1999, pp. 111–27.

Levin, Christoph. 2003. "Das Alter des Deborahlieds," pp. 124–41, in *Fortschreibungen: Gesammelte Studien zum Alten Testament* [BZAW 316]. Berlin and New York: De Gruyter.

Lindars, Barnabas, S.S.F. 1995. *Judges 1–5: A New Translation and Commentary*. Edinburgh: T&T Clark.

Lloyd, Michael. 1992. *The Agon in Euripides*. Oxford: Clarendon Press.

Lloyd-Jones, Hugh. 1996. *Sophocles: Fragments (Loeb Classical Library)*. Cambridge, MA: Harvard University Press.

López-Ruiz, Carolina. 2010. *When the Gods Were Born: Greek Cosmogonies and the Near East*. Cambridge, MA: Harvard University Press.

———. 2011. "A Hangover of Cosmic Proportions: OF *222* and Its Mythical Context." In de Jáuregui et al., pp. 99–104.

Louden, Bruce. 1993. "Pivotal Contrafactuals in Homeric Epic." *Classical Antiquity* 12: 181–98.

———. 1999. *The Odyssey: Structure, Narration, and Meaning*. Baltimore: Johns Hopkins University Press.

———. 2005. "The Gods in Epic, or the Divine Economy," pp. 90–104, in *A Companion to Ancient Epic*, ed. John Miles Foley. Oxford: Blackwell.

———. 2006. *The Iliad: Structure, Myth, and Meaning*. Baltimore: Johns Hopkins University Press.

———. 2007. "Reading through *The Alcestis* to *The Winter's Tale*." *Classical and Modern Literature* 27(2): 7–30.

———. 2009. "*Retrospective Prophecy* and *the Vision* in *Aeneid* 6 and the Book of Revelation." *International Journal of the Classical Tradition* 16: 1–18.

———. 2011a. *Homer's Odyssey and the Near East*. Cambridge: Cambridge University Press.

———. 2011b. "Is There Early Recognition between Penelope and Odysseus? Book 19 in the Larger Context of the *Odyssey*." *College Literature* 38(2): 76–100.

———. 2013. "Iapetós and Japheth: Hesiod's *Theogony*, *Iliad* 15.187–93, and Genesis 9–10." *Illinois Classical Studies* 38: 1–22.

———. 2014. "Hesiod's *Theogony* and the Book of Revelation 4 and 12," pp. 258–77, in The Bible and *Hellenism*, eds. Thomas L. Thompson and Philippe Wajdenbaum. London: Routledge.

———. 2016. "Agamemnon and the Hebrew Bible." *Svensk Exegetisk Årsbok* 81: 1–24.

———. 2018. "*Iliad* 11: Healing, Healers, Nestor, and Medea," pp. 151–64, in *Yearbook of Ancient Greek Epic*, Vol. 2.

Luschnig, C. A. E. and H. M. Roisman. 2003. *Euripides' Alcestis: With Notes and Commentary*. Norman: University of Oklahoma Press.

MacDonald, Dennis R. 2015. *The Gospels of Homer: Imitations of Greek Epic in Mark and Luke-Acts*. Lanham, MD: Rowman & Littlefield.

Maeir, Aren M. 2013. "Philistia Transforming: Fresh Evidence from Tell es-Safi/Gath on the Transformational Trajectory of the Philistine Culture." In Killebrew and Lehmann, 2013, pp. 191–242.

Malkin, Irad. 1996. "Nymphs," p. 1056, in *The Oxford Classical Dictionary*, 3rd ed., eds. Simon Hornblower and Anthony Spawforth. Oxford: Oxford University Press.

Mann, C. S. 1986. *The Anchor Bible: Mark: A New Translation with Introduction and Commentary*. Garden City, NY: Doubleday.

Marquis, Timothy Luckritz. 2013. *Transient Apostle: Paul, Travel, and the Rhetoric of Empire*. New Haven, CT: Yale University Press.

Martin, James D. 1975. *The Cambridge Bible Commentary: The Book of Judges*. Cambridge: Cambridge University Press.

Martindale, Charles, ed. 1997. *The Cambridge Companion to Vergil*. Cambridge: Cambridge University Press.

Masterman, E. W. G. 1956. "Myrrh." In Orr et al., Vol. II, 1976, pp. 2102–3.

Mastronarde, Donald J. 1979. *Contact and Discontinuity: Some Conventions of Speech and Action on the Greek Tragic Stage*. Berkeley: University of California Press.

———. 2002. *Euripides* Medea. Cambridge: Cambridge University Press.

McCarter, P. Kyle Jr. 1984. *The Anchor Bible: II Samuel: A New Translation with Introduction, Notes and Commentary*. Garden City, NY: Doubleday.

———. 1985. *The Anchor Bible: I Samuel: A New Translation with Introduction, Notes & Commentary*. Garden City, NY: Doubleday.

McClure, Laura K. 2017. *A Companion to Euripides*. Hoboken, NJ: Wiley.

Merkelbach, R. and M. L. West. 1967. *Fragmenta Hesiodea*. Oxford: Clarendon Press.

Metzger, Bruce M. and Michael D. Coogan. 1993. *The Oxford Companion to the Bible*. New York: Oxford University Press.

Metzger, Isobel MacKay. 1993. "Rachel." In Metzger and Coogan, 1993, pp. 641–42.

Mobley, Gregory. 2005. *The Empty Men: The Heroic Tradition*. New Haven, CT: Yale University Press.

Montari, Franco, Antonios Rengakos, and Christos C. Tsagalis, eds. 2012. *Homeric Contexts: Neoanalysis and the Interpretation of Oral Poetry*. Berlin: De Gruyter.

Montari, Montari. 2015. *The Brill Dictionary of Ancient Greek*. Leiden, The Netherlands, and Boston: Brill.

Morgan, Teresa. 2007. *Literate Education in the Hellenistic and Roman World*. Cambridge: Cambridge University Press.

Morris, Sarah P. 2001. "Potnia Aswiya: Anatolian Contributions to Greek Religion." In Laffineur and Hägg, 2001, pp. 423–34.

Mueller, Melissa. 2010. "Athens in a Basket: Naming, Objects, and Identity in Euripides' *Ion*." *Arethusa* 43: 365–402.

Muraoka, T. 2002. *A Greek-English Lexicon of the Septuagint: Chiefly of the Pentateuch and the Twelve Prophets*. Louvain, Paris, and Dudley, MA: Peeters.

Nathanson, Barbara Geller. 1993. "Aqedah." In Metzger and Coogan, 1993, 43–44.

Niditch, Susan. 2008. *Judges: A Commentary*. Louisville, KY: Westminster John Knox Press.

Orr, James. 1976. "Cleopas," p. 669, in *The International Standard Bible Encyclopedia*, Vol. II, gen. ed. James Orr. Grand Rapids, MI: Eerdmans Publishing.

Otis, Brooks. 1966. "The Odyssean Aeneid and the Iliadic Aeneid." In Commager 1966, pp. 89–106.

Owen, A. S. 1939. *Euripides Ion: Edited with Introduction and Commentary*. Bedminster, UK: Bristol Classical Press.

Padilla, Mark W. 1999. *Rites of Passage in Ancient Greece: Literature, Religion, Society*. Lewisburg, KY: Bucknell University Press.

Pagels, Elaine. 2012. *Revelations: Visions, Prophecy, & Politics in the Book of Revelation*. New York: Viking.

Parker, L. P. E. 2007. *Euripides Alcestis: Edited with Introduction and Commentary*. Oxford: Oxford University Press.

Parker, Robert. 2017. *Greek Gods Abroad: Names, Natures, and Transformation*. Sather Classical Lectures, 72. Oakland: University of California Press.

Parker, Simon B. 1997. *Ugaritic Narrative Poetry*. Atlanta, GA: Society of Biblical Literature.

Patch, James A. 1976. "Goats' Hair," pp. 1249–50 in The *International Standard Bible Encyclopedia*, Vol. II, gen. ed James Orr. Grand Rapids, MI: Eerdmans Publishing.

Paulson, Johannes. 1962. *Index Hesiodeus*. Hildesheim, Germany: Georg Olms Verlagsbuchhandlung.

Perkell, Christine, ed. 1999. *Reading Vergil's Aeneid: An Interpretive Guide*. Norman: University of Oklahoma Press.

Phillips, Anthony. 1973. *Deuteronomy*. Cambridge: Cambridge University Press.

Pittard, Wayne T. 1998. "Before Israel: Syria-Palestine in the Bronze Age." In Coogan, 1998, pp. 33–77.

Propp, William H., Baruch Halpern, and David Noel Freedman. 1990. *The Hebrew Bible and Its Interpreters: Biblical and Judaic Studies. Volume 1*. Winona Lake, IN: Eisenbrauns.

———. 1998. *The Anchor Bible: Exodus 1–18: A New Translation with Introduction and Commentary*. New York: Doubleday.

Putnam, Michael C. J. 2005. "Vergils Aeneid." In Foley, 2005, pp. 452–75.

Quinn, Stephanie, ed. 2000. *Why Vergil? A Collection of Interpretations*. Wauconda, IL: Bolchazy-Carducci.

Race, William H. 1993. "First Appearances in the *Odyssey*." *Transactions of the American Philological Association* 123: 79–107.

———. 1997. *Pindar: Olympian Odes; Pythian Odes. Loeb Classical Library*. Cambridge, MA: Harvard University Press.

Reece, Steve. 1993. *The Stranger's Welcome: Oral Theory and the Aesthetics of the Homeric Hospitality Scene*. Ann Arbor: University of Michigan Press.

Rhodes, P. J. 1981. *A Commentary on the Aristotelian* Athenaion Politeia. Oxford: Clarendon Press.

Richardson, Nicholas. 1993. *The Iliad: A Commentary, Volume VI: Books 21–24*. Cambridge: Cambridge University Press.

———. 2010. *Three Homeric Hymns: To Apollo, Hermes, and Aphrodite*. Cambridge: Cambridge University Press.

Robbins, V. K. 1996. *Exploring the Texture of Texts*. Valley Forge, PA: Trinity Press International.

Roberts, David Francis. 1949. "Javan," p. 52, in *The International Standard Bible Encyclopedia*, Vol. III, gen. ed. James Orr. Grand Rapids, MI: Eerdmans Publishing.

Roisman, Hanna. 2011. "Hecuba." In Finkelberg, 2011, pp. 334–35.

Römer, Thomas C. 1998. "Why Would the Deuteronomists Tell About the Sacrifice of Jephthah's Daughter?" *JSOT* 77: 27–38.

Rosenmeyer, Thomas G. 1963. *The Masks of Tragedy: Essays on Six Dramas*. Austin: University of Texas Press.

Sandnes, Karl Olva. 2009. *The Challenge of Homer: School, Pagan Poets and Early Christianity*. London: T&T Clark International.

Sasson, Jack M. 2014. *The Anchor Yale Bible: Judges 1–12*. New Haven, CT: Yale University Press.

Saxonhouse, Arelene, W. 1986. "Myths and the Origins of Cities: Reflections on the Authochthony Theme in Euripides' Ion." Euben, 1986, pp. 252–73.

Schenk, C. E. 1939. "Jael," pp. 1557–58, in The *International Standard Bible Encyclopedia*, Vol. III, gen. ed. James Orr. Grand Rapids, MI: Eerdmans Publishing.

Scully, Stephen. 2015. *Hesiod's Theogony: From Near Eastern Creation Myths to Paradise Lost*. Oxford: Oxford University Press.

Segal, Charles. 1999. "Euripides' Ion: Generational Passage and Civic Myth." In= Padilla, 1999, pp. 67–108.

Shinan, Avigdor and Yair Zakovitch. 2012. *From Gods to God: How the Bible Debunked, Suppressed, or Changed Ancient Myths & Legends*, trans. Valerie Zakovitch. Philadelphia, PA: Jewish Society Publication.

Singer, Itamar. 2013. "The Philistines in the Bible: A Short Rejoinder to a New Perspective." In Killebrew and Lehmann, 2013, pp. 19–28.

Smith, Jean Edward. 2016. *Bush*. New York: Simon & Schuster.

Smith, Mark S. 1990. *The Early History of God: Yahweh and the Other Deities in Ancient Israel*. San Francisco, CA: Harper Collins.

———. 2001. *The Origins of Biblical Monotheism: Israel's Polytheistic Background and the Ugaritic Texts*. New York: Oxford University Press.

———. 2008. *God in Translation: Deities in Cross-Cultural Discourse in the Biblical World*. Grand Rapids, MI: Eerdmans Publishing.

———. 2014. *Poetic Heroes: Literary Commemorations of Warriors and Warrior Culture in the Early Biblical World*. Grand Rapids, MI: Eerdmans Publishing.

Smith, Riggs Alden. 2005. *The Primacy of Vision in Virgil's Aeneid*. Austin: University of Texas Press.

Sparks, H. F. D. 1974. *The Johannine Synopsis of the Gospels*. New York: Harper & Row.

Sparks, Kenton L. 2005. *Ancient Texts for the Study of the Hebrew Bible*. Peabody, MA: Hendrickson Publishers.

Speiser, E. A. 1962. *The Anchor Bible: Genesis, Introduction, Translation, and Notes*. New York: Doubleday.

Spronk, Klaas. 2010. "The Book of Judges as a Late Construct," pp. 15–28, in *Historiography and Identity (Re)formulation in Second Temple Historiographical Literature*, ed. Louis Jonker. London: T&T Clark.

———. 2015. "Comparing the Book of Judges to Greek Literature," pp. 261–71, in *Open-Mindedness in the Bible and Beyond: A Volume of Studies in Honour of Bob Becking* (*Library of Hebrew Bible/Old Testament Studies* 616). London: T&T Clark.

Stager, Lawrence E. 1991. "When Canaanites and Philistines Ruled Ashkelon." *Biblical Archaeology Review* 17(2). http://cojs.org/when-canaanites-and-philistines-ruled-ashkelon/.

Suggs, M. Jack. 1992. *The Oxford Study Bible*, eds. M. Jack Suggs, Katharine Doob Sakenfeld, and James R. Mueller. New York: Oxford University Press.

Sweet, John. 1993. "The Antichrist" and "Revelation, The Book of." In Metzger and Coogan, 1993, pp. 31–32, 651–55.

Taylor, John. 2007. *Classics and the Bible: Hospitality and Recognition*. London: Duckworth.

Thayer, Joseph Henry. *A Greek-English Lexicon of the New Testament (Complete and Unabridged)*. Grand Rapids, MI: Zondervan.

Thompson, Marianne Meye. 2006. "The Gospel According to John." In Barton, 2006, pp. 182–200.

Turkeltaub, Daniel. 2017. "Hecuba." In McClure, 2017, pp. 136–51.

van Daalen, David H. 1993. "Six Hundred Sixty-Six." In Metzger and Coogan, 1993, pp. 699–700.

van der Toorn, Karel. 2007. *Scribal Culture and the Making of the Hebrew Bible*. Cambridge, MA: Harvard University Press.

van Nortwick, Thomas. 2011. "Agamemnon." In Finkelberg, 2011, pp. 14–16.

Wadjenbaum, Philippe. 2011. *Argonauts of the Desert: Structural Analysis of the Hebrew Bible*. London: Routledge.

Watkins, Calvert. 1995. *How to Kill a Dragon: Aspects of Indo-European Poetics.* New York: Oxford University Press.

Watson, Duane F. 1992. *Persuasive Artistry: Studies in New Testament Rhetoric in Honor of George A. Kennedy.* Sheffield, UK: Sheffield Academic Press.

Webb, Barry G. 1987. *The Book of Judges: An Integrated Reading* (JSOT Supplement 46). Sheffield, UK: JSOT Press.

Weinfeld, Moshe. 1988. "The Promise to the Patriarchs and Its Realization: An Analysis of Foundation Stories." In Heltzer and Lipinski, 1988, pp. 353–69.

———. 1993. *The Promise of the Land: The Inheritance of the Land of Canaan by the Israelites.* Berkeley: University of California Press.

West, M. L. 1966. *Hesiod: Theogony.* Oxford: Clarendon Press.

———. 1997. *The East Face of Helicon: West Asiatic Elements in Greek Poetry and Myth.* Oxford: Clarendon Press.

———. 2001. "Atreus and Attarasiyas." *Glotta* 77: 262–66.

———. 2003. *Greek Epic Fragments.* Loeb Classical Library. Cambridge, MA: Harvard University Press.

———. 2005. "*Odyssey* and *Argonautica*." *Classical Quarterly* 55: 39–64.

West, S. 1988. "*Books I–IV*": *A Commentary on Homer's Odyssey*, Vol. 1, eds. A. Heubeck, S. West, and J. B. Hainsworth. Oxford: Oxford University Press.

Westermann, Claus. 1976. *The Promises to the Fathers: Studies on the Patriarchal Narratives*, trans. David E. Green. Philadelphia, PA: Fortress Press.

Whitaker, Robyn J. 2015. "The Poetics of Ekphrasis: Vivid Description and Rhetoric in the Apocalypse." In Alkier et al., 2015, pp. 227–40.

White, L. Michael. 2010. *Scripting Jesus: The Gospels in Rewrite.* New York: HarperCollins.

Whitman, Cedric H. 1958. *Homer and the Heroic Tradition.* New York: W. W. Norton.

———. 1974. *Euripides and the Full Circle of Myth.* Cambridge, MA: Harvard University Press.

Whitmarsh, Tim. 2015. *Battling the Gods: Atheism in the Ancient World.* New York: Alfred A. Knopf.

Wohl, Victoria. 2015. *Euripides and the Politics of Form.* Princeton, NJ: Princeton University Press.

Woodard, Roger D. 2014. *The Textualization of the Greek Alphabet.* Cambridge and New York: Cambridge University Press.

Wordelman, Amy L. 1994. "The Gods Have Come Down: Images of Historical Lycaonia and the Literary Construction of Acts 14." PhD dissertation, Princeton University.

Wuellner, W. 1992. "The Rhetorical Genre of Jesus' Sermon in Luke 12:1–13:9." In Watson, 1992, pp. 93–118.

Yadin, Azzan. 2004. "Goliath's Armor and Israelite Collective Memory." *Vetus Testamentum* LIV 3: 373–95.

Yasur-Landau, Assaf. 2001. "The Mother(s) of All Philistines? Aegean Enthroned Deities of the 12th–11th Century Philistia." In Laffineur and Hägg, 2001, pp. 329–43.

———. 2010. *The Philistines and Aegean Migration at the End of the Late Bronze Age.* Cambridge: Cambridge University Press.

Index

For Product Safety Concerns and Information please contact our EU
representative GPSR@taylorandfrancis.com
Taylor & Francis Verlag GmbH, Kaufingerstraße 24, 80331 München, Germany